Beyond Silenced Voices

SUNY Series

FRONTIERS IN EDUCATION

Philip G. Altbach, Editor

The Frontiers in Education Series draws upon a range of disciplines and approaches in the analysis of contemporary educational issues and concerns. Books in the series help to reinterpret established fields of scholarship in education by encouraging the latest synthesis and research. A special focus highlights educational policy issues from a multidisciplinary perspective. The series is published in cooperation with the Graduate School of Education, State University of New York at Buffalo.

Class, Race, and Gender in American Education
—Lois Weis (ed.)

Excellence and Equality: A Qualitatively Different Perspective on Gifted and Talented Education
—David M. Fetterman

Change and Effectiveness in Schools: A Cultural Perspective
—Gretchen B. Rossman, H. Dickson Corbett, and William A. Firestone

The Curriculum: Problems, Politics, and Possibilities
—Landon E. Beyer and Michael W. Apple (eds.)

The Character of American Higher Education and Intercollegiate Sport
—Donald Chu

Crisis in Teaching: Perspectives on Current Reforms
—Lois Weis, Philip G. Altbach, Gail P. Kelly, Hugh G. Petrie, and Sheila Slaughter (eds.)

The High Status Track: Studies of Elite Schools and Stratification
—Paul William Kingston and Lionel S. Lewis (eds.)

The Economics of American Universities: Management, Operations, and Fiscal Environment
—Stephen A. Hoenack and Eileen L. Collins (eds.)

Beyond Silenced Voices

Class, Race, and Gender in
United States Schools

Lois Weis
Michelle Fine
Editors

State University of New York Press

Harvard Educational Review has kindly granted reprint rights for the following articles that appear in this volume:

Michelle Fine, "Sexuality, Schooling, and Adolescent Females: The Missing Discourse of Desire"

Jim Cummins, "Empowering Minority Students: A Framework for Intervention"

Lisa Delpit, "The Silenced Dialogue: Power and Pedagogy in Educating Other People's Children"

Published by
State University of New York Press, Albany

© 1993 State University of New York

For information, address State University of New York
Press, State University Plaza, Albany, N.Y., 12246

Production by E. Moore
Marketing by Fran Keneston

Library of Congress Cataloging-in-Publication Data

Beyond silenced voices : class, race, and gender in United States
  schools / edited by Lois Weis and Michelle Fine.
      p.   cm — (SUNY series, frontiers in education)
    Includes bibliographical references and index.
    ISBN 0-7914-1285-7. — ISBN 0-7914-1286-5 (pbk.)
    1. Discrimination in education—United States. 2. Sex
discrimination in education—United States. 3. Sexism in education–
–United States. 4. Minorities—Education—United States. 5. Women–
–Education—United States. 6. Working class—Education—United
States. 7. Power (Social sciences) 8. Educational equalization–
— United States. I. Weis, Lois. II. Fine, Michelle. III. Series
LC212.2.B49   1993
370.19′342′0973—dc20   91-46125
                                                           CIP

10 9 8 7 6 5 4 3 2

For our children

Sam Finesurrey
Sara Asrat
Jessica Asrat

Contents

Contents

PART II
FROM THE MARGINS TO THE CENTER:
BEYOND SILENCED VOICES

Acknowledgments

We would like to thank a number of people who helped us put this volume together. Sharon Smith, Cynthia Boyd, Lisa Johnston, and Jeanne Ferry at the Graduate School of Education, State University of New York at Buffalo, provided invaluable help, as did Donna Leitner, Sari Locker, and Elizabeth Sayre at the Graduate School of Education, University of Pennsylvania. Lois Patton and Priscilla Ross of SUNY Press also provided help in bringing this volume into production. Both have been sources of intellectual and personal support and helped to make this book what it is.

We would like to dedicate this volume to our children, Sam Finesurrey and Sara and Jessica Asrat, with the hope that they will not be silenced and will have the strength and courage to be part of the struggle to break the silencing of others.

MICHELLE FINE
LOIS WEIS

Introduction

This volume began as an attempt to collect essays on the practices, and consequences, of silencing in public schools. We had both witnessed and written about such practices and determined that an academic volume was needed in which a set of essays together could unravel the dynamics of power and privilege that nurture, sustain, and legitimate silencing. Once we solicited articles from friends, and from others whose work we had admired from afar about the multiple forms of public silencing, we soon realized that silencing, as a practice, does not totally work—that the move to silence is an often ineffective and ironic move of power. From within the very centers of structured silence can be heard the most critical and powerful, if excluded, voices of teachers and students in public education. Further, we soon recognized that our volume would need to move "beyond silencing," not only by listening to those who had been institutionally banished from the center to the margins, but by deconstructing those policies and practices that have historically encoded power, privilege, and marginality in our public schools.

This text, then, is constructed around these two political projects. The first set of essays examines selected policies, discourse, and practices that enable the *structuring of silence*. These essays critically challenge institutional practices that create the structuring of silence and then discount, through delegitimation, the voices of those excluded. The essays, for example, examine racist hiring practices performed in the name of "affirmative action," classist tracking practices institutionalized in the name of "giftedness," and sexist curriculum delivered in the name of "sex education." By analyzing select policies and practices that sustain silencing, typically couched within a discourse of what is for the "common good," and by unraveling who has been privileged by these practices and policies, the deeply institutionalized character of silencing becomes visible.

1

But to move "beyond silenced voices," we need to understand not only the oppressive nature of policies, discourses, and practices that silence, but also those that act to solicit and listen closely to the words, critiques, dreams, and fantasies of those who have dwelt historically on the margins. The second section of this collection, "From the Margins to the Center: Beyond Silenced Voices," introduces a set of essays in which the voices of children and adolescents who have been expelled from the centers of their schools and the centers of our culture are invited to speak as interpreters—as political critics of the economy and schooling, and race, class, and gender relations, and also as political creators of adolescent cultures. In this section we hear the voices of lesbian and gay students who have been assaulted in their schools and are organizing as a community of political activists; we hear young men and women, across racial, ethnic, and class lines, struggling for identities amidst the radically transforming conditions of late twentieth-century capitalism; and we hear African American teachers trying to make sense of a public education system deeply fractured along race and class lines. These essays, as a collection, force us to listen closely to the *discursive undergrounds* of students and adults that flourish within the margins of our public schools. These voices, once marginalized, need to be heard and centered—if we are serious about schools as a democratic public sphere, if we are sincere in our commitment to multicultural and feminist education, and if we want to understand and interrupt the perversions and pleasures of power, privilege, and marginalization in public schooling.

Finally, we are eager, with this text, to reach broadly audiences who would and audiences who would not initially be interested in questions of race, class, and gender in schooling. We presume that some of you will teach, many will parent, and some will be engaged as community activists working within social movements. And so, in this text, we take quite seriously bell hooks's class for "plain talk"—for talk that captures everyday words and for talk that breaks out of the dichotomy splitting academic language from the language of real people's lives and struggles. For if we did not stay within "plain talk," we would merely be replaying, as ventriloquists, voices from the margin, rearticulating them in a style and form accessible only to the privileged. We ourselves would then be structuring silence—once again. As bell hooks argues,

> It is a false dichotomy which suggests that academics and/or intellectuals can only speak to one another, that we cannot hope to speak with the masses. What is true is that we make choices, that we choose voices to hear and voices to silence. If I do not speak in a language that can be understood, then there is little chance for dialogue. This issue of language and behavior is a central contradiction in all radical intellectuals, particularly those who

are members of oppressed groups, must continually conform and work to resolve. One of the clear and present dangers that exists when we move outside our class of origin, our collective ethnic experience, and enter hierarchal institutions which daily reinforce domination by race, sex and class, is that we gradually assume a mindset similar to those who dominate and oppress, that we lose critical consciousness because it is not reinforced or affirmed by the environment. We must be ever vigilant. It is important that we know who we are speaking to, who we most want to hear us, who we most long to move, motivate, and touch with our words.[1]

THE ESSAYS

In the first six essays the authors examine select policies and practices that have served to structure silence. These chapters roam broadly over the territories of race/ethnicity, gender, and social class, providing examples of the ways in which traditional and accepted policies and practices of silencing work in schools. Roslyn Arlin Mickelson, Stephen Samuel Smith, and Melvin L. Oliver take up the question of affirmative action in hiring academic faculty, paying particular attention to the ways in which seemingly "neutral" criteria serve to exclude African American candidates from the pool of the "qualified."

Mara Sapon-Shevin examines academic discourse and policies stemming from this discourse, piercing the power of the "gifted" label in a society tired of the language of equal opportunity and seeking strategies to preserve privilege among those historically enshrined with such privilege. Walter Haney examines the ways in which standardized tests work against students of color, despite claims by statisticians that there is an absence of test bias. Haney pries open the question of "unfairness" through a critical examination of the practice of "high stakes" testing in the United States, and the ways in which these test results have been used consistently against the academic and economic well-being of people of color.

Michelle Fine takes us into the realm of curriculum practice, where she travels through a sex education classroom, asking what is privileged as "natural," "normal," and "right" within the curriculum and the classroom and, conversely, what is shadowed, buried, hidden, and/or trivialized. Jim Cummins offers a theoretical framework for analyzing minority students' failure in school and the reasons behind the failure of past educational reform efforts aimed at this population. Cummins brings us into the world of language minority students and suggests that the educational failure of these students is linked to the extent to which schools reflect, or interrupt, the power relations that exist within the broader society. Those schools that legitimate the language of the students rather than attempt to silence this language through policy or practice are, he argues, the most successful.

Lisa Delpit, in the last essay in this section, examines the "culture of power" that exists in society, and, by extension, in educational institutions. Through focusing on the debate over process-product-oriented versus skills-oriented instruction for urban youth, Delpit concludes that teachers must teach all students the explicit and implicit rules of power as a first step toward a more just society. Her work sensitizes us to the ways in which academic discourse and practice emanating from this discourse serve to silence certain segments of the population.

In the second section, "From the Margins to the Center: Beyond Silenced Voices," we take seriously the notion that people have, in spite of the policies and practices of silencing, been able to create voice within educational institutions. It is these multifaceted voices that we must, as persons interested in the creation of democratic public spheres, be able to hear.

Carol Gilligan analyzes the developmental processes by which adolescent females come to bury both their political and their personal resistances at the moment when their bodies "fill out" and the culture of femininity envelops. Silenced, we hear, are their passions and the power of their collective rebellion. Linda Christian-Smith offers an examination of how middle- and working-class young women, ages twelve through fifteen, from diverse racial and ethnic backgrounds, construct their gender, class, racial, age, and sexual identities while reading romance fiction in school. Far from determining in any holistic sense their identities, however, young women partially accept traditional gender sentiments embedded within the novels and at the same time express a desire to move beyond them.

R. W. Connell unravels "masculinities" as they are constructed by a group of young unemployed working-class men and a group of more affluent men involved in "green" politics, that is, social action around environmental issues. Connell details the production of masculinities and argues that our inattention to do so up to now renders the male as a shield against which the "other" is always constructed and deconstructed.

Richard Friend provides an essay on/with adolescent lesbian women and gay men attending high schools. He seeks to understand at once the resounding silences in schools eclipsing multiple sexualities, as well as the tortured shouts of "faggot" as they resonate down high school halls. The text stretches to hear how young men and women construct their own identities and link up with social movements in the midst of tortured silencing. Friend reminds us of pockets of silencing and exclusion among otherwise privileged groups, and insists that the voice of class and race privilege must be further nuanced along the lines of sexual orientation.

Lois Weis narrates a story about white working-class male students angry about the loss of their relative privilege in a society that seeks to remedy past injustices and at the same time is constricted by virtue of economic restructuring. Weis argues that by virtue of the braiding of the twin privileges of whiteness and maleness and the potential loss of these privileges as we move into the 1990s, white working-class youth are ideally situated to become recruits for secular New Right ideology.

Robert Stevenson and Jeanne Ellsworth invite us to hear the voices of working-class white adolescents who have dropped out of school. Expressing neither the rich critique voiced by adolescent dropouts of color, nor enjoying the rich sense of entitlement displayed by white middle- and upper-class peers, white working-class dropouts, lacking ideologies by which they can explain, justify, or even organize on the basis of their class and race position, retreat to self-hatred, regrets, and muted social challenge.

Michele Foster takes us into the arena of teachers, offering a set of narratives collected from older "outstanding" African American teachers. These teachers provide biographies of the history of race and class relations in U.S. schools, the policies of integration, and the problematic legacy of reform in education.

Also working in the area of race, Jody Cohen suggests that young people's experiences, questions, and critiques of the meanings of race/ethnicity in this society are essential to developing an approach to multicultural education. Based on interviews with African American teenagers, Cohen opens up a discussion of race through a conversation between social theorists and these teens, who, rather than unproblematically agreeing on the definition of race, move in and out of various definitions, rooting race both biologically and socially.

William Tierney invites us into the world of Native American college students, a topic almost wholly excluded from academic literature. It is the silencing and opening of Native American voice and experiences in higher education that Tierney begins to pierce.

In the final essay, Cameron McCarthy examines the difference between and within mainstream and radical approaches to racial inequality in the educational literature. McCarthy contends that race and racism have not been adequately theorized in the literature, having been silenced by academics, and takes up this charge by developing a nonsynchronous theory of race relations in school and society. McCarthy's analysis offers a way of focusing on race, thus overcoming the silence in our theories on one of the most constitutive of all dynamics.

This volume, then, sits as testimony to the powerful press for silencing and yet, at the same time, its failure. While some of these essays examine how, through policies and practices, voices are marginalized and shut out, they, in even more compelling detail, document the relentless desire and ability to be heard and to survive.

It is our shared sense that public schools, as democratic public spheres, have an obligation to work with all students, teachers, and parents, to listen and understand, and to open up the structured silences imposed on those non-privileged. Those pushed to the margins are struggling for voice at the same time as those with privilege are mounting their energies to call for exclusive hegemonic voice. This "chorus of differences" now litters our schools, but could be so much more thoughtfully incorporated into the educational life of schooling. We wish to encourage attention to these voices, ever mindful and delighted that they flourish in harmony and in conflict. It is with this sentiment that we welcome you into this text, to imagine, with us, what "could be" if public schools were a truly democratic public sphere.

Part One

Structuring Silence:
Policies and Practice

ROSLYN ARLIN MICKELSON
STEPHEN SAMUEL SMITH
MELVIN L. OLIVER

Chapter One

Breaking through the Barriers: African American Job Candidates and the Academic Hiring Process

In 1990 Professor Derrick Bell took an indefinite unpaid leave of absence from his position at Harvard Law School to protest the institution's failure to find a "qualified" female, African American legal scholar. His dramatic action called national attention to the racial crisis in higher education, one aspect of which is the paucity of African American faculty. The proportion of university faculty members who are African American has barely risen from 3 percent in the early 1960s to an estimated 3.3 percent in 1989.[1]

In this chapter we explore how academic hiring practices affect the opportunities available to African Americans. Our focus is on the way faculty search committees choose finalists from the pool of applicants.[2] We report the findings from a national study of African American graduate students that suggests that commonly used procedures for initially assessing candidates are poor measures of "quality" and reflect structural barriers that adversely affect the job prospects of Blacks. In this respect, we argue, the barriers facing African Americans in academia bear some striking similarities to the obstacles they face in other labor markets. Those similarities make the renewed debate about affirmative action relevant to academic hiring practices.

THE PERSISTENCE OF RACISM IN THE ACADEMY

Given the tendency of some academics to idealize their workplaces as bastions of racial enlightenment, it is important to note that faculty hiring itself has never been free of the racism that has long characterized U.S. society. Two stories illustrate how academic hiring practices have sometimes exemplified the seamier aspect of race relations in this country. They also illustrate how the lines between individual and structural racism are sometimes blurred.

The first concerns the biologist Ernest Everett Just. A 1907 magna cum laude, Phi Beta Kappa graduate of Dartmouth College with a degree in English and science, Just was eagerly sought as an instructor by both Howard University and Morehouse College.[3] Just chose Howard, where, after first teaching English, he became an instructor in a newly formed zoology major and subsequently became a teacher and administrator in Howard's medical school. He fought many racist obstacles to gain advanced training at the Marine Biology Laboratory at Woods Hole, Massachusetts. There he came to the attention of its director, Frank Lilly, who was also chair of the department of biology at the University of Chicago. Impressed with Just's intelligence and lab skills, Lilly arranged to have Just's work at Woods Hole count toward earning a doctorate at the University of Chicago. After several years of working at Howard, attending summer institutes at Woods Hole, and studying at the University of Chicago, Just earned his Ph.D. in 1916. His dissertation was the basis of a series of articles on cell structure that were published in top biology journals.

Although he had an outstanding record of publications and had made important scientific contributions, Just was never seriously considered for a position at any of the major research institutions (which at that time were invariably predominantly white universities). Even those with whom he had worked and who knew him well wrote recommendations like "very good for a Negro, but not for a white," "very well qualified to be a teacher in a colored university." The only white university to seriously consider Just was Brown, but in the end it concluded that he would have been "just ideal except for his race."[4]

Just's contributions to science have, of course, outlived many of those individuals who offered these evaluations. Given the racist attitudes, such as those expressed with regard to Just, among decision makers in higher education, it is not surprising that African Americans were hardly ever found in major white colleges and universities before the 1940s and continue to appear so infrequently today. De la Luz Reyes and Halçon describe painfully similar racist practices and attitudes faced by Hispanics in the current academic job market.[5]

Lest it be thought that such outrageous bigotry has completely disappeared from the academy, the case of Reginald Clark illustrates it has not. In the mid 1980s Clark was denied tenure by Claremont Graduate School, one of six colleges in the prestigious private consortium, Claremont Colleges. In his successful racial bias lawsuit, Clark showed that the all-white faculty evaluated his work against different scholarly criteria than those used for granting tenure for the others in the department.[6] His highly praised book *Family Life and School Achievement: Why Poor Black Children Succeed or Fail* was discredited by his review committee as "too close to his dissertation," and his journal articles were said to be of insufficient quality and quantity for tenure to be granted.[7] During the course of the trial it was revealed that at the time he was denied tenure, no African American, Native American, Hispanic, or Asian American had ever been granted tenure by Claremont Graduate School.

Perhaps the most dramatic evidence presented during the trial was Clark's testimony about a conversation he inadvertently overheard. While previewing a film for a class in one room, Clark heard through an air duct the deliberations of the tenure and review committee that was discussing his case in the next one. The long, emotional, and heated discussion touched on a variety of factors that the committee planned to use to justify denying Clark tenure. In the words of one member, "White people have rights, too." Another speaker said, "We're a private school, and we're not under pressure to have minorities." Another person said about him, "We all agree he has the potential for greatness, perhaps," but then added, "I really don't know how I would feel working with a Black man."[8]

It is difficult to know how prevalent are practices similar to the ones exposed by Reginald Clark. Between 1969 and 1984, 225 faculty discrimination suits were brought, with one-fifth resulting in a victory for the plaintiff.[9] At a minimum, these data, along with the chilling similarity between the experiences of Just and Clark, should dispel any Pollyannish optimism that the academy—as enlightened as it supposedly is—has purged its hiring and promotion practices of the most blatant forms of individual racism. They also illustrate how raw bigotry can seep into and contaminate seemingly meritocratic structural procedures.

AFFIRMATIVE ACTION: ATTEMPTS TO OPEN THE ACADEMY

Affirmative action became part of the employment practices of higher education in the 1960s and 1970s as part of a larger societal effort to address a long history of discrimination in hiring practices. Adding special impetus to such developments were the protests and demands of African American students and their allies in regard to racism and sexism in higher education.[10]

Affirmative action guidelines were designed to address primarily the structural sources of discrimination in hiring.

The passage of the Civil Rights Act of 1964 and amendments to Title VII in 1972 set the legal basis for affirmative action in higher education.[11] Combined with several executive orders issued by President Lyndon B. Johnson and requirements for federal contracts issued by the Office of Federal Contract Compliance, universities were no longer as free to use racial exclusionary practices in the hiring of faculty and the admission of students as they had been historically. Job openings now had to be widely advertised, and written evidence of the good-faith efforts of the university to increase the pool of minority applicants had to be provided. Federal contracts and grants, which provided significant income to the medical and scientific enterprises of most research-oriented universities, were subject to compliance review that monitored the affirmative action efforts of the institution in general.[12] The Adams case of 1971, which called for faculty desegregation as an adjunct to mandatory student body desegregation, contributed to the process of faculty diversification.[13]

The barriers facing minorities in university employment are best understood in the context of those that exist throughout the occupational structure. The important role of affirmative action guidelines in breaking through structural barriers to employment throughout the occupational structure has been carefully discussed by Braddock and McPartland in their analysis of social networks and access to the labor market.[14] They identified specific job barriers facing women and minorities at three stages of the employment process: recruitment, job entry (selection), and job promotion. Using a national survey of employers, they found that minority candidates were significantly disadvantaged because the informal social networks used by employers to recruit entry-level employees were segregated. Braddock and McPartland found that for middle-level and upper-level jobs that require specialized knowledge and advanced education, employers use screening information about the type and reputation of the applicant's college program, the applicant's grades, and recommendations from college officials.[15] Because at all levels of the occupational structure, employers extensively use inexpensive and less time-consuming informal candidate-recruitment practices, Braddock and McPartland concluded that the segregated informal networks constitute an important racial barrier at the job candidate stage."[16] Recent work by Coverdill confirms these findings.[17] His work also demonstrates the greater importance of job contacts to Black males compared to white males for obtaining a job.

Braddock and McPartland argue that racially segregated social networks are maintained in part because they are tied to the racial segregation of neighborhoods and public schools and also because of white misunderstanding of the sources of racial group differences. The tendency of employers to use the simplest and least expensive methods for recruitment, namely, informal social networks, often creates the primary conditions for racial exclusionary barriers in employment at all levels of the occupational structure.[18]

THE MERITOCRATIC RHETORIC OF FACULTY HIRING

Although Braddock and McPartland's research examines barriers to employment throughout the occupational structure, there are a number of parallel processes in higher education. Just as employers use the time and money expedience of social networks (job contacts) to identify the pool of potential job candidates, faculty search committees, faced with hundreds of applications and limited recruitment time and funds, also use indirect measures of candidate suitability. These indirect measures include both the social networks of job candidates, namely their referees, and the reputation of the university that awarded the applicant her or his Ph.D. Because minorities continue to have less access to the most powerful and prestigious academic networks as well as to the most elite graduate schools than do majority males, they are structurally disadvantaged with regard to academic hiring.

This structural disadvantage faced by minority candidates is masked by the allegedly meritocratic nature of academic searches. That merit is the putative value guiding the selection of university faculty cannot be denied. What *can* be questioned is the ability of whatever bodies evaluate and select candidates for faculty positions to make judgments based on a set of meritocratic criteria. Analyzed from a sociological perspective, the selection process appears to be less an expression of positive choices and more the result of negative choices, where inappropriate and supposedly less-qualified candidates are weeded out and the most qualified candidates buoy to the top of the list.[19]

THE FALLACY OF SELECTION BY INSTITUTIONAL PROXY

Proponents argue that a system that allows an autonomous faculty to choose its peers within the context of meritocratic criteria is the best protection that minorities have against biases in the selection process.[20] When selection is based on neutral, objective, universalistic, and achievement-based criteria, the argument states, Blacks and other disadvantaged minorities are protected against the intrusion of particularistic and biased practices that have previously excluded them. This presumes, of course, that there is a consensus as to what constitutes merit. However, this presumption disregards an

established literature[21] that finds the search process to be plagued by precisely the opposite—"objective standards are often vague, inconsistent, and
weighted toward subjective judgments."[22] The implementation of meritocratic principles is thwarted somewhere between rhetoric and reality.

To understand just where the disjuncture between rhetoric and implementation occurs, we look more closely at the search process itself. Two very
good studies offer considerable insight into this process.[23] One describes the
operation of academic searches before affirmative action, and the other describes post-affirmative-action efforts. Both studies show that the results of
searches continue to be the same. Among new Ph.D.'s who rise to the top of
lists of qualified candidates are graduates from the most elite universities who
are recommended by the most eminent people in their field and who were, in
many cases, encouraged to apply by members of the hiring faculty.

How does this occur? The power of institutional reputation (and likewise
department reputation) is crucial to the selection process, because of the inability of faculty committees to agree upon the factors that constitute "excellence in research and teaching." Academic disciplines and specializations
differ as to the degree to which excellence can be recognized. There is greater
consensus in the physical and natural sciences on what constitutes good
work. The social sciences and humanities are fragmented by varying schools
of thought and paradigms—so much so that consensus is difficult, if not impossible, to achieve. It is in this way that institutional prestige becomes a
proxy that can take the place of—or at least supplement—a candidate's claim
for excellence in the face of shifting and elusive standards of scholarship.
From the outset, the search process becomes biased, not toward individual
merit, as the ideology of meritocracy would have us believe, but toward institutional reputation. Institutional reputation or prestige becomes a proxy for
the qualifications of the candidate.

In addition to the attention paid to institutional proxies of merit, faculties
tend to rely heavily on the sources of recommendations that accompany a
candidate's application. Given an inability to reliably evaluate a candidate's
record in the light of conflicting or unclear standards, what becomes important is the nature and source of an applicant's supporting letters. They testify
to the referee's perceptions of a candidate's abilities and potentials. But more
importantly, to the degree that the referee is personally well known, the more
influence the recommendation will have. Thus Caplow and McGee argue that
"personal influence among networks of colleagues" is the most important
carrier of the prestige that really counts.[24] In other words, the academic market is not an objective competitive system, but rather a system of sponsored
mobility where patronage from established scholars at elite institutions is the
important indicator of potential merit.[25]

That such a system radically departs from the model of meritocracy seems evident. Smelser and Content argue that what in actuality occurs is a succession of exclusions.[26] What is of interest to us is that the built-in biases of such a system tend to *exclude* more African American scholars than to *include* them. In part, this is a consequence of the sponsored character of the search. In a quasi-objective manner, each discipline can claim to have knowledge of the best universities in a particular field. However, when institutional reputation is used as an exclusionary criterion, the end result is to unfairly exclude those Blacks who do not have access to such prestigious institutions.

African Americans and other minorities suffer because most lack the sustenance of initial privilege. They often suffer severe difficulties conquering personal and institutional barriers in their quest for academic success. Davidson's poignant essay "The Furious Passage of the Black Graduate Student," while twenty years old, still resonates with the experience of many African Americans who have survived graduate school.[27] A 1977 report of the National Academy of Science indicates that Blacks are less likely to earn their Ph.D.'s from the top-rated institutions and that the proportion earned from that tier is less than their proportion of the total degrees conferred.[28] In a more recent study Thomas obtained similar results.[29]

Because it is almost impossible for a student to gain access to a powerful and prestigious mentor unless he or she attends an elite university where these professors teach, African Americans are less likely to have such individuals as their referees. Referees are the analogues of the social networks or job contacts researchers found to be so important in the general labor market. In both instances, given the tendencies for these networks to be race, class, and gender segregated, minority job seekers are disadvantaged.

If one disregards the overwhelming evidence that access to elite graduate programs and prestigious faculty is linked to race, class, and gender, one might argue that the most qualified individuals attend the most prestigious institutions and are trained by the best professors in the field and that, therefore, institutional proxy for candidate quality is not only reasonable, it is an accurate and efficient device for identifying the merit of candidates for faculty positions. And if this is true, affirmative action guidelines are, indeed, unnecessary. But this is an empirical issue. In view of this, we explore several questions: Are there differences in quality among Black graduate students in variously ranked graduate institutions? Do their backgrounds differ so as to confirm the notion that students from better institutions also come from more privileged backgrounds? Do students from variously ranked graduate schools differ in aspirations for career success?

These questions test directly the assumptions that undergird present-day academic search practices. To the degree that we find differences among students, the current search process may well be the best way to identify minority talent. Such a finding will lend support to the use of institutional proxies as an indirect measure of potential talent. To the degree that we do not find such differences, we can argue that the search process is not meritocratic and affects African Americans unfairly by overlooking an important source of Black scholarly resources in nonelite institutions of graduate training.

A STUDY OF AFRICAN AMERICAN GRADUATE STUDENTS

The Data and Sample

Data used in this study come from surveys administered to participants in the National Study of Black College Students (NSBCS).[30] The instruments gathered comprehensive information on the respondents' background, achievements, experiences, attitudes, and aspirations. For more details about the methods, sample, and data, see Allen, Epps, and Haniff's *College in Black and White*.[31] Our sample consists of all graduate and professional school students enrolled in the universities that participated in the NSBCS in 1981 and 1982. Our sample consists of 387 students from the top rank of universities, 224 students from the middle rank, and 122 students from the lower rank, a total of 733 graduate and professional students. We discuss the basis for institutional ranking below.[32]

Variables

We used a performance-based model to examine the issue of quality differences among African American graduate students. What skills are necessary for successful careers in academia? What factors are academic search committees likely to accept as evidence of a candidate's potential merit? Four factors come to mind. First, we considered the student's academic performance as measured by grade point average. Outstanding grades indicate that a student has mastered the necessary coursework and subsequently has obtained the skills, theoretical background, and knowledge to do good work in an academic discipline.[33] Second, we looked at the receipt of fellowships, research assistantships, and grants; this step is a precursor to the competitive process of securing the grants and prized fellowships that are a part of a successful academic career. Third, we noted the presentation of research papers at conferences and professional meetings. Finally, we considered the publication of scholarly articles and books. A combination of these four factors constitutes our indicator of quality.[34]

Respondents' quality index scores (QUALITY), our dependent variable, range from a low of 0.5 to a high of 8.0. The formula for ascertaining each student's score on our quality index works as follows: A first-year student with a high grade point average and a research grant would receive a score of 4.5 (GPA > 3.0 [2.0] + grant [2.5] = 4.5), whereas a third-year student would receive a score of 3.5 for the same accomplishments (GPA > 3.0 [1.5] + grant [2.0] = 3.5).[35] In this way we weight the scale to the length of our respondents' graduate careers. We also adapt this formula to the extremes of our scales. Extraordinary first-year students with high grades, grants, publications, and paper presentations—of which there are several in the sample—can surpass the 8.0 on the scale. In these circumstances, we truncate their scores to 8.0. Certain respondents, primarily a few first-year graduate students have not presented papers and have no grants or publications. In addition, their grade point average is below 3.0. To prevent their quality index score from receiving a value of zero, which would cause their case to be dropped from the analysis, we assign them a score of 0.5 in order to retain their cases.

We created our university rank variable (RANK) by dividing the eight graduate training institutions that participated the NSBCS into three groups based on the national reputations of their graduate departments. The top group represents institutions that in our sample of schools, across every discipline, have highly ranked departments whose size and influence have made them traditional suppliers of faculty for other elite institutions. This group includes the Universities of Michigan at Ann Arbor, Wisconsin at Madison, and North Carolina at Chapel Hill. Universities in the middle category have nationally ranked departments but are not consistently as strong as those in the first group. This category includes the University of California at Los Angeles, Arizona State, and SUNY–Stony Brook. The lowest-ranked group, which includes Memphis State and Eastern Michigan University, represents schools without national reputations and with relatively new graduate programs. These institutions, located for the most part in urban areas, developed most rapidly in the 1960s, when expansion in higher education was common. Although they have recruited high-quality faculty, they have yet to gain more than regional (and in some cases local) recognition as important graduate institutions.

In addition to these key variables, in order to elaborate our model, we introduce into our analysis a series of individual and structural variables that are traditionally related to academic achievement. These are students' gender (GENDER), marital status (MARITAL), presence of young children in the home (KIDS), father's education (DADED), father's occupation (DADOCC), mother's education (MOMED), mother's occupation (MOMOCC), respondent's age at first full-time job (AGE), the type of first job (FIRSTJOB), and the respondent's motivation to succeed in a chosen career (HUNGER).

FINDINGS

Differences in Quality

We began our data analysis with a series of analyses of variance that examined mean differences in quality index scores for students who attended differently ranked graduate institutions. The first ANOVA revealed that the average score on the quality measure for students from the lower-ranked schools (3.35) was only slightly lower than for those from the middle- and top-ranked schools (3.51 and 3.59). Table 1.1 shows that the differences were not statistically significant.

The analyses of variance also showed that institutional differences are less important than certain individual attributes in predicting how well students will perform in graduate school. Two of these important attributes are marital status and gender. As table 1.1 shows, married students and men have higher mean scores on our index of quality than do women and single graduate students. Both gender and marital status differences in graduate students' performance are statistically significant (gender, $p < .0001$; marital status, $p < .05$). Overall, the analyses of variance show that high-caliber Black graduate students are found not only in the highest-ranking institutions but also in the lowest-ranking ones. Our analyses indicate that marital status and gender are better predictors of student quality than rank of graduate institution.

Differences in Background

Implicit in the academic search process is the assumption that the best and brightest African American students, like their white male counterparts, attend the best universities and become the best Ph.D.'s. This assumption implies that the educational attainment process for Blacks in academia is similar to that for whites. The evidence regarding white students reveals a strong relationship among family background, academic achievement, and the prestige of the university.[36] Can we find evidence of this educational attainment process in our sample of Black graduate students? Our analyses indicate that this is not the case.

Among Black students at the variously ranked schools in our sample, parental occupational and educational backgrounds can be quite diverse (see table 1.1). For example, the mean educational level of the mothers and fathers of students from the highest- and lowest-ranked graduate schools in our study

TABLE 1.1
Summary of Means and Standard Deviations of Selected Variables

Dependent Variable	N	Mean	Standard Deviation	F
Student Quality Index				.492
High rank	387	3.51	2.16	
Medium rank	224	3.59	2.11	
Low rank	122	3.35	2.23	
Student Quality Index				10.48***
Male	320	3.80	2.28	
Female	413	3.28	4.14	
Student Quality Index				4.28*
Single	427	3.37	4.53	
Married	219	3.74	5.01	
Father's Education (1 to 6 scale)				4.13**
High rank	375	2.93	1.48	
Medium rank	219	2.59	2.12	
Low rank	118	2.95	2.20	
Mother's Education (1 to 6 scale)				9.79***
High rank	386	3.10	1.31	
Medium rank	221	2.67	1.32	
Low rank	126	3.00	1.34	
Father's Occupation (Duncan SEI)				.82
High rank	345	40.40	28.75	
Medium rank	194	36.18	26.17	
Low rank	106	42.30	28.75	
Mother's Occupation (Duncan SEI)				1.47
High rank	338	40.51	24.94	
Medium rank	179	36.64	24.04	
Low rank	110	39.74	24.44	
Age at First Job				10.42***
High rank	285	20.40	9.78	
Medium rank	197	20.72	9.40	
Low rank	92	18.91	14.02	
Occupational Prestige of First Job (Duncan SEI)				5.57*
High rank	243	51.95	21.18	
Medium rank	151	56.11	17.31	
Low rank	106	42.34	28.75	
Motivation to Succeed ("Hunger")				1.159
High rank	222	3.60	2.25	
Medium rank	127	3.61	1.91	
Low rank	76	3.88	1.51	

* p = <.05
** p = <.01
*** p = <.001

are virtually the same (2.93 versus 2.95 for father's education, and 3.10 compared to 3.00 for mother's education). Black students attending the middle-ranked schools appear to come from social backgrounds in which the parents are less well educated and hold lower-status jobs than parents of Blacks from both lower- and higher-ranked schools.

African American graduate students from all social backgrounds appear to attend a variety of graduate schools. Students in our sample from the lowest-ranked universities worked full-time at a much earlier age (18.91) than did students from either the middle or highest category (20.71 and 20.40). Furthermore, they were likely to have less prestigious first jobs than their counterparts at elite universities ($p < .05$). Yet the marked differences in students' family backgrounds do not seem to influence their quality index scores.

Motivational Differences

Inherent in the notion that the best students train at the most prestigious universities is the assumption that students at elite universities are the most highly motivated and therefore aspire to the highest accomplishments in their chosen field. To test whether this difference exists among graduate students in our sample, we examined an item related to this theme that appeared in the NSBCS. Students were asked the following question:

> After you are in the profession which will be your life's work, when do you think you will be able to consider yourself successful enough so that you can relax and stop trying so hard to get ahead?

Students could choose one of five answers, which ranged from "when you are doing well enough to stay in the profession" (scored 1) to "when you are recognized as one of the top persons in the profession" (scored 5). We labeled this the "hunger for success" question: How motivated are these students to achieve at the highest levels possible? According to assumptions inherent in the evaluation of graduate students for jobs in the market today, the hungriest students are assumed to be found among those at the most elite institutions.

The data, however, indicate that the sample of students from elite universities are no more likely to be hungry for success than those from less prestigious schools. Although not statistically significant, mean HUNGER scores for students from the less high ranked schools are higher (3.88) than for students at the most highly ranked schools (3.60). Once again, our data offer no evidence to support the notion that academic potential, this time in the form of highly motivated Black students, is found exclusively in the narrow group of elite universities.

There are a number of limitations in the NSBCS data that make a definitive test of the our argument difficult. For example, we would like to be able to compare students across disciplines, because we are aware that some disciplines can be more affected by the institutional resources that students have available to them than are others. Our data do not permit us to make these comparisons. Second, our sample of universities includes only public universities. Had we included elite private schools like Stanford, Harvard, Yale, or the University of Chicago, our student population, hence our findings, may have been different. Finally, we are aware of the problems inherent in attempts to operationalize a construct like student quality. The analyses presume that grades are equivalent across institutions. Our results might have been different if we had controlled for the number and quality of the respondent's articles and presentations. Our measure of student quality is a rather crude and preliminary attempt to tap a fairly complex phenomenon. Yet even with these flaws, we submit this research as evidence that fresh, new African American academic talent is not isolated in prestigious graduate programs, but is dispersed broadly throughout higher education.

DISCUSSION AND CONCLUSION

The study reported in this essay suggests that the practice by search committees of using institutional reputation and referee prestige as proxies for candidate quality can adversely affect the job prospects of African Americans. Using data from the NSBCS, we examined the assumption that African American graduate students from elite schools are superior to those from lesser ranked universities in terms of their academic promise, social background, and motivation to succeed. Given a performance-based model of quality, our data show that there are minimal differences in the quality of students, their background, and their motivation to succeed. The assumption that the cream of academic talent rises to the top of the academic hierarchy may conceivably be true for majority males, but it is false for African Americans. The cry often heard in faculty search committees that qualified minorities cannot be found is one that should be amended to "properly sponsored and credentialed" minority Ph.D.'s cannot be found.

These findings have several important implications. First, they indicate striking similarities between the structural barriers in the academic job market and those in the occupational structure as a whole. As discussed earlier, Braddock and McPartland's analysis of social networks and access to labor markets indicated minorities were significantly disadvantaged because the informal networks used by employers tend to be racially segregated.[37] Segregated informal networks constitute an important racial barrier for job candidates. Similarly, minority applicants for faculty positions are disadvantaged by their unequal access to powerful and prestigious academic mentors and elite universities.

Second, our findings illuminate the broader debate about affirmative action. Although controversial from the beginning, affirmative action policies have come under increasing attack during the Reagan and Bush years.[38] Most of the attacks involve two analytically distinct kinds of claims. The first is usually an empirical one that points to the alleged shortcomings of affirmative action policies in order to challenge their very existence. The second is a more theoretical one and hinges on the presumed pernicious consequences of any employment policy that is not based exclusively on putative meritocratic criteria.

Into the first category fall claims that affirmative action policies largely assist the most privileged members of minority groups, such as the highly educated middle class.[39] Other critics argue that affirmative action programs imply the inferiority of the targeted groups and thus set into action psychosocial processes that produce self-doubt and lowered performance.[40] Undoubtedly, there is some merit in both these claims. It is certainly true that affirmative action policies have disproportionately benefited advantaged members of minority groups. Likewise, some social science research suggests a link between token or solo employee status and minority self-doubt.[41] But acknowledging the partial merit of these claims is not equivalent to saying that affirmative action has failed or is useless. That is because affirmative action policies are at most only partially responsible for the negative outcomes attributed primarily to them by these critics. For example, the restructured, deindustrialized economy is a crucial component of any explanation of the failure of non-college-educated minority workers to get good jobs.[42] Likewise, even in the absence of affirmative action programs, cultural stereotypes lead many white Americans to perceive African Americans as less competent.[43] In combination with organizational arrangements like token or solo status, these negative stereotypes can contribute to lower minority self-esteem and performance. But even if these unintended negative consequences can be attributed partially to affirmative action, this is hardly a reason for jettisoning the policies. Far better to develop policies that help whites deal with racial stereotypes as well as alter the organization of the workplace so as to not place African Americans in token or solo statuses. Moreover, affirmative action policies that bring additional minorities into a workplace help build a critical mass so that token status and negative stereotypes are more difficult to sustain. A similar conclusion emerges from our work. To be sure, the use of institutional proxy as an indicator of candidate "merit" undermines the effectiveness of affirmative action guidelines for faculty searches. But that is not an argument for throwing out the baby with the bath water.

In talking about a candidate's suitability for a position, we are led to the second kind of claim against affirmative action: the alleged pernicious social consequences of any hiring policy not based solely on a candidate's merit. Such policies, it is claimed, constitute reverse discrimination and provoke white backlash. There is more than a bit of self-serving hypocrisy in such claims. For example, warnings about the possibilities of "backlash" have historically been used to intimidate the disadvantaged from taking action to redress any of their grievances. And it is not just the likes of Ronald Reagan and George Bush who pointedly obscure the differences among quotas, goals, and affirmative action guidelines. Nonetheless, this claim touches an area of legitimate concern that cannot be completely dismissed by the flip, albeit largely true, retort that particular kinds of preferential policies (such as federal housing policies, mortgage assistance, targeted compensations for specific groups like farmers and veterans, or college admission for children of wealthy alumni) have long been the functional equivalent of affirmative action for whites. A more thorough reply points to the difficulty of assessing "merit" and the even greater difficulties in establishing criteria that are simultaneously meritocratic and race neutral. Moreover, demanding that all people be treated meritocratically in a society in which the political economy is highly unequal, serves to perpetuate and aggravate inequality. The perfect illustration of this point is the process by which most workers attain a job.

Assessing the merit of a job applicant is a difficult matter. Detailed work histories, aptitude tests, and trial employment periods are expensive. The economics literature on discrimination in labor-market processes calls "signaling" what sociologists identify as "statistical discrimination"—that is, employer use of ascriptive characteristics of race and gender as proxies for worker reliability, job experience, proper demeanor, and work ethic attitudes.[44] Coverdill argues that because of statistical discrimination, job contacts are even more important for minority males in the process of getting a job. The job contact can provide information to an employer about the applicant that can intervene and counteract the negative race stereotypes.[45] But because social networks remain largely segregated by race, class, and gender, the role of social networks in employment tends to perpetuate employment discrimination by race, class, and gender. This, then, is hardly meritocratic.

The academic search process entails similar dynamics, where the imperatives of time and the difficulty of directly assessing candidate merit lead also to the use of signals and social networks, in this case, the use of institutional reputation and referee prestige. African Americans continue to be less likely to become part of these social networks. Consequently, the use of these indirect measures of candidate suitability tends to perpetuate the racial crisis in higher education. Again, this requires an enormous stretch of the imagination to consider it a meritocratic process.

Employment policies and practices do not exist in a vacuum; they operate in a society whose racial divisions overlap those of class and income. That is why if establishing criteria for assessing an applicant's quality is difficult, defining criteria that are simultaneously meritocratic and race neutral is even harder. Search committees may apply the criterion of institutional proxy equally to all the candidates who submit applications. But when African American graduate students do not have the same access to elite universities as do majority males, the results of faculty searches will tend to underidentify the number of qualified African Americans as finalists for academic positions.

Our argument has had two parts. In the first we attempted to demonstrate that, contrary to popular belief, the outcomes of the academic search process tend to be elitist not meritocratic ones. The second part of our argument sought to show why the use of institutional proxy is simply an inaccurate way of assessing African American candidates' potentials. We wish to conclude by bringing the discussion back to the importance of affirmative action. The labor market processes we have described belie claims that meritocratic hiring practices are, in fact, the norm. Affirmative action guidelines continue to be necessary in order to break through the structural barriers that we have described at length. Our findings suggest also that the academic search process needs to be redesigned to minimize, if not eliminate, the use of institutional proxy as a measure of candidate merit. As Alvarez notes, when universities face real shortages of resources, "the cognitive fictions by which social stratification is made legitimate or justifiable are likely to receive vigorous endorsement."[46] And indeed, the irony of current attacks against affirmative action is that, just at the time when the recruitment and promotion of minority faculty has assumed great public interest, the ideology of meritocracy has become all the more vigorously defended and promoted in the halls of academia.

Chapter Two

Gifted Education and the Protection of Privilege: Breaking the Silence, Opening the Discourse

---

INTRODUCTION

The emperor was told that he was being woven beautiful clothing that could not be seen by silly folks, only by wise people, and he paid the weavers lots of money to weave him a suit. When the weavers brought the clothes to the emperor, he could see nothing, of course, but not wanting to be thought a silly man, he pretended to dress himself in invisible clothes. Those who watched the emperor parade naked did not want to be thought fools either, so they said nothing. When, finally, one honest little boy blurted out the truth, the emperor ran naked and embarrassed back to his castle, but alas, by then the weavers were gone, and so was the money.

The story of gifted education is a lot like the story of the emperor's new clothes; vast looms have been constructed to weave a cloth that we can't actually see, children have been identified and labeled, special programs have been organized and evaluated, and not wanting to be thought fools, not wanting to appear disrespectful or envious or unappreciative of the beautiful weave, many of us have remained silent. As in the story, increasing amounts of money are spent to support gifted education, but unlike the story, the weavers are not leaving town; firmly entrenched within powerful governmental and educational positions, solidly supported by current economic and political rhetoric, they will continue to maintain that their clear vision

25

allows them to see what the rest of us do not, that gifted education is a just, democratic way to provide for children's individual needs and meet the needs of society.

Declaring that there is something undemocratic about gifted education, something fundamentally wrong with labeling a small group of children in a way that entitles them to a highly differentiated, almost always superior, education is a bit like saying that the emperor has no clothes—it is both patently obvious to many and yet not something we talk about. It is striking that some of the most obvious critiques of gifted education rarely find a public voice.

This chapter examines some of the stated rationales for gifted education and relates those rationales to the rhetoric of protection that has been used to silence and marginalize critics. I will explore both how criticism is avoided within schools and what happens when the silence is broken and a critical discourse is begun. This chapter concludes with an analysis of ways in which an open exploration of merit and value could be developed, and must be developed if our schools and society are to achieve educational and societal equity.

SITUATING GIFTED EDUCATION BEYOND CRITIQUE

Elaborate critiques of tracking and differentiated instruction have been offered. Oakes's landmark book *Keeping Track*[1] provides extensive and elegant testimony to the ways in which schools both create and perpetuate existing social and educational stratification by providing children with vastly different educations and possibilities. Many others have also explored the ways in which race, class, and gender often become the key determinants of students' educational futures, and there is growing acknowledgment of the prejudicial and often devastating effects of such differentiation.[2] Since gifted programs represent the ultimate tracking, the selection of a small group of students who are provided with highly differentiated, often segregated, special educational programming, it is striking that most critiques of tracking and the sorting/selection role of schools do not directly address gifted education. Although race, class, and gender are increasingly regarded as illegitimate criteria for differentiation, grouping by ability has been relatively immune from such critique.[3]

How can we account for this silence? One might argue that critiques of gifted education are excluded from more general tracking discussions because their discriminatory effects are so obvious, so flagrantly apparent, that criticism of gifted education is subsumed under broader critiques. But perhaps there is more. The metaphor of the emperor's new clothes may be particularly revealing; I will describe here several of the major arguments used to promote and defend gifted education, all of which serve a priori to limit the credibility of potential critics. Within the traditional rhetoric that surrounds gifted education and the ways in which the discourse is framed, questioning the desirability of such programs is judged un-American, unenlightened, and unsophisticated, the action of those too stupid or too shortsighted to appreciate the elegant texture of the Emperor's new cape. Thus, potential critiques become caught in the rhetoric of gifted advocates, trapped by assumptions they may not share.

The following are some of the common arguments raised when the need for gifted programs is questioned.

These Kids Are Special; You Wouldn't Understand

In discussions about gifted children, it is not uncommon to hear people talk and act as though giftedness were a tangible characteristic of behavior, personality, or genetic makeup that can be objectively and reliably identified. We speak, for example, about "finding gifted children" and about "identifying gifted children," about "talent searches" and about screening for ability. By describing a group of children in ways that emphasize their differences from typical or "normal" children, we are encouraged to believe that giftedness is something foreign, outside our daily, commonsense frameworks. The parent who exclaims, "Well, I knew my daughter was very smart, but I had no idea she was gifted," provides evidence of the ways in which official, scientific-sounding, technical terminology replaces our commonsense ways of talking about and thinking about children's differences and further legitimizes differentiation.[4]

In reality, identifying a category of children as "gifted" represents a decision. It is a decision to attend to specific variables of performance or achievement and to label those who display them as gifted. It is a decision to establish an arbitrary cutoff point along a continuum of scores or behaviors and to then act as though those above that point are qualitatively rather than quantitatively different from those below. Csikszentmihalyi and Robinson illustrate how the measurement of giftedness through IQ testing leads to debates about whether 3 percent of the population or 5 percent is actually gifted and where those cutoffs should be made. They explain that such questions (3 or 5 percent?) can have either "naturalistic" or "attributional" meanings: The naturalistic assumption is that giftedness is a natural fact, and therefore the number of gifted children can be counted, as one might count white herons or panda bears. If this is the sense in which people are asking the question, the question is meaningless. The attributional assumption recognizes that giftedness is not an objective fact but a result jointly constituted by social expectations and individual abilities. From this perspective, it is obvious that the question "What proportion of the population is 'gifted'?" means "What proportion of the population have we agreed to call 'gifted'?"[5]

By acting as though giftedness were an objective reality, rather than a decision, we silence discussion about that decision. Since the most common way of identifying children as gifted is through intelligence testing, that process itself (which must be administered by a certified school psychologist or clinician) leads to the silencing of those who are not licensed or credentialed. Anyone can talk about which children are "smart," but when evaluation and labeling are based on science, when the label is not *smart* but *gifted and talented,* then lay conversation, debate, or rebuttal is muted.

Not only is giftedness assumed by many to be objectively verifiable, but, for many, this assumption is linked to a belief in the inborn, hereditary nature of intelligence, thus further linking the identification process to "science" and further removing the decision from common discourse. According to this position, we are not defining intelligence or making decisions about what kinds of skills we value, but simply identifying and labeling inherent, immutable human characteristics, some of which happen to be highly valued. Selden has written about the extent to which biology has been used to legitimate other forms of inequality, specifically in the eugenics movement;[6] if biology is destiny, then identifying peoples' genetics, biological makeup, and educational options is descriptive, objective, and neutral, rather than evaluative, arbitrary, and value-laden. Thus, identifying children as gifted is generally seen as an essentially benign, if not beneficial, process—now we have found these children and can attend to them properly—and while discussions about accuracy and reliability have been prominent, the validity of the category has rarely been challenged.

Although the extent to which mental retardation can be seen to be a social construct—a shared decision to see and describe things in a certain way—has received increasing attention,[7] this extension has not been made to children labeled as "gifted." Logically, if IQ scores are questionably valid, unidimensional, and not educationally useful for students at the low end of the spectrum, it would be surprising for those same IQ scores to be valid, complete, and educationally significant at the other end of the spectrum. But the parallels have not been made clear; while it has become increasingly unacceptable to "send children to the dungeon" (isolated in segregated special education classes), a similar uproar has not been raised about the justice of sending only some children to the tower.

By focusing on the accuracy of the IQ tests administered, and on correlations between IQ and other standardized achievement measures, the focusing question has become "Is this child really gifted?" rather than the more challenging questions, "How was the decision made to call this child 'gifted' and why?" or "What are the consequences of labeling this child as 'gifted'?"

It's Only Fair to Treat Different Children Differently

Gifted children have been described as the most underserved minority group in the country, as "deprived" and as suffering "psychological damage and permanent impairment of their abilities to function well."[8] Gifted advocates have argued that it is only right to treat children differently who are so different from typical children. Judge Alfred Gitelson's decision in a Los Angeles superior court case reads, in part:

> Equal education is the foundation of the right to be a human being. . . . This does not mean that any child or any other gifted child having a greater capacity to learn may or shall be deprived of his or her opportunity of learning more. It does mean that every child shall have the equal opportunity to learn to the best of his or her ability. That opportunity must be made available on equal terms.[9]

By adopting a rhetoric of special needs that parallels that of special education, gifted advocates encourage us to view gifted children as needing and deserving services that are different from those typically provided; just as blind children need instruction in braille, hearing impaired children need to learn sign language, and children labeled as "mentally retarded" need differentiated instruction, gifted children need educational programs tailored to their unique skills and abilities. The Marland Report defines gifted and talented children as follows:

> Gifted and talented children are those identified by professionally qualified persons who by virtue of outstanding abilities are capable of high performance. These children require differentiated educational programs and services beyond those normally provided by the regular school program in order to realize their contribution to self and society.[10]

Much of the advocacy material in support of gifted education draws direct parallels with other special education categories, arguing that P.L. 94–142 mandated that all handicapped children be provided with a free, appropriate, public education, and that gifted children deserve no less. This argument, is, of course, highly related to the belief that giftedness represents an objective characteristic and that one should not discriminate against people simply because they are born different. This equity argument is further buttressed by the belief that, just as a handicapped child can occur in any family, regardless of race, ethnicity, or economic or social background, giftedness (if it is an organic, or biological, characteristic) can "happen" to anyone. Since, according to this logic, everyone has an equal chance of being gifted, and some children from terrible backgrounds and impoverished families do make it into gifted programs, the educational system must be fair and open; just as we would not consider it appropriate to deny services to children with cystic fibrosis, even though almost all of them are white, how can we think of denying gifted programs to gifted children, even though a disproportionate number of them are white, upper middle class? Gallagher and Weiss, in describing America's "love-hate relationship with giftedness and talent," state that "we revere the gifted individual who has risen from humble background. We are proud to live in a society where talent can triumph over poor environment or limited family status."[11]

The belief in random distribution of giftedness ("You never know where you'll find these kids") also fuels the talent-search mentality and the use of standardized tests in order to uncover exceptionality, at the same time that it ignores which children do well on standardized tests and the very nonrandom distribution of who gets into gifted programs. Freedman, in discussing the identification of children categorized as talented in art, links the talent-search mentality to the rhetoric of public responsibility; it is important to our society to identify and specially educate talented children, and since this is much too important a job to be left to teachers, it must be objectified through testing. Freedman explains how the discrimination of talent was objectified and tested, with the assumption that appraisal through testing would reveal natural merit.[12]

Not all advocates focus entirely on heredity and on natural talent; however, those gifted advocates who do acknowledge the crucial role of the environment and of education in producing "giftedness" often do so in terms of the further urgency of finding and nurturing native talent, lest it be wasted. Gallagher and Weiss, for example, argue that

> we have tried to find methods to uncover the talent that will always be there, just as one might lift up a basket and find a lantern shining beneath it. A contradictory explanation, however, is more in line with known facts. Since ability in young children is the product of both environment and native ability, a poor environment experienced over time can substantially reduce, or even eliminate, the high talent or ability originally present. The notion that superior talent can, in fact, be suppressed or destroyed lends additional urgency to the need to discover ways to provide stimulating educational experiences.[13]

Later in the same monograph, Gallagher and Weiss acknowledge that one of the unsolved programs in gifted education is "the concept of giftedness as a genetic trait."

> Quite clearly giftedness is, in part, a genetic trait, as a substantial body of evidence indicates. There is also a substantial body of evidence to suggest

that it is not only genetics, but genetics married to opportunity, that produces gifted children. Such a finding may make educators breathe more easily, because it enables them to explain troublesome differences shown by research but not widely understood. There have been major sex, racial, and ethnic differences in the proportions of youngsters identified as gifted and talented. When one adds opportunity to the formula, then such differences become understandable and explainable.[14]

The "troublesome differences" alluded to above are the gross inequalities in who gets labeled as "gifted"; conceptualizing giftedness as "genetics married to opportunity" may make such differences more tolerable to some, but these differences actually confirm the ways in which differentiated opportunities further compound whatever inequalities children bring to school. Such arguments fail to address the fact that while a poor environment over time (as described above) certainly can suppress and destroy those with "superior talent," there are unquestionably negative effects of poor educational opprtunities on all children. The "urgency of discovering ways to provide stimulating educational experiences" should not hinge on finding and developing those with "superior talents."

Gifted Children Face Special Challenges

Historically, attempts to garner support for gifted children on the basis of their unique and special needs have not always been successful; there are no gifted poster children, and it has been difficult to make broadly based appeals on behalf of children whom some see as uniquely privileged. In order to draw support for this group of "underserved" children, gifted advocates have adopted alternative strategies for appealing for public sympathy. One is to make a case for the pain experienced by those who are exceptionally bright. In their book *Guiding the Gifted Child,* Webb, Meckstroth, and Tolan attempt to convey the frustrations that gifted children experience in their daily lives; they argue that the pain of a gifted child having to live in a "normal" world can be equated with what a normal person would have to experience in a world of retarded people:

> Imagine living in a world where the average IQ was 50 or 60, where most others are actually retarded. Imagine that there is no other world to live in, and much of the world's productions are, in fact, mediocre. The challenge, then, is whether we could learn to live gladly in that world, with personal contentment, sharing, and joy, or whether we would be angry, depressed, withdrawn and miserable . . . perhaps finally deciding that such a life was not worth living.[15]

Other effects of "unrecognized giftedness" are listed as everything from inattention, restlessness, mischievous behavior, hyperactivity, withdrawal, imaginary illness, and refusal to attend school, for the individual, and the loss of talent and leadership, for the country.[16]

When this rhetoric is challenged as inaccurate and not conducive toward developing positive attitudes toward differences (including toward those labeled as "retarded"),[17] the counteraccusation is leveled that failure to be sympathetic to the plight of the gifted, who must "suffer fools gladly," denies the pain of those who have been treated poorly because of their differences:

> Sapon-Shevin treats the label "gifted" as though it were a badge of admission to an exclusive club whose members have advantages over nonmembers, so that everyone naturally wishes to belong. One wonders how many parents she has listened to, how many times she has heard the stories we hear from all over the country of children rejected by classmates, put down by defensive teachers, "taken down a peg" by adults and age peers, and taunted with names like "smarty-pants," "nerd," "brain" and "weirdo." For children, unusual intellectual abilities are more likely to be felt as burdens than as gifts. . . . It is difficult to get support for gifted children in pain when the prevailing attitude (even among professionals who work for the gifted) is that gifted children are lucky, privileged and better off than anyone else.[18]

Attempts to be thoughtful about the ways in which advocates solicit support for gifted education and the consequences of such rhetoric are dismissed as insensitivity and a failure to recognize the ways in which gifted children are at risk rather than legitimate questions about institutional inequity.

The Nation Needs to Cultivate the Talents of Gifted Children

Currently, the most prominent argument in support of gifted education is that educating the "best and the brightest" is in the best interests of our national economy. Although many gifted advocates begin with the equity argument cited above—that these children deserve and require differential treatment—they also recognize that given current economic and educational realities, this strategy may not be effective. At a meeting of an association of parents of gifted children, one gifted advocate, in explaining her strategy for garnering support for gifted programs, said:

> I can't compete on an emotional level for gifted children. If my neighbor brings her Down's syndrome child, I get nothing. I sell gifted children to the legislature on the basis of producing a labor force—economic issues. (Overheard at a session of The Ohio Personnel and Guidance Association annual meeting, April 1982.)

Thus, gifted children become economic hedges in an increasingly competitive market, and advocates argue that we're not doing this for the kids themselves, we're doing this for all of us. We're not giving them special education because they're worth more, but because they're worth more to us.

The rhetoric of economic necessity, fueled by the spate of national reports that forecast dire futures for America, is powerful. Although most of the national reports give at least lip service to the "twin" goals of excellence and equality, some reports, such as that of the Heritage Foundation, state explicitly that our crisis of excellence stems directly from a misguided emphasis on equity and equality issues.[19]

Gifted advocacy material abounds with the language of economics, including the need to "invest" in gifted students and thus insure a comfortable future. Freedman articulates well the relationship between the belief in the existence of artistic "talent" as a tangible characteristic and the exploitation of such talent for societal benefit:

A search for talent in school emerged because the qualities of a talented child (exceptional skills, middle class values and leadership capabilities) were thought analogous to money. Talent was something you either had or you didn't. It was finite and could be wasted. Children diagnosed as talented would become financially successful if directed in a special way. To give certain children extra attention was considered equitable, not only because it allowed those born to be great to become so, but because it was an efficient means to improve society. Because a prosperous society was assumed to be made up of successful individuals, unnurtured talent became a public concern.[20]

Thus, we owe it to ourselves to invest in gifted children. Although many educators (including many gifted educators) would no doubt be uncomfortable stating that certain children simply "deserve" more (and would argue that they are receiving something different, and not necessarily something "more"), talking about the need to use gifted children as a way of ensuring the continued preeminence of the United States as an economic and political force seems somehow more acceptable. Fetterman, for example, makes a strong plea for increased funding for gifted education by arguing that "this educational arena must become a national priority if we are to survive and prosper in the international marketplace,"[21] that we must "maximize our scarce resources where they have the highest probability of success,"[22] and that by ignoring the fact that other countries spend more than we do on gifted students, we are in danger of "educational complacency and neglect in global economy."[23]

This argument is occasionally buttressed by the espoused belief that gifted education can revitalize the entire educational system, providing models of good instruction that can trickle down to regular classrooms:

> Gifted and talented education programs offer a model of academic and administrative excellence that is generalizable to the mainstream of the American educational system.[24]

This is an appealing notion. As I have argued elsewhere,[25] much of gifted education is laudatory and desirable, but there is no convincing evidence that "investing" in gifted children will trickle down to other students unless programs are expressly designed to do so. Gifted programs have provided schools with ways of conducting educational triage—a form of damage control—saving those children for whom mediocre education would not be tolerated by their parents and allowing the inadequate mainstream to remain virtually untouched. Just as excellent special education programs are now seen by many as undesirable because they do not address the quality of mainstream education, many gifted programs do little to improve regular schools and regular classroom teaching.

The very ways in which gifted education is defined, funded, and implemented seem to mitigate against remaking the educational system under the influence of gifted education. The belief in giftedness as a thing apart, the reification of the category of giftedness, decreases the probability that educators will generalize from "what's good for the gifted" to "what's good for everyone." The growth of the gifted industry—books and journals of gifted education, organizations of parents of gifted children, conferences on gifted education, teacher education programs for teachers of the gifted, and even a toy catalogue called "the Gifted Children's Catalog"—all provide evidence of the growing separateness and discreteness of the category, not of its use as a model for all education.

Current economic exigencies and the nervous push for excellence at the cost of equity also belie the belief that gifted programs will somehow benefit all children. In fact, some gifted advocates are explicit about the need for parents of gifted children to compete for funding with other groups:

> Parents of the gifted must take an active role, and they must fight harder on the legislative battleground. They yield all too readily to other pressures, accepting meekly the excuses that other problems are more urgent. Parents of the gifted are particularly intimidated by the expressed needs of the disadvantaged and the handicapped. Apparently we are determined to use larger and larger bandages to help unfortunate children, but will not train the one group that has the capacity to solve their problems.[26]

Pitting disability rights groups against gifted groups for the same limited piece of educational pie draws attention away from the limited resources committed to education, but does little to build alliances and bridges, does not help educators and parents find the common ground of school-wide educational reform, and cannot promote the kinds of discourse about educational funding and national priorities necessary for massive, wide-scale societal reform.

"THE SUBJECT NEVER COMES UP": THE DISCOURSE OF SILENCE

The seemingly well-formulated, comprehensive arguments in support of gifted education and the ways in which protests are effaced, the almost ritualized call and response—argument and defense—might make one assume that gifted education programs are the result of a conspiracy theory, a well-articulated plan to reproduce existing social and economic groups through differentiated instruction and differential allocation of school resources. I do not believe that gifted education is the result of a five-year plan for promoting elitism or even an articulated desire to promote meritocracy; indeed, many of the practices of gifted education are implemented out of genuinely positive motives—to help children, to reduce the pain of difference, to increase achievement—and these positive motives, juxtaposed with the results of their implementation, make the resulting structures all the more contradictory and confusing. But the ways in which gifted education is conceptualized, the kinds of language that support its implementation, and the social and educational sanctions on its critique have resulted in the system we have now—grossly inequitable and highly prejudicial.

What are the hegemonic principles that maintain gifted education and meritocratic schooling in place? Apple has stated that "hegemony is constituted by our very day to day practices. It is our whole assemblage of commonsense meaning and actions that make up the social world as we know it, a world in which the internal curricular, teaching and evaluative characteristics of educational institutions partake."[27]

The commonsense meanings—and not so commonsense meanings—that hold gifted education in place are numerous. Some of these—beliefs about fairness, justice, allocation of resources, intelligence, and differentness—have already been articulated. But there are other beliefs and practices of education and schooling that maintain gifted education structures: Myths about the value of homogeneous grouping, bifurcated teacher education programs (for regular or special children), educational funding policies, and school structures that divide and separate, all help to maintain the gifted education system. But what keeps these practices, beliefs, and structures from being critically examined, rejected, or modified? There seems to be a conspiracy of a different kind—a conspiracy of silence.

For all of us, within our families, communities, and societies, there are things that we have learned not to talk about, questions we have been encouraged not to raise, areas in which the discourse has been silenced. Prominent among these forbidden topics in schools is any open discussion about children's difference, our comfort or discomfort with elitism, and our notions of what constitutes fairness and justice.

Fine, in describing the kind of silencing that surrounds high school dropouts, explains:

> If silencing is about who can and cannot speak, it is also about what can and cannot be spoken. Inside public schools, particularly low-income public schools, there persists a systematic commitment not to name those aspects of social life or of schooling that activate social anxieties—particularly anxieties of teachers and administrators who are often from different social classes, racial and ethnic groups, and neighborhoods than the children they teach. With important moments of exception, school-based silencing precludes conversation about social controversy and social inequity. . . . When I asked a white teacher why she does not discuss racism in her classrooom of black and Hispanic students, I was told, "It would demoralize the children." When I asked the principal why he preferred that I not mention dropping out to students I interviewed, he replied, "If you say it, they will do it."[28]

Although the social anxieties that are raised by talking about the implications of gifted education may appear to be different from those raised by talking about school dropouts, there are some clear parallels. The rhetoric surrounding dropouts deals with what should happen to students who do poorly, what they are "worth" and what they deserve; gifted education raises parallel issues of difference and merit—what should happen to students who do well, and what are they worth and what do they deserve? Both discussions force participants to consider the role of schools in selecting and sorting children according to certain features and inevitably lead to painful examinations of the inequitable ways in which various school outcomes are related to social class, race, ethnicity, and economic level.

Fine discusses the particular anxieties raised when teachers and administrators come from different social classes and racial and ethnic groups; when teachers and administrators are of the same social class and live in the same neighborhood, and must daily interact with students who have not been chosen for special programs, different anxieties are aroused. Not only is gifted education advocated and marketed in ways that marginalize criticism, but more direct forms of silencing occur as well, as teachers, parents, and students learn not to talk about structures that directly affect their lives.

Examining the responses of regular classroom teachers to the identification of students as gifted and talented reveals some of the ways in which certain kinds of discussion are silenced. In a recent study I conducted, teachers were asked how they explain the selection process (based largely on standardized testing) to parents, and how they dealt with student questions about the program.[29]

Most of the teachers reported that parents rarely questioned their decisions, that some of the parents didn't even seem to know that the program existed, and that as the years go by, fewer and fewer parents asked any questions. One teacher who lives in the community and frequently sees parents at football and basketball games says that she is sometimes asked by parents why their child was not chosen for the program, and how difficult it is for her.

The lack of discussion with parents about the existence and meaning of the Enrichment Program closely parallels the lack of discussion with students. Teachers were asked if children ever inquired about where other students were going, and then, specifically, if they ever asked when they would go or when it would be their turn.

Some teachers said that the children simply ''never ask,'' and many of the teachers seemed quite relieved that there was limited discussion about the issue and added parenthetic comments such as ''They're good about it, they don't ask'' or ''I don't have any problems with them—they don't ask.'' At one level, teachers painted a picture of acceptance and nonchalance about the program; since many children left the room for other special services like speech and remedial reading, teachers felt that students were largely oblivious to this particular departure.

Other teachers, however, described how children had asked more at the beginning of the year, but had stopped asking as the year went on, and one teacher reported her efforts to minimize the disruption and the questions occasioned by having students pulled out:

> I just said they just go to a special class for a few minutes and then when they get back we have their milk and crackers set out for them and they just go right to their table and join in with the rest of the class so it's not disruptive.

Other teachers reported that students did ask about why certain children were chosen, and when it would be their turn. Teachers' responses revealed a range of detail, comfort, and perspective. While some teachers told children that they might get a chance to go someday, several teachers said explicitly that they preferred not to talk about it. One teacher said that she avoids talking about it because it might "put ideas in their head," and another described how she tried to "distract" children from the issues. One commented, "I try not to make it a big issue because I think the more I explain in front of them the more I take the questions."

One teacher reported how she is purposely kind of "vague" so that she doesn't label children unnecessarily, and another teacher explained, "I don't usually answer them in verbatim," so that she can avoid "shooting them down" if the possibility of their going is small. Most of the teachers were not eager to engage their students in a discussion of the program or how children were chosen; they were relieved when children were easily placated, and they did not make the selection process explicit. One teacher said both: "I play it down, keep it low key, so they don't have a lot of time to wish they were going." A first-grade teacher explained, "They've never asked and I don't say anything." Only one teacher (of the thirty-six interviewed) talked to her class about the selection process, told them that there were many different ways of being intelligent and that selection was based on the score on one test and didn't mean that much. None of the teachers reported being forthright with parents about their misgivings. Even the teacher who was most distressed about the selection process and described in elaborate detail the "heartbreak" involved in letting some children in and telling others they weren't chosen, nonetheless told parents that the admission requirements were based on Stanford Tests and that their child's scores were not sufficient and that the child probably couldn't handle the work.

The teacher interviews from this study are just one indication of the silencing process in action; teachers, parents, and students alike have learned not to talk about "it," not to talk about differences in ability, differences in treatment, about what sometimes looks like favoritism and about who makes decisions and how. More than one teacher commented that many parents were not even aware that there was a gifted program, and one teacher reported that those children who were not "in tune" would probably never ask, because they were oblivious to the program. Not only was the process hidden, but knowledge that there was a process was also not openly shared. Just as Fine described, in the passage quoted earlier, those in positions of power were reluctant to discuss the process for fear that questions might be raised, or "ideas" might be put into heads; it seems ironic, at best, that having children ask questions and get ideas are two outcomes to be avoided within schools.

WHEN THE SILENCE IS BROKEN:
A COMMUNITY CONFRONTS TRACKING

Sometimes, however, the silence is broken, and tracking and differentiation become the objects of close scrutiny and critique. The publication of

Locked In/Locked Out: Tracking and Placement Practices in Boston Public Schools by the Massachusetts Advocacy Center[30] and the response to its publication provide a window on what happens on such occasions, when public school administrators and the public are forced to confront the reality of children's day-to-day school experiences. The report details the tracking and ability grouping that occur within the Boston Public Schools, with particular attention to the harmful effects on "the most vulnerable, racial and linguistic minorities, children with special needs, and the poor."[31] The report documents grouping practices in elementary schools, the negative effects of segregated special education programs and bilingual programs, and the ways in which the district's high schools provide vastly different curricular opportunities to different groups of students (closely linked, of course, to racial and economic variables). Additionally, the report makes a strong plea for detracking the schools and for developing ways of teaching that embrace and capitalize on heterogeneity within inclusive schools.

The district's three "exam schools" (those available to students only through a competitive examination), Boston Latin School, Latin Academy, and Boston Technical High School, come under particularly close scrutiny. The report documents discrimination at two levels: the disproportionately small numbers of students of color at Boston Latin School (BLS) and evidence of further resegregation within BLS as well, with disproportionate numbers of white students assigned to honors mathematics classes and honors English classes within the school, while students of color are served in general classes. While there are Black, Hispanic, and Asian students within the competitive schools, many of those students still do not have access to the highest-level programs. *Locked In/Locked Out* concludes with a comprehensive set of "Recommendations for Action," including detracking elementary schools, broadening curricular options for all students and implementing strategies such as cooperative learning, team teaching, and interdisciplinary curriculum in order to better meet the needs of heterogeneous groups of learners; the report proposes restructuring the three exam schools by changing the assignment procedure from an examination score to a more inclusive parent/student choice program parallel to that which takes place at the other high schools, so that these schools could serve a more diverse group of learners.

The community response to the publication of *Locked In/Locked Out* was rapid; the local newspaper published many parental letters in support of the special program offered at the exam schools, and the Boston Latin School held a meeting and issued a seven-page response to the report,[32] taking issue with both the document's basic assumptions and its recommendations for detracking and school restructuring. The BLS responded that *Locked In/Locked Out* "distorts the range and nature of students' need," "exaggerates the extent and impact of tracking and homogeneous grouping in the school system,"

and denies the differences among students, which demand differentiated programming and which cannot be met by "best practice," a term they believe
implies an "educational melting pot from which will emerge a 'state of the
art' 'best practice' that will buoy all students upward together." In responding to the report's documentation of the ways in which BLS "creams off the
academically talented" from other schools and from other districts, the response's authors actually confirm the accusation; they state that "the examination schools have credibility with people who are very critical of the
school system and would not make use of it otherwise." In other words,
keeping the exam school as it is allows the district to keep and attract more
privileged, wealthier, more powerful parents (and their children) within the
district, in spite of the overall poor quality of the rest of the schools.[33]

Just as arguments in support of gifted education quickly move from equity to economics, arguments in favor of maintaining segregated gifted programs (such as the one at BLS) argue for the particular needs of the students
they serve, emphasize the ways in which these students are different from
typical students, and ultimately, when pushed, argue that such programs and
such schools are economically and politically advantageous for the districts in
which they exist. When challenged, critics are accused of being insensitive to
individual differences and to the need for differentiated programming; there
seems to be little acknowledgment that sensitivity to individual difference and
differentiated educational needs do not necessarily mandate segregated, homogeneously grouped programs.

OPENING THE DISCUSSION:
EXPLORING MERITOCRACY, DEMOCRACY, AND JUSTICE

If the goal were an open exploration of the full ramifications of selecting
and differentially serving students labeled as "gifted," one would need to
open up a dialogue with teachers, with parents, and with students, and with
the whole community. There are ways to break the silence about gifted education, to explore fully the ways in which gifted programs both reflect and
perpetuate meritocratic ways of viewing people and their differences.

At a recent teacher in-service on cooperative learning, I talked about the
values of working with heterogeneous groups in order to promote a sense of
community, explore the meanings of democratic citizenship, and build relationships of interdependence among children. Several of the teachers at this
private, economically homogeneous school, which prides itself on the prestigious colleges to which its students are routinely admitted, were troubled by
the apparent contradictions between valuing and nurturing diversity and interdependence and the school's rhetoric of individual achievement and high

standards. One teacher articulated her discomfort before the group: "It seems like we would really have to be clear about what our own values are in this area before we could implement this kind of teaching, wouldn't we. . . . ? I mean it would be hard to promote cooperation with our students if we don't really believe in it."

This kind of discourse is generally silenced—sometimes self-censored—because it is painful. It involves addressing uncomfortable topics, revealing personal biases and beliefs, and standing up for what may be unpopular positions. But it is this kind of discourse that must be opened.

At the Barbara Taylor School in Harlem, a multiracial, independent elementary school that challenges the barriers of racism, sexism, and homophobia in order to make children change agents in their own worlds, a teacher also challenged another kind of prejudice by asking the middle-grade children who in her class was smart.

> The children looked around the room, smiled and a few raised their hands. The teacher asked them how they knew they were smart? What was the history of their smartness? How did it get produced? The students expressed very individualistic, privatized understandings of their abilities to do well in school. The teacher pointed out how their learning was in fact a very collective process. No one had learned alone and isolated from others.[34]

The teacher then continued by asking the children what their smartness was good for, exploring how smartness came between them and was the source of put-downs and comparisons. When one child suggested that the children who were faster at learning could teach those that weren't, the teacher said that they would have to do a lot of work on race, class, and gender differences in order for that to work well, since she thought that people had lots of assumptions about who they could learn from.

If children are to develop a sense of social justice, a sense of control over their own lives, and a sense of responsibility to others, they must be engaged in this kind of open and far-reaching exploration. What do they think it means for someone to be called "gifted"? How do they think children who are different (along a number of parameters) should be treated? Is different treatment fair or unfair? What is the difference between sameness and fairness? What should be the relationship among children who are different and have different skills and abilities? The list of questions is endless, and rather than opening up new areas of conflict, such discussions can help to contextualize, deepen, and broaden children's understandings about the nature of schooling, and of society. Discussing such issues with children will not "put ideas in their heads," will not introduce notions of injustice and inequality; any student in a class with three reading groups is already painfully aware of how he or she stands relative to classmates, who is "smart" and who is "stupid," and how these differences are addressed within schools.

I recently asked two third graders what they thought of a proposal to group children homogeneously in their elementary school. One girl responded immediately, "I think it's a terrible idea." When I asked why, she responded, "First of all, it would hurt a lot of children's feelings, and second of all, who would the slower children learn from?" The other third grader concurred and added, "And besides, there wouldn't be anyone in the bottom class, because everybody is good at something." It is clear that our reluctance to engage children in this kind of dialogue reflects our own deep discomfort with tracking and elitism, and not their inability to wrestle with complex topics such as differentiation, heterogeneity, and mutual interdependence.

Opening such a discussion with parents is equally essential, although difficult in different ways. Parents of children labeled "gifted" often push for differentiated programming for their offspring; recognizing the inadequacies of the public schools, they are proud, relieved, and grateful when their children are provided with enriched, challenging, high-status programming. Since current models of school organization and funding have often pitted parents against one another, and most advocacy groups are designated by label (*parents of the handicapped, parents of gifted children*), there has been little impetus for or support of shared or joint advocacy for broad-scale, inclusive educational reform.

But parents are engageable; at a recent meeting that I attended, a district administrator explained the gifted program to parents of children whose high test scores had made them eligible for the program. Many of the parents had questions; one parent wondered about the effects of the *gifted* label on other, nonlabeled siblings; another inquired about how the child would feel about being pulled out of his regular class and how that would affect peer relations; and several parents asked about the quality of the regular education program in which their gifted child was served most of the time, and their nongifted children all of the time. In many ways, parents of children labeled as "gifted" could be perfectly situated to initiate and sustain efforts to address educational changes for all students; if they were convinced that their child's individual needs could still be met within the mainstream of general education, they might be able to muster financial, educational, and political resources to support such changes.

As Dewey said,

> What the best and wisest parent wants for his own child, that must be the community want for all of its children. Any other ideal for our schools is narrow and unlovely; acted upon, it destroys our democracy.[35]

Gifted education is certainly not the only example of meritocratic, inequitable educational programming within schools, but its tangible, blatant nature can provide us with an entrée into the discussion, a window of opportunity for deconstructing and disassembling more pervasive inequities. Terminating gifted programs will not inevitably and automatically lead to improvements in general education, but challenging such programs could mobilize the power of those parents who would not tolerate a poor education for their children. The future of public schooling hangs delicately in the balance; if parents of gifted children are forced to throw in their child's lot with those of "nongifted children," then either underresourced, ill-equipped, substandard schools will be challenged by the demands of powerful, influential parents, or we will witness an even larger mass exodus of middle-class children to private schools. Either way, we will be forced as a society to confront our values and to ask ourselves what we want for all children and what role we expect the schools to play in creating an educated citizenry for democracy.

In dealing with the racial and class segregation within urban schools, Fine lists four strategies for addressing such inequalities: empowering teachers and paraprofessionals; desegregating teachers by race/ethnicity and students by race/ethnicity, social class and disability labels; implementing curricula and pedagogy that value students and their communities and recognize social inequities as problematic and worthy of academic investigation; and involving the perspectives of parents, community members, and advocates.[36] Each of these goals also applies to deconstructing gifted education and breaking through the silence that has surrounded its implementation. Empowering teachers and other school staff would mean letting them make decisions about how best to deal with the diversity of students within their own schools and classrooms rather than relying on standardized tests that label and remove certain students to segregated settings. The goal of desegregating schools in all ways, so that students are educated in heterogeneous settings where they come to appreciate and value diversity, is directly applicable to the problem of gifted education. As Fine states: "Public schooling in a context in which students and faculty are exclusively white and middle class is essentially inadequate education if our goal is to build critical, sensitive and participatory citizens."[37] Problematizing social inequities and making them the subject of academic exploration and involving the community in such discussion means talking about merit, intelligence, testing, gifted programs, differential skills, and social justice. It means exploring gifted programs openly with students, parents, teachers, and the community. And that might mean not having them at all.

Maintaining silence about gifted education and its role in creating a new meritocracy has removed from public discourse the tensions between unequal distribution of economic status and the mythology that schools represent the great equalizing force in society in which every child has an equal chance at success and achievement. We have obscured the reality of gross inequalities in educational opportunities and resources in America, only one example of which is that certain children are much more likely to end up in gifted programs where they will receive enriched curricular opportunities. By critically exploring gifted education, we can break the silence; there is little time, and the stakes are very high.

WALTER HANEY

Chapter Three

Testing and Minorities

INTRODUCTION

Standardized tests have often been used to the disadvantage of racial, ethnic, and language minorities in the United States. Standardized tests have not always worked to the disadvantage of such groups, but because of many instances in which tests have been used to deny opportunities to minorities or to depict them as somehow inferior or less able than majority individuals, standardized testing has often been viewed with suspicion, if not downright opposition, by many minority individuals. In this chapter, I review how this situation has come to be and describe the concepts of bias and fairness, which are deeply intertwined in issues of standardized testing and in particular with how standardized tests are used with and affect minority groups and individuals. In conclusion I explain why, despite many statistical studies indicating an absence of test bias defined in terms of differential validity for minority versus nonminority individuals, many uses of tests may be unfair or biased against minorities in the nontechnical meaning of these terms. First several explanations of terminology and territory are needed.

Regarding terminology, the phrase *standardized test* is used to refer mainly to tests of cognitive skills, which have been systematically developed and are administered so that examinees are given the same directions, questions, and time limits. To be standardized also means that a test's results are scored in a standard or uniform way. While most standardized tests in the United States at present are paper-and-pencil and multiple choice in format, the term *standardized test* also includes open-ended exercises (as in an essay

45

test, where examinees have to create, rather than simply select, an answer) and nonverbal tests (such as block-sorting tests, which are sometimes used to test cognitive development of young children).

The term *minority* is used here to refer to ethnic, racial, and language minorities generally and specifically to Black Americans, Hispanic Americans, Asian Americans, and American Indians. Standardized testing does of course have considerable import for other minority groups, but we focus on these groups here for two simple reasons. First, these are groups that have been clearly recognized as minority groups in government legislation and surveys. Second, there is considerable evidence available as to how these groups score on and are affected by testing programs. While this chapter does not devote much attention to the manner in which standardized tests affect opportunities of women as compared with men, in some instances standardized testing does in similar ways limit the educational and other opportunities of women.

Regarding territory, issues of standardized testing and minorities are of considerable complexity and range. Testing programs vary in many important respects at preschool, school, college, and employment levels, and there is no way that testing programs and practices at all these levels, as they affect minorities, can be described thoroughly in one chapter. Thus in this chapter we seek to describe the more general issues regarding testing that are relevant to educational opportunities of minorities across a range of levels of education.

HISTORY

Standardized tests became prominent in schools of the United States mainly after Alfred Binet's invention in 1905 of a standardized scale for measuring intelligence, and especially after World War I, when wide publicity was given to use of a revision of the Binet scale—modified for group administration—in classifying Army recruits.[1] From almost the beginning of the story of standardized testing in American education come examples of standardized testing programs being used to limit the opportunities and standing of minorities in the United States. In his history of the civil rights movement in the United States leading up to the landmark Supreme Court decision in *Brown v. Board of Education of Topeka* in 1954, Kluger, for example, points out that as early as 1913 intelligence tests had been used to demonstrate the supposed mental inferiority of Blacks in the United States.[2]

An even clearer example of racist interpretation of test results occurred after World War I. During the Great War, as it was then called, psychologists had developed the Army Alpha and Beta tests for screening army recruits. While the extent to which the WWI army tests were actually used in making decisions about recruits is unclear, what is clear is that after the war, the test data were used by social scientists to draw highly negative (and, as later became clear, almost entirely racist) conclusions about ethnic and racial minorities. Carl Brigham, for example, who was then a young professor at Princeton University (and later creator of the Scholastic Aptitude Test), used the Army data in *A Study of American Intelligence*. On the basis of his "objective" and "scientific" analysis of Army data, showing ethnic minorities and immigrants to score lower than whites, Brigham argued for a policy to restrict the immigration of inferior races and to prevent the "continued propagation of defective strains in the present population."[3]

Though such views were opposed by some social scientists (such as Beardsley Ruml and Horace Mann Bond) and journalists (such as Walter Lippman), it was not until decades later that such racist interpretations of the WWI data were widely discredited.[4] What was clear in retrospect was that patterns of average group scores on the Army tests that had been interpreted as indicating innate differences in intelligence reflected patterns of social and educational opportunities (including familiarity with the English language) more than anything about race groups per se. Northern Blacks, for example, tended to score higher on the Army tests than southern whites. But in the early 1920s, the racist interpretations fit well with the xenophobia and racism of the time.[5]

Though such racist interpretations of test scores may have served to reinforce racial and ethnic stereotypes and thus indirectly affected opportunities of minorities, probably the strongest direct influence of testing on the educational opportunities of minority pupils in the United States came about through the use of test results to track students into different ability groups in both elementary and secondary schools. Specialized educational programs for students with special characteristics (deafness, blindness, non-English-speaking) were fairly commonplace in the United States well before the turn of the century, and at least as early as 1910 many school systems were using Binet tests to help identify "feebleminded" children in need of special educational programs.[6] Such instances appear to have dealt, however, with relatively small numbers of exceptional cases, and the testing involved was done individually.

However, after the apparent success of the World War I Army testing, and as the numbers of students enrolled in schools of the United States were increasing rapidly, group-administered intelligence testing was advocated for all school children so that they might be grouped into homogeneous ability groups and thereby schools might better deal with students' individual differences. Stanford University professor Lewis Terman was probably the preeminent advocate of using group-administered intelligence tests to track students, as early as the first grade, into ability groups. In *Intelligence Tests and School Reorganization,* Terman advocated the tracking of students into homogeneous groups based on ability, with an ideal tracking system providing for five groups: the "gifted" (the top 2.5 percent of students), the "bright" (the next 15 percent); the "average" (65 percent); the "slow" (15 percent); and the "special" (the bottom 2.5 percent).[7] While little evidence is available on the extent to which Terman's recommendation for five separate groupings of students by ability was adopted by schools, what is clear is that group-administered intelligence tests were widely adopted as early as the mid 1920s and were used mainly to track students into homogeneous ability groups. Homogeneous grouping of students by ability appears to have continued as a widespread practice in schools of the United States for at least the next half century, and surveys indicate that standardized tests of intelligence and achievement were extremely widely used in placing students into such homogeneous ability groups.

The role of tests in ability grouping or tracking was documented, for example, in a series of surveys about testing in the 1960s. When a national sample of secondary school administrators was surveyed about the importance of various reasons for using standardized tests in their schools, over 90 percent indicated that the following reasons for testing were fairly or very important:

• To help in guiding pupils into appropriate curricula
• To help students gain a better understanding of their strengths and weaknesses
• To help in educational and vocational counseling of students[8]

More recent work on tracking practices of schools continues to indicate that tracking decisions are based largely (albeit sometimes indirectly) on test results.[9]

Though available evidence is largely indirect, it seems clear that these practices (using test scores to judge students' abilities and to group them into homogeneous ability groups or tracks) and attitudes (educators' viewing test scores as the most accurate indicator of student ability) have had a widespread impact in limiting the educational opportunities of minority students in American schools for most of the twentieth century. This is because, on the average, minority students have widely been shown to score lower than non-minority students on standardized tests of ability and achievement.

The ways in which low test scores may have limited the opportunities of minorities are myriad. However, this chapter focuses mainly on the way in which testing is involved in tracking or ability grouping of students at the secondary school level. This focus is adopted for two reasons. One is simply that the tracking of students at this level is more obvious and widespread than at other levels. The other is that inequities in educational opportunities begin to be much more obvious at the secondary level of education than they are at the elementary level. Before discussing the connection between testing and tracking in more detail, we briefly summarize some of the wide-ranging evidence concerning differential performance of minorities and nonminorities on standardized tests, and then point out that testing may contribute to the differential school completion rates of minorities and nonminorities, irrespective of the tracking issue.

Differential Performance

A wide range of studies of standardized test scores over the last three-quarters of a century have shown that the average scores (on tests of both achievement and "ability") of minorities are substantially below the average scores of whites in the United States. Reports of the WWI testing of recruits showed, for example, that while the mean "mental age" of whites was around thirteen, the average scores of Italians, Poles, and Negroes were all in the range of ten to eleven.[10] Fifty years later, in the Coleman report on the Equality of Educational Opportunity Survey in 1966, a large national sample of children were tested in grades one, three, six, nine, and twelve, and notable differences between racial and ethnic groups were found at every grade level:

> At grade 12, the rank ordering of the [race/ethnic] groups in terms of median scores on the verbal ability tests was whites, Oriental-Americans, Mexican Americans, Indian Americans, Puerto Ricans, and blacks. On a scale with a mean of 50 and a standard deviation of 10, the median 12th grade verbal ability scores for these six groups were 52.1, 49.6, 43.8, 43.7, 43.1 and 40.9, respectively. Although there is a great deal of overlap in the distribution of scores for all groups, the above differences in medians were large indeed.[11]

In 1971, a report on minority access to higher education noted that

> virtually every test that purports to measure educational aptitude or achievement reveals that the mean of the scores of minority youth is about one standard deviation below the mean of the scores of the rest of the population.[12]

The standard deviation (commonly represented by the Greek letter sigma, σ) is a measure of variability, or spread, in a set of data, such as test scores. Because different kinds of tests employ various numerical scales for reporting results, scores on different kinds of tests are often compared using the standard deviation as a basis of comparison. The standard deviation is simply the square root of the variance of a distribution, and variance is easily calculated by summing the squares of the deviations of each value in a distribution from the average or mean of the distribution and then dividing by the number of cases or values in the distribution.[13] If test scores are normally distributed—and norm-referenced tests are constructed so as to help yield normal distributions of scores—a 1.0 standard deviation difference in the average scores of two groups means that only about 16 percent of the lower-scoring group would have scores equal to or higher than the mean of the higher-scoring group.

In his review of literature on bias in mental testing in 1980, Jensen elaborated on average Black-white differences in test scores in terms of the standard deviation unit:

> Standardized intelligence tests of practically every description show an average white-black difference of very close to one standard deviation, with over 90 percent of the published studies reporting differences between $\frac{2}{3}\sigma$ and $1\frac{1}{3}\sigma$, which on the IQ scale (with $\sigma = 15$) is between 10 and 20 IQ points, with a mean of 15 IQ points.[14]

Gaps between average scores of minority and nonminority individuals show up not just on so-called intelligence or ability tests and general achievement tests. They also show up on competency tests used for grade promotion and high school graduation, college admissions tests, military admissions tests, licensing and certification tests, and employment tests.[15] Studies of the National Teacher Examination (NTE) in the 1980s, for example showed that the average Black-white difference on the NTE subtests was about 1.4 to 1.5 standard deviations.[16]

The consistency with which average test score differences between whites and minorities have been reported may well have contributed to genetic and racist interpretations as to the origins of such group differences. Genetic interpretations as to the origins of group differences have long been largely discredited. In the 1930s, for example, one British physician ridiculed simplistic genetic interpretations of group differences by likening them to the taking of family pedigrees of mining accident victims—all of whom were male, and who tended to have relatives who also had suffered such accidents—to conclude that "the tendency to have mining accidents is the product of a sex-linked gene."[17]

Nevertheless, since remnants of genetic interpretations of Black-white differences in test scores do persist, it is worth pointing out that the findings from the National Assessment of Educational Progress (NAEP) between 1970 and 1988 clearly belie such interpretations. Consider, for example, findings from the NAEP regarding differences in reading proficiency:

> Trend information from the five NAEP reading assessments conducted during the 1970s and 1980s reveals that the average performance gap between

White and Black students has been reduced at all three age levels—particularly at age 17. These findings reflect, at least in part, the dramatic gains in performance made by Black 17-year-olds, an especially noteworthy achievement given that the dropout rate among Black high-school students has been declining since 1970.[18]

NAEP results are reported on an unusual scale, so it is not possible to compare them directly to other sorts of findings regarding group differences in test scores mentioned previously. However, given the distribution of NAEP scores, it is clear that the decrease in the Black-white performance gap has narrowed by approximately one-third of a standard deviation.[19] A decrease of this magnitude in a period of less than twenty years, far too short a time in which to see widespread genetic changes, is highly significant given fairly consistent results going back more than half a century of Black-white differences on general ability and achievement tests of roughly a full standard deviation.[20] As mentioned previously, average group differences of one full standard deviation imply that only about 16 percent of Blacks score above the mean of whites, but an average group difference of two-thirds of a standard deviation implies that about 25 percent of Blacks score above the mean of whites.

School Completion

As late as 1940 most young Americans did not complete high school. Even so, there has always been a significant difference in the median years of schooling attained by most minorities and nonminorities. In 1950, for example, the median years of school completed by Black men aged twenty-five to twenty-nine was about 7.5, while for young white men the comparable figure was slightly over 12. Since 1950, the school completion gap between Blacks and whites has narrowed considerably, but although there has been a rapid rise in high school completion among Blacks over the last forty years, in 1980 about one-quarter of young Black adults had not completed high school, as opposed to only slightly over 10 percent of whites.[21]

Thus by the 1960s, when high school completion had become the norm rather than the exception, failure to complete high school came to be recognized as a severe disadvantage and was usually labeled as "dropping out." In 1964, for example, a national conference on education and deprivation identified the "disadvantaged" as the one-third of high school entrants who did not complete high school and noted that a majority of these were Puerto Ricans, Mexican Americans, Blacks, and whites who had moved to urban areas.[22]

More recently, as high school graduation has become more nearly universal, the topic of school dropouts has become of more concern.[23] Though there is no universally accepted means of measuring school dropout rates, whatever means are employed generally show that dropout rates are higher among minorities than among whites. For example, 1985 data from the Bureau of the Census indicated a 14 percent dropout rate among eighteen- and nineteen-year-olds overall, but a 17 percent dropout rate among Blacks and a 31 percent dropout rate among Hispanics in this age group.[24]

The causal connections between standardized testing and failure to complete high school are not clear, but what is clear is that the same groups that tend to score low on standardized tests are those having greater risk of dropping out of school. Research on causes of school dropouts indicates that among the factors increasing likelihood of dropping out are being retained in grade, experiencing failure in school, and low self-esteem. If tests are widely used as indicators of school ability, it certainly seems likely that testing programs may well contribute to these factors that have been shown to increase likelihood of dropping out of school. While this connection is far from clear, at least one study has cited circumstantial evidence to suggest that competency testing programs "may give students at risk of dropping out an extra push out the school door."[25]

More recently, Cawthorne showed the way in which a high school graduation test in the Boston public schools could have prevented many minority students from receiving their high school diplomas. The Boston School Committee had mandated a policy requiring that all high school students attain a particular score on the Metropolitan Achievement Test (MAT) in order to graduate. Preliminary results of MAT scores released in the fall of 1989 indicated that 40 percent of high school seniors would not meet this requirement (and over 50 percent of seniors, if the Boston exam schools were not included). What Cawthorne did was to interview students at two schools to find out why many "good" kids who "were doing everything their schools asked of them" had failed the test. He found that many of these students were minority and/or bilingual youngsters with good grades (several were honor roll students, and some had already been accepted to college). Though all the students interviewed could read, some said they "did not test well" or read English so slowly that they were unable to finish the test (though by working long hours on their school assignments they were able to do well on school work). Others simply had not been given reasonable notice about the importance of the test. According to interviews, many of these "good" students who had done everything else their high schools asked of them but had failed the new graduation test would not have returned to school another year simply to pass the test requirement. Clearly, many of the cases documented by Cawthorne were ones in which the Boston graduation test policy would have given minority students a significant "push out the school door," were it not for the fact that just as Cawthorne was conducting his research, the Boston School Committee rescinded its graduation testing policy.[26]

Tracking

Even when students complete high school, a major cause of inequality in educational opportunity is tracking. As previously noted, testing has clearly been employed in homogeneous ability grouping of students for most of this century. Also, while Terman's plan for five school tracks was never widely accepted, tripartite tracking at the high school level has been very widely employed in high schools of the United States. Three different national surveys in the 1960s and 1970s, for example, indicated that nationwide the distribution of students in high school programs was that some 30 to 40 percent of students were enrolled in academic or college preparatory high school tracks, some 35 to 50 percent were enrolled in general high school programs, and 14 to 16 percent were enrolled in vocational or business high school programs.[27] Though tracking of students within schools may be most obvious at the high school level, where the differentiation between college prep, general, and vocational programs is widely recognized, less obvious means of tracking or streaming students exist at the junior high and elementary levels of education. Indeed, forms of tracking are widely practiced as early as kindergarten and first-grade years, whereby children are retained in kindergarten or placed in transitional kindergarten–grade 1 classes, often on the basis of so-called readiness tests.[28]

Whatever the exact extent of tracking of students by "ability" below the high school level—and tracking may well exist in practice if not in policy—what is clear is the connection between tracking and minorities' educational opportunities at the high school level. First, as previously recounted, test scores have long been documented to be a primary basis for placement into high school tracks. Second, and as noted above, there are longstanding and widely documented differences in the average test scores of minorities and nonminorities (usually defined as whites). Given these two facts, it is hardly surprising that minorities are underrepresented in the highest-level high school track, namely, the college preparatory or academic track. Using data from National Longitudinal Surveys from the late 1960s, for example, Grasso and Shea found that 46 percent of white youth in grades eleven and twelve were in college preparatory curriculum programs as compared with only 28 percent of Black youth.[29] More recently, a study of secondary school tracking in six racially mixed schools found that white students were disproportionately enrolled in the highest-level English and math classes and minorities disproportionately underenrolled in such classes.[30]

These findings are largely predictable, given what we know about the distribution of minority versus white test scores. If a school is composed of 20 percent minority and 80 percent nonminority students, if there is a one standard deviation difference between the average test scores of minorities and those of nonminorities in the school, and if those scores were to be used in selecting the top-scoring 40 percent of all students for the college preparatory track, it is entirely predictable that about 45 percent of nonminorities, but less than 20 percent of the minority students, will be in the high track.[31]

Tracking clearly has ramifications for students' learning. Students placed in "lower ability," or noncollege, tracks tend to take courses that are less academically demanding and with teachers who tend to expect less learning from their students. Thus even though test scores used to place students in different school tracks actually may reflect initial differences in learning, the practice of educational tracking tends to perpetuate and reinforce preexisting performance differences.[32] Jones and colleagues,[33] for example, in analyzing national data from the 1980s, have found that Black students tend to take fewer math courses in high school than whites, and that the variation in math courses, together with other background variables, explains half of the Black-white differences in grade-twelve math scores.[34]

What is also clear is that even after graduation from high school (a level of school attainment, as noted earlier, reached by proportionately fewer minorities than nonminorities), whether or not one graduates from a college preparatory or academic high school program clearly affects not just chances of attending college, but also future economic and broader social well-being.[35] Thus testing is clearly implicated in sorting and selection processes of the educational system of the United States that have limited the educational and social opportunities of minorities.

It should be noted that, contrary to this conclusion, many have argued that tests do not create the inequalities associated with school attainment and tracking, but merely reflect the broader social and economic inequalities that often afflict minorities in the United States. In this regard it is often said that standardized tests are not biased against minorities and ought not be blamed for accurately reflecting broader inequalities that often lead to lower school performance—or lower "academic abilities"—among minorities than among nonminorities. I address these arguments below, in discussing the topics of bias and fairness. However, before I do so, three additional points are worth adding.

First, though the role of testing in limiting opportunities of minorities is sometimes complex and indirect, the close connection between testing and limitation of opportunities of minorities via tracking has been established in several federal court decisions. In the case of *Hobsen v. Hansen* (1967), for example, plaintiffs charged that the use of IQ tests in ability tracking in the schools of the District of Columbia (DC) resulted in the disproportionate placement of Black students in the lower ability tracks. In this case the court ruled that the tracking via IQ testing constituted illegal segregation and banned the use of IQ tests in the DC schools. A second case concerning testing and tracking was that of *Larry P. v. Riles,* brought in federal court in California. At issue in this case was the use of IQ tests in placement of children into classes for the "educably mentally retarded" (EMR), which resulted in disproportionate placement of black children into such classes. While the story of the *Larry P.* case is a long one (transcripts of testimony in the case ran to more than ten thousand pages), all that we note here is that in ruling in favor of the plaintiffs in 1979, the trial judge said, in part, that

> defendants have utilized standardized intelligence tests that are racially and culturally biased, have a discriminatory impact against black children and have not been validated for the purpose of essentially permanent placement of blacks into educationally dead end, isolated and stigmatizing classes for the so-called "educably mentally retarded."[36]

A second general point worth noting is that on occasion lower test scores of minorities have been used not to depict them as somehow inferior or to limit their educational or other social opportunities, but as evidence of the disadvantages often suffered by minorities in American society. Perhaps the preeminent example of such use of test scores was in the 1960s, when lower performance of minority and inner-city children was used to bolster arguments for the war on poverty and to help propel passage of the landmark Elementary and Secondary Education Act of 1965, via which federal funds were allocated to help improve the education of children in districts serving large proportions of educationally disadvantaged children.[37] This example, perhaps more than any of the statistical issues described in the following discussion of test bias, illustrates the important point that the typically lower test scores of minorities need not necessarily work to their disadvantage or to the depiction of lower-scoring groups as somehow inferior. Instead it is how people, institutions, and society generally have made sense of and used standardized tests that has worked to their disadvantage.

Since testing has, however, so often worked to the disadvantage of minorities, it is hardly surprising that at least since the 1960s, standardized testing programs in the United States have often been opposed by minority groups. In 1968, the National Association of Black Psychologists, for example, passed a resolution calling for study of the use of tests "to maintain and justify the practice of systematically denying economic opportunities to Black youth." Pending the finding from such a study, the Association called for a moratorium on comparative testing. In 1972 and 1974, the National Association for the Advancement of Colored People (NAACP) in its national convention called for the cessation of standardized tests whenever tests have "not been corrected for cultural bias."[38]

In addition to such organized opposition to tests, some surveys have indicated that minority individuals view tests much more negatively than do whites. In a survey of graduate and professional school students (who obviously had succeeded fairly well in testing and the educational process, because they all were engaged in postcollege education), for example, Baird found that 96 percent of Black respondents agreed with the statement that admissions test content "is biased against blacks and other minorities."[39]

BIAS

Given that tests have often been used to the disadvantage of minorities and that charges of cultural bias and unfairness have often been leveled at standardized tests, it is hardly surprising that the topics of bias and fairness in testing have drawn much attention since the 1960s. Before recounting how these topics have been treated, it is vital to point out that a large semantic problem has caused considerable misunderstanding concerning bias and fairness in testing.

In the general lexicon, the word *bias* refers to a bent, drift, leaning, or inclination that inhibits impartial judgment, and the word *fairness* (at least in the meanings of the word relevant to testing) means free of favoritism or bias, just to all parties, or equitable. Thus in common language the terms *bias* and *fairness* are closely connected. Indeed, some dictionaries list the word *unbiased* as a synonym for *fair*, and *biased* as an antonym for *fair*. However, among most specialists in testing—who are sometimes called "psychometricians"—*bias* means something quite different from unfairness. In *Bias in Mental Testing*, for example, Jensen writes that "bias is clearly distinguished from the concept of 'unfairness' "(454). Thus in order to understand the controversy over bias and unfairness, it is vital to appreciate the fact that when nonspecialists and advocates of minority interests commonly talk about test bias, they mean something quite different than what testing specialists mean. When an advocate of minority interests says that a test is biased, and a testing expert says that the same test is not biased, they both may be correct. They just mean different things in using the same word. In order to appreciate the difference, let us first recount what testing specialists typically mean by the phrase *test bias;* later, when recounting issues of fairness, I return to the issue of bias as understood in the common lexicon.

The word *bias* has been applied to tests in several different ways,[40] but among testing specialists the term *test bias* has most commonly been used to refer to differential validity.[41] Thus the question of whether tests are biased against minorities is frequently translated into the question of whether or not tests are less valid for minority individuals than for nonminorities. The most common means of investigating whether test results are biased (that is, whether they have differential validity for different groups) is to look at whether or not test scores have less predictive validity for minorities than for nonminorities. Bias of tests in terms of predictive validity is usually studied using the statistical techniques of correlation and regression analysis, whereby some criterion measure such as school grades is compared with test scores.

Both correlation and regression analyses are commonly employed techniques with which to examine the degree of association between two or more variables. A correlation coefficient may vary from $+1$ to 0 to -1. A correlation of zero between two variables means that there is no relationship or association between values of the two variables. If two variables show a correlation of close to $++1$, this means that they are strongly associated—as one variable increases, the other increases also. A correlation of negative one (-1) means that the variables are inversely related—as the value of one increases, the value of the other decreases.

Regression analysis is another way in which to examine the relationship between two variables. A regression equation takes the form of a linear equation (such as those commonly studied in high school algebra):

$$Y = a + bX + c$$

where: Y = a criterion variable, such as school grades in studies of test validity

a = the intercept or value of Y when the value of $X = 0$

X = the test score;

b = the regression coefficient, or slope, which indicates how much the criterion measure Y is expected to change as a result of a one-point change in test score X; and

c = an error term (and hence in the testing literature is usually denoted with the Greek letter epsilon, ϵ.)

In order to validate tests, researchers often look at the correlation or regression relations between test scores and various criterion measures with which tests ought to show some relationship if the test scores are really reflecting what the test is presumed to measure. Thus the tests that are intended to measure intelligence or scholastic aptitude or even reading ability are often examined in conjunction with school grades, since it is assumed that if a test is really measuring such attributes, test scores ought to show a positive relationship with how well students do in school (we should note that many criticisms have been made of grades as an appropriate criterion measure, but for the moment we omit this issue).

The most common examples of such studies are those examining the relationships between college admissions test scores and students' freshman year grade point average after they have been admitted to college. A summary of over six hundred studies of the predictive validity of the Scholastic Aptitude Test (SAT), for example, showed that the median correlation between SAT verbal scores (SATV) and freshman grade point average (FGPA) was 0.36 and the median correlation between SAT math (SATM) scores and FGPA was 0.35. In contrast the correlation between high school record (HSR) and FGPA among the same six hundred students was 0.48.[42] The combination of SATV, SATM, and HSR showed a median correlation with FGPA of 0.55. A more recent summary of research over the last two decades on prediction of college grades substantiates these general patterns, with HSR having slightly greater power to predict FGPA than college admission test scores, but with the combination of test scores and HSR having greater predictive power than either used alone.[43]

Correlation analysis has also been used to study the relationship between test scores and school grades and between test scores and teachers' ratings of pupils. As long ago as 1919, for example, Terman reported results from studies carried out in his revision of the original Binet intelligence scale. Teachers were asked to rate their students' intelligence on a five-point scale, and in an analysis of results for about a thousand pupils, Terman found that the correlation between intelligence test results and teachers' ratings of intelligence was 0.48.[44] Many additional studies have been carried out to examine the correlations between test results and school grades. While results vary among studies, the general pattern across studies is for test scores to correlate with high school grades, on average, in the range of 0.45 to 0.60.[45]

Given these kinds of results, it is commonly assumed that a test showing a correlation of 0.50 or greater as a predictor of grades is entirely satisfactory, for as one testing expert pointed out, it is very unusual for a validity coefficient to rise above 0.60.[46] What is noteworthy regarding such validity coefficients, however, is that they actually indicate a relatively low degree of predictive power. A correlation coefficient of 0.50 means that test scores "explain" or account for 25 percent of the variability in student grade point averages (since the square of the correlation coefficient, or R^2, represents the amount of variance explained). In contrast, people's height explains much more of the variance in their weight. Though common experience tells us that height is a highly imperfect predictor of people's weight—people of the same height can be fat or skinny—height is actually a much better predictor of weight than test scores are of scholastic success as measured by grades. Therefore it makes far less sense, from a predictive point of view, to use test scores in isolation to predict students' success in school than to use people's height as a means of identifying fat people.[47]

Correlational Studies of Test Bias

The same techniques used to study the predictive validity of tests have also been used to study the question of test bias. Thus there have been numerous studies of how test scores correlate with various criterion measures for minority versus nonminority individuals. Pfeifer and Sedlacek, for example, studied the relationships between SAT scores and freshman grades at the University of Maryland and found that correlations for Blacks were similar to those found among University of Maryland students generally.[48] A review of many such correlational studies of the relationship between SAT scores and FGPA for Black students as compared with all students indicates that the correlations for Blacks (at either predominantly Black or predominantly white colleges) are not much different from those for students generally.[49] Similarly others have compared SAT-FGPA correlations for Hispanic versus white students and concluded that there do not seem to be large or consistent differences in such correlations.[50] An example of another such correlational analysis for younger students is that of McCandless, Roberts, and Starnes. They studied the relationships among achievement and intelligence test scores and grades for seventh-grade children in Atlanta public schools. They found that the correlations between test scores and grades were as high or higher for Black students as for white students.[51]

Correlation statistics thus have long been commonly used in studying test validity generally and the possibility of differential test validity for different kinds of students. In part this is a historical accident,[52] but correlational techniques are also popular for analyzing test data, for the practical reason that one can calculate correlation coefficients on test scores measured using different scales and still obtain comparable correlation coefficients all falling in the range of -1.00 to $+1.00$. The problem with correlations as a means of summarizing the relationship between variables is that correlation coefficients can mask highly different kinds of relationships among variables.[53]

Regression Analyses of Test Bias

Partly as a result of this weakness in correlation analysis, most recent studies of test bias have not employed simple correlational analysis, but instead have employed regression analysis (sometimes in addition to correlation analyses). Specifically, in order to examine whether or not test results may be biased against minorities, investigators have conducted separate regression analyses for majority and minority groups, using a criterion variable (such as college or school grades) regressed against test scores. Having conducted such separate regression analyses, they then check to see whether the regression relations (the intercepts, or a's, in the regression equations; the slopes, or b's; and the variability, or c's) are significantly different for majority and minority groups. In the Pfeifer and Sedlacek study on University of Maryland students mentioned earlier, for example, regression analyses were performed separately for Blacks and whites, using SAT verbal and math scores (SATV, SATM) and high school grade point average (HSGPA) to predict freshman grade point averages. They found that SAT scores used in conjunction with high school record did not have less validity for Blacks than whites in predicting freshman grades at the University of Maryland.

Summaries of this sort of regression analysis research on the question of test bias have generally concluded that tests are not biased against minorities. Jensen, for example, concluded his review of research on possible test bias, defined in terms of regression relations in prediction equations calculated separately for minorities and nonminorities, by saying that "in the vast majority of studies, the regressions of criterion performance on test scores do not differ for blacks and whites."[54] Linn reaches similar conclusions in his review of differential prediction for ability tests generally, as does Donlon in his review of studies of the predictive validity of the SAT for different groups.[55]

In sum, then, according to a number of reviews of research on test bias defined in terms of differential correlation and/or regression relations, the conclusion seems universal. Correlation and regression analyses of the validity of test scores for predicting things such as grades in school, performance on other tests—and even workers' performance on the job—generally do not show systematic differences in the predictive power of tests for minorities (with the most often studied minority being Blacks) and nonminorities (usually defined as whites or a general sample of all individuals regardless of race or ethnicity).

FAIRNESS

Rather than elaborating further on this line of research on test bias, it is useful to return to two points made earlier. The first is the semantic problem noted previously, namely, that such technical analyses employing regression statistics to try to identify test bias in terms of differential prediction may be largely irrelevant to the common meaning of the word *bias*. Though a test may be unbiased in the sense that it does not show differential predictive power for minorities versus nonminorities, it still may be biased in the sense that its use results in unfairness. In a moment I explain how it is that a test may be "technically" unbiased but still unfair in use and thus biased in the commonsense usage of the word *bias*. But it is also important to point out that such unfairness becomes apparent only when we consider the manner in which test results are *used*. As I explain later, this is a topic that analysts such as Jensen and Linn appear not to have considered closely.

As long ago as 1971, Robert Thorndike showed how a test could be unbiased (in terms of not having different regression relations between test scores and criterion measures for major versus minor groups), but could at the same time still be unfair to minorities in terms of how it was used.[56] The situation he described is illustrated in figure 3.1. In this situation, the test and criterion data for majority and minority groups fall along a common regression line. However, the average differences between the two groups are larger on the test than on the criterion measure. Illustrated in figure 3.1, as in Thorndike's original example, is the case in which "the minor group differs

FIGURE 3.1
Unfair Selection with an Unbiased Test

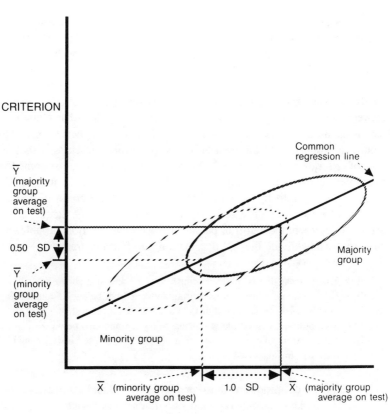

from the major group by only half a standard deviation on the criterion variable, while differing by a full standard deviation on the test."[57] Given such a situation (and a couple of assumptions commonly made about test score distributions), it can be shown that though only about 16 percent of minority group members would exceed the majority group average test score, about 31 percent would exceed the majority group average on the criterion variable. Under such a situation, any overall cutoff score that might be chosen on the test to select people would be unfair to minority group members in the sense that it would have the consequence of selecting lower proportions of minorities scoring high on the criterion. Thorndike went on to elaborate:

> If one defines "fair" use of a test . . . as providing each group the same opportunity for admission to training or to a job as would be represented by the proportion of the group falling above a specified criterion score on the correlated variable of training or job performance, then it does not matter particularly whether the slope of the regression of criterion score on the test differs in the two groups. Having set a standard for the major group, one independently sets a critical score that will admit the required percent from the minor group (i.e. the percentage of the group which that have been found to achieve the specified criterion score). (68)

Because Thorndike suggested here that whatever the regression relations between criterion and test scores, fair selection implies that "qualifying scores set on a test be set at levels that will qualify applicants in the two groups in proportion to the fraction of the two groups reaching a specified level of criterion performance."[58] This model of fair selection has come to be called the "constant ratio model of fair selection." This model may be illustrated by referring to figure 3.2, which represents a scatterplot of X and Y data. If X* is used to represent the cutoff or passing score on the test and Y* is used to represent the cutoff or passing score on the criterion variable, then these two scores divide the XY distribution into four quadrants:

A = True passes, that is, cases scoring above Y* and also above X*
B = False failures, that is, cases scoring above Y* but below X* and thus misclassified on the based of the cutoff score on the test
C = True failures, that is, cases scoring below Y* and also below X*
D = False passes, that is, cases scoring below Y* and also above X* and thus also misclassified[59]

Given these definitions as illustrated in figure 3.2 and summarized in table 3.1, Thorndike's constant ratio model of fair selection suggests that whatever the regression relations between Y and X for minority and majority

FIGURE 3.2
Models of Fair Selection

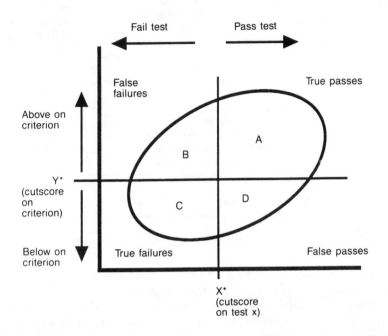

groups, the X* and Y* cutoff scores ought to be set so that the ratio of $\frac{(A+D)}{(A+B)}$ is equal for majority and minority groups.

Thorndike's article helped point attention to the fundamental point that a test in and of itself may not be biased or unfair, but rather it is how test scores are interpreted or used that is likely to yield bias or unfairness. It also led others to suggest alternative models of fair selection (or what some called "models of group parity"). In 1973, Cole proposed what came to be called the "conditional probability model of fair selection."[60] She argued that an alternative definition of fairness is that for "both minority and majority groups whose members can achieve a satisfactory criterion score (i.e., score above Y* on the criterion variable) there should be the same probability of selection regardless of group membership" (240). In other words, the passing scores on the test (X*) ought to be set so that the ratio $\frac{(A)}{(A+B)}$ is equal for minority and majority group members.

A third model of fair selection was proposed by Linn in 1973. He suggested that another plausible model of fairness would be to select people so that those selected (i.e., scoring above the test cutoff score X*) should have the same probability of success on the criterion (i.e., score above Y*)

TABLE 3.1
Alternative Definitions of Fair Selection or Group Parity Models (see Figure 3.3)

Model	Source	Criterion of Fairness Across Major and Minor Groups	Ratios to be Equalized for Major and Minor Groups
Constant ratio	Thorndike, 1971	Equalize ratio of passes to those truly above criterion	$\dfrac{A+D}{A+B}$
Conditional probability	Cole, 1973	Equalize true passes as proportion of all truly above criterion	$\dfrac{A}{A+B}$
Equal probability	Linn, 1973	Equalize true passes as proportion of all passes	$\dfrac{A}{A+D}$
Converse constant ratio	Peterson & Novick, 1976	Equalize failures as proportion of all below criterion	$\dfrac{B+C}{C+D}$
Converse conditional probability	Peterson & Novick, 1976	Equalize true failures as proportion of all below criterion	$\dfrac{C}{C+D}$
Converse equal probability	Peterson & Novick, 1976	Equalize true failures as proportion of all failures	$\dfrac{C}{B+C}$

regardless of group membership. This model meant that one ought to equalize the ratio $\frac{(A)}{(A+D)}$ for the majority and minority groups.

However as Peterson and Novick pointed out in 1976,[61] each of these three models of fair selection has a logical complement, which they labeled "converse models." Each of these converse models is summarized in table 3.1. Peterson and Novick noted that though each of these six models of group parity has a certain intuitive appeal, in specific situations they can imply quite different cutoff or passing scores (X^*). In a follow-up article, Novick and Ellis argued that group parity models of fairness toward groups identified on the basis of race, ethnicity or other group characteristics are "socially undesirable" in that within minority groups, the group parity models result in an "inverse relationship between disadvantage and compensation."[62] Later, Jensen discounted the group parity models of fair selection as amounting to quota systems and as dependent on "a philosophical position regarding the way test scores should be used."[63] These critics of the group parity models also argued for the theoretical attractiveness of "expected utility" or "decision theory" models, which, instead of leaving philosophical assumptions implicit, force the decision maker to make assumptions explicit in terms of utilities associated with different kinds of correct and incorrect classifications for different kinds of individuals.

The development of the various models of fairness in selection may seem highly theoretical and far removed from actual practice of using tests in schools, in college admissions, and in employment. They do, however, help to clarify several different issues concerning the use of standardized tests with minorities. First, these models make eminently clear that despite many statistical studies of tests' possible bias defined in terms of predictive validity, unfairness of tests for minorities results not simply from the tests themselves, but from how they are used.

Second, testing specialists such as Jensen and others cited previously have not paid close attention to how tests are actually used in making decisions about students. Though the academic literature concerning test bias has focused heavily on the value of test scores for making statistical predictions (using correlation and regression analyses) about majority versus minority individuals, it is clear that most colleges and schools do not use tests to make such statistical predictions about students. For example, though the membership of the College Board consists of twenty-five hundred colleges and schools, and despite the fact that since 1964 the College Board has offered a free validity study service to help colleges perform validity studies on the SAT, each year from 1964 through 1982, less than two hundred colleges availed themselves of this free service.[64] Thus it is clear that instead of using test scores to make statistical predictions about applicants, most colleges use less sophisticated methods in employing test results to make decisions about students—according to one recent survey, around 40 percent of four-year public colleges and universities reported using a cutoff score on the SAT.[65] And if colleges having access to free validity studies conduct predictive validity studies infrequently, it seems even less likely that elementary and secondary schools employ such studies in using test scores to make decisions about placing students into ability tracks. Thus if test validity and fairness reside not so much in the tests themselves as in how they are used, the literature concerning predictive power of tests in regression equations is somewhat irrelevant to use of tests by schools and colleges.

We do know that both schools and colleges classify students into two or more broad categories (e.g., at the secondary school level, college prep, general, or vocational tracks; and regarding college admissions, admit or reject). We also know that both schools and colleges employ both students' grades and standardized test scores in classifying students in these ways. Therefore in considering the implications of testing for the educational opportunities of minorities, it is useful to examine the relationship between test scores and grades in making categorical classifications of students.

Test Scores versus Grades

A considerable amount of evidence shows that minorities tend to rank better (relative to whites or to all students irrespective of race or ethnicity) on grades as opposed to test scores. Table 3.2 illustrates this general pattern for

TABLE 3.2
National Profile of SAT Takers 1988

	SAT Verbal	SAT Math	Test of Standard Written English	High School Grade Point Average
Total				
Mean	428	476	43	3.07
Standard deviation	109	120	10.8	0.66
Subgroups				
Means and deviations				
Males	435	498	42.3	3.02
Deviation from total group	0.06	0.18	−0.06	−0.08
Females	422	455	43.7	3.13
Deviation from total group	−0.06	−0.18	0.06	0.09
American Indians	393	435	39.8	2.88
Deviation from total group	−0.32	−0.34	−0.30	−0.29
Asian Americans	408	522	39.9	3.25
Deviation from total group	−0.18	0.38	−0.29	0.27
Blacks	353	384	35.6	2.79
Deviation from total group	−0.69	−0.77	−0.69	−0.42
Hispanic Mexican Americans	382	428	39.4	3.05
Deviation from total group	−0.42	−0.40	−0.33	−0.03
Puerto Ricans	355	402	34.8	2.99
Deviation from total group	−0.67	−0.62	−0.76	−0.12
Other Hispanics	387	433	NA	NA
Deviation from total group				
Whites	445	490	44.9	3.11
Deviation from total group	0.16	0.12	0.18	0.06

Source: College Board 1988

all students who took the SAT in 1988. Specifically, the table shows the means and the standard deviations on the SATV, the SATM, the Test of Standard Written English (TSWE), and high school GPA for the total group of SAT test takers in 1988 and then shows the subgroup means and deviations from the total group means in terms of standard deviation units (i.e., the total group means minus the subgroup mean, and this difference is then divided by the standard deviation of the total group).

Before I discuss the patterns shown in table 3.2 for different racial/ethnic groups, consider the data shown for males and females who took the SAT in 1988. These data shows that males scored somewhat higher than females on the SATV and the SATM, but that females scored higher on the Test of Standard Written English and on high school grade point average. For instance, though the overall average of the total group of SAT takers on the SATV was

428, females on average scored 422 and males 435. As the data in table 3.2 indicate, this means that females were 0.06 standard deviation units below the total group mean on the SATV, but that males were 0.06 standard deviation units above the total group mean on the SATV.

Inspection of table 3.2 shows that for almost all minority racial/ethnic groups for which the College Board reports data (specifically American Indians, Blacks, Mexican Americans, and other Hispanics), on the average almost all scored relatively lower on the SATV, SATM, and TSWE (from 0.30 to 0.77 standard deviations below the total mean) than on high school grade point average (0.03 to 0.42 standard deviation [SD] units below the total mean). The notable exception to this general pattern was for Asian American students, who, while scoring 0.18 SD units below the overall mean on the SATV, scored 0.38 standard deviation units *above* the total mean on the SATM.

These data show clearly that the situation described theoretically by Thorndike in 1971, in which a minority group scores 1.0 standard deviation below the majority group on a test but only 0.50 of a standard deviation below on a criterion measure, is very similar to what these data on SAT takers reveal about minorities' performance on the SAT and TSWE relative to their performance as indicated by high school grade point average. Minorities generally (with the notable exception of Asian Americans on the SATM) score relatively worse on the SAT than on high school grades.

Before elaborating on these data, it should be noted that though based on more than a million SAT takers in 1988, because the GPA data summarized here are based on students' self-reports, their accuracy may well be questioned, particularly since there is some evidence that the validity of self-reported high school GPA has slightly lower power to predict success in college than high school GPA reported by institutions.[66] However, other studies that do not rely on measures of GPA reported by students show similar patterns. In the 1971 study mentioned earlier by Pfeifer and Sedlacek concerning students attending the University of Maryland, for example, data reported indicate that Blacks score about 0.87 standard deviations below whites on the SATV and 1.09 SD below whites in the SATM, but only 0.42 SD units below whites on high school GPA. Also in the study of seventh-grade students in the Atlanta public schools by McCandless, Roberts, and Starnes, data reported indicate that while Black students scored 0.66 SD units below whites on an intelligence test and 0.62 SD units below whites on a standardized achievement test, they scored only 0.22 SD units below whites in terms of average teachers' grades.[67]

Given these patterns, it is worth returning to the ideas of fair selection and group parity discussed earlier. Let us suppose that there is a 0.8 standard deviation difference between the averages of majority and minority groups on a standardized test, but only a 0.40 difference in their grade averages. Assuming that the major group comprises 80 percent of the total population and the minority group 20 percent and that there is an overall correlation of 0.50 between test scores and GPA, let us consider what would happen if we wished to select the top 40 percent (for example, for placement into a college preparatory track in high school or admission into a selective college). Given such a scenario, if we were to select the top 40 percent on the basis of test scores, we would select about 45 percent of the majority group, but less than 20 percent of the minority group. On the other hand, if we were to base our selection not on the test, but on GPA, we would be selecting about 43 percent of the majority group and about 28 percent of the minority group. In other words, basing placement or selection decisions on GPAs has a much less disparate impact on selection rates of minorities than selection on the basis of test scores. Given the scenario just described, selecting students on the basis of GPA increases the chances of minorities' being selected by about 40 percent as opposed to selecting students on the basis of test scores (the 28 percent of minorities selected by GPA is 40 percent greater than the 20 percent selected by test scores).

The perspective suggested in Thorndike's constant ratio model of fair selection provides another picture of what happens under such a situation. Selection of the top 40 percent of scorers on the test would yield about 110 percent of majority individuals who were actually in the top 40 percent on grades, but only about 82 percent of minority individuals who were in the top 40 percent on grades.

These results—that is, the greater negative impact on selection rates of minorities when selection is based on test results rather than on grades—follows directly from the general pattern apparent in the research literature, namely, that minorities generally do better relative to whites on grades as compared with standard test results. This phenomenon was examined in considerable detail with respect to college admissions testing by Crouse and Truesheim in their book *The Case against the SAT.*[68] Through a variety of statistical analyses, using a set of nationally representative data on Blacks and whites, they showed that even if regression prediction equations are used to make categorical classifications about individuals, the use of test scores in addition to grades tends to work against Black students and fails to improve overall forecasting accuracy regarding such classifications.

Why Not Use Grades?

If test scores generally show greater adverse impact on minorities than grades, and if grades also tend to have more validity for predicting students' future success in school or college, an obvious question arises. If we are concerned with enhancing the educational opportunities of minorities, why not simply make decisions about students' placement in high school tracks and admission to college strictly on the basis of grades and other information without using test scores?

One of the main reasons is that grades themselves have been shown for many decades to have numerous weaknesses.[69] Indeed, historically one of the main arguments for relying more heavily on test results as opposed to teachers' grades was that research showed that teachers' grades were not highly reliable. When given the same paper to grade, different teachers—or even the same teacher on different occasions—gave sharply different grades.[70] Also, research has shown that grading standards vary across schools and across fields of study. Moreover, considerable research has indicated that there are systematic differences in the grading of males and females, with females tending to earn higher grades, and some research has indicated that teachers' expectations about students—which presumably may influence the grades they give—are based partly on students' socioeconomic backgrounds.[71]

Additional evidence of the unreliability of grades became apparent in the 1970s, a time of apparent grade inflation. While college admissions test scores were declining, student grade point averages were increasing. One national survey of high school students in the late 1970s, for example, found that even students who reported spending zero hours per week on homework reported getting mostly Bs and Cs for grades.[72] Also, some research has shown that minorities may be graded differently than whites. For example, one study reported that some elementary school teachers graded essays differently depending on whether or not they thought the student authors were male or female, or Black or white.[73] Also, as previously noted, college admission tests have long been supported by research indicating that while high school grades (or ranks) generally predict freshman grades better than admission test scores, admissions test scores do add significantly to the predictive power of grades.

At the same time, despite the vagaries of grading practices in schools and colleges, it is clear that *average* grades earned by students do reflect something real and stable about students that is not reflected fully in test scores. Studies have shown, for example, that the correlations between college grades received in one semester predict the grade average in the next semester with a correlation of about 0.60[74]—significantly greater than the correlation between college admissions tests with college grades.

One explanation for what is reflected in college grades that is not reflected in test scores is that grades in part show how well students learn what it is that they are taught. Standardized tests, because they are used with students in many classes and schools, are not well matched to the material taught in any one class or school. Grade averages also may reflect students' motivation and willingness to work hard. One study has shown, for example, that time spent on homework is correlated with high school grades, even after controlling for "ability" test scores.[75]

In sum, according to evidence concerning scholastic success at levels ranging from junior high school through college, minorities tend to show up relatively better on grade point average than on standardized test scores. Though grades have been widely criticized as unreliable indicators of scholastic achievement, when averaged across several different courses (for example, those taken in one semester), GPA has fairly consistently been shown to have as much or greater power to predict future grades as have test scores. Before I suggest what to make of these somewhat contradictory findings, it is important to point out the limitations of predictive validity studies—be they of test scores or of grade averages.

THE PROBLEM WITH PREDICTIVE VALIDITY

The criticisms by testing specialists such as Jensen and Novick of fair selection models as being dependent on particular philosophical assumptions must be extended to point out that *any* use of test results inevitably carries philosophical assumptions. Note for instance that any study of test results that seeks to establish tests' validity in terms of their power to predict how well students will do in school or college in the future carries an implicit assumption that the purpose of educational institutions is to base decisions using test scores on students' predicted future performance. But as Alexander Astin has pointed out with regard to college admissions, "To defend selective admissions on the grounds that aptitude tests and high school grades predict performance is perhaps to miss the main point of education."[76] Astin argues that a more important criterion for determining the utility of admissions tests and educational programs ought to be whether or not students learn and acquire skills and knowledge that are of value either to themselves or to society.

Though Astin's focus in making this point was on postsecondary education, it is particularly relevant to elementary and secondary education and how tests and other information about students are used at these levels. Regarding public schooling at the elementary level (and increasingly at the secondary level, since dropping out of high school is now looked upon with disapprobation), there is broad social commitment in the United States to educating all students. In contrast, there is no similar social commitment to educating all students beyond the secondary level. Hence, since college education is somewhat selective, it makes some sense to evaluate college admissions tests in terms of their power to predict who will do best in college.

But this logic is simply not relevant to precollege education where there is a broad commitment to educate all students, rather than simply educating the ones who are predicted to do best. Thus there is fairly widespread agreement that at the elementary and secondary levels, the value of test information for purposes of special placements of students ought to be judged in terms of the benefits derived from such placements. Even as staunch a defender of mental tests as Jensen has written that the only justification for placement of students into alternative treatments (such as special education classes or ability tracks) is "evidence that alternative treatments are more beneficial to the individuals assigned to them than would be the case if everyone got the same treatment."[77] Predictive validity evidence is entirely irrelevant to this issue. For as Astin has pointed out, testing students at one point and then retesting or grading them later may show the initial test results to have extremely high "validity" for predicting the later scores or grades, even though the students may not have benefited or changed at all.

This suggests that in contrast to predictive validity evidence, which is widely cited to bolster the use of test results in educational decision making, we ought to pay far more attention to the *educational validity* of test results and other kinds of information about students. By "educational validity" I mean the extent to which information not just predicts individuals' future status, but instead helps to educate them—that is, helps them improve and grow.

From this perspective, a major question arises as to what it is that is reflected in students' average grades that is not reflected in test scores. While teachers' grades do have many weaknesses from the point of view of representing reliable and valid measurements (as mentioned, they seem to be affected by factors such as students' sex, socioeconomic factors, and programs of study), it is possible that they may have more educational validity than standardized test scores, in the sense that they may be more reflective of how much students improve and grow in their coursework than are standardized test results. While we have not found any direct evidence to support—or to refute—this possibility, if teachers' grades are based mainly on student work in their courses, it seems likely that they may be more reflective of student change than are standardized test scores, for the simple reason that the content of standardized tests are not matched to the curriculum content of particular courses.

From the point of view of educational policy generally, how to answer the question posed in the previous section ("Why not use grades?") requires a determination as to whether what is reflected in grade averages that is not reflected in test scores is something that we wish to value and promote. Even if students' grade averages do not fully reflect how much they learn in their courses, they may reflect characteristics like attendance, willingness to work hard, and perseverance, which, while not cognitive skills, are attributes that we, as educators or as a society, wish to reward and promote. If so, this clearly argues for placing greater weight on grades than on test scores in making educational decisions about students.

CONCLUSION

In this chapter I have shown that though standardized test results have historically been used to the disadvantage of minorities in the United States, considerable statistical evidence indicates that test results do not have less predictive validity for minorities than nonminorities. Then I explained the manner in which test results, even if not statistically biased against minorities in terms of showing differential predictive validity in correlation or regression analyses, may still be used unfairly in making classifications of students if there are larger minority-nonminority differences on test results than on relevant criterion measures.

Having reviewed these concepts generally, I next showed that there is considerable evidence that minority-nonminority differences on standardized test results are larger than on grade point averages. Thus when greater weight is placed on test results in making educational decisions, the results may be unfair—or, in the common lexicon, biased—against minorities, relative to how opportunities would be allocated on the basis of grades rather than test results.

Having come this far I then addressed the obvious question as to why not simply avoid using test results and base decisions about students on grade averages rather than on test scores. Part of the answer to this question is that grading practices of teachers have been shown to have many imperfections, but also there appears to be considerable uncertainty as to what it is that is reflected in grade averages that is not reflected in student learning as measured by standardized tests. From the point of view of educational as opposed to predictive validity, we suggested that to the extent that grade averages reflect increases in learning or attributes such as perseverance and hard work, general educational policies ought to place greater weight on grade averages and less on test scores.

In conclusion it is important to point out that even if the relatively higher performance of minorities generally on grades than on tests is indicative of nothing more than imperfections in the grading practices of our nation's schools and colleges, this differential performance gap still presents a major dilemma of procedural fairness. Suppose, for example, that the relatively higher standing of minorities, on the average, on grades than on tests reflects simply lower expectations that schools and teachers generally hold out for minorities. If it does, then it demonstrates a different sort of unfairness or bias against minority students in the United States.

As I have shown, minority students have long been disproportionately classified into lower "ability" tracks in schools of the United States, and differential expectations are placed on students in different ability tracks—with lower expectations placed on the students in lower tracks, which are disproportionately inhabited by minority students. If this is so, minorities still have ample cause for concern about making decisions about individuals on the basis of test results, for it represents a sort of procedural unfairness by which students are judged on one set of standards—grades—on a week-to-week and course-to-course basis, on which they perform relatively well. But when it comes to making more important and longer-term decisions, such as ability tracking or college admissions, a different standard is employed, on which they show up relatively less well. It thus may be the story writ large of the students whom Cawthorne interviewed in Boston. They did well on everything that their schools asked of them—but when it came time to make an important decision about their futures, they were confronted with a test that simply did not correspond well with what their schools had been expecting of them or with how their schools had been evaluating them.

Whichever explanation for the differential gap between minorities and nonminorities on standardized tests versus grade averages is more true, it likely would not be in the best interests of the educational opportunities of minorities in the United States to do away with use of standardized tests and rely strictly on grades for making decisions about students. After all, standardized tests have *sometimes* been used to document the educational disadvantages of minorities in the United States, and it must be remembered that historically such disadvantages long preceded the introduction of standardized tests into the schools and colleges of the United States and that many minority individuals experience significant social and economic disadvantages long before they encounter standardized tests or schools. What needs to be opposed is the use of tests that serve to justify and perpetuate social and educational disadvantages of minorities. And from a more positive perspective, what is needed is to use test results not so much to make decisions about individual students, as to examine critically how our schools are serving their interests. It is to use tests, as the National Commission on Testing and Public Policy recently recommended, not as gatekeepers to close off opportunities, but as gateways to open them up and to examine critically the performance of our nation's education institutions.

MICHELLE FINE

Chapter Four

Sexuality, Schooling, and Adolescent Females: The Missing Discourse of Desire*

Since late 1986, popular magazines and newspapers have printed steamy stories about education and sexuality. Whether the controversy surrounds sex education or school-based health clinics (SBHCs), public discourses of adolescent sexuality are represented forcefully by government officials, New Right spokespersons, educators, "the public," feminists, and health-care professionals. These stories offer the authority of "facts," insights into the political controversies, and access to unacknowledged fears about sexuality.[1] Although the facts usually involve the adolescent female body, little has been heard from young women themselves.

This article examines these diverse perspectives on adolescent sexuality and, in addition, presents the views of a group of adolescent females. The article is informed by a study of numerous current sex education curricula, a year of negotiating for inclusion of lesbian and gay sexuality in a citywide sex education curriculum, and interviews and observations gathered in New York City sex education classrooms.[2] The analysis examines the desires, fears, and fantasies which give structure and shape to silences and voices concerning sex education and school-based health clinics in the 1980s.

Despite the attention devoted to teen sexuality, pregnancy, and parenting in this country, and despite the evidence of effective interventions and the widespread public support expressed for these interventions,[3] the systematic implementation of sex education and SBHCs continues to be obstructed by the controversies surrounding them.[4] Those who resist sex education or SBHCs often present their views as based on rationality and a concern for protecting the young. For such opponents, sex education raises questions of promoting promiscuity and immorality, and of undermining family values. Yet the language of the challenges suggests an affect substantially more profound and primitive. Gary Bauer, Undersecretary of Education in the U.S. Department of Education, for example, constructs an image of immorality littered by adolescent sexuality and drug abuse:

> There is ample impressionistic evidence to indicate that drug abuse and promiscuity are not independent behaviors. When inhibitions fall, they collapse across the board. When people of any age lose a sense of right and wrong, the loss is not selective. . . . [T]hey are all expressions of the same ethical vacuum among many teens.[5]

Even Surgeon General C. Everett Koop, a strong supporter of sex education, recently explained: "[W]e have to be as explicit as necessary. . . . You can't talk of the dangers of snake poisoning and not mention snakes."[6] Such commonly used and often repeated metaphors associate adolescent sexuality with victimization and danger.

Yet public schools have rejected the task of sexual dialogue and critique, or what has been called "sexuality education." Within today's standard sex education curricula and many public school classrooms, we find: (1) the authorized suppression of a discourse of female sexual desire; (2) the promotion of a discourse of female sexual victimization; and (3) the explicit privileging of married heterosexuality over other practices of sexuality. One finds an unacknowledged social ambivalence about female sexuality which ideologically separates the female sexual agent, or subject, from her counterpart, the female sexual victim. The adolescent woman of the 1980s is constructed as the latter. Educated primarily as the potential victim of male sexuality, she represents no subject in her own right. Young women continue to be taught to fear and defend in isolation from exploring desire, and in this context there is little possibility of their developing a critique of gender or sexual arrangements.

PREVAILING DISCOURSES OF FEMALE SEXUALITY INSIDE PUBLIC SCHOOLS

> If the body is seen as endangered by uncontrollable forces, then presumably this is a society or social group which fears change—change which it perceived simultaneously as powerful and beyond its control.[7]

Public schools have historically been the site for identifying, civilizing, and containing that which is considered uncontrollable. While evidence of sexuality is everywhere within public high schools—in the halls, classrooms, bathrooms, lunchrooms, and the library—official sexuality education occurs sparsely: in social studies, biology, sex education, or inside the nurse's office. To understand how sexuality is managed inside schools, I examined the major discourses of sexuality which characterize the national debates over sex education and SBHCs. These discourses are then tracked as they weave through the curricula, classrooms, and halls of public high schools.

The first discourse, *sexuality as violence,* is clearly the most conservative, and equates adolescent heterosexuality with violence. At the 1986 American Dreams Symposium on education, Phyllis Schlafly commented: "Those courses on sex, abuse, incest, AIDS, they are all designed to terrorize our children. We should fight their existence, and stop putting terror in the hearts and minds of our youngsters." One aspect of this position, shared by women as politically distinct as Schlafly and the radical feminist lawyer Catherine MacKinnon, views heterosexuality as essentially violent and coercive.[8] In its full conservative form, proponents call for the elimination of sex education and clinics and urge complete reliance on the family to dictate appropriate values, mores, and behaviors.

Sexuality as violence presumes that there is a causal relationship between official silence about sexuality and a decrease in sexual activity—therefore, by not teaching about sexuality, adolescent sexual behavior will not occur. The irony, of course, lies in the empirical evidence. Fisher, Byrne, and White have documented sex-negative attitudes and contraceptive use to be negatively correlated. In their study, sex-negative attitudes do not discourage sexual activity, but they do discourage responsible use of contraception. Teens who believe sexual involvement is wrong deny responsibility for contraception. To accept responsibility would legitimate "bad" behavior.[9] By contrast, Fisher et al. found that adolescents with sex-positive attitudes tend to be both more consistent and more positive about contraceptive use. By not teaching about sexuality, or by teaching sex-negative attitudes, schools apparently will not forestall sexual activity, but may well discourage responsible contraception.[10]

The second discourse, *sexuality as victimization,* gathers a much greater following. Female adolescent sexuality is represented as a moment of victimization in which the dangers of heterosexuality for adolescent women (and, more recently, of homosexuality for adolescent men) are prominent. While sex may not be depicted as inherently violent, young women (and today, men) learn of their vulnerability to potential male predators.

To avoid being victimized, females learn to defend themselves against disease, pregnancy, and "being used." The discourse of victimization supports sex education, including AIDS education, with parental consent. Suggested classroom activities emphasize "saying no," practicing abstinence, enumerating the social and emotional risks of sexual intimacy, and listing the possible diseases associated with sexual intimacy. The language, as well as the questions asked and not asked, represents females as the actual and potential victims of male desire. In exercises, role plays, and class discussions, girls practice resistance to trite lines, unwanted hands, opened buttons, and the surrender of other "bases" they are not prepared to yield. The discourses of violence and victimization both portray males as potential predators and females as victims. Three problematic assumptions underlie these two views:

— First, female subjectivity, including the desire to engage in sexual activity, is placed outside the prevailing conversation.[11]
— Second, both arguments present female victimization as contingent upon unmarried heterosexual involvement—rather than inherent in existing gender, class, and racial arrangements.[12] While feminists have long fought for the legal and social acknowledgment of sexual violence against women, most have resisted the claim that female victimization hinges primarily upon sexual involvement with men. The full range of victimization of women—at work, at home, on the streets—has instead been uncovered. The language and emotion invested in these two discourses divert attention away from structures, arrangements, and relationships which oppress women in general, and low-income women and women of color in particular.[13]
— Third, the messages, while narrowly anti-sexual, nevertheless buttress traditional heterosexual arrangements. These views assume that as long as females avoid premarital sexual relations with men, victimization can be avoided. Ironically, however, protection from male victimization is available primarily through marriage—by coupling with a man. The paradoxical message teaches females to fear the very men who will ultimately protect them.

    The third discourse, *sexuality as individual morality,* introduces explicit notions of sexual subjectivity for women. Although quite judgmental and moralistic, this discourse values women's sexual decisionmaking as long as the decisions made are for premarital abstinence. For example, Secretary of Education William Bennett urges schools to teach "morality literacy" and to educate towards "modesty," "chastity," and "abstinence" until marriage. The language of self-control and self-respect reminds students that sexual immorality breeds not only personal problems but also community tax burdens.
    The debate over morality in sex education curricula marks a clear contradiction among educational conservatives over whether and how the state may intervene in the "privacy of families." Non-interventionists, including Schlafly and Onalee McGraw, argue that educators should not teach about

sexuality at all. To do so is to take a particular moral position which subverts the family. Interventionists, including Koop, Bennett, and Bauer, argue that schools should teach about sexuality by focusing on "good values," but disagree about how. Koop proposes open discussion of sexuality and the use of condoms, while Bennett advocates "sexual restraint".[14] Sexuality in this discourse is posed as a test of self-control; individual restraint triumphs over social temptation. Pleasure and desire for women as sexual subjects remain largely in the shadows, obscured from adolescent eyes.

The fourth discourse, a *discourse of desire*, remains a whisper inside the official work of U.S. public schools. If introduced at all, it is as an interruption of the ongoing conversation.[15] The naming of desire, pleasure, or sexual entitlement, particularly for females, barely exists in the formal agenda of public schooling on sexuality. When spoken, it is tagged with reminders of "consequences"—emotional, physical, moral, reproductive, and/ or financial.[16] A genuine discourse of desire would invite adolescents to explore what feels good and bad, desirable and undesirable, grounded in experiences, needs, and limits. Such a discourse would release females from a position of receptivity, enable an analysis of the dialectics of victimization and pleasure, and would pose female adolescents as subjects of sexuality, initiators as well as negotiators.[17]

In Sweden, where sex education has been offered in schools since the turn of the century, the State Commission on Sex Education recommends teaching students to "acquire a knowledge . . . [which] will equip them to experience sexual life as a source of happiness and joy in fellowship with other [people]".[18] The teachers' handbook goes on, "The many young people who wish to wait [before initiating sexual activity] and those who have had early sexual relations should experience, in class, [the feeling] that they are understood and accepted".[19] Compare this to an exercise suggested in a major U.S. metropolitan sex education curriculum: "Discuss and evaluate: things which may cause teenagers to engage in sexual relations before they are ready to assume the responsibility of marriage".[20]

A discourse of desire, though seldom explored in U.S. classrooms, does occur in less structured school situations. The following excerpts, taken from group and individual student interviews, demonstrate female adolescents' subjective experiences of body and desire as they begin to articulate notions of sexuality.

In some cases young women pose a critique of marriage:

I'm still in love with Simon, but I'm seeing Jose. He's OK but he said, "Will you be my girl?" I hate that. It feels like they own you. Like I say to a girlfriend, "What's wrong? You look terrible!" and she says, "I'm married!" (Millie, a 16-year-old student from the Dominican Republic)

In other cases they offer stories of their own victimization:

> It's not like last year. Then I came to school regular. Now my old boyfriend,
> he waits for me in front of my building every morning and he fights with
> me. Threatens me, gettin' all bad. . . . I want to move out of my house and
> live 'cause he ain't gonna stop no way. (Sylvia, age 17, about to drop out of
> twelfth grade)

Some even speak of desire:

> I'm sorry I couldn't call you last night about the interview, but my boy-
> friend came back from [the] Navy and I wanted to spend the night with him,
> we don't get to see each other much. (Shandra, age 17, after a no-show for
> an interview)

In a context in which desire is not silenced, but acknowledged and discussed,
conversations with adolescent women can, as seen here, educate through a
dialectic of victimization and pleasure. Despite formal silencing, it would be
misleading to suggest that talk of desire never emerges within public schools.
Notwithstanding a political climate organized around the suppression of this
conversation, some teachers and community advocates continue to struggle
for an empowering sex education curriculum both in and out of the high
school classroom.

Family life curricula and/or plans for a school-based health clinic have
been carefully generated in many communities. Yet they continue to face loud
and sometimes violent resistance by religious and community groups, often
from outside the district lines.[21] In other communities, when curricula or
clinics have been approved with little overt confrontation, monies for training
are withheld. For example, in New York City in 1987, $1.7 million was ini-
tially requested to implement training on the Family Life education curriculum. As sex educators confronted community and religious groups, the
inclusion of some topics as well as the language of others were continually
negotiated. Ultimately, the Chancellor requested only $600,000 for training,
a sum substantially inadequate to the task.[22]

In this political context many public school educators nevertheless continue to take personal and professional risks to create materials and foster
classroom environments which speak fully to the sexual subjectivities of
young women and men. Some operate within the privacy of their classrooms,
subverting the official curriculum and engaging students in critical discussion. Others advocate publicly for enriched curricula and training. A few
have even requested that community-based advocates *not* agitate for official
curricular change, so "we [teachers] can continue to do what we do in the

classroom, with nobody looking over our shoulders. You make a big public deal of this, and it will blow open."[23] Within public school classrooms, it seems that female desire may indeed be addressed when educators act subversively. But in the typical sex education classroom, silence, and therefore distortion, surrounds female desire.

The blanketing of female sexual subjectivity in public school classrooms, in public discourse, and in bed will sound familiar to those who have read Luce Irigaray and Helene Cíxous.[24] These French feminists have argued that expressions of female voice, body, and sexuality are essentially inaudible when the dominant language and ways of viewing are male. Inside the hegemony of what they call The Law of the Father, female desire and pleasure can gain expression only in the terrain already charted by men.[25] In the public school arena, this constriction of what is called sexuality allows girls one primary decision—to say yes or no—to a question not necessarily their own. A discourse of desire in which young women have a voice would be informed and generated out of their own socially constructed sexual meanings. It is to these expressions that we now turn.

The Bodies of Female Adolescents: Voices and Structured Silences

If four discourses can be distinguished among the many positions articulated by various "authorities," the sexual meanings voiced by female adolescents defy such classification. A discourse of desire, though absent in the "official" curriculum, is by no means missing from the lived experiences or commentaries of young women. This section introduces their sexual thoughts, concerns, and meanings, as represented by a group of Black and Latina female adolescents—students and dropouts from a public high school in New York City serving predominantly low-income youths. In my year at this comprehensive high school I had frequent opportunity to speak with adolescents and listen to them talk about sex. The comments reported derive from conversations between the young women and their teachers, among themselves, and with me, as researcher. During conversations, the young women talked freely about fears and, in the same breath, asked about passions. Their struggle to untangle issues of gender, power, and sexuality underscores the fact that, for them, notions of sexual negotiation cannot be separated from sacrifice and nurturance.

The adolescent female rarely reflects simply on sexuality. Her sense of sexuality is informed by peers, culture, religion, violence, history, passion, authority, rebellion, body, past and future, and gender and racial relations of power.[26] The adolescent woman herself assumes a dual consciousness—at once taken with the excitement of actual/anticipated sexuality and consumed with anxiety and worry. While too few safe spaces exist for adolescent

women's exploration of sexual subjectivities, there are all too many dangerous spots for their exploitation.

Whether in a classroom, on the street, at work, or at home, the adolescent female's sexuality is negotiated by, for, and despite the young woman
herself. Patricia, a young Puerto Rican woman who worried about her
younger sister, relates: "You see, I'm the love child and she's the one born
because my mother was raped in Puerto Rico. Her father's in jail now, and
she feels so bad about the whole thing so she acts bad." For Patricia, as for
the many young women who have experienced and/or witnessed sexual violence, discussions of sexuality merge representations of passion with violence. Often the initiator of conversation among peers about virginity,
orgasm, "getting off," and pleasure, Patricia mixed sexual talk freely with
references to force and violence. She is a poignant narrator who illustrates,
from the female adolescent's perspective, that sexual victimization and desire
coexist.[27]

Sharlene and Betty echo this braiding of danger and desire. Sharlene explained: "Boys always be trying to get into my panties," and Betty added: "I
don't be needin' a man who won't give me no pleasure but take my money
and expect me to take care of him." This powerful commentary on gender
relations, voiced by Black adolescent females, was inseparable from their
views of sexuality. To be a woman was to be strong, independent, and reliable—but not too independent for fear of scaring off a man.

Deidre continued this conversation, explicitly pitting male fragility
against female strength: "Boys in my neighborhood ain't wrapped so tight.
Got to be careful how you treat them. . . ." She reluctantly admitted that perhaps it is more important for Black males than females to attend college,
"Girls and women, we're stronger, we take care of ourselves. But boys and
men, if they don't get away from the neighborhood, they end up in jail, on
drugs or dead . . . or wack [crazy]."

These young women spoke often of anger at males, while concurrently
expressing a strong desire for male attention: "I dropped out 'cause I fell in
love, and couldn't stop thinking of him." An equally compelling desire was
to protect young males—particularly Black males—from a system which
"makes them wack." Ever aware of the ways that institutional racism and the
economy have affected Black males, these young women seek pleasure but
also offer comfort. They often view self-protection as taking something away
from young men. Lavanda offered a telling example: "If I ask him to use a
condom, he won't feel like a man."

In order to understand the sexual subjectivities of young women more
completely, educators need to reconstruct schooling as an empowering context in which we listen to and work with the meanings and experiences of

gender and sexuality revealed by the adolescents themselves. When we refuse that responsibility, we prohibit an education which adolescents wholly need and deserve. My classroom observations suggest that such education is rare.

Ms. Rosen, a teacher of a sex education class, opened one session with a request: "You should talk to your mother or father about sex before you get involved." Nilda initiated what became an informal protest by a number of Latino students: "Not our parents! We tell them one little thing and they get crazy. My cousin got sent to Puerto Rico to live with her religious aunt, and my sister got beat 'cause my father thought she was with a boy." For these adolescents, a safe space for discussion, critique, and construction of sexualities was not something they found in their homes. Instead, they relied on school, the spot they chose for the safe exploration of sexualities.

The absence of safe spaces for exploring sexuality affects all adolescents. It was paradoxical to realize that perhaps the only students who had an in-school opportunity for critical sexual discussion in the comfort of peers were the few students who had organized the Gay and Lesbian Association (GALA) at the high school. While most lesbian, gay, or bisexual students were undoubtedly closeted, those few who were "out" claimed this public space for their display and for their sanctuary. Exchanging support when families and peers would offer little, GALA members worried that so few students were willing to come out, and that so many suffered the assaults of homophobia individually. The gay and lesbian rights movement had powerfully affected these youngsters, who were comfortable enough to support each other in a place not considered very safe—a public high school in which echoes of "faggot!" fill the halls.

In the absence of an education which explores and unearths danger and desire, sexuality education classes typically provide little opportunity for discussions beyond those constructed around superficial notions of male heterosexuality.[28] Male pleasure is taught, albeit as biology. Teens learn about "wet dreams" (as the onset of puberty for males), "erection" (as the preface to intercourse), and "ejaculation" (as the act of inseminating). Female pleasures and questions are far less often the topic of discussion. Few voices of female sexual agency can be heard. The language of victimization and its underlying concerns—"Say No," put a brake on his sexuality, don't encourage—ultimately deny young women the right to control their own sexuality by providing no access to a legitimate position of sexual subjectivity. Often conflicted about self-representation, adolescent females spend enormous amounts of time trying to "save it," "lose it," convince others that they have lost or saved it, or trying to be "discreet" instead of focusing their energies in ways that are sexually autonomous, responsible, and pleasurable. In classroom observations, girls who were heterosexually active rarely spoke, for fear of being ostracized.[29] Those who were heterosexual virgins had the same worry. And most students who were gay, bisexual, or lesbian remained closeted, aware of the very real dangers of homophobia.

Occasionally, the difficult and pleasurable aspects of sexuality were discussed together, coming either as an interruption, or because an educational context was constructed. During a social studies class, for example, Catherine, the proud mother of two-year-old Tiffany, challenged an assumption underlying the class discussion—that teen motherhood devastates mother and child; "If I didn't get pregnant I would have continued on a downward path, going nowhere. They say teenage pregnancy is bad for you, but it was good for me. I know I can't mess around now, I got to worry about what's good for Tiffany and for me."

Another interruption came from Opal, a young Black student. Excerpts from her hygiene class follow.

Teacher: Let's talk about teenage pregnancy.
Opal: How come girls in the locker room say, "You a virgin?" and if you say "Yeah" they laugh and say "Ohh, you're a virgin. . . ." And some Black teenagers, I don't mean to be racial, when they get ready to tell their mothers they had sex, some break on them and some look funny. My friend told her mother and she broke all the dishes. She told her mother so she could get protection so she don't get pregnant.
Teacher: When my 13-year-old (relative) asked for birth control I was shocked and angry.
Portia: Mothers should help so she can get protection and not get pregnant or diseases. So you was wrong.
Teacher: Why not say "I'm thinking about having sex?"
Portia: You tell them after, not before, having sex but before pregnancy.
Teacher (now angry): Then it's a fait accompli and you expect my compassion? You have to take more responsibility.
Portia: I am! If you get pregnant after you told your mother and you got all the stuff and still get pregnant, you the fool. Take up hygiene and learn. Then it's my responsibility if I end up pregnant. . . .
                              —Field Note, October 23, Hygiene Class

Two days later, the discussion continued.

Teacher: What topics should we talk about in sex education?
Portia: Organs, how they work.
Opal: What's an orgasm?
[laughter]
Teacher: Sexual response, sensation all over the body. What's analogous to the male penis on the female?

Theo: Clitoris.
Teacher: Right, go home and look in the mirror.
Portia: She is too much!
Teacher: Why look in the mirror?
Elaine: It's yours.
Teacher: Why is it important to know what your body looks like?
Opal: You should like your body.
Teacher: You should know what it looks like when it's healthy, so you can recognize problems like vaginal warts.

—Field Note, October 25, Hygiene Class

The discourse of desire, initiated by Opal but evident only as an interruption, faded rapidly into the discourse of disease—warning about the dangers of sexuality.

It was in the spring of that year that Opal showed up pregnant. Her hygiene teacher, who was extremely concerned and involved with her students, was also quite angry with Opal: "Who is going to take care of that baby, you or your mother? You know what it costs to buy diapers and milk and afford child care?"

Opal, in conversation with me, related, "I got to leave [school] 'cause even if they don't say it, them teachers got hate in their eyes when they look at my belly." In the absence of a way to talk about passion, pleasure, danger, and responsibility, this teacher fetishized the latter two, holding the former two hostage. Because adolescent females combine these experiences in their daily lives, the separation is false, judgmental, and ultimately not very educational.

Over the year in this high school, and in other public schools since, I have observed a systematic refusal to name issues, particularly issues that caused adults discomfort. Educators often projected their discomfort onto students in the guise of "protecting" them.[30] An example of such silencing can be seen in a (now altered) policy of the school district of Philadelphia. In 1985 a student informed me, "We're not allowed to talk about abortion in our school." Assuming this was an overstatement, I asked an administrator at the District about this practice. She explained, "That's not quite right. If a student asks a question about abortion, the teacher can define abortion, she just can't discuss it." How can definition occur without discussion, exchange, conversation, or critique unless a subtext of silencing prevails?[31]

Explicit silencing of abortion has since been lifted in Philadelphia. The revised curriculum now reads:

Options for unintended pregnancy:
(a) adoption
(b) foster care

(c) single parenthood
(d) teen marriage
(e) abortion

A footnote is supposed to be added, however, to elaborate the negative consequences of abortion. In the social politics which surround public schools, such compromises are apparent across cities.

The New York City Family Life Education curriculum reads similarly:

List: The possible options for an unintended pregnancy. What considerations should be given in the decision on the alternatives?
—adoption
—foster care
—mother keeps baby
—elective abortion

Discuss:
—religious viewpoints on abortion
—present laws concerning abortion
—current developments in prenatal diagnosis and their implication for abortion issues
—why abortion should not be considered a contraceptive device

List: The people or community services that could provide assistance in the event of an unintended pregnancy

Invite: A speaker to discuss alternatives to abortion; for example, a social worker from the Department of Social Services to discuss foster care.[32]

One must be suspicious when diverse views are sought only for abortion, and not for adoption, teen motherhood, or foster care. The call to silence is easily identified in current political and educational contexts.[33] The silence surrounding contraception and abortion options and diversity in sexual orientations denies adolescents information and sends the message that such conversations are taboo—at home, at church, and even at school.

In contrast to these "official curricula," which allow discussion and admission of desire only as an interruption, let us examine other situations in which young women were invited to analyze sexuality across categories of the body, the mind, the heart, and of course, gender politics.

Teen Choice, a voluntary counseling program held on-site by non-Board of Education social workers, offered an instance in which the complexities of pleasure and danger were invited, analyzed, and braided into discussions of sexuality. In a small group discussion, the counselor asked of the seven ninth graders, "What are the two functions of a penis?" One student responded,

"To pee!" Another student offered the second function: "To eat!" which was followed by laughter and serious discussion. The conversation proceeded as the teacher asked, "Do all penises look alike?" The students explained, "No, they are all different colors!"

The freedom to express, beyond simple right and wrong answers, enabled these young women to offer what they knew with humor and delight. This discussion ended as one student insisted that if you "jump up and down a lot, the stuff will fall out of you and you won't get pregnant," to which the social worker answered with slight exasperation that millions of sperm would have to be released for such "expulsion" to work, and that of course, it wouldn't work. In this conversation one could hear what seemed like too much experience, too little information, and too few questions asked by the students. But the discussion, which was sex-segregated and guided by the experiences and questions of the students themselves (and the skills of the social worker), enabled easy movement between pleasure and danger, safety and desire, naiveté and knowledge, and victimization and entitlement.

What is evident, then, is that even in the absence of a discourse of desire, young women express their notions of sexuality and relate their experiences. Yet, "official" discourses of sexuality leave little room for such exploration. The authorized sexual discourses define what is safe, what is taboo, and what will be silenced. This discourse of sexuality mis-educates adolescent women. What results is a discourse of sexuality based on the male in search of desire and the female in search of protection. The open, coed sexuality discussions so many fought for in the 1970s have been appropriated as a forum for the primacy of male heterosexuality and the preservation of female victimization.

THE POLITICS OF FEMALE SEXUAL SUBJECTIVITIES

In 1912, an education committee explicitly argued that "scientific" sex education "should . . . keep sex consciousness and sex emotions at the minimum".[34] In the same era G. Stanley Hall proposed diversionary pursuits for adolescents, including hunting, music, and sports, "to reduce sex stress and tension . . . to short-circuit, transmute it and turn it on to develop the higher powers of the men [sic]".[35] In 1915 Orison Marden, author of *The Crime of Silence,* chastised educators, reformers, and public health specialists for their unwillingness to speak publicly about sexuality and for relying inappropriately on parents and peers, who were deemed too ignorant to provide sex instruction.[36] And in 1921 radical sex educator Maurice Bigelow wrote:

Now, most scientifically-trained women seem to agree that there are no corresponding phenomena in the early pubertal life of the normal young woman
who has good health (corresponding to male masturbation). A limited number of mature women, some of them physicians, report having experienced
in the pubertal years localized tumescence and other disturbances which
made them definitely conscious of sexual instincts. However, it should be
noted that most of these are known to have had a personal history including
one or more such abnormalities such as dysmenorrhea, uterine displacement, pathological ovaries, leucorrhea, tuberculosis, masturbation, neuras-
thenia, nymphomania, or other disturbances which are sufficient to account
for local sexual stimulation. In short such women are not normal.[37]

In the 1950s public school health classes separated girls from boys. Girls
"learned about sex" by watching films of the accelerated development of
breasts and hips, the flow of menstrual blood, and then the progression of
venereal disease as a result of participation in out-of-wedlock heterosexual
activity.

Thirty years and a much-debated sexual revolution later,[38] much has
changed. Feminism, the Civil Rights Movement, the disability and gay rights
movements, birth control, legal abortion with federal funding (won and then
lost), and reproductive technologies are part of these changes.[39] Due both to
the consequences of, and the backlashes against, these movements, students
today do learn about sexuality—if typically through the representations of
female sexuality as inadequacy or victimization, male homosexuality as a
story of predator and prey, and male heterosexuality as desire.

Young women today know that female sexual subjectivity is at least not
an inherent contradiction. Perhaps they even feel it is an entitlement. Yet
when public schools resist acknowledging the fullness of female sexual subjectivities, they reproduce a profound social ambivalence which dichotomizes
female heterosexuality.[40] This ambivalence surrounds a fragile cultural distinction between two forms of female sexuality: *consensual* sexuality, representing consent or choice in sexuality, and *coercive* sexuality, which
represents force, victimization, and/or crime.[41]

During the 1980s, however, this distinction began to be challenged. It
was acknowledged that gender-based power inequities shape, define, and
construct experiences of sexuality. Notions of sexual consent and force, except in extreme circumstances, became complicated, no longer in simple
opposition. The first problem concerned how to conceptualize power asymmetries and consensual sexuality. Could *consensual* female heterosexuality be
said to exist within a context replete with structures, relationships, acts, and
threats of female victimization (sexual, social, and economic)?[42] How could
we speak of "sexual preference" when sexual involvement outside of heterosexuality may seriously jeopardize one's social and/or economic well-

being?[43] Diverse female sexual subjectivities emerge through, despite, and because of gender-based power asymmetries. To imagine a female sexual self, free of and uncontaminated by power, was rendered naive.[44]

The second problem involved the internal incoherence of the categories. Once assumed fully independent, the two began to blur as the varied practices of sexuality went public. At the intersection of these presumably parallel forms—coercive and consensual sexualities—lay "sexual" acts of violence and "violent" acts of sex. "Sexual" acts of violence, including marital rape, acquaintance rape, and sexual harassment, were historically considered consensual. A woman involved in a marriage, on a date, or working outside her home "naturally" risked receiving sexual attention; her consent was inferred from her presence. But today, in many states, this woman can sue her husband for such sexual acts of violence; in all states, she can prosecute a boss. What was once part of "domestic life" or "work" may, today, be criminal. On the other hand, "violent" acts of sex, including consensual sadomasochism and the use of violence-portraying pornography, were once considered inherently coercive for women.[45] Female involvement in such sexual practices historically had been dismissed as nonconsensual. Today such romanticizing of a naive and moral "feminine sexuality" has been challenged as essentialist, and the assumption that such a feminine sexuality is "natural" to women has been shown to be false.[46]

Over the past decade, understandings of female sexual choice, consent, and coercion have grown richer and more complex. While questions about female subjectivities have become more interesting, the answers (for some) remain deceptively simple. Inside public schools, for example, female adolescents continue to be educated as though they were the potential *victims* of sexual (male) desire. By contrast, the ideological opposition represents only adult married women as fully consensual partners. The distinction of coercion and consent has been organized simply and respectively around age and marital status—which effectively resolves any complexity and/or ambivalence.

The ambivalence surrounding female heterosexuality places the victim and subject in opposition and derogates all women who represent female sexual subjectivities outside of marriage—prostitutes, lesbians, single mothers, women involved with multiple partners, and particularly, Black single mothers.[47] "Protected" from this derogation, the typical adolescent woman, as represented in sex education curricula, is without any sexual subjectivity. The discourse of victimization not only obscures the derogation, it also transforms socially distributed anxieties about female sexuality into acceptable, and even protective, talk.

The fact that schools implicitly organize sex education around a concern for female victimization is suspect, however, for two reasons. First, if female victims of male violence were truly a social concern, wouldn't the victims of rape, incest, and sexual harassment encounter social compassion, and not suspicion and blame? And second, if sex education were designed primarily to prevent victimization but not to prevent exploration of desire, wouldn't there be more discussions of both the pleasures and relatively fewer risks of disease or pregnancy associated with lesbian relationships and protected sexual intercourse, or of the risk-free pleasures of masturbation and fantasy? Public education's concern for the female victim is revealed as deceptively thin when real victims are discredited, and when nonvictimizing pleasures are silenced.

This unacknowledged social ambivalence about heterosexuality polarizes the debates over sex education and school-based health clinics. The anxiety effectively treats the female sexual victim as though she were a completely separate species from the female sexual subject. Yet the adolescent women quoted earlier in this text remind us that the female victim and subject coexist in every woman's body.

TOWARD A DISCOURSE OF SEXUAL DESIRE AND SOCIAL ENTITLEMENT: IN THE STUDENT BODIES OF PUBLIC SCHOOLS

I have argued that silencing a discourse of desire buttresses the icon of woman-as-victim. In so doing, public schooling may actually disable young women in their negotiations as sexual subjects. Trained through and into positions of passivity and victimization, young women are currently educated away from positions of sexual self-interest.

If we re-situate the adolescent woman in a rich and empowering educational context, she develops a sense of self which is sexual as well as intellectual, social, and economic. In this section I invite readers to imagine such a context. The dialectic of desire and victimization—across spheres of labor, social relations, and sexuality—would then frame schooling. While many of the curricula and interventions discussed in this paper are imperfect, data on the effectiveness of what *is* available are nevertheless compelling. Studies of sex education curricula, SBHCs, classroom discussions, and ethnographies of life inside public high schools demonstrate that a sense of sexual and social entitlement for young women *can* be fostered within public schools.

Sex Education as Intellectual Empowerment

Harris and Yankelovich polls confirm that over 80 percent of American adults believe that students should be educated about sexuality within their public schools. Seventy-five percent believe that homosexuality and abortion should be included in the curriculum, with 40 percent of those surveyed by Yankelovich et al. (N = 1015) agreeing that 12-year-olds should be taught about oral and anal sex.[48]

While the public continues to debate the precise content of sex education, most parents approve and support sex education for their children. An Illinois program monitored parental requests to "opt out" and found that only 6 or 7 of 850 children were actually excused from sex education courses.[49] In a California assessment, fewer than 2 percent of parents disallowed their children's participation. And in a longitudinal 5-year program in Connecticut, 7 of 2,500 students requested exemption from these classes.[50] Resistance to sex education, while loud at the level of public rhetoric and conservative organizing, is both less vocal and less active within schools and parents' groups.[51]

Sex education courses are offered broadly, if not comprehensively, across the United States. In 1981, only 7 of 50 states actually had laws against such instruction, and only one state enforced a prohibition.[52] Surveying 179 urban school districts, Sonnenstein and Pittman found that 75 percent offered some sex education within senior and junior high schools, while 66 percent of the elementary schools offered sex education units. Most instruction was, however, limited to 10 hours or less, with content focused on anatomy.[53] In his extensive review of sex education programs, Kirby concludes that less than 10 percent of all public school students are exposed to what might be considered comprehensive sex education courses.[54]

The progress on AIDS education is more encouraging, and more complex,[55] but cannot be adequately reviewed in this article. It is important to note, however, that a December 1986 report released by the U.S. Conference of Mayors documents that 54 percent of the 73 largest school districts and 25 state school agencies offer some form of AIDS education.[56] Today, debates among federal officials—including Secretary of Education Bennett and Surgeon General Koop—and among educators question *when* and *what* to offer in AIDS education. The question is no longer *whether* such education should be promoted.

Not only has sex education been accepted as a function of public schooling, but it has survived empirical tests of effectiveness. Evaluation data demonstrate that sex education can increase contraceptive knowledge and use.[57] In terms of sexual activity (measured narrowly in terms of the onset or frequency of heterosexual intercourse), the evidence suggests that sex education does not instigate an earlier onset or increase of such sexual activity[58] and may, in fact, postpone the onset of heterosexual intercourse.[59] The data for pregnancy rates appear to demonstrate no effect for exposure to sex education alone.[60]

Sex education as constituted in these studies is not sufficient to diminish teen pregnancy rates. In all likelihood it would be naive to expect that sex education (especially if only ten hours in duration) would carry such a "long arm" of effectiveness. While the widespread problem of teen pregnancy must be attributed broadly to economic and social inequities,[61] sex education remains necessary and sufficient to educate, demystify, and improve contraceptive knowledge and use. In conjunction with material opportunities for enhanced life options, it is believed that sex education and access to contraceptives and abortion can help to reduce the rate of unintended pregnancy among teens.[62]

School-Based Health Clinics: Sexual Empowerment

The public opinion and effectiveness data for school-based health clinics are even more compelling than those for sex education. Thirty SBHCs provide on-site health care services to senior, and sometimes junior, high school students in more than 18 U.S. communities, with an additional 25 communities developing similar programs.[63] These clinics offer, at a minimum, health counseling, referrals, and follow-up examinations. Over 70 percent conduct pelvic examinations,[64] approximately 52 percent prescribe contraceptives, and 28 percent dispense contraceptives.[65] None performs abortions, and few refer for abortions.

All SBHCs require some form of general parental notification and/or consent, and some charge a nominal fee for generic health services. Relative to private physicians, school-based health clinics and other family planning agencies are substantially more willing to provide contraceptive services to unmarried minors without specific parental consent (consent in this case referring explicitly to contraception). Only one percent of national Planned Parenthood affiliates require consent or notification, compared to 10 percent of public health department programs and 19 percent of hospitals.[66]

The consequences of consent provisions for abortion are substantial. Data from two states, Massachusetts and Minnesota, demonstrate that parental consent laws result in increased teenage pregnancies or increased numbers of out-of-state abortions. The Reproductive Freedom Project of the American Civil Liberties Union, in a report which examines the consequences of such consent provisions, details the impact of these statutes on teens, on their familial relationships, and ultimately, on their unwanted children.[67] In an analysis of the impact of Minnesota's mandatory parental notification law from 1981 to 1985, this report documents over 7,000 pregnancies in teens aged 13–17, 3,500 of whom "went to state court to seek the right to confidential abortions, all at considerable personal cost." The report also notes that many of the pregnant teens did not petition the court, "although their entitlement and need for confidential abortions was as strong or more so than the teenagers who made it to court. . . . Only those minors who are old enough and wealthy enough or resourceful enough are actually able to use the court bypass option".[68]

These consent provisions, with allowance for court bypass, not only increase the number of unwanted teenage pregnancies carried to term, but also extend the length of time required to secure an abortion, potentially endangering the life of the teenage woman, and increasing the costs of the abortion. The provisions may also jeopardize the physical and emotional well-being of some young women and their mothers, particularly when paternal consent is required and the pregnant teenager resides with a single mother. Finally, the consent provisions create a class-based health care system. Adolescents able to afford travel to a nearby state, or able to pay a private physician for a confidential abortion, have access to an abortion. Those unable to afford the travel, or those who are unable to contact a private physician, are likely to become teenage mothers.[69]

In Minneapolis, during the time from 1980 to 1984 when the law was implemented, the birth rate for 15- to 17-year-olds increased 38.4 percent, while the birth rate for 18- and 19-year-olds—not affected by the law—rose only .3 percent.[70] The state of Massachusetts passed a parental consent law which took effect in 1981. An analysis of the impact of that law concludes that ". . . the major impact of the Massachusetts parental consent law has been to send a monthly average of between 90 and 95 of the state's minors across state lines in search of an abortion. This number represents about one in every three minor abortion patients living in Massachusetts".[71] These researchers, among others, write that parental consent laws could have more devastating effects in larger states, from which access to neighboring states would be more difficult.

The inequalities inherent in consent provisions and the dramatic consequences which result for young women are well recognized. For example, twenty-nine states and the District of Columbia now explicitly authorize minors to grant their own consent for receipt of contraceptive information and/or services, independent of parental knowledge or consent.[72] More recently, consent laws for abortion in Pennsylvania and California have been challenged as unconstitutional.

Public approval of SBHCs has been slow but consistent. In the 1986 Yankelovich survey, 84 percent of surveyed adults agree that these clinics should provide birth control information; 36 percent endorse dispensing of contraceptives to students.[73] In 1985, Harris found that 67 percent of all respondents, including 76 percent of Blacks and 76 percent of Hispanics, agree that public schools should establish formal ties with family planning clinics for teens to learn about and obtain contraception.[74] Mirroring the views of the general public, a national sample of school administrators polled by the Education Research Group indicated that more than 50 percent believe birth control should be offered in school-based clinics; 30 percent agree that parental permission should be sought, and 27 percent agree that contraceptives should be dispensed, even if parental consent is not forthcoming. The discouraging news is that 96 percent of these respondents indicate that their districts do not presently offer such services.[75]

Research on the effectiveness of SBHCs is consistently persuasive. The three-year Johns Hopkins study of school-based health clinics found that schools in which SBHCs made referrals and dispensed contraceptives noted an increase in the percentage of "virgin" females visiting the program as well as an increase in contraceptive use. They also found a significant reduction in pregnancy rates: There was a 13 percent increase at experimental schools after 10 months, versus a 50 percent increase at control schools; after 28 months, pregnancy rates decreased 30 percent at experimental schools versus a 53 percent increase at control schools. Furthermore, by the second year, a substantial percentage of males visited the clinic (48 percent of males in experimental schools indicated that they "have ever been to a birth control clinic or to a physician about birth control," compared to 12 percent of males in control schools). Contrary to common belief, the schools in which clinics dispensed contraceptives showed a substantial postponement of first experience of heterosexual intercourse among high school students and an increase in the proportion of young women visiting the clinic prior to "first coitus."[76]

Paralleling the Hopkins findings, the St. Paul Maternity and Infant Care Project found that pregnancy rates dropped substantially in schools with clinics, from 79 births/1,000 (1973) to 26 births/1,000 (1984). Teens who delivered and kept their infants had an 80 percent graduation rate, relative to approximately 50 percent of young mothers nationally. Those who stayed in school reported a 1.3 percent repeat birth rate, compared to 17 percent nationally. Over three years, pregnancy rates dropped by 40 percent. Twenty-five percent of young women in the school received some form of family planning and 87 percent of clients were continuing to use contraception at a 3-year follow-up. There were fewer obstetric complications; fewer babies were born at low birth weights; and prenatal visits to physicians increased relative to students in the control schools.[77]

Predictions that school-based health clinics would advance the onset of sexual intimacy, heighten the degree of "promiscuity" and incidence of pregnancy, and hold females primarily responsible for sexuality were countered by the evidence. The onset of sexual intimacy was postponed, while contraception was used more reliably. Pregnancy rates substantially diminished and, over time, a large group of males began to view contraception as a shared responsibility.

It is worth restating here that females who received family planning counseling and/or contraception actually postponed the onset of heterosexual intercourse. I would argue that the availability of such services may enable females to feel they are sexual agents, entitled and therefore responsible, rather than at the constant and terrifying mercy of a young man's pressure to "give in" or of a parent's demands to "save yourself." With a sense of sexual agency and not necessarily urgency, teen girls may be less likely to use or be used by pregnancy.[78]

Nontraditional Vocational Training: Social and Economic Entitlement

The literature reviewed suggests that sex education, access to contraception, and opportunities for enhanced life options, in combination,[79] can significantly diminish the likelihood that a teenager will become pregnant, carry to term, and/or have a repeat pregnancy, and can increase the likelihood that she will stay in high school through graduation.[80] Education toward entitlement—including a sense of sexual, economic, and social entitlement—may be sufficient to affect adolescent girls' views on sexuality, contraception, and abortion. By framing female subjectivity within the context of social entitlement, sex education would be organized around dialogue and critique, SB-HCs would offer health services, options counseling, contraception, and abortion referrals, and the provision of real "life options" would include nontraditional vocational training programs and employment opportunities for adolescent females.[81]

In a nontraditional vocational training program in New York City designed for young women, many of whom are mothers, participants' attitudes toward contraception and abortion shifted once they acquired a set of vocational skills, a sense of social entitlement, and a sense of personal competence.[82] The young women often began the program without strong academic skills or a sense of competence. At the start, they were more likely to express more negative sentiments about contraception and abortion than when they completed the program. One young woman, who initially held strong anti-abortion attitudes, learned that she was pregnant midway through her carpentry apprenticeship. She decided to abort, reasoning that now that she has a future, she can't risk losing it for another baby.[83] A developing sense of social entitlement may have transformed this young woman's view of reproduction, sexuality, and self.

The Manpower Development Research Corporation (MDRC), in its evaluation of Project Redirection[84] offers similar conclusions about a comprehensive vocational training and community-based mentor project for teen mothers and mothers-to-be. Low-income teens were enrolled in Project Redirection, a network of services designed to instill self-sufficiency, in which community women served as mentors. The program included training for what is called "employability," Individual Participation Plans, and peer group sessions. Data on education, employment, and pregnancy outcomes were collected at 12 and 24 months after enrollment. Two years after the program began, many newspapers headlined the program as a failure. The data actually indicated that at 12 months, the end of program involvement, Project Redirection women were significantly *less likely* to experience a repeat pregnancy than comparison women; *more likely* to be using contraception; *more likely* to be in school, to have completed school, or to be in the labor force; and twice as likely (20 percent versus 11 percent, respectively) to have earned a Graduate Equivalency Diploma. At 24 months, however, approximately one year out of the program, Project and comparison women were virtually indistinguishable. MDRC reported equivalent rates of repeat pregnancies, dropout, and unemployment.

The Project Redirection data demonstrate that sustained outcomes cannot be expected once programs have been withdrawn and participants confront the realities of a dismal economy and inadequate child care and social services. The data confirm, however, the effectiveness of comprehensive programs to reduce teen pregnancy rates and encourage study or work as long as the young women are actively engaged. Supply-side interventions—changing people but not structures or opportunities—which leave unchallenged an inhospitable and discriminating economy and a thoroughly impoverished child care/social welfare system are inherently doomed to long-term failure. When such programs fail, the social reading is that "these young women can't be helped." Blaming the victim obscures the fact that the current economy and social welfare arrangements need overhauling if the sustained educational, social, and psychological gains accrued by the Project Redirection participants are to be maintained.

In the absence of enhanced life options, low-income young women are likely to default to early and repeat motherhood as a source of perceived competence, significance, and pleasure. When life options are available, however, a sense of competence and "entitlement to better" may help to prevent second pregnancies, may help to encourage education, and, when available, the pursuit of meaningful work.[85]

Femininity May Be Hazardous to Her Health: The Absence of Entitlement

Growing evidence suggests that women who lack a sense of social or sexual entitlement, who hold traditional notions of what it means to be female— self-sacrificing and relatively passive—and who undervalue themselves, are disproportionately likely to find themselves with an unwanted pregnancy and to maintain it through to motherhood. While many young women who drop out, pregnant or not, are not at all traditional in these ways, but are quite feisty and are fueled with a sense of entitlement, it may also be the case that young women who do internalize such notions of "femininity" are disproportionately at risk for pregnancy and dropping out.[86]

The Hispanic Policy Development Project reports that low-income female sophomores who, in 1980, expected to be married and/or have a child by age 19 were disproportionately represented among nongraduates in 1984. Expectations of early marriage and childbearing correspond to dramatic increases (200 to 400 percent) in nongraduation rates for low-income adolescent women across racial and ethnic groups.[87] These indicators of traditional notions of womanhood bode poorly for female academic achievement.

The Children's Defense Fund recently published additional data which demonstrate that young women with poor basic skills are three times more likely to become teen parents than women with average or above-average basic skills. Those with poor or fair basic skills are four times more likely to have more than one child while a teen; 29 percent of women in the bottom skills quintile became mothers by age 18 versus 5 percent of young women in the top quintile. While academic skill problems must be placed in the context of alienating and problematic schools, and not viewed as inherent in these young women, those who fall in the bottom quintile may nevertheless be the least likely to feel entitled or in control of their lives. They may feel more vulnerable to male pressure or more willing to have a child as a means of feeling competent.[88]

My own observations, derived from a year-long ethnographic study of a comprehensive public high school in New York City, further confirm some of these conclusions. Six months into the ethnography, new pregnancies began showing. I noticed that many of the girls who got pregnant and carried to term were not those whose bodies, dress, and manner evoked sensuality and experience. Rather, a number of the pregnant women were those who were quite passive and relatively quiet in their classes. One young woman, who granted me an interview anytime, washed the blackboard for her teacher, rarely spoke in class, and never disobeyed her mother, was pregnant by the spring of the school year.[89]

Simple stereotypes, of course, betray the complexity of circumstances under which young women become pregnant and maintain their pregnancies. While U.S. rates of teenage sexual activity and age of "sexual initiation" approximate those of comparable developed countries, the teenage pregnancy, abortion, and childbearing rates in the United States are substantially higher. In the United Sates, teenagers under age fifteen are at least five times more likely to give birth than similarly aged teens in other industrialized nations.[90] The national factors which correlate with low teenage birthrates include adolescent access to sex education and contraception, and relative equality in the distribution of wealth. Economic and structural conditions which support a class-stratified society, and which limit adolescent access to sexual information and contraception, contribute to inflated teenage pregnancy rates and birthrates.

This broad national context acknowledged, it might still be argued that within our country, traditional notions of what it means to be a woman—to remain subordinate, dependent, self-sacrificing, compliant, and ready to marry and/or bear children early—do little to empower women or enhance a sense of entitlement. This is not to say that teenage dropouts or mothers tend to be of any one type. Yet it may well be that the traditions and practices of "femininity" as commonly understood may be hazardous to the economic, social, educational, and sexual development of young women.

In summary, the historic silencing within public schools of conversations about sexuality, contraception, and abortion, as well as the absence of a discourse of desire—in the form of comprehensive sex education, school-based health clinics, and viable life options via vocational training and placement—all combine to exacerbate the vulnerability of young women whom schools, and the critics of sex education and SBHCs, claim to protect.

CONCLUSION

Adolescents are entitled to a discussion of desire instead of the anit-sex rhetoric which controls the controversies around sex education, SBHCs, and AIDS education. The absence of a discourse of desire, combined with the lack of analysis of the language of victimization, may actually retard the development of sexual subjectivity and responsibility in students. Those most "at risk" of victimization through pregnancy, disease, violence, or harassment—all female students, low-income females in particular, and non-heterosexual males—are those most likely to be victimized by the absence of critical conversation in public schools. Public schools can no longer afford to maintain silence around a discourse of desire. This is not to say that the silencing of a discourse of desire is the primary root of sexual victimization, teen motherhood, and the concomitant poverty experienced by young and low-income females. Nor could it be responsibly argued that interventions initiated by public schools could ever be successful if separate from economic and social development. But it is important to understand that by providing education, counseling, contraception, and abortion referrals, as well as meaningful educational and vocational opportunities, public schools could play an essential role in the construction of the female subject—social and sexual.

And by not providing such an educational context, public schools contribute to the rendering of substantially different outcomes for male and female students, and for male and female dropouts.[91] The absence of a thorough sex education curriculum, of school-based health clinics, of access to free and confidential contraceptive and abortion services, of exposure to information about the varieties of sexual pleasures and partners, and of involvement in sustained employment training programs may so jeopardize the educational and economic outcomes for female adolescents as to constitute sex discrimination. How can we ethically continue to withhold educational treatments we know to be effective for adolescent women?

Public schools constitute a sphere in which young women could be offered access to a language and experience of empowerment. In such contexts, "well-educated" young women could breathe life into positions of social critique and experience entitlement rather than victimization, autonomy rather than terror.

Chapter Five

Empowering Minority Students: A Framework for Intervention*

During the past twenty years educators in the United States have implemented a series of costly reforms aimed at reversing the pattern of school failure among minority students. These have included compensatory programs at the preschool level, myriad forms of bilingual education programs, the hiring of additional aides and remedial personnel, and the institution of safeguards against discriminatory assessment procedures. Yet the dropout rate among Mexican-American and mainland Puerto Rican students remains between 40 and 50 percent compared to 14 percent for whites and 25 percent for blacks.[1] Similarly, almost a decade after the passage of the nondiscriminatory assessment provision of PL94–142,[2] we find Hispanic students in Texas overrepresented by a factor of 300 percent in the "learning disabilities" category.[3]

I have suggested that a major reason previous attempts at educational reform have been unsuccessful is that the relationships between teachers and students and between schools and communities have remained essentially unchanged. The required changes involve *personal redefinitions* of the way classroom teachers interact with the children and communities they serve. In other words, legislative and policy reforms may be necessary conditions for effective change, but they are not sufficient. Implementation of change is dependent upon the extent to which educators, both collectively and individually, redefine their roles with respect to minority students and communities.

The purpose of this paper is to propose a theoretical framework for examining the types of personal and institutional redefinitions that are required to reverse the pattern of minority student failure. The framework is based on a series of hypotheses regarding the nature of minority students' educational difficulties. These hypotheses, in turn, lead to predictions regarding the probable effectiveness, or ineffectiveness, of various interventions directed at reversing minority students' school failure.

The framework assigns a central role to three inclusive sets of interactions of power relations: (1) the classroom interactions between teachers and students, (2) relationships between schools and minority communities, and (3) the intergroup power relations within the society as a whole. It assumes that the social organization and bureaucratic constraints within the school reflect not only broader policy and societal factors but also the extent to which *individual educators* accept or challenge the social organization of the school in relation to minority students and communities. Thus, this analysis sketches directions for change for policymakers at all levels of the educational hierarchy and, in particular, for those working directly with minority students and communities.

THE POLICY CONTEXT

Research data from the United States, Canada, and Europe vary on the extent to which minority students experience academic failure.[4] For example, in the United States, Hispanic (with the exception of some groups of Cuban students), Native American, and Black students do poorly in school compared to most groups of Asian-American (and white) students. In Canada, Franco-Ontarian students in English language programs have tended to perform considerably less well academically than immigrant minority groups,[5] while the same pattern characterizes Finnish students in Sweden.[6]

The major task of theory and policy is to explain the pattern of school success and failure among minority students. This task applies both to students whose home language and culture differ from those of the school and wider society (language minority students) and to students whose home language is a version of English but whose cultural background is significantly different from that of the school and wider society, such as many Black and Hispanic students from English language backgrounds. With respect to language-minority students, recent policy changes in the United States have been based on the assumption that a major cause of students' educational difficulty is the switch between the language of the home and the language of the school. Thus, the apparently plausible assumption that students cannot learn in a language they do not understand gave rise in the late sixties and early seventies to bilingual education programs in which students' home language was used in addition to English as an initial medium of school instruction.[7]

Bilingual programs, however, have met with both strong support and vehement opposition. The debate regarding policy has revolved around two intuitively appealing assumptions. Those who favor bilingual education argue that children cannot learn in a language they do not understand, and, therefore, L1 (first language) instruction is necessary to counteract the negative effects of a home/school linguistic mismatch. The opposition contends that bilingual education is illogical in its implication that less English instruction will lead to more English achievement. It makes more sense, the opponents argue, to provide language-minority students with maximum exposure to English.

Despite the apparent plausibility of each assumption, these two conventional wisdoms (the "linguistic mismatch" and "insufficient exposure" hypotheses) are each patently inadequate. The argument that language minority students fail primarily as a result of a home/school language switch is refuted by the success of many minority students whose instruction has been totally through a second language. Similarly, research in Canada has documented the effectiveness of "French immersion programs" in which English background (majority language) students are instructed largely through French in the early grades as a means of developing fluent bilingualism. In spite of the home/school language switch, students' first language (English) skills develop as well as those of students whose instruction has been totally through English. The fact that the first language has high status and is strongly reinforced in the wider society is usually seen as an important factor in the success of these immersion programs.[8]

The opposing "insufficient exposure" hypothesis, however, fares no better with respect to the research evidence. In fact, the results of virtually every bilingual program that has been evaluated during the past fifty years show either no relationship or a negative relationship between amount of school exposure to the majority language and academic achievement in that language.[9] Evaluations of immersion programs for majority students show that students perform as well in English academic skills as comparison groups despite considerably less exposure to English in school. Exactly the same result is obtained for minority students. Promotion of the minority language entails no loss in the development of English academic skills. In other words, language minority students instructed through the minority language (for example, Spanish) for all or part of the school day perform as well in English academic skills as comparable students instructed totally through English.

These results have been interpreted in terms of the "interdependence hypothesis," which proposes that to the extent that instruction through a minority language is effective in developing academic proficiency in the minority language, transfer of this proficiency to the majority language will occur given adequate exposure and motivation to learn the majority language.[10]

The interdependence hypothesis is supported by a large body of research from bilingual program evaluations, studies of language use in the home, immigrant student language learning, correlational studies of L1–L2 (second language) relationships, and experimental studies of bilingual information processing.[11]

It is not surprising that the two conventional wisdoms inadequately account for the research data, since each involves only a one-dimensional linguistic explanation. The variability of minority students' academic performance under different social and educational conditions indicates that many complex, interrelated factors are at work.[12] In particular, sociological and anthropological research suggests that status and power relations between groups are an important part of any comprehensive account of minority students' school failure.[13] In addition, a variety of factors related to educational quality and cultural mismatch also appear to be important in mediating minority students' academic progress.[14] These factors have been integrated into the design of a theoretical framework that suggests the changes required to reverse minority student failure.

A THEORETICAL FRAMEWORK

The central tenet of the framework is that students from "dominated" societal groups are "empowered" or "disabled" as a direct result of their interactions with educators in the schools. These interactions are mediated by the implicit or explicit role definitions that educators assume in relation to four institutional characteristics of schools. These characteristics reflect the extent to which (1) minority students' language and culture are incorporated into the school program; (2) minority community participation is encouraged as an integral component of children's education; (3) the pedagogy promotes intrinsic motivation on the part of students to use language actively in order to generate their own knowledge; and (4) professionals involved in assessment become advocates for minority students rather than legitimizing the location of the "problem" in the students. For each of these dimensions of school organization the role definitions of educators can be described in terms of a continuum, with one end promoting the empowerment of students and the other contributing to the disabling of students.

The three sets of relationships analyzed in the present framework—majority/minority societal group relations, school/minority community relations, educator/minority student relations—are chosen on the basis of hypotheses regarding the relative ineffectiveness of previous educational reforms and the directions required to reverse minority group school failure. Each of these relationships will be discussed in detail.

INTERGROUP POWER RELATIONS

When the patterns of minority student school failure are examined from an international perspective, it becomes evident that power and status relations between minority and majority groups exert a major influence on school performance. An example frequently given is the academic failure of Finnish students in Sweden, where they are a low-status group, compared to their success in Australia, where they are regarded as a high-status group.[15] Similarly, Ogbu reports that the outcast Burakumin perform poorly in Japan but as well as other Japanese students in the United States.[16]

Theorists have explained these findings using several constructs. Cummins, for example, discusses the "bicultural ambivalence" (or lack of cultural identification) of students in relation to both the home and school cultures.[17] Ogbu discusses the "caste" status of minorities that fail academically and ascribes their failure to economic and social discrimination combined with the internalization of the inferior status attributed to them by the dominant group.[18] Feuerstein attributes academic failure to the disruption of intergenerational transmission processes caused by the alienation of a group from its own culture.[19] In all three conceptions, widespread school failure does not occur in minority groups that are positively oriented towards both their own and the dominant culture, that do not perceive themselves as inferior to the dominant group, and that are not alienated from their own cultural values.

Within the present framework, the *dominant* group controls the institutions and reward systems within society; the *dominated* group is regarded as inherently inferior by the dominant group and denied access to high-status positions within the institutional structure of the society.[20] As described by Ogbu, the dominated status of a minority group exposes them to conditions that predispose children to school failure even before they come to school.[21] These conditions include limited parental access to economic and educational resources, ambivalence toward cultural transmission and primary language use in the home, and interactional styles that may not prepare students for typical teacher/student interaction patterns in school.[22] Bicultural ambivalence and less effective cultural transmission among dominated groups are frequently associated with a historical pattern of colonization and subordination by the dominant group. This pattern, for example, characterizes Franco-Ontarian students in Canada, Finns in Sweden, and Hispanic, Native, and Black groups in the United States.

Different patterns among other societal groups can clearly be distinguished.[23] Detailed analysis of patterns of intergroup relations go beyond the scope of this paper. However, it is important to note that the minority groups characterized by widespread school failure tend overwhelmingly to be in a dominated relationship to the majority group.[24]

Empowerment of Students

Students who are empowered by their school experiences develop the ability, confidence, and motivation to succeed academically. They participate competently in instruction as a result of having developed a confident cultural identity as well as appropriate school-based knowledge and interactional structures.[25] Students who are disempowered or "disabled" by their school experiences do not develop this type of cognitive/academic and social/emotional foundation. Thus, student empowerment is regarded as both a mediating construct influencing academic performance and as an outcome variable itself.[26]

Although conceptually the cognitive/academic and social/emotional (identity-related) factors are distinct, the data suggest that they are extremely difficult to separate in the case of minority students who are "at risk" academically. For example, data from both Sweden and the United States suggest that minority students who immigrate relatively late (about ten years of age) often appear to have better academic prospects than students of similar socioeconomic status born in the host country.[27] Is this because their L1 cognitive/academic skills on arrival provide a better foundation for L2 cognitive/academic skills acquisition, or alternatively, because they have not experienced devaluation of their identity in the societal institutions, namely schools of the host country, as has been the case of students born in that setting?

Similarly, the most successful bilingual programs appear to be those that emphasize and use the students' L1.[28] Is this success due to better promotion of L1 cognitive/academic skills or to the reinforcement of cultural identity provided by an intensive L1 program? By the same token, is the failure of many minority students in English-only immersion programs a function of cognitive/academic difficulties or of students' ambivalence about the value of their cultural identity?[29]

These questions are clearly difficult to answer; the point to be made, however, is that for minority students who have traditionally experienced school failure, there is sufficient overlap in the impact of cognitive/academic and identity factors to justify incorporating these two dimensions within the notion of "student empowerment," while recognizing that under some conditions each dimension may be affected in different ways.

Schools and Power

Minority students are disabled or disempowered by schools in very much the same way that their communities are disempowered by interactions with societal institutions. Since equality of opportunity is believed to be a given, it is assumed that individuals are responsible for their own failure and are,

FIGURE 5.1
Empowerment of Minority Students: A Theoretical Framework

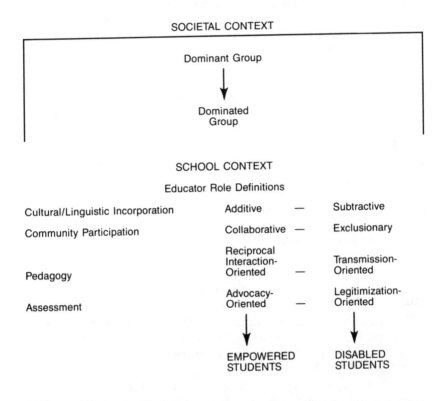

SOCIETAL CONTEXT

Dominant Group

Dominated
Group

SCHOOL CONTEXT

Educator Role Definitions

Cultural/Linguistic Incorporation	Additive —	Subtractive
Community Participation	Collaborative —	Exclusionary
Pedagogy	Reciprocal Interaction-Oriented —	Transmission-Oriented
Assessment	Advocacy-Oriented —	Legitimization-Oriented

EMPOWERED
STUDENTS

DISABLED
STUDENTS

therefore, made to feel that they have failed because of their own inferiority, despite the best efforts of dominant-group institutions and individuals to help them.[30] This analysis implies that minority students will succeed educationally to the extent that the patterns of interaction in school reverse those that prevail in the society at large.

Four structural elements in the organization of schooling contribute to the extent to which minority students are empowered or disabled. As outlined in figure 5.1, these elements include the incorporation of minority students' culture and language, inclusion of minority communities in the education of their children, pedagogical assumptions and practices operating in the classroom, and the assessment of minority students.

Cultural/linguistic incorporation. Considerable research data suggest that, for dominated minorities, the extent to which students' language and culture are incorporated into the school program constitutes a significant predictor of academic success.[31] As outlined earlier, students' school success appears to reflect both the more solid cognitive/academic foundation developed through intensive L1 instruction and the reinforcement of their cultural identity.

Included under incorporation of minority group cultural features is the adjustment of instructional patterns to take account of culturally conditioned learning styles. The Kamehameha Early Education Program in Hawaii provides strong evidence of the importance of this type of cultural incorporation. When reading instruction was changed to permit students to collaborate in discussing and interpreting texts, dramatic improvements were found in both reading and verbal intellectual abilities.[32]

An important issue to consider at this point is why superficially plausible but patently inadequate assumptions, such as the "insufficient exposure" hypothesis, continue to dominate the policy debate when virtually all the evidence suggests that incorporation of minority students' language and culture into the school program will at least not impede academic progress. In other words, what social function do such arguments serve? Within the context of the present framework, it is suggested that a major reason for the vehement resistance to bilingual programs is that the incorporation of minority languages and cultures into the school program confers status and power (jobs, for example) on the minority group. Consequently, such programs contravene the established pattern of dominant/dominated group relations. Within democratic societies, however, contradictions between the rhetoric of equality and the reality of domination must be obscured. Thus, conventional wisdoms such as the insufficient exposure hypothesis become immune from critical scrutiny, and incompatible evidence is either ignored or dismissed.

Educators' role definitions in relation to the incorporation of minority students' language and culture can be characterized along an "additive-subtractive" dimension.[33] Educators who see their role as adding a second language and cultural affiliation to their students' repertoire are likely to empower students more than those who see their role as replacing or subtracting students' primary language and culture. In addition to the personal and future employment advantages of proficiency in two languages, there is considerable, though not conclusive, evidence that subtle educational advantages result from continued development of both languages among bilingual students. Enhanced metalinguistic development, for example, is frequently found in association with additive bilingualism.[34]

It should be noted that an additive orientation does not require the actual teaching of the minority language. In many cases a minority language class may not be possible for reasons such as low concentration of particular groups of minority students. Educators, however, communicate to students and parents in a variety of ways the extent to which the minority language and culture are valued within the context of the school. Even within a monolingual school context, powerful messages can be communicated to students regarding the validity and advantages of language development.

Community participation. Students from dominated communities will be empowered in the school context to the extent that the communities themselves are empowered through their interactions with the school. When educators involve minority parents as partners in their children's education, parents appear to develop a sense of efficacy that communicates itself to children, with positive academic consequences.

Although lip service is paid to community involvement through Parent Advisory Committees (PAC)[35] in many education programs, these committees are frequently manipulated through misinformation and intimidation.[36] The result is that parents from dominated groups retain their powerless status, and their internalized inferiority is reinforced. Children's school failure can then be attributed to the combined effects of parental illiteracy and lack of interest in their children's education. In reality, most parents of minority students have high aspirations for their children and want to be involved in promoting their academic progress.[37] However, they often do not know how to help their children academically, and they are excluded from participation by the school. In fact, even their interaction through L1 with their children in the home is frequently regarded by educators as contributing to academic difficulties.[38]

Dramatic changes in children's academic progress can be realized when educators take the initiative to change this exclusionary pattern to one of collaboration. The Haringey project in Britain illustrates just how powerful the effects of simple interventions can be.[39] In order to assess the effects of parental involvement in the teaching of reading, the researchers established a project in the London borough of Haringey whereby all children in two primary level experimental classes in two different schools read to their parents at home on a regular basis. The reading progress of these children was compared with that of children in two classes in two different schools who were given extra reading instruction in small groups by an experienced and qualified teacher who worked four half-days at each school every week for the two years of the intervention. Both groups were also compared with a control group that received no treatment.

All the schools were in multiethnic areas, and there were many parents who did not read English or use it at home. It was found, nevertheless, to be both feasible and practicable to involve nearly all the parents in educational activities such as listening to their children read, even when the parents were nonliterate and largely non-English-speaking. It was also found that, almost without exception, parents welcomed the project, agreed to hear their children read, and completed a record card showing what had been read.

The researchers report that parental involvement had a pronounced effect on the students' success in school. Children who read to their parents made significantly greater progress in reading than those who did not engage in this type of literacy sharing. Small-group instruction in reading, given by a highly competent specialist, did not produce improvements comparable to those obtained from the collaboration with parents. In contrast to the home collaboration program, the benefits of extra reading instruction were least apparent for initially low-achieving children.

In addition, the collaboration between teachers and parents was effective for children of all initial levels of performance, including those who, at the beginning of the study, were failing in learning to read. Teachers reported that the children showed an increased interest in school learning and were better behaved. Those teachers involved in the home collaboration found the work with parents worthwhile, and they continued to involve parents with subsequent classes after the experiment was concluded. It is interesting to note that teachers of the control classes also adopted the home collaboration program after the two-year experimental period.

The Haringey project is one example of school/community relations; there are others. The essential point, however, is that the teacher's role in such relations can be characterized along a *collaborative-exclusionary* dimension. Teachers operating at the collaborative end of the continuum actively encourage minority parents to participate in promoting their children's academic progress both in the home and through involvement in classroom activities. A collaborative orientation may require a willingness on the part of the teacher to work closely with mother-tongue teachers or aides in order to communicate effectively, in a noncondescending way, with minority parents. Teachers with an exclusionary orientation, on the other hand, tend to regard teaching as *their* job and are likely to view collaboration with minority parents as either irrelevant or detrimental to children's progress.

Pedagogy. Several investigators have suggested that many "learning disabilities" are pedagogically induced in that children designated "at risk" frequently receive intensive instruction which confines them to a passive role and induces a form of "learned helplessness".[40] This process is illustrated in a microethnographic study of fourteen reading lessons given to West Indian Creole-speakers of English in Toronto, Canada.[41] It was found that teachers' constant correction of students' miscues prevented students from focusing on the meaning of what they were reading. Moreover, the constant corrections fostered dependent behavior because students knew that whenever they paused at a word the teacher would automatically pronounce it for them. One student was interrupted so often in one of the lessons that he was able to read only one sentence, consisting of three words, uninterrupted. In contrast to a pattern of classroom interaction which promotes instructional dependence, teaching that empowers will aim to liberate students from instruction by encouraging them to become active generators of their knowledge. As Graves has demonstrated, this type of active knowledge generation can occur when, for example, children create and publish their own books within the classroom.[42]

Two major pedagogical orientations can be distinguished. These differ in the extent to which the teacher retains exclusive control over classroom interaction as opposed to sharing some of this control with students. The dominant instructional model in North American schools has been termed a transmission model.[43] This model incorporates essentially the same assumptions about teaching and learning that Freire has termed a "banking" model of education.[44] This transmission model will be contrasted with a "reciprocal interaction" model of pedagogy.

The basic premise of the transmission model is that the teacher's task is to impart knowledge or skills that she or he possesses to students who do not yet have these skills. This implies that the teacher initiates and controls the interaction, constantly orienting it towards the achievement of instructional objectives. For example, in first- and second-language programs that stress pattern repetition, the teacher presents the materials, models the language patterns, asks questions, and provides feedback to students about the correctness of their response. The curriculum in these types of programs focuses on the internal structure of the language or subject matter. Consequently, it frequently focuses predominantly on surface features of language or literacy such as handwriting, spelling, and decoding, and emphasizes correct recall of content taught by means of highly structured drills and workbook exercises. It has been argued that a transmission model of teaching contravenes central principles of language and literacy acquisition and that a model allowing for reciprocal interaction among students and teachers represents a more appropriate alternative.[45]

A central tenet of the reciprocal interaction model is that "talking and writing are means to learning".[46] The use of this model in teaching requires a genuine dialogue between student and teacher in both oral and written modalities, guidance and facilitation rather than control of student learning by the teacher, and the encouragement of student/student talk in a collaborative learning context. This model emphasizes the development of higher level cognitive skills rather than just factual recall, and meaningful language use by students rather than the correction of surface forms. Language use and development are consciously integrated with all curricular content rather than taught as isolated subjects, and tasks are presented to students in ways that generate intrinsic rather than extrinsic motivation. In short, pedagogical approaches that empower students encourage them to assume greater control over setting their own learning goals and to collaborate actively with each other in achieving these goals.

The development of a sense of efficacy and inner direction in the classroom is especially important for students from dominated groups whose experiences so often orient them in the opposite direction. Wong-Fillmore has reported that Hispanic students learned considerably more English in classrooms that provided opportunities for reciprocal interaction with teachers and peers.[47] Ample opportunities for expressive writing appear to be particularly significant in promoting a sense of academic efficacy among minority students.[48] As expressed by Daiute:

> Children who learn early that writing is not simply an exercise gain a sense of power that gives them confidence to write—and write a lot. . . . Beginning writers who are confident that they have something to say or that they can find out what they need to know can even overcome some limits of training or development. Writers who don't feel that what they say matters have an additional burden that no skills training can help them overcome.[49]

The implications for students from dominated groups are obvious. Too often the instruction they receive convinces them that what they have to say is irrelevant or wrong. The failure of this method of instruction is then taken as an indication that the minority student is of low ability, a verdict frequently confirmed by subsequent assessment procedures.

Assessment. Historically, assessment has played the role of legitimizing the disabling of minority students. In some cases assessment itself may play the primary role, but more often it has been used to locate the "problem" within the minority student, thereby screening from critical scrutiny the subtractive nature of the school program, the exclusionary orientation of teachers towards minority communities, and transmission models of teaching that inhibit students from active participation in learning.

This process is virtually inevitable when the conceptual base for assessment is purely psychoeducational. If the psychologist's task is to discover the causes of a minority student's academic difficulties and the only tools at his or her disposal are psychological tests (in either L1 or L2), then it is hardly surprising that the child's difficulties will be attributed to psychological dysfunctions. The myth of bilingual handicaps that still influences educational policy was generated in exactly this way during the 1920s and 1930s.

Recent studies suggest that despite the appearance of change brought about by PL 94–142, the underlying structure of assessment processes has remained essentially intact. Mehan, Hertweck, and Meihls, for example, report that psychologists continued to test children until they "found" the disability that could be invoked to "explain" the student's apparent academic difficulties.[50] Diagnosis and placement were influenced frequently by factors related to bureaucratic procedures and funding requirements rather than to students' academic performance in the classroom. Rueda and Mercer have also shown that designation of minority students as "learning disabled" as compared to "language impaired" was strongly influenced by whether a psychologist or a speech pathologist was on the placement committee.[51] In other words, with respect to students' actual behavior, the label was essentially arbitrary. An analysis of more than four hundred psychological assessments of minority students revealed that although no diagnostic conclusions were logically possible in the majority of assessments, psychologists were most reluctant to admit this fact to teachers and parents.[52] In short, the data suggest that the structure within which psychological assessment takes place orients the psychologist to locate the cause of the academic problem within the minority student.

An alternative role definition for psychologists or special educators can be termed an "advocacy" or "delegitimization" role.[53] In this case, their task must be to delegitimize the traditional function of psychological assessment in the educational disabling of minority students by becoming advocates for the child in scrutinizing critically the societal and educational context within which the child has developed.[54] This involves locating the pathology within the societal power relations between dominant and dominated groups, in the reflection of these power relations between school and communities, and in the mental and cultural disabling of minority students that takes place in classrooms. These conditions are a more probable cause of the 300 percent overrepresentation of Texas Hispanic students in the learning disabled category than any intrinsic processing deficit unique to Hispanic children. The training of psychologists and special educators does not prepare them for this advocacy or delegitimization role. From the present perspective, however, it must be emphasized that discriminatory assessment is carried out by well-intentioned individuals who, rather than challenging a socioeducational system that tends to disable minority students, have accepted a role definition and an educational structure that makes discriminatory assessment virtually inevitable.[55]

EMPOWERING MINORITY STUDENTS:
THE CARPINTERIA EXAMPLE

The Spanish-only preschool program of the Carpenteria School District, near Santa Barbara, California, is one of the few programs in the United States that explicitly incorporates the major elements hypothesized in previous sections to empower minority students. Spanish is the exclusive language of instruction, there is a strong community involvement component, and the program is characterized by a coherent philosophy of promoting conceptual development through meaningful linguistic interaction.

The proposal to implement an intensive Spanish-only preschool program in this region was derived from district findings showing that a large majority of the Spanish-speaking students entering kindergarten each year lacked adequate skills to succeed in the kindergarten program. On the School Readiness Inventory, a districtwide screening measure administered to all incoming kindergarten students, Spanish-speaking students tended to average about eight points lower than English-speaking students (approximately 14.5 compared to 23.0, averaged over four years from 1979 to 1982) despite the fact that the test was administered in students' dominant language. A score of 20 or better was viewed by the district as predicting a successful kindergarten year for the child. Prior to the implementation of the experimental program, the Spanish-background children attended a bilingual preschool program—operated either by Head Start or the Community Day Care Center—in which both English and Spanish were used concurrently but with strong emphasis on the development of English skills. According to the district kindergarten teachers, children who had attended these programs often mixed English and Spanish into a "Spanglish."

The major goal of the experimental Spanish-only preschool program was to bring Spanish-dominant children entering kindergarten up to a level of readiness for school similar to that attained by English-speaking children in the community. The project also sought to make parents of the program participants aware of their role as the child's first teacher and to encourage them to provide specific types of experiences for their children in the home.

The preschool program itself involved the integration of language with a large variety of concrete and literacy-related experiences. As summarized in the evaluation report: "The development of language skills in Spanish was foremost in the planning and attention given to every facet of the pre-school day. Language was used constantly for conversing, learning new ideas, concepts and vocabulary, thinking creatively, and problem-solving to give the children the opportunity to develop their language skills in Spanish to as high a degree as possible within the structure of the pre-school day".[56]

Participation in the program was on a voluntary basis and students were screened only for age and Spanish-language dominance. Family characteristics of students in the experimental program were typical of other Spanish-speaking families in the community; more than 90 percent were of low socioeconomic status, and the majority worked in agriculture and had an average educational level of about sixth grade.

The program proved to be highly successful in developing students' readiness skills, as evidenced by the average score of 21.6 obtained by the

1982–83 incoming kindergarten students who had been in the program, compared to the score of 23.2 obtained by English-speaking students. A score of 14.6 was obtained by Spanish-speaking students who experienced the regular bilingual preschool program. In 1983–84 the scores of these three groups were 23.3, 23.4, and 16.0, respectively. In other words, the gap between English-background and Spanish-background children in the Spanish-only preschool had disappeared; however, a considerable gap remained for Spanish-background students for whom English was the focus of preschool instruction.

Of special interest is the performance of the experimental program students on the English and Spanish versions of the Bilingual Syntax Measure (BSM), a test of oral syntactic development.[57] Despite the fact that they experienced an exclusively Spanish preschool program, these students performed better than the other Spanish-speaking students in English (and Spanish) on entry to kindergarten in 1982 and at a similar level in 1983. On entrance to grade one in 1983, the gap had widened considerably, with almost five times as many of the experimental-program students performing at level 5 (fluent English) compared to the other Spanish-background students (47 percent vs. 10 percent).[58]

The evaluation report suggests that

> although project participants were exposed to less *total* English, they, because of their enhanced first language skill and concept knowledge were better able to comprehend the English they were exposed to. This seems to be borne out by comments made by kindergarten teachers in the District about project participants. They are making comments like, "Project participants appear more aware of what is happening around them in the classroom," "They are able to focus on the task at hand better" and "They demonstrate greater self-confidence in learning situations." All of these traits would tend to enhance the language acquisition process.[59]

Campos and Keatinge also emphasize the consequences of the preschool program for parental participation in their children's education.[60] They note that, according to the school officials, "the parents of project participants are much more aware of and involved in their child's school experience than nonparticipant parents of Spanish speakers. This is seen as having a positive impact on the future success of the project participants—the greater the involvement of parents, the greater the chances of success of the child".[61]

The major relevance of these findings for educators and policymakers derives from their demonstration that educational programs *can* succeed in preventing the academic failure experienced by many minority students. The corollary is that failure to provide this type of program constitutes the disabling of minority students by the school system. For example, among the students who did not experience the experimental preschool program, the typical pattern of low levels of academic readiness and limited proficiency in both languages was observed. These are the students who are likely to be referred for psychological assessment early in their school careers. This assessment will typically legitimize the inadequate educational provision by attributing students' difficulties to some vacuous category, such as learning disability. By contrast, students who experienced a preschool program in which (a) their cultural identity was reinforced, (b) there was active collaboration with parents, and (c) meaningful use of language was integrated into every aspect of daily activities were developing high levels of conceptual and linguistic skills in *both* languages.

CONCLUSION

In this article I have proposed a theoretical framework for examining minority students' academic failure and for predicting the effects of educational interventions. Within this framework the educational failure of minority students is analyzed as a function of the extent to which schools reflect or counteract the power relations that exist within the broader society. Specifically, language-minority students' educational progress is strongly influenced by the extent to which individual educators become advocates for the promotion of students' linguistic talents, actively encourage community participation in developing students' academic and cultural resources, and implement pedagogical approaches that succeed in liberating students from instructional dependence.

The educator/student interactions characteristic of the disabling end of the proposed continua reflect the typical patterns of interaction that dominated societal groups have experienced in relation to dominant groups. The intrinsic value of the group is usually denied, and "objective" evidence is accumulated to demonstrate the group's "inferiority." This inferior status is then used as a justification for excluding the group from activities and occupations that entail societal rewards.

In a similar way, the disabling of students is frequently rationalized on the basis of students' "needs." For example, minority students need maximum exposure to English in both the school and home; thus, parents must be told not to interact with children in their mother tongue. Similarly, minority children need a highly structured drill-oriented program in order to maximize time spent on tasks to compensate for their deficient preschool experiences. Minority students also need a comprehensive diagnostic/prescriptive assessment in order to identify the nature of their "problem" and possible remedial interventions.

This analysis suggests a major reason for the relative lack of success of the various educational bandwagons that have characterized the North American crusade against underachievement during the past twenty years. The individual role definitions of educators and the institutional role definitions of schools have remained largely unchanged despite "new and improved" programs and policies. These programs and policies, despite their cost, have simply added a new veneer to the outward facade of the structure that disables minority students. The lip service paid to initial L1 instruction, community involvement, and nondiscriminatory assessment, together with the emphasis on improved teaching techniques, have succeeded primarily in deflecting attention from the attitudes and orientation of educators who interact on a daily basis with minority students. It is in these interactions that students are disabled. In the absence of individual and collective educator role redefinitions, schools will continue to reproduce, in these interactions, the power relations that characterize the wider society and make minority students' academic failure inevitable.

To educators genuinely concerned about alleviating the educational difficulties of minority students and responding to their needs, this conclusion may appear overly bleak. I believe, however, that it is realistic and optimistic, as directions for change are clearly indicated rather than obscured by the overlay of costly reforms that leave the underlying disabling structure essentially intact. Given the societal commitment to maintaining the dominant/dominated power relationships, we can predict that educational changes threatening this structure will be fiercely resisted. This is in fact the case for each of the four structural dimensions discussed earlier.[62]

In order to reverse the pattern of widespread minority group educational failure, educators and policymakers are faced with both a personal and a political challenge. Personally, they must redefine their roles within the classroom, the community, and the broader society so that these role definitions result in interactions that empower rather than disable students. Politically, they must attempt to persuade colleagues and decisionmakers—such as school boards and the public that elects them—of the importance of redefining institutional goals so that the schools transform society by empowering minority students rather than reflect society by disabling them.

Chapter Six

The Silenced Dialogue: Power and Pedagogy in Educating Other People's Children*

A Black male graduate student who is also a special education teacher in a predominantly Black community is talking about his experiences in predominantly white university classes:

> There comes a moment in every class where we have to discuss "The Black Issue" and what's appropriate education for Black children. I tell you, I'm tired of arguing with those White people, because they won't listen. Well, I don't know if they really don't listen or if they just don't believe you. It seems like if you can't quote Vygotsky or something, then you don't have any validity to speak about your *own* kids. Anyway, I'm not bothering with it anymore, now I'm just in it for a grade.

A Black woman teacher in a multicultural urban elementary school is talking about her experiences in discussions with her predominantly white fellow teachers about how they should organize reading instruction to best serve students of color:

> When you're talking to White people they still want it to be their way. You can try to talk to them and give them examples, but they're so headstrong, they think they know what's best for *everybody*, for *everybody's* children. They won't listen, White folks are going to do what they want to do *anyway*.

119

It's really hard. They just don't listen well. No, they listen, but they don't *hear*—you know how your mama used to say you listen to the radio, but you *hear* your mother? Well they don't *hear* me.

So I just try to shut them out so I can hold my temper. You can only beat your head against a brick wall for so long before you draw blood. If I try to stop arguing with them I can't help myself from getting angry. Then I end up walking around praying all day "Please Lord, remove the bile I feel for these people so I can sleep tonight." It's funny, but it can become a cancer, a sore.

So, I shut them out. I go back to my own little cubby, my classroom, and I try to teach the way I know will work, no matter what those folk say. And when I get Black kids, I just try to undo the damage they did.

I'm not going to let any man, woman, or child drive me crazy—White folks will try to do that to you if you let them. You just have to stop talking to them, that's what I do. I just keep smiling, but I won't talk to them.

A soft-spoken Native Alaskan woman in her forties is a student in the Education Department of the University of Alaska. One day she storms into a Black professor's office and very uncharacteristically slams the door. She plops down in a chair and, still fuming, says, "Please tell those people, just don't help us anymore! I give up. I won't talk to them again!"

And finally, a Black woman principal who is also a doctoral student at a well-known university on the West Coast is talking about her university experiences, particularly about when a professor lectures on issues concerning educating Black children:

If you try to suggest that that's not quite the way it is, they get defensive, then you get defensive, then they'll start reciting research.

I try to give them my experiences, to explain. They just look and nod. The more I try to explain, they just look and nod, just keep looking and nodding. They don't really hear me.

Then, when it's time for class to be over, the professor tells me to come to his office to talk more. So I go. He asks for more examples of what I'm talking about, and he looks and nods while I give them. Then he says that that's just my experiences. It doesn't really apply to most Black people.

It becomes futile because they think they know everything about everybody. What you have to say about your life, your children, doesn't mean anything. They don't really want to hear what you have to say. They wear blinders and earplugs. They only want to go on research they've read that other White people have written.

It just doesn't make any sense to keep talking to them.

Thus was the first half of the title of this text born—"The Silenced Dialogue." One of the tragedies in the field of education is that scenarios such as these are enacted daily around the country. The saddest element is that the individuals that the Black and Native American educators speak of in these statements are seldom aware that the dialogue *has* been silenced. Most likely the white educators believe that their colleagues of color did, in the end, agree with their logic. After all, they stopped disagreeing, didn't they?

I have collected these statements since completing a recently published article.[1] In this somewhat autobiographical account, entitled "Skills and Other Dilemmas of a Progressive Black Educator," I discussed my perspective as a product of a skills-oriented approach to writing and as a teacher of process-oriented approaches. I described the estrangement that I and many teachers of color feel from the progressive movement when writing-process advocates dismiss us as too "skills oriented." I ended the article suggesting that it was incumbent upon writing-process advocates—or indeed, advocates of any progressive movement—to enter into dialogue with teachers of color, who may not share their enthusiasm about so-called new, liberal, or progressive ideas.

In response to this article, which presented no research data and did not even cite a reference, I received numerous calls and letters from teachers, professors, and even state school personnel from around the country, both Black and white. All of the white respondents, except one, have wished to talk more about the question of skills versus process approaches—to support or reject what they perceive to be my position. On the other hand, *all* of the non-white respondents have spoken passionately on being left out of the dialogue about how best to educate children of color.

How can such complete communication blocks exist when both parties truly believe they have the same aims? How can the bitterness and resentment expressed by the educators of color be drained so that the sores can heal? What can be done?

I believe the answer to these questions lies in ethnographic analysis, that is, in identifying and giving voice to alternative world views. Thus, I will attempt to address the concerns raised by white and Black respondents to my article "Skills and Other Dilemmas".[2] My charge here is not to determine the best instructional methodology; I believe that the actual practice of good teachers of all colors typically incorporates a range of pedagogical orientations. Rather, I suggest that the differing perspectives on the debate over "skills" versus "process" approaches can lead to an understanding of the alienation and miscommunication, and thereby to an understanding of the "silenced dialogue."

In thinking through these issues, I have found what I believe to be a connecting and complex theme: what I have come to call "the culture of power." There are five aspects of power I would like to propose as given for this presentation:

1. Issues of power are enacted in classrooms.
2. There are codes or rules for participating in power; that is, there is a "culture of power."
3. The rules of the culture of power are a reflection of the rules of the culture of those who have power.
4. If you are not already a participant in the culture of power, being told explicitly the rules of that culture makes acquiring power easier.
5. Those with power are frequently least aware of—or least willing to acknowledge—its existence. Those with less power are often most aware of its existence.

The first three are by now basic tenets in the literature of the sociology of education, but the last two have seldom been addressed. The following discussion will explicate these aspects of power and their relevance to the schism between liberal educational movements and that of non-White, non-middle-class teachers and communities.[3]

1. *Issues of power are enacted in classrooms.* These issues include: the power of the teacher over the students; the power of the publishers of textbooks and of the developers of the curriculum to determine the view of the world presented; the power of the state in enforcing compulsory schooling; and the power of an individual or group to determine another's intelligence or "normalcy." Finally, if schooling prepares people for jobs, and the kind of job a person has determines her or his economic status and, therefore, power, then schooling is intimately related to that power.

2. *There are codes or rules for participating in power; that is, there is a "culture of power."* The codes or rules I'm speaking of relate to linguistic forms, communicative strategies, and presentation of self; that is, ways of talking, ways of writing, ways of dressing, and ways of interacting.

3. *The rules of the culture of power are a reflection of the rules of the culture of those who have power.* This means that success in institutions—schools, workplaces, and so on—is predicated upon acquisition of the culture of those who are in power. Children from middle-class homes tend to do better in school than those from non-middle-class homes because the culture of the school is based on the culture of the upper and middle classes—of those in power. The upper and middle classes send their children to school with all the accoutrements of the culture of power; children from other kinds of families operate within perfectly wonderful and viable cultures but not cultures that carry the codes or rules of power.

4. *If you are not already a participant in the culture of power, being told explicitly the rules of that culture makes acquiring power easier.* In my work

culturally implicit codes – within OK — between ??? (handwritten annotation)

within and between diverse cultures, I have come to conclude that members of any culture transmit information implicitly to co-members. However, when implicit codes are attempted across cultures, communication frequently breaks down. Each cultural group is left saying, "Why don't those people say what they mean?" as well as, "What's wrong with them, why don't they understand?"

Anyone who has had to enter new cultures, especially to accomplish a specific task, will know of what I speak. When I lived in several Papua New Guinea villages for extended periods to collect data, and when I go to Alaskan villages for work with Alaskan Native communities, I have found it unquestionably easier—psychologically and pragmatically—when some kind soul has directly informed me about such matters as appropriate dress, interactional styles, embedded meanings, and taboo words or actions. I contend that it is much the same for anyone seeking to learn the rules of the culture of power. Unless one has the leisure of a lifetime of "immersion" to learn them, explicit presentation makes learning immeasurably easier.

And now, to the fifth and last premise:

5. *Those with power are frequently least aware of—or least willing to acknowledge—its existence. Those with less power are often most aware of its existence.* For many who consider themselves members of liberal or radical camps, acknowledging personal power and admitting participation in the culture of power is distinctly uncomfortable. On the other hand, those who are less powerful in any situation are most likely to recognize the power variable most acutely. My guess is that the white colleagues and instructors of those previously quoted did not perceive themselves to have power over the non-white speakers. However, either by virtue of their position, their numbers, or their access to that particular code of power of calling upon research to validate one's position, the white educators had the authority to establish what was to be considered "truth" regardless of the opinions of the people of color, and the latter were well aware of that fact.

A related phenomenon is that liberals (and here I am using the term "liberal" to refer to those whose beliefs include striving for a society based upon maximum individual freedom and autonomy) seem to act under the assumption that to make any rules or expectations explicit is to act against liberal principles, to limit the freedom and autonomy of those subjected to the explicitness.

I thank Fred Erickson for a comment that led me to look again at a tape by John Gumperz[4] on cultural dissonance in cross-cultural interactions. One of the episodes showed an East Indian interviewing for a job with an all-white committee. The interview was a complete failure, even though several of the interviewers appeared to really want to help the applicant. As the interview

"cultural dissonance" (handwritten annotation)

rolled steadily downhill, these "helpers" became more and more indirect in their questioning, which exacerbated the problems the applicant had in performing appropriately. Operating from a different cultural perspective, he got fewer and fewer clear clues as to what was expected of him, which ultimately resulted in his failure to secure the position.

I contend that as the applicant showed less and less aptitude for handling the interview, the power differential became ever more evident to the interviewers. The "helpful" interviewers, unwilling to acknowledge themselves as having power over the applicant, became more and more uncomfortable. Their indirectness was an attempt to lessen the power differential and their discomfort by lessening the power-revealing explicitness of their questions and comments.

When acknowledging and expressing power, one tends towards explicitness (as in yelling to your 10-year-old, "Turn the radio down!"). When de-emphasizing power, there is a move toward indirect communication. Therefore, in the interview setting, those who sought to help, to express their egalitarianism with the East Indian applicant, became more and more indirect—and less and less helpful—in their questions and comments.

In literacy instruction, explicitness might be equated with direct instruction. Perhaps the ultimate expression of explicitness and direct instruction in the primary classroom is Distar. This reading program is based on a behaviorist model in which reading is taught through the direct instruction of phonics generalizations and blending. The teacher's role is to maintain the full attention of the group by continuous questioning, eye contact, finger snaps, hand claps, and other gestures, and by eliciting choral responses and initiating some sort of award system.

When the program was introduced, it arrived with a flurry of research data that "proved" that all children—even those who were "culturally deprived"—could learn to read using this method. Soon there was a strong response, first from academics and later from many classroom teachers, stating that the program was terrible. What I find particularly interesting, however, is that the primary issue of the conflict over Distar has not been over its instructional efficacy—usually the students did learn to read—but the expression of explicit power in the classroom. The liberal educators opposed the methods—the direct instruction, the explicit control exhibited by the teacher. As a matter of fact, it was not unusual (even now) to hear of the program spoken of as "fascist."

I am not an advocate of Distar, but I will return to some of the issues that the program—and direct instruction in general—raises in understanding the differences between progressive white educators and educators of color.

To explore those differences, I would like to present several statements typical of those made with the best of intentions by middle-class liberal educators. To the surprise of the speakers, it is not unusual for such content to be met by vocal opposition or stony silence from people of color. My attempt here is to examine the underlying assumptions of both camps.

"I want the same thing for everyone else's children as I want for mine." To provide schooling for everyone's children that reflects liberal, middle-class values and aspirations is to ensure the maintenance of the status quo, to ensure that power, the culture of power, remains in the hands of those who already have it. Some children come to school with more accoutrements of the culture of power already in place—"cultural capital," as some critical theorists refer to it[5]—some with less. Many liberal educators hold that the primary goal for education is for children to become autonomous, to develop fully who they are in the classroom setting without having arbitrary, outside standards forced upon them. This is a very reasonable goal for people whose children are already participants in the culture of power and who have already internalized its codes.

But parents who don't function within that culture often want something else. It's not that they disagree with the former aim, it's just that they want something more. They want to ensure that the school provides their children with discourse patterns, interactional styles, and spoken and written language codes that will allow them success in the larger society.

It was the lack of attention to this concern that created such a negative outcry in the Black community when well-intentioned white liberal educators introduced "dialect readers." These were seen as a plot to prevent the schools from teaching the linguistic aspects of the culture of power, thus dooming Black children to a permanent outsider caste. As one parent demanded, "My kids know how to be Black—you all teach them how to be successful in the white man's world."

Several Black teachers have said to me recently that as much as they'd like to believe otherwise, they cannot help but conclude that many of the "progressive" educational strategies imposed by liberals upon Black and poor children could only be based on a desire to ensure that the liberals' children get sole access to the dwindling pool of American jobs. Some have added that the liberal educators believe themselves to be operating with good intentions, but that these good intentions are only conscious delusions about their unconscious true motives. One of Black anthropologist John Gwaltney's informants reflects this perspective with her tongue-in-cheek observation that the biggest difference between Black folks and white folks is that Black folks *know* when they're lying![6]

Let me try to clarify how this might work in literacy instruction. A few years ago I worked on an analysis of two popular reading programs, Distar and a progressive program that focused on higher-level critical thinking skills. In one of the first lessons of the progressive program, the children are introduced to the names of the letter *m* and *e*. In the same lesson they are then taught the sound made by each of the letters, how to write each of the letters, and that when the two are blended together they produce the word *me*.

As an experienced first-grade teacher, I am convinced that a child needs to be familiar with a significant number of these concepts to be able to assimilate so much new knowledge in one sitting. By contrast, Distar presents the same information in about forty lessons.

I would not argue for the pace of the Distar lessons; such a slow pace would only bore most kids—but what happened in the other lesson is that it merely provided an opportunity for those who already knew the content to exhibit that they knew it, or at most perhaps to build one new concept onto what was already known. This meant that the child who did not come to school already primed with what was to be presented would be labeled as needing "remedial" instruction from day one; indeed, this determination would be made before he or she was ever taught. In fact, Distar was "successful" because it actually *taught* new information to children who had not already acquired it at home. Although the more progressive system was ideal for some children, for others it was a disaster.

I do not advocate a simplistic "basic skills" approach for children outside of the culture of power. It would be (and has been) tragic to operate as if these children were incapable of critical and higher-order thinking and reasoning. Rather, I suggest that schools must provide these children the content that other families from a different cultural orientation provide at home. This does not mean separating children according to family background, but instead, ensuring that each classroom incorporate strategies appropriate for all the children in its confines.

And I do not advocate that it is the school's job to attempt to change the homes of poor and non-white children to match the homes of those in the culture of power. That may indeed be a form of cultural genocide. I have frequently heard schools call poor parents "uncaring" when parents respond to the school's urging, that they change their home life in order to facilitate their children's learning, by saying, "But that's the school's job." What the school personnel fail to understand is that if the parents were members of the culture of power and lived by its rules and codes, then they would transmit those codes to their children. In fact, they transmit another culture that children must learn at home in order to survive in their communities.

"Child-centered, whole language, and process approaches are needed in order to allow a democratic state of free, autonomous, empowered adults, and because research has shown that children learn best through these methods." People of color are, in general, skeptical of research as a determiner of our

fates. Academic research has, after all, found us genetically inferior, culturally deprived, and verbally deficient. But beyond that general caveat, and despite my or others' personal preferences, there is little research data supporting the major tenets of process approaches over other forms of literacy instruction, and virtually no evidence that such approaches are more efficacious for children of color.[7]

Although the problem is not necessarily inherent in the method, in some instances adherents of process approaches to writing create situations in which students ultimately find themselves held accountable for knowing a set of rules about which no one has ever directly informed them. Teachers do students no service to suggest, even implicitly, that "product" is not important. In this country, students will be judged on their product regardless of the process they utilized to achieve it. And that product, based as it is on the specific codes of a particular culture, is more readily produced when the directives of how to produce it are made explicit.

If such explicitness is not provided to students, what it feels like to people who are old enough to judge is that there are secrets being kept, that time is being wasted, that the teacher is abdicating his or her duty to teach. A doctoral student in my acquaintance was assigned to a writing class to hone his writing skills. The student was placed in the section led by a white professor who utilized a process approach, consisting primarily of having the students write essays and then assemble into groups to edit each others' papers. That procedure infuriated this particular student. He had many angry encounters with the teacher about what she was doing. In his words:

> I didn't feel she was teaching us anything. She wanted us to correct each others' papers and we were there to learn from her. She didn't teach anything, absolutely nothing.
>
> Maybe they're trying to learn what Black folks knew all the time. We understand how to improvise, how to express ourselves creatively. When I'm in a classroom, I'm not looking for that, I'm looking for structure, the more formal language.
>
> Now my buddy was in [a] Black teacher's class. And that lady was very good. She went through and explained and defined each part of the structure. This [white] teacher didn't get along with that Black teacher. She said that she didn't agree with her methods. But *I* don't think that White teacher *had* any methods.

When I told this gentleman that what the teacher was doing was called a process method of teaching writing, his response was, "Well, at least now I know that she *thought* that she was doing *something*. I thought she was just a fool who couldn't teach and didn't want to try."

This sense of being cheated can be so strong that the student may be completely turned off to the educational system. Amanda Branscombe, an accomplished white teacher, recently wrote a letter discussing her work with working-class Black and white students at a community college in Alabama. She had given these students my "Skills and Other Dilemmas" article [8] to read and discuss, and wrote that her students really understood and identified with what I was saying. To quote her letter:

> One young man said that he had dropped out of high school because he failed the exit exam. He noted that he had then passed the GED without a problem after three weeks of prep. He said that his high school English teacher claimed to use a process approach, but what she really did was hide behind fancy words to give herself permission to do nothing in the classroom.

The students I have spoken of seem to be saying that the teacher has denied them access to herself as the source of knowledge necessary to learn the forms they need to succeed. Again, I tentatively attribute the problem to teachers' resistance to exhibiting power in the classroom. Somehow, to exhibit one's personal power as expert source is viewed as disempowering one's students.

Two qualifiers are necessary, however. The teacher cannot be the only expert in the classroom. To deny students their own expert knowledge *is* to disempower them. Amanda Branscombe, when she was working with Black high school students classified as "slow learners," had the students analyze RAP songs to discover their underlying patterns. The students became the experts in explaining to the teacher the rules for creating a new RAP song. The teacher then used the patterns the students identified as a base to begin an explanation of the structure of grammar, and then of Shakespeare's plays. Both student and teacher are expert at what they know best.

The second qualifier is that merely adopting direct instruction is not the answer. Actual writing for real audiences and real purposes is a vital element in helping students to understand that they have an important voice in their own learning processes. Siddle[9] examines the results of various kinds of interventions in a primarily process-oriented writing class for Black students. Based on readers' blind assessments, she found that the intervention that produced the most positive changes in the students' writing was a "mini-lesson" consisting of direct instruction about some standard writing convention. But what produced the *second* highest number of positive changes was a subsequent student-centered conference with the teacher. (Peer conferencing in this group of Black students who were not members of the culture of power produced the least number of changes in students' writing. However, the classroom teacher maintained—and I concur—that such activities are necessary to introduce the elements of "real audience" into the task, along with more teacher-directed strategies.)

"It's really a shame but she (that Black teacher upstairs) seems to be so au-thoritarian, so focused on skills and so teacher directed. Those poor kids never seem to be allowed to really express their creativity. (And she even yells at them.)" This statement directly concerns the display of power and author-ity in the classroom. One way to understand the difference in perspective be-tween Black teachers and their progressive colleagues on this issue is to explore culturally influenced oral interactions.

In *Ways With Words,* Shirley Brice Heath quotes the verbal directives given by the middle-class "townspeople" teachers:

—"Is this where the scissors belong?"
—"You want to do your best work today."[10]

By contrast, many Black teachers are more likely to say:

—"Put those scissors on that shelf."
—"Put your name on the papers and make sure to get the right answer for each question."

Is one oral style more authoritarian than another?

Other researchers have identified differences in middle-class and working-class speech to children. Snow et al.[11], for example, report that working-class mothers use more directives to their children than do middle- and upper-class parents. Middle-class parents are likely to give the directive to a child to take his bath as, "Isn't it time for your bath?" Even though the utterance is couched as a question, both child and adult understand it as a directive. The child may respond with "Aw Mom, can't I wait until . . . ," but whether or not negotiation is attempted, both conversants understand the intent of the utterance.

By contrast, a Black mother, in whose house I was recently a guest, said to her eight-year-old son, "Boy, get your rusty behind in that bathtub." Now I happen to know that this woman loves her son as much as any mother, but she would never have posed the directive to her son to take a bath in the form of a question. Were she to ask, "Would you like to take your bath now?" she would not have been issuing a directive but offering a true alternative. Con-sequently, as Heath suggests, upon entering school the child from such a fam-ily may not understand the indirect statement of the teacher as a direct command. Both white and Black working-class children in the communities

Heath studied "had difficulty interpreting these indirect requests for adherence to an unstated set of rules".[12]

But those veiled commands are commands nonetheless, representing true power, and with true consequences for disobedience. If veiled commands are ignored, the child will be labeled a behavior problem and possibly officially classified as behavior disordered. In other words, the attempt by the teacher to reduce an exhibition of power by expressing herself in indirect terms may remove the very explicitness that the child needs to understand the rules of the new classroom culture.

A Black elementary school principal in Fairbanks, Alaska, reported to me that she has a lot of difficulty with Black children who are placed in some White teachers' classrooms. The teachers often send the children to the office for disobeying teacher directives. Their parents are frequently called in for conferences. The parents' response to the teacher is usually the same: "They do what I say; if you just *tell* them what to do, they'll do it. I tell them at home that they have to listen to what you say." And so, does not the power still exist? Its veiled nature only makes it more difficult for some children to respond appropriately, but that in no way mitigates its existence.

I don't mean to imply, however, that the only time the Black child disobeys the teacher is when he or she misunderstands the request for certain behavior. There are other factors that may produce such behavior. Black children expect an authority figure to act with authority. When the teacher instead acts as a "chum," the message sent is that this adult has no authority, and the children react accordingly. One reason this is so is that Black people often view issues of power and authority differently than people from mainstream middle-class backgrounds.[13] Many people of color expect authority to be earned by personal efforts and exhibited by personal characteristics. In other words, "the authoritative person gets to be a teacher because she is authoritative." Some members of middle-class cultures, by contrast, expect one to achieve authority by the acquisition of an authoritative role. That is, "the teacher is the authority because she is the teacher."

In the first instance, because authority is earned, the teacher must consistently prove the characteristics that give her authority. These characteristics may vary across cultures, but in the Black community they tend to cluster around several abilities. The authoritative teacher can control the class through exhibition of personal power; establishes meaningful interpersonal relationships that garner student respect; exhibits a strong belief that all students can learn; establishes a standard of achievement and "pushes" the students to achieve that standard; and holds the attention of the students by incorporating interactional features of Black communicative style in his or her teaching.

By contrast, the teacher whose authority is vested in the role has many more options of behavior at her disposal. For instance, she does not need to express any sense of personal power because her authority does not come from anything she herself does or says. Hence, the power she actually holds may be veiled in such questions/commands as "Would you like to sit down now?" If the children in her class understand authority as she does, it is mutually agreed upon that they are to obey her no matter how indirect, soft-spoken, or unassuming she may be. Her indirectness and soft-spokenness may indeed be, as I suggested earlier, an attempt to reduce the implication of overt power in order to establish a more egalitarian and non-authoritarian classroom atmosphere.

If the children operate under another notion of authority, however, then there is trouble. The Black child may perceive the middle-class teacher as weak, ineffectual, and incapable of taking on the role of being the teacher; therefore, there is no need to follow her directives. In her dissertation, Michelle Foster quotes one young Black man describing such a teacher:

> She is boring, bo::ing. She could do something creative. Instead she just stands there. She can't control the class, doesn't know how to control the class. She asked me what she was doing wrong. I told her she just stands there like she's meditating. I told her she could be meditating for all I know. She says that we're supposed to know what to do. I told her I don't know nothin' unless she tells me. She just can't control the class. I hope we don't have her next semester. [14]

But of course the teacher may not view the problem as residing in herself but in the student, and the child may once again become the behavior-disordered Black boy in special education.

What characteristics do Black students attribute to the good teacher? Again, Foster's dissertation provides a quotation that supports my experience with Black students. A young Black man is discussing a former teacher with a group of friends:

> We had fu::n in her class, but she was mean. I can remember she used to say, "Tell me what's in the story, Wayne." She pushed, she used to get on me and push me to know. She made us learn. We had to get in the books. There was this tall guy and he tried to take her on, but she was in charge of that class and she didn't let anyone run her. I still have this book we used in her class. It's a bunch of stories in it. I just read one on Coca-Cola again the other day. [15]

To clarify, this student was *proud* of the teacher's "meanness," an attribute he seemed to describe as the ability to run the class and pushing and expecting students to learn. Now, does the liberal perspective of the negatively authoritarian Black teacher really hold up? I suggest that although all "explicit" Black teachers are not also good teachers, there are different attitudes in different cultural groups about which characteristics make for a good teacher. Thus, it is impossible to create a model for the good teacher without taking issues of culture and community context into account.

And now to the final comment I present for examination:

"Children have the right to their own language, their own culture. We must fight cultural hegemony and fight the system by insisting that children be allowed to express themselves in their own language style. It is not they, the children, who must change, but the schools. To push children to do anything else is repressive and reactionary." A statement such as this originally inspired me to write the "Skills and Other Dilemmas" article. It was first written as a letter to a colleague in response to a situation that had developed in our department. I was teaching a senior-level teacher education course. Students were asked to prepare a written autobiographical document for the class that would also be shared with their placement school prior to their student teaching.

One student, a talented young Native American woman, submitted a paper in which the ideas were lost because of technical problems—from spelling to sentence structure to paragraph structure. Removing her name, I duplicated the paper for a discussion with some faculty members. I had hoped to initiate a discussion about what we could do to ensure that our students did not reach the senior level without getting assistance in technical writing skills when they needed them.

I was amazed at the response. Some faculty implied that the student should never have been allowed into the teacher education program. Others, some of the more progressive minded, suggested that I was attempting to function as gatekeeper by raising the issue and had internalized repressive and disempowering forces of the power elite to suggest that something was wrong with a Native American student just because she had another style of writing. With few exceptions, I found myself alone in arguing against both camps.

No, this student should not have been denied entry to the program. To deny her entry under the notion of upholding standards is to blame the victim for the crime. We cannot justifiably enlist exclusionary standards when the reason this student lacked the skills demanded was poor teaching at best and institutionalized racism at worst.

However, to bring this student into the program and pass her through without attending to obvious deficits in the codes needed for her to function effectively as a teacher is equally criminal—for though we may assuage our own consciences for not participating in victim blaming, she will surely be accused and convicted as soon as she leaves the university. As Native Alas-

deny entry ⇒ no!,
deny need for other attributes ⇒ No!

kans were quick to tell me, and as I understood through my own experience in the Black community, not only would she not be hired as a teacher, but those who did not hire her would make the (false) assumption that the university was putting out only incompetent Natives and that they should stop looking seriously at any Native applicants. A white applicant who exhibits problems is an individual with problems. A person of color who exhibits problems immediately becomes a representative of her cultural group.

No, either stance is criminal. The answer is to *accept* students but also to take responsibility to *teach* them. I decided to talk to the student and found out she had recognized that she needed some assistance in the technical aspects of writing soon after she entered the university as a freshman. She had gone to various members of the education faculty and received the same two kinds of responses I met with four years later: faculty members told her either that she should not even attempt to be a teacher, or that it didn't matter and that she shouldn't worry about such trivial issues. In her desperation, she had found a helpful professor in the English Department, but he left the university when she was in her sophomore year.

We sat down together, worked out a plan for attending to specific areas of writing competence, and set up regular meetings. I stressed to her the need to use her own learning process as insight into how best to teach her future students those "skills" that her own schooling had failed to teach her. I gave her some explicit rules to follow in some areas; for others, we devised various kinds of journals that, along with readings about the structure of the language, allowed her to find her own insights into how the language worked. All that happened two years ago, and the young woman is now successfully teaching. What the experience led me to understand is that pretending that gatekeeping points don't exist is to ensure that many students will not pass through them.

Now you may have inferred that I believe that because there is a culture of power, everyone should learn the codes to participate in it, and that is how the world should be. Actually, nothing could be further from the truth. I believe in a diversity of style, and I believe the world will be diminished if cultural diversity is ever obliterated. Further, I believe strongly, as do my liberal colleagues, that each cultural group should have the right to maintain its own language style. When I speak, therefore, of the culture of power, I don't speak of how I wish things to be but of how they are.

I further believe that to act as if power does not exist is to ensure that the power status quo remains the same. To imply to children or adults (but of course the adults won't believe you anyway) that it doesn't matter how you talk or how you write is to ensure their ultimate failure. I prefer to be honest with my students. Tell them that their language and cultural style is unique and wonderful but that there is a political power game that is also being played, and if they want to be in on that game there are certain games that they too must play.

But don't think that I let the onus of change rest entirely with the students. I am also involved in political work both inside and outside of the educational system, and that political work demands that I place myself to influence as many gatekeeping points as possible. And it is there that I agitate for change—pushing gatekeepers to open their doors to a variety of styles and codes. What I'm saying, however, is that I do not believe that political change toward diversity can be effected from the bottom up, as do some of my colleagues. They seem to believe that if we accept and encourage diversity within classrooms of children, then diversity will automatically be accepted as gatekeeping points.

I believe that will never happen. What will happen is that the students who reach the gatekeeping points—like Amanda Branscombe's student who dropped out of high school because he failed his exit exam—will understand that they have been lied to and will react accordingly. No, I am certain that if we are truly to effect societal change, we cannot do so from the bottom up, but we must push and agitate from the top down. And in the meantime, we must take the responsibility to *teach*, to provide for students who do not already possess them, the additional codes of power.[16]

But I also do not believe that we should teach students to passively adopt an alternate code. They must be encouraged to understand the value of the code they already possess as well as to understand the power realities in this country. Otherwise they will be unable to work to change these realities. And how does one do that?

Martha Demientieff, a masterly Native Alaskan teacher of Athabaskan Indian students, tells me that her students, who live in a small, isolated, rural village of less than two hundred people, are not aware that there are different codes of English. She takes their writing and analyzes it for features of what has been referred to by Alaskan linguists as "Village English," and then covers half a bulletin board with words or phrases from the students' writing, which she labels "Our Heritage Language." On the other half of the bulletin board she puts the equivalent statements in "standard English," which she labels "Formal English."

She and the students spend a long time on the "Heritage English" section, savoring the words, discussing the nuances. She tells the students, "That's the way we say things. Doesn't it feel good? Isn't it the absolute best way of getting that idea across?" Then she turns to the other side of the board. She tells the students that there are people, not like those in their village, who judge others by the way they talk or write.

We listen to the way people talk, not to judge them, but to tell what part of the river they come from. These other people are not like that. They think everybody needs to talk like them. Unlike us, they have a hard time hearing what people say if they don't talk exactly like them. Their way of talking and writing is called "Formal English."

We have to feel a little sorry for them because they have only one way to talk. We're going to learn two ways to say things. Isn't that better? One way will be our Heritage way. The other will be Formal English. Then, when we go to get jobs, we'll be able to talk like those people who only know and can only really listen to one way. Maybe after we get the jobs we can help them to learn how it feels to have another language, like ours, that feels so good. We'll talk like them when we have to, but we'll always know our way is best.

Martha then does all sorts of activities with the notions of Formal and Heritage or informal English. She tells the students,

> In the village, everyone speaks informally most of the time unless there's a potlatch or something. You don't think about it, you don't worry about following any rules—it's sort of like how you eat food at a picnic—nobody pays attention to whether you use your fingers or a fork, and it feels *so* good. Now, Formal English is more like a formal dinner. There are rules to follow about where the knife and fork belong, about where people sit, about how you eat. That can be really nice, too, because it's nice to dress up sometimes.

The students then prepare a formal dinner in the class, for which they dress up and set a big table with fancy tablecloths, china, and silverware. They speak only Formal English at this meal. Then they prepare a picnic where only informal English is allowed.

She also contrasts the "wordy" academic way of saying things with the metaphoric style of Athabaskan. The students discuss how book language always uses more words, but in Heritage language, the shorter way of saying something is always better. Students then write papers in the academic way, discussing with Martha and with each other whether they believe they've said enough to sound like a book. Next, they take those papers and try to reduce the meaning to a few sentences. Finally, students further reduce the message to a "saying" brief enough to go on the front of a T-shirt, and the sayings are put on little paper T-shirts that the students cut out and hang throughout the room. Sometimes the students reduce other authors' wordy texts to their essential meanings as well.

The following transcript provides another example. It is from a conversation between a Black teacher and a Southern Black high school student named Joey, who is a speaker of Black English. The teacher believes it very important to discuss openly and honestly the issues of language diversity and power. She has begun the discussion by giving the student a children's book written in Black English to read.

Teacher: What do you think about that book?
Joey: I think it's nice.
Teacher: Why?
Joey: I don't know. It just told about a Black family, that's all.
Teacher: Was it difficult to read?
Joey: No.
Teacher: Was the text different from what you have seen in other books?
Joey: Yeah. The writing was.
Teacher: How?
Joey: It use more of a southern-like accent in this book.
Teacher: Uhm-hmm. do you think that's good or bad?
Joey: Well, uh, I don't think it's good for people down this a way, cause that's the way they grow up talking anyway. They ought to get the right way to talk.
Teacher: Oh. So you think it's wrong to talk like that?
Joey: Well . . . [*Laughs*]
Teacher: Hard question, huh?
Joey: Uhm-hmm, that's a hard question. But I think they shouldn't make books like that.
Teacher: Why?
Joey: Because they not using the right way to talk and in school they take off for that and li'l chirren grow up talking like that and reading like that so they might think that's right and all the time they getting bad grades in school, talking like that and writing like that.
Teacher: Do you think they should be getting bad grades for talking like that?
Joey: [*Pauses, answers very slowly*] No . . . No.
Teacher: So you don't think that it matters whether you talk one way or another?
Joey: No, not long as you understood.
Teacher: Uhm-hmm. Well, that's a hard question for me to answer, too. It's, ah, that's a question that's come up in a lot of schools now as to whether they should correct children who speak the way we speak all the time. Cause when we're talking to each other we talk like that even though we might not talk like that when we get into other situations, and who's to say whether it's—
Joey: [*Interrupting*] Right or wrong.
Teacher: Yeah.
Joey: Maybe they ought to come up with another kind of . . . maybe Black English or something. A course in Black English. Maybe Black folks would be good in that cause people talk, I mean Black people talk like that, so . . . but I guess there's a right way and wrong way to talk, you know, not regarding what race. I don't know.

Teacher: But who decided what's right or wrong?
Joey: Well that's true . . . I guess White people did.
[*Laughter. End of tape.*]

Notice how throughout the conversation Joey's consciousness has been raised by thinking about codes of language. This teacher further advocates having students interview various personnel officers in actual workplaces about their attitudes toward divergent styles in oral and written language. Students begin to understand how arbitrary language standards are, but also how politically charged they are. They compare various pieces written in different styles, discuss the impact of different styles on the message by making translations and back translations across styles, and discuss the history, apparent purpose, and contextual appropriateness of each of the technical writing rules presented by their teacher. *And* they practice writing different forms to different audiences based on rules appropriate for each audience. Such a program not only "teaches" standard linguistic forms, but also explores aspects of power as exhibited through linguistic forms.

Tony Burgess, in a study of secondary writing in England by Britton, Burgess, Martin, McLeod, and Rosen, suggests that we should not teach "iron conventions . . . imposed without rationale or grounding in communicative intent," . . . but "critical and ultimately cultural awarenesses".[17] Courtney Cazden calls for a two-pronged approach:

1. Continuous opportunities for writers to participate in some authentic bit of the unending conversation . . . thereby becoming part of a vital community of talkers and writers in a particular domain, and
2. Periodic, temporary focus on conventions of form, taught as cultural conventions expected in a particular community.[18]

Just so that there is no confusion about what Cazden means by a focus on conventions of form, or about what I mean by "skills," let me stress that neither of us is speaking of page after page of "skill sheets" creating compound words or identifying nouns and adverbs, but rather about helping students gain a useful knowledge of the conventions of print while engaging in real and useful communicative activities. Kay Rowe Grubis, a junior high school teacher in a multicultural school, makes lists of certain technical rules for her eighth graders' review and then gives them papers from a third grade to "correct." The students not only have to correct other students' work, but also tell them why they have changed or questioned aspects of the writing.

A village teacher, Howard Cloud, teaches his high school students the conventions of formal letter writing and the formulation of careful questions in the context of issues surrounding the amendment of the Alaska Land

Claims Settlement Act. Native Alaskan leaders hold differing views on this issue, critical to the future of local sovereignty and land rights. The students compose letters to leaders who reside in different areas of the state seeking their perspectives, set up audioconference calls for interview/debate sessions, and, finally, develop a videotape to present the differing views.

To summarize, I suggest that students must be *taught* the codes needed to participate fully in the mainstream of American life, not by being forced to attend to hollow, inane, decontextualized subskills, but rather within the context of meaningful communicative endeavors; that they must be allowed the resource of the teacher's expert knowledge, while being helped to acknowledge their own "expertness" as well; and that even while students are assisted in learning the culture of power, they must also be helped to learn about the arbitrariness of those codes and about the power relationships they represent.

I am also suggesting that appropriate education of poor children and children of color can only be devised in consultation with adults who share their culture. Black parents, teachers of color, and members of poor communities must be allowed to participate fully in the discussion of what kind of instruction is in their children's best interest. Good liberal intentions are not enough. In an insightful study entitled "Racism without Racists: Institutional Racism in Urban Schools," Massey, Scott, and Dornbusch found that under the pressures of teaching, and with all intentions of "being nice," teachers had essentially stopped attempting to teach Black children. In their words: "We have shown that oppression can arise out of warmth, friendliness, and concern. Paternalism and a lack of challenging standards are creating a distorted system of evaluation in the schools".[19] Educators must open themselves to, and allow themselves to be affected by, these alternative voices.

In conclusion, I am proposing a resolution for the skills/process debate. In short, the debate is fallacious; the dichotomy is false. The issue is really an illusion created initially not by teachers but by academics whose world view demands the creation of categorical divisions—not for the purpose of better teaching, but for the goal of easier analysis. As I have been reminded by many teachers since the publication of my article, those who are most skillful at educating Black and poor children do not allow themselves to be placed in "skills" or "process" boxes. They understand the need for both approaches, the need to help students to establish their own voices, but to coach those voices to produce notes that will be heard clearly in the larger society.

The dilemma is not really in the debate over instructional methodology, but rather in communicating across cultures and in addressing the more fundamental issue of power, of whose voice gets to be heard in determining what is best for poor children and children of color. Will Black teachers and parents continue to be silenced by the very forces that claim to "give voice" to our

The dilemma!!

children? Such an outcome would be tragic, for both groups truly have something to say to one another. As a result of careful listening to alternative points of view, I have myself come to a viable synthesis of perspectives. But both sides do need to be able to listen, and I contend that it is those with the most power, those in the majority, who must take the greater responsibility for initiating the process.

To do so takes a very special kind of listening, listening that requires not only open eyes and ears, but open hearts and minds. We do not really see through our eyes or hear through our ears, but through our beliefs. To put our beliefs on hold is to cease to exist as ourselves for a moment—and that is not easy. It is painful as well, because it means turning yourself inside out, giving up your own sense of who you are, and being willing to see yourself in the unflattering light of another's angry gaze. It is not easy, but it is the only way to learn what it might feel like to be someone else and the only way to start the dialogue.

There are several guidelines. We must keep the perspective that people ① are experts on their own lives. There are certainly aspects of the outside world of which they may not be aware, but they can be the only authentic chroniclers of their own experience. We must not be too quick to deny their interpretations, or accuse them of "false consciousness." We must believe ② that people are rational beings, and therefore always act rationally. We may not understand their rationales, but that in no way militates against the existence of these rationales or reduces our responsibility to attempt to apprehend them. And finally, we must learn to be vulnerable enough to allow our ③ world to turn upside down in order to allow the realities of others to edge themselves into our consciousness. In other words, we must become ethnographers in the true sense.

Teachers are in an ideal position to play this role, to attempt to get all of the issues on the table in order to initiate true dialogue. This can only be done, however, by seeking out those whose perspectives may differ most, by learning to give their words complete attention, by understanding one's own power, even if that power stems merely from being in the majority, by being unafraid to raise questions about discrimination and voicelessness with people of color, and to listen, no, to *hear* what they say. I suggest that the results of such interactions may be the most powerful and empowering coalescence yet seen in the educational realm—for *all* teachers and for *all* the students they teach.

The Issue!!!

Part Two

From the Margins to the Center: Beyond Silenced Voices

Chapter Seven

Joining the Resistance: Psychology, Politics, Girls, and Women*

IN THE MUSEUM

It is Tuesday. It is raining. And the Theater, Writing, and Outing Club is going to the museum. Eight eleven-year-old girls, members of the sixth grade at the Atrium School in Watertown, Massachusetts, and two women, psychologists interested in girls' development, climb into the school van and begin to make their way through the rain-washed streets into the city. It is June. School is over for the year. The sixth grade has graduated, and the girls from the class have returned for a week of outings, writing, and theater work, designed to strengthen healthy resistance and courage. They gather in the coatroom of the Fine Arts Museum, shedding backpacks and raincoats, retrieving notebooks; they are ready. Today, I explain, they are to be investigative reporters; their assignment is to find out how girls and women appear in this museum.

"Naked," Emma says, without hesitation. A current of recognition passes swiftly, silently, through the group. Like Dora, Freud's patient, who remembers standing in the Dresden art gallery for two-and-a-half hours in front of the Sistine Madonna, Emma will be transfixed by the images of women, by their nakedness in this cool, marble building. Later, when asked to write a conversation with one of the women, Emma chooses a headless, armless Greek statue, weaving into the conventions of polite childhood conversation her two burning questions: Are you cold? and Would you like some clothes?[1]

But why am I telling you this story? I am interested in the relationship between political resistance and psychological resistance—both highly charged subjects in the twentieth century. And I have observed a moment of resistance that occurs in girls' lives at the edge of adolescence. Emma's playfully innocent, slightly irreverent conversation with the statue in the museum bespeaks her interest in the scenes that lie behind the paintings and sculpture that she is seeing—an inquiry into relationships between artists and models: what each is doing and feeling and thinking; a curiosity about the psychological dimensions of this connection between men and women. The statue's response—"I have no money"—to the question about whether she wants some clothes, reveals how readily this inquiry becomes political and sets up the dynamic I wish to follow: the tendency in girls' lives at adolescence for a resistance that is essentially political—an insistence on knowing what one knows and a willingness to be outspoken—to turn into a psychological resistance: a reluctance to know what one knows and a fear that such knowledge, if spoken, will endanger relationships and threaten survival.

Freud located this intersection between psychology and politics— between the child's desire for relationships and for knowledge and the cultural prohibitions on knowing and seeing—as a turning point in boys' early childhood, and named it "the Oedipus complex," after Sophocles' tragedy about knowledge and blindness.[2] In studying girls' development, my colleagues and I have observed a comparable turning point in girls' lives at the time of adolescence.[3] This is the time when girls' desire for relationships and for knowledge comes up against the wall of Western culture, and a resistance breaks out that is, I will claim, potentially of great human value.

Let me return for a moment to the museum and record the doubling of voice and vision that characterizes girls' perception and conversation. Mame's eye for the disparity between outside and inside, between calm surface and explosive laughter, is evident as she describes the painting of "Reverend John Atwood and his family." His two oldest daughters, she writes, sustaining the possessive, "have no expression. They're just staring straight ahead, but one of them looks like she is going to burst out laughing." His wife, she concludes on a more somber note, "looks very worn and tired." By paying close attention to the human world around them and following the changing weather of relationships and the undercurrents of thoughts and feelings, girls come to discern patterns, to notice repeating sequences and to hear familiar rhythms and thus find under the surface of the apparent disorder of everyday living an order that is the psychological equivalent of the Mandelbrot equations of the new chaos physics.

Yet girls' "unpaid-for-education"—Virginia Woolf's name for "that understanding of human beings and their motives which . . . might be called psychology,"[4] leaves girls with knowledge that may well run counter to what they are told by those in authority. So that they are often left, in effect, with two truths, two versions of a story, two voices revealing two points of view. Malka, perhaps reflecting this experience, writes not one but two conversations between herself and the Queen of Babylon. The first is the official version. Speaking in the voice of a reporter, Malka addresses the Queen in a manner befitting her station. "Hello Madam," she says to the woman in the painting, who is brushing her hair while receiving news of the revolt, "What is it like ruling so great a land?" "Glorious," the Queen replies, "It is great fun, although," she adds with a yawn, "it does tax time and strength sometimes." In the second conversation, Malka speaks in her own voice to this bored, haughty Queen, asking her simply: "Whatchya doing?" The Queen, in a sudden reversal of priorities, replies: "Brushing my hair. I was interrupted this morning by a revolt."

Whose agenda, what is important, what can be spoken, and what is tacitly to be ignored—looked at but not seen, heard but not listened to? The play of girls' conversation, the questions and comments that dart in and out like minnows, followed by looks, scanning faces, and listening to what happens, seeing what follows, taking the pulse, the temperature of the human climate—is anyone upset? What is permitted, admitted (in both senses of the word)? Conflict erupts among girls like lightning—something has happened, someone has stepped over a line. Rejection—the thin dark line of rejection: not you; we—whoever "we" are—do not want to be with you.

Girls' questions about who wants to be with whom are to them among the most important questions, and they take sharp notice throughout the day of the answers given to these questions, as revealed through nuance and gesture, voice and glances, seating arrangements, choices of partners, the responses of adult women and men, the attitudes of authorities in the world. Emma's voice in saying that the nudes are naked, Mame's voice in speaking about the irreverence of the daughter and the tiredness of the mother in Reverend John Atwood's family, Malka's voice in revealing by reversing the relationship between hair-brushing and quelling revolts, are the same three voices that are suppressed in the first published version of Anne Frank's diary—the excised passages that reveal that Anne has looked at and seen her own naked body, that she has recorded disturbing thoughts and feelings about her mother, and that she knows from her reading whose activities people record and imbue with value and is disturbed by the disparate attention given to the courage and suffering of women and men. On 15 June, 1944, in one of the deleted passages, she writes:

A question that has been raised more than once and that gives me no inner peace is why did so many nations in the past, and often still now, treat women as inferior to men? Everyone can agree how unjust this is, but that is not enough for me, I would also like to know the cause of the great injustice. . . . It is stupid enough of women to have borne it all in silence for such a long time, since the more centuries this arrangement lasts, the more deeply rooted it becomes. . . . Many people, particularly women, but also men, now realize for how long this state of affairs has been wrong, and modern women demand the right of complete independence! But that's not all, respect for woman, that's going to have to come as well! . . . Soldiers and war heroes are honored and celebrated, explorers acquire immortal fame, martyrs are revered, but how many will look upon woman as they would upon a soldier? . . . Women are much braver, much more courageous soldiers, struggling and enduring pain for the continuance of humankind, than all the freedom-fighting heroes with their big mouths![5]

That girls' knowledge—of the body, of relationships, and of the world and its values—and girls' irreverence provide the grounds for resistance has been known since the time of *Lysistrata*.

IF ONLY WOMEN . . .

In 411 B.C.E., in the midst of the disastrous war between Athens and Sparta, Aristophanes plays out a plan for ending the war in the bawdy comedy, *Lysistrata*. If only women, he thinks, who are able to see the absurdity of men's fighting, who are wise, moreover, in the ways of human bodies and psyches, and who can have an effect on men, would take the salvation of Greece into their hands, they could, he imagines, stop the violence. At the opening of the play, Lysistrata calls the women of Athens and Sparta together, preparing to explain her plan, and the voice and expressions of this classical rendition of a peacemaking woman resonate strongly with the voices and gestures of eleven-year-old girls in the twentieth century.

"I am angry . . . I am very angry and upset," Sarah says, protesting with her whole face and body. Somberness gathers across her eyebrows, joining them together as she says directly: "I was treated by Ted like trash." Tension is in the air. Sarah and Emma walk back and forth across the room, heads down, arms around each other's shoulders. The social texture has suddenly become dark, opaque, like sudden shadows, hurt feelings easily moving to tears, then out, talking, contact, an opening, light and shadow, the play of relationships, the somberness that gathered across Sarah's face moves off, dissipates . . . the girls line up chairs, dragging them into a row, two chairs apiece, bottoms on one, feet on another. They open their journals and begin writing.

"What's bothering you [Lysistrata]?" Calonice says at the beginning of Act One, in Alan Somerstein's 1973 Penguin Classics translation. "Don't screw up your face like that. It really doesn't suit you, you know, knitting your eyebrows up like a bow." "Sorry, Calonice, but I'm furious. I'm disappointed in womankind." Lysistrata is upset because the women of Athens and Sparta have not shown up for her meeting—and she knows they would do so at once for Bacchus. Calonice, taking on the task of speaking to someone who is too angry to listen, reminds Lysistrata that "it is not so easy for a wife to get out of the house."[6]

The women come, and Lysistrata explains that if women will vow to give up sex until men vow to give up fighting, they should succeed in bringing about peace—in essence by substituting the mutual pleasures of sex for men's single-minded pursuit of violence.

The strategy is as follows: The women will do everything in their power to arouse the desire of their husbands and lovers, and then they will run out of their houses and lock themselves up in the Acropolis. The plan succeeds brilliantly in the theater. The Peloponnesian War, however, continues.

Virginia Woolf, in her darkly cautious and brilliantly far-reaching essay *Three Guineas,* asks: Is there a way in which women can help men prevent what has historically been the male act of war—the violence that, whatever its causes, leaves in its wake a litter of dead bodies and ruined houses? And she lays out a three-step passage for "the daughters of educated men," leading out of the private houses of their fathers and into the public world where they will form "a Society of Outsiders." The steps that Woolf sees as essential are university education and admission to the professions, so that women will gain what is to be their leverage: the power of independent opinion supported by independent income. Because women's experiences in living and women's relation to the tradition differ from men's, Woolf believes that women may succeed in "finding new words and creating new methods,"[7] and in this way may help men to break what otherwise is a vicious cycle of domination and violence.

The dangers inherent in this passage are what Woolf calls "adultery of the brain" and "brain-selling," or writing "what you do not want to write for the sake of money"—practices that are engendered by university education and professional training and that create and let loose upon the world "anaemic, vicious and diseased progeny."[8] And the deeply knotted dilemma that lies at the center of Woolf's vision and of women's psychological development is how can girls both enter and stay outside of, be educated in and then change, what has for centuries been a man's world? Yet, if "the public and the private worlds are inseparably connected, . . . [if] the tyrannies and servilities of the one are the tyrannies and servilities of the other,"[9] if we live in one world and cannot dissociate ourselves from one another, and if the psychology of fathers that has ruled the private house is writ large in society's legal codes and moral orders and supported by the ever-present threat of what is considered to be a legitimate use of force or violence, how can daughters be anywhere other than inside and outside of these structures?

Girls' doubling of voice and vision is a response to this situation—to being at once inside and outside of the world they are entering as young women. And this dizzying ability to see and to speak in two ways also enables girls to resist the pressures and the temptations they face simply to fit themselves into the world in which they are living by taking on a male perspective. This taking-on of an androcentric point of view is the central lesson girls coming of age are taught by more or less well-meaning men and women both at home and at school as well as through the various media for transmitting cultural norms and values; and if girls learn to make what seems a simple correction—like the algebraic corrections that they are learning in school, or geometric corrections, or "foreign languages," then they can tune their voices and align their visions with androcentric cultural traditions and enter without changing what has been called "the human conversation." Once this correction is made, however, the cultural framework becomes invisible, and then, as one wise twelve-year-old girl observed, "you don't have to think."

RESISTANCE

Five psychological truths:

1. What is unvoiced or unspoken, because it is out of relationship, tends to get out of persepctive and to dominate psychic life.
2. The hallmarks of loss are idealization and rage, and under the rage, immense sadness. ("To want and want and not to have.")[10]
3. What is dissociated or repressed—known and then not known—tends to return, and return, and return.
4. The logic of the psyche is an associative logic—the free-falling logic of dreams, poetry, and memory—as well as a formal logic of classification and control.
5. One learns the answers to one's own questions.

Anna at twelve, tall, thin, her dark hair cut short, her green eyes looking steadily out of a quiet and somewhat wary face, raises the question: How can you tell if what people are saying is true, "if what they are saying about you, if they really mean it, or if they are just doing it to be mean, and it's hard to tell, I mean, with a lot of people you can't tell how they are." What she is trying to understand is the difference between the surface banter of teasing, making fun, putting people down that went on among her friends (although she does not know if they are really her friends) at the public school she went to, and being mean, "really mean," or cruel. At her new school—a girls' school, Anna notices that everyone is "nice," and she feels good about herself when she is "nice to people or . . . not being mean," and bad about herself when she is mean or hurts people, but "sometimes you just can't help it." Anna feels that people can tell how she feels, even when "inside I'm really sad about something but outside I'm trying to be happy," because "if you're feeling sad, you just can't make yourself happy."[11]

Malka writes about the disparity between inside and outside after the outing club's trip to Plum Island—a beach and bird sanctuary on Boston's north shore:

> A sand castle, life on a small scale. Kingdoms rise and fall, water ebbs in and out. Water rises, in and out. Channels, pools, castles, forests. The outside view. But on the inside—are babies being born? Are children playing? Are crafts being learned? Are people being married? Are battles being fought? Are people dying? Love, fun, smiling, and crying. Life. A sand castle.

At the edge of adolescence, girls draw attention to the disparity between an insider's view of life, which they are privy to in childhood, and an outside view, intimating that the insider's knowledge is in danger of being washed out or giving way. The connection between inside and outside becomes explicitly a focus of attention when girls reach adolescence and become subjected to a kind of voice and ear training, designed to make it clear what voices people like to listen to in girls and what girls can say without being called, in today's vernacular, "stupid," or "rude." On a daily basis, girls receive lessons on what they can let out and what they must keep in, if they do not want to be spoken about by others as mad or bad, or simply told they are wrong. Anna, dealing with this problem of containment, says that she would like to be "just a better person or have better ways of thinking" and explains:

> Sometimes I will get really mad, and I can outburst or something, and I can't be like that . . . I have to learn how to work with people, because sometimes I just get really mad at people who can't understand what I am saying, and I get so exasperated. It is like, "Why can't you just . . . ? What's wrong with you? Why can't you see this my way?" And I have to really go for what I want though. I can't let this stuff take over me. And I have to, you kind of have to fight to get what you want.

In essence, Anna states the problem of resistance as a problem of relationship. She feels pressure to hold herself in, "not to be like that . . . [not

to] get really mad," or, even worse, "outburst." At the same time, she realizes she must not let go of what she wants, that "I can't let this stuff take
over me." One resistance is psychological and will lead Anna to take herself
out of relationship, not to fight for what she wants but to become "nice" and,
as she now views it, "successful." The other resistance is political, and, by
staying in relationship, Anna will come into conflict with others.

Anna struggles between these two forms of resistance at the age of
twelve. With her mother, she experiences the central dilemma of relationship:
how to speak honestly and also stay in connection with others. When they go
shopping for clothes, Anna explains,

> She will pull something out and she'll say, "Well, what do you think of it?"
> And then if I say I don't like it, then she'll get really mad, and she'll put it
> back. . . . And then, she'll forget about what happens when I really give her
> my opinion, and then she'll say, "Tell me what you really think about it."
> And then she gets mad when I tell her. . . . And I'll say, "Well, you don't
> really want it because you already screamed at me when I gave it."

Eleven-year-old Tessie articulates the importance of voicing conflicts in
relationships, explaining why it is necessary to "tell someone about it" so
that you are "telling it from both sides" and can "*hear* the [other] person's
point of view."

> When you are having an argument . . . and you just keep it inside you and
> don't tell anyone, you never hear the person's point of view. And if you are
> telling someone about it, you are telling it from both sides and so you hear
> what my mother said, or what my brother said. And the other person can
> say, well, you might be mad, but your mom was right, and you say, yeah,
> I know. So when you say it out loud, you have to listen.

Tessie also observes that fighting—by which she means verbal conflict or
voicing disagreement—is good for relationships: "Fighting is what makes relationships go on," in the face of trouble, and "the more fights you get in and
the more it goes on . . . the stronger it gets because the more you can talk
with that person." The subtlety of Tessie's understanding of how people
come to know one another and what kind of knowledge is necessary if friends
are not to hurt one another's feelings is evident as she explains that it is
through fighting, rather than "just saying 'I'm sorry' to them," that you
learn "how that person feels," and then you know how "not to hurt their
feelings." Yet fights also carry with them the danger of not speaking, and
"then you seem to grow apart."[12]

I emphasize this detailed, specific psychological knowledge based on
careful listening and sustained observation and characterized by finely

wrought distinctions—a naturalist's rendering of the human world—because girls' knowledge, when brought into the public world, is often dismissed as trivial or seen as transgressive, with the result that girls are told repeatedly not to speak, not to say anything, or at least not to talk in public about what they know.

Asked at twelve whether she has changed as a learner, Anna explains that she has come to think about things that she never thought about before, meaning the origins of things, which formerly she just took for granted because "you just kind of trusted the teacher," like 2 + 2 = 4, or the letters of the alphabet. "You don't sit there and say, 'A—what a dumb letter.' You don't think about it."

Now, thinking about thinking and about different ways people "look at something," Anna says you might think someone is "crazy," but, struggling with the problem of difference—the problem of relationship and also of relativism—"that is their opinion . . . as long as it's not going to hurt anybody." As a scholarship student in a private school, she is acutely aware of difference and wonders about how she fits into this world where "it's just friendly and everything is nice. It is really nice, I think," and where to her delight she is encouraged to speak—for Anna, an irresistible invitation. "Most of the time," Anna concludes at twelve, "I'm in a pretty good mood, and sometimes I'm not. Sometimes I am mad at the world."

When Anna is interviewed at age thirteen, as an eighth grader, her interview is peppered with "I don't know" (spoken now over three times as often as the previous year, increasing from twenty-one times at age twelve to sixty-seven at age thirteen, with no corresponding increase in the length of the interview transcript). Anna is struggling explicitly with a reluctance to know what she knows and an inclination to suppress her knowledge and go along with the group. Asked about whether she has work that she loves, this child who loves learning and loves school says, "Reading and singing . . . and I can just sort of get lost in them and not have to think about things." Talking about herself as a knower, she observes that "you can interpret things differently" and describes the way thoughts and feelings cascade differently from different beginnings, so that depending on where you start from—for example, in reading a poem—you arrive at different end points.

But now conformity has a hold on Anna as she begins to feel like a member of her new school, not only a top student but also a part of her class. She watches others to see which way to go and does not, she says, "massively disagree on anything." With friends, if she disagreed, she would be "kind of mad at myself, have kind of a messed up feeling." With adults, "they would overpower me most of the time." Anna is learning to bring herself into line with the world around her, to bring herself into agreement with others so as not to mess up relationships with friends or experience the helplessness of being overpowered by adults. Paradoxically, for the sake of relationship and also for protection, she is disconnecting her self from others.

At fourteen, in ninth grade, Anna bursts out, becoming outspoken and drawing the interviewer's attention to the change she hears in her voice: "I used to be really quiet and shy and everything, and now I am really loud." Again, the phrase "I don't know" has increased, doubling from 67 to 135,[13] but now it punctuates a tale of resistance that is clearly political: an insistence on knowing what she knows and writing the paper she wants to write, even though she knows it will make her English teacher angry. "I see things from a lot of points of view," Anna explains, and calling her ability to see from different viewpoints "creative" now rather than "crazy," she tells the following story.

The class was asked to write a hero legend, and Anna did not see the hero in the same way as her teacher: "There was a ladeedah hero who went and saved all humankind." Anna explains,

> If you see this hero from a different viewpoint, from a different standpoint, everyone could be a hero. So I wanted to write it from a Nazi standpoint, like Hitler as hero, and she really did not go for that at all. And I started to write, and she got really mad, and she was, like, I am afraid you are going to come out sounding like a little Nazi.

Anna's solution was to write two papers, two versions of the hero legend: "a ladeedah legend and the one I wanted to write." She turned both papers in to her teacher along with a letter explaining her reasons. "She gave me an A on the normal one. I gave her the other one because I just had to write it. It sort of made me mad."

Anna wrote about Hitler "from the point of view of a little boy who was joining one of those groups that they had, and he was so proud to have a uniform and he went to try to salute. . . . It did not come out about Hitler as much as about the reasons for Hitler,"—which interested Anna, who was part German and whose father had been unemployed. In addition, Anna has seen, by watching her father and her brothers' easy resort to what she calls "brute force" in the face of frustration, how the need to appear strong or heroic can cover over vulnerability and lead to violence. To Anna, the hero legend is an understandable but dangerous legend.

In choosing to disagree openly with her teacher and, in Woolf's terms, not to sell her writing or commit adultery of the brain, Anna said she was "just really mad" and that her teacher "was just narrow-minded" in her insistence that Hitler was an "anti-hero" rather than a hero.

"It was an urge," Anna says ". . . . I had to write that paper because I was so mad. . . . I had to write it to explain it to her, you know; I just had to. . . . I just had to make her understand."

This urgent need to "make her understand," the overwhelming desire for human connection—to bring one's own inner world of thoughts and feelings into relationship with the thoughts and feelings of others—feels very pressing to girls who fight for authentic relationships and who resist being shut up, put down, turned away, ignored. Anna's friend went to talk with the teacher on Anna's behalf, and her mother encouraged her to write the paper but to do so in a way that would not antagonize the teacher. In the end, Anna concludes that her teacher "probably saw it as more annoying than anything else." What she learned from this experience, she said, "was not to antagonize people," her mother's caution. In fact, she was able to both speak and not antagonize people—in part, she suspects, because she had not been heard, because her teacher did not understand, but also because her teacher, however annoyed, was willing to listen and read both papers.

Anna at fourteen sees the framework of the worlds she lives in. Painfully, she has become aware of the inconsistencies in the school's position on economic differences—where money is available and where it isn't, the limits of the meritocracy that is espoused. And seeing inconsistencies, she becomes riveted by the disparity between the names of things and the realities and plays with the provocation of being literal in an effort to call things by their right names.

At fifteen, Anna begins to ask some literal questions about the order that is taken to be unquestionable in the world she lives in—questions about religion and about violence. And she discovers that her questions are often not welcomed and her opinions met with silence; in the midst of an intensely controversial classroom conversation, she notices that "there were a bunch of people who just sat there like stones and listened."

Anne Frank, in one of the suppressed diary entries, comments on the silences that surround the subject of sex. On 18 March 1944, at the age of fourteen, she writes:

> Parents and people in general are very strange when it comes to [sexual matters]. Instead of telling their daughters as well as their sons everything when they are 12 years old, they send the children out of the room during such conversations and leave them to find things out for themselves. If the parents notice later on that the children have learned things anyway, then they assume that the children know either more or less than they actually do. . . . Grownups do come up against an important obstacle, although I'm sure the obstacle is no more than a very small barrier, they believe that children will stop looking on marriage as something sacred and pure when it dawns on them that in most cases the purity is nothing more than eyewash.[14]

What puzzles Anna is the reluctance of people to speak about cruelty and violence. Like Anne Frank, she notes the readiness of adults to cover over what they do not want children to look at—so that children, especially as they reach adolescence, are encouraged, tacitly, not to know what they see or not to listen to what they hear, or to see everything as "nice." And yet Anna is also bothered by her mother's refusal to wash over the realities of her life and confused by what she is taking in—in part because of the disparity between what women are saying in the two worlds that she lives in.

The acuity of Anna's perception is striking, and her description of life in her family is almost identical to Glen Elder and Avshalom Caspi's depiction of families living under economic hardship, where fathers are unemployed and emotionally volatile, and where mothers and daughters bond. Anna's family constellation (herself and younger brothers) matches the picture for maximal psychological risk in children, given the consistent finding that when families are under stress, the children who are most psychologically in danger are boys in early childhood and girls at adolescence.[15] Anna's relationship with her mother thus seems critical to Anna's resilience. Her closeness with her mother and the openness of their conversation is sometimes painful. Anna feels her mother's feelings "gnawing at" her. And it is sometimes confusing for Anna to know how her mother thinks and feels. She realizes that her mother's is "only one viewpoint," and she does not "know how much of it is dramatized." And yet, she "can see that a lot of what my Mom says is true."

"You can't see someone like my Dad," she says, as an eleventh grader in the fifth year of the study, returning to a question she introduced at the start, "without realizing how easily people are taken in." At school, she has "gotten a glimpse" behind the scenes and seen women whom she saw as nice and compassionate "give away their color," after which, she astutely observes, "all you can see is that part." "It is awful," she says, despairing at the capacity of people to cover over reality, the chameleon-like way her father changes his voice when,

> in the midst of screaming and yelling and ranting and raving at everyone in our house, the phone rings: "Hello"—like that. And it is really awful. Everyone thinks he is the strongest person, and when you see the other side you just get so annoyed when people do that.

"I could," Anna muses, "probably give *the* best senior speech in the world in terms of shocking people, but people just don't, you know, it is so different, because there is just no one," she says with adolescent fervor, "no one who has to deal with anywhere near the same thing [as I do]." The violent outbursts of her father toward her brothers have brought social service agencies to the house; her brother's violence toward her mother has brought the police. Because of the social class difference, Anna may think that hers is the only family (in her school) where violence happens. And yet, she concludes, "Pollyanna"—that epitome of the nice girl—"would have problems. . . . Thinking that life is peaches and cream is not realistic. It's not real. . . . It really grates on you when you have someone around you that is like Pollyanna . . . that is really scary, you know; you can't deal with someone like that." The niceness that governs and sustains the school that she goes to cannot admit the world that she knows from experience—and Anna knows it. They are, she says, "totally different outlooks on life."

In the real world, Anna begins, "I have a bunch of friends that I talk to and, you know, they understand and everything, but it is not very many people. This school," she concludes, "is not the real world." Anna, who loves school, wants to take everything that there is to take, to know everything she can know about the world—to know Chinese and Latin as well as French and English. She does not know how to imagine her future: whether she will enter the world that the people in her school think of as "normal"—the world that is reflected in the norms—or whether she will join Woolf's Outsiders' Society and, armed with an independent income to support her independent opinions,

> will be one of those people who go through college and get a Ph.D. and I'll live at the bottom of a mountain in Montana. Just one of those weird people. Have a chicken farm. I don't know. Then I will just write books or something,

remaining, as Woolf envisioned, "outside (and) experiment[ing] not with public means in public but with private means in private."[16]

PSYCHOLOGY AND POLITICS: PERFECT GIRLS AND DISSIDENTS

"The anxious bird," Jorie Graham writes in her poem, "The Age of Reason,"

> . . . in the wild
> spring green
> is *anting*, which means,
> in my orchard
> he has opened his wings
> over a furious
>
> anthill and will take up
> into the delicate

ridges of quince-yellow
feathers
a number of tiny, angry
creatures

that will inhabit him, bewildered
no doubt,
travelling deep
into the air
on this feathery planet
new life . . .

We don't know why
they do it.
At times they'll take on
almost anything
that burns, spreading
their wings

over coals, over cigarette
butts,
even, mistakenly, on bits
of broken glass.
Meanwhile the light keeps
stroking them

as if it were love.

The poem is an inquiry about love. Love means opening; it means taking in. And Graham asks the question: What, in the name of love, is taken in? The world of nature, with its ever-present reminder of death—"The garden / continues its work / all round them, the gradual / openings that stand / for death." And the world humans cultivate, the stories that grow in the hothouse of culture: "Under the plastic / groundcover the human / garden grows: help-sticks / and knots, row / after row. Who wouldn't want / to take / into the self / something that burns / or cuts, or wanders / lost / over the body?"

Who would, or wouldn't, in the name of love, take in films like Werner Herzog's *Woyzek,* where

the hero whom
we love
who is mad has
murdered

the world, the young
woman
who is his wife,
and loved her,
and covered himself
with blood,

he grows frightened
by how quickly
she softens and takes on the shape
of the soil.

The emphasized lines, the short lines of this poem, in their staccato insistence telling, flashing, a warning to women, like Emilia in the brothel scene of *Othello* desperately trying to tell Desdemona before it is too late what she needs to know about what Othello is thinking, and feeling, Graham's words capturing the essence of that warning, like nautical flags flying or newspaper headlines: *murdered / woman / and loved her/ with blood.* How often, how far, do we take this truth in? How do philosophers reason about this, what are reasonable answers to the poet's questions: "How far is true / enough? / How far into the earth / can vision go and / still be / love?"[17]

When eleven-year-old Tessie is asked, at the end of November, what stays with her in looking back over the past year, she says, "The summer, things that we do in the summer . . . like the sailing that we do and all the fun that I had going swimming and doing different things." Asked how she would describe herself to herself, Tessie says simply, "I like myself." Pleasure runs through Tessie's life like water flowing, swirling around her friends in the summer, her fights with her brother, swimming, reading, writing stories, her closeness with her mother, her special relationship with her father, who "always wanted a daughter," her confidence and pleasure—in taking care of children, in throwing sawdust on a classmate who has made her angry, in deciding it was worth it to get into trouble, in helping people with difficult things or problems, in meeting new people, "that's fun, you get to know more people as you go on."

But Tessie also has taken in, in the name of love, an image of perfection, exemplified by her grandmother, the person she admires:

She is *always* smiling and *always* laughing. She's *always* doing something helpful. I don't know. She goes to a nursing home, and she writes letters for people who can't write letters. . . . She *always* has things made and *always* has little things for little kids. . . . She makes big terrariums and everything that she sells at the Church fair, and she enjoys what she is doing, she loves

her grandchildren and her children. And she seems to be an *always* happy
person and *always* willing to help you and everything. (emphasis added)

The repeated word, *always,* catches the stillness at the center of this frozen
image; Tessie's free-flowing world has suddenly stopped.

Ellen, at eleven, asked whether there is someone whom she admires, describes a variant of this image—a perfect girl who seems an offshoot of the
always good woman, and the repeated word *really* in her description suggests
that Ellen may question whether what she is seeing is real.

there is this girl in our class who is perfect. . . . She's *really* tall, tall, *not
really* tall, she's tall, and is pretty and she's good at everything. You could
say something, and she could do it perfectly. And she's smart, and she is
good at any sport, and she's good at art, and she's good at everything. She's
like a person I know, like my mother's friend in college. She's good at everything. There is not one thing she cannot do. She's *really* nice and . . .
she's *always* being herself.

Claudia, the astute nine-year-old narrator of Toni Morrison's novel *The
Bluest Eye,* sums up "this disrupter of seasons," the girl who enters the late
elementary school classroom and "enchanted the entire school."[18]

The familiarity of this girl, her regular appearance at the edge of adolescence in girls' lives and in women's novels, signals a shift in the cultural
framework that is key to the psychology and politics of girls' adolescence.
Suddenly girls feel the presence of a standard that does not come out of their
experience and an image that, because embodied, calls into question the reality that they have lived in—the moving, changing world of thoughts and
feelings, relationships and people. Feeling the mesmerizing presence of the
perfect girl, girls have entered the world of the hero legend and experience
the imposition of a framework that seemingly comes out of nowhere—a
worldview superimposed on girls but grounded in the psychology of men.
With the arrival of the perfect girl, who exemplifies the incredible, girls are
in danger of losing their world. But they are also in danger, in the world of
the hero legend, if they continue to know what they know, and especially if
they say it in public. What once seemed ordinary to girls—speaking, difference, anger, conflict, fighting, bad as well as good thoughts and feelings,
now seems treacherous: laced with danger, a sign of imperfection, a harbinger
of being left out, not chosen.

Like the hero or the superheroes of boys' early childhood, the perfect girl
of girls' early adolescence is an emblem of loss—signifying an idealization
that replaces relationship, covering over a rage that is unspeakable and a sadness that seems endless, and thus marking an inner division or psychic

chasm: a taking of the self out of relationship in the name of love. This is the move enacted by the hand that censored Anne Frank's diary, removing her slightly from the reader (especially the puritanical American reader), imposing a kind of innocence or psychological virginity, so that she—who knew so much—would appear more perfect or more acceptable or more protected in the eyes of the world by seeming to know less than she knew. The evidence covered over reveals the extent of Anne's connection with her body, with desire, with her mother, and with the world she lived in—a world that contained both the story of Woyzeck and the Nazis. Living in the midst of real terror, she had not lost her world.

If girls' knowledge of reality is politically dangerous, it is both psychologically and politically dangerous for girls not to know what is going on—or to render themselves innocent by disconnecting themselves from their bodies, that repository of experience and desire, and thus, in essence, disassociating themselves from themselves, from relationships and from what they know about the world. Because girls are encouraged to make this disconnection at the time of their adolescence, girls' dissent at this time becomes psychologically essential, and potentially healing for boys as well. And yet at adolescence, girls' knowledge and girls' passion are bound to make trouble in the world girls are entering.

When Rosie is interviewed at age fourteen, her vitality is infectious. She speaks openly in the privacy of the interview setting about desire as sexual—in somewhat the same tentative yet resolute manner that Anne Frank describes in preparing to speak about her body ("When the subject [of what a naked girl looks like] comes up again," she says to herself in her diary, "how in heaven's name will you be able to explain what things are like [down there] without using examples? Shall I try it out here in the meantime? Well then get on with it!").[19] Rosie's pleasure in her body and her exuberance at age fourteen are unmistakable. At the same time, she is in trouble at school for her outspokenness, her irreverence, and her refusal, despite her evident brightness, to be the perfect student.

At fifteen, when Rosie and her boyfriend are caught having sex together, Rosie felt embarrassed and scared about what was going to happen to her, and also worried about disillusioning her professionally successful and ambitious Latina mother, who "had this image of me . . . as close to the perfect child." Asked to describe this perfect child, she says, without hesitation: "She gets straight As and has a social life, but still gets home exactly on the dot, on time, and does everything her parents say, and keeps her room neat." I ask Rosie: "Are there girls like this?" She says, "Perhaps; saints." "Do saints have sex?" I wonder aloud, thinking of Rosie. "I don't know," she begins, and then fills in her solution: "If they want, as long as they don't get caught; as long as nobody knows."

Once her mother knew, Rosie "hunted her down and . . . made her talk to me. And it wasn't like a battle or anything. . . . I just wanted to talk to her and see what she had to say." Like Anna, who wants to connect her own with her teacher's view of the hero, by "making her understand," Rosie wants to discover what connections are possible between herself and her mother, what her mother is willing to say.

Rosie's clarity, her playfulness, her irreverence in refusing to disembody saints, and her courage in staying in her own body, coexist with confusion about the world she lives in. Despite her efforts, she cannot find the emotional center—the place where desire or passion or pleasure live in her mother's busy life. From her mother, she takes in the caution that she must be more careful about her body, more attentive to the warning signals and the flags of danger. Perhaps the seemingly disembodied perfect girl whom her mother and teachers envision she could be really exists and is admirable, exemplifying the way Rosie should live in order to take care of herself in a world where imperfection often means rejection and where, more darkly, sex can be fatal, love can mean murder, and fighting can mean violence.

At the end of *Oedipus Rex,* that psychological telling of the hero legend, after the truth about family relations has been uncovered (that Oedipus has unwittingly murdered his father and married his mother, and that it was his mother who [cannily, uncannily?] game him away to the herdsman), Oedipus blinds himself, Jocasta strangles herself, their sons run off to become kings and war against one another, and their daughters are summoned to accompany their father in his blindness. A quick scanning of Sophocles' *tableau vivant* of life in the patriarchal family suggests that the wounds that fathers suffer in early childhood infect their daughters in adolescence. Yet in a play that is filled with riddles and questions—where the chorus asks about Jocasta's silence ("How could the Queen whom Lauis won, / Be silent when that deed was done?"),[20] no one asks on behalf of the daughters: Why did Oedipus blind himself?

WOMEN TEACHING GIRLS

It is September, and the sky over New England is Fra Angelico blue. Lyn Brown and I are flying to Cleveland, to talk with the Laurel School teachers about our research with the girls they are teaching. It is the beginning of the second year of the project, and the library fills as we enter, the faculty sitting in short rows crossing the room with a long aisle running down the center. School—the microcosm in children's lives of the public world, the public space that Hannah Arendt sees as the crux of democracy, the place where the natality and plurality, the ever new and always different nature of the human condition can flourish.

The school is governed by an honor code, which is working well, according to the school's recent evaluation, maintaining an order of living where people can bring themselves and leave their things in safety. In the privacy of the research interview, girls spoke about the honor code from a different angle, describing dilemmas of relationship that arose in the wake of honor code violations; how, they wondered, could they stay in connection with themselves and also be in connection with others? Since there seemed no way to speak about these problems of relationship in the public arena, many girls had publicly agreed to an honor code that they did not believe in.[21] And, taking matters of public governance into their own hands, girls took them into a private world of relationships and settled them in private places, drawing on that psychological knowledge—that intricate physics of relationship—that girls learn by keeping an eye on the human weather and following the constant play of relationships, thoughts, feelings, and actions as it moves across the sky of the day.

This girls' school, like a perfectly run household, was being governed as if effortlessly. In fact, it was being run by an underground society of girls whose knowledge and activities on behalf of the school were for the most part unseen and unnamed. I say: "If we want to educate girls who as women will participate fully as citizens in a democratic state, then it would seem beneficial to name girls' activities which are sustaining the school's public welfare and also to encourage girls to treat matters of public governance as political questions and to deal publicly with their differences and their disagreement."

To my right, in front, a women—small bones, white hair, intense face concentrating energy as her thoughts and feelings connect with sound and come out into the air of the room on her voice—says: "How can we help girls learn to deal with disagreement in public, when we"—she looked across the rows, quickly scanning faces of her colleagues, women and men—"when we," meaning now women, "cannot deal with disagreement in public ourselves?"

Silence washed the room. The research was uncovering the underground. Girls' voices, recorded in private and amplified in the public space of the school, were resonating with women teachers, encouraging women to ask: What were they teaching girls about relationships, about speaking, about conflict, about difference, about political and psychological resistance?

Two questions about relationship clarified a woman's position: Where am I in relation to the tradition that I am practicing and teaching? and Where am I in relation to girls, the next generation of women? Are women vessels through which the culture passes? Are women oracles of the disciplines, conveying, like the oracle of Apollo—the priestess who voiced the wisdom of the Delphic oracle—the wisdom of male gods? Provocative questions, but it is the relationship between girls and women that proves to be transformative, and most specifically, the relationship of women to girls at the edge of adolescence.

Education is the time-honored, nonviolent means of social change, the alternative to revolution. And education at present in this country is largely in the hands of women, who, as mothers, teachers, and therapists, are directly in contact with people's desires for relationships and for knowledge, and also in touch with the resistance. Perhaps women are currently in a position to constitute an Outsiders' Society.

The old question stirs: What if women . . . irrepressible question! Half the population in every generation. Could women, as Madeline Grumet envisions, turn the practice of teaching—a relational practice par excellence—from "women's work" into "the work of women," so that instead of leading what Grumet calls "the great escape" from the daily rhythms of the maternal order to the clock time of the paternal state,[22] women would institute a new order (using private means in private, as Woolf would have it) by teaching a different knowledge and creating a different practice of human relationships?

At the beginning of the second act of *Lysistrata*, Lysistrata despairs; the women are leaving the Acropolis and rushing home to their husbands. "I know you miss your husbands," she says, "but don't you realize that they miss you as well? . . . Be strong sisters," she enjoins the women. "There is an oracle that we will triumph if only we don't fall out among ourselves."[23]

Sara Ruddick heals what is a major division both within and among women—the division between mother and resister—by defining a women's politics of resistance that is relationally rather than heroically conceived. This practice of resistance is rooted in the body (its vulnerability, its promise, its power) and is a practice of "preservative love." Taking her cue from the Madres of Argentina and the women of Chile, Ruddick describes a resistance to loss that takes its imperative from the singularity of human being and the irreplaceability of human relationships, rather than from claims to immortality or superhuman strength. If only women would make a shift within their existing practice as mothers, separating out those elements that support militarism (the worshipping of martyrs and heros) from those that subvert it (women's irreverent language of loyalty, love, and outrage), women could move readily, Ruddick suspects, "from denial to truthfulness, from parochialism to solidarity, from inauthenticity to active responsibility."[24] In short, women could move from psychological to political resistance.

Central to this journey is a recovery of anger as the political emotion par excellence—the bellweather of oppression, injustice, bad treatment; the clue that something is wrong in the relational surround (a fin on the horizon, a sudden darkening, a bad shadow). Teresa Bernardez, writing about women and anger from the two-culture vantage point of an Argentinean born, North American psychotherapist, reminds her reader that cultural injunctions against anger in women turn into psychological inhibitions that "prevent rebellious acts," with the result that women come to feel complicit in their own misery. The process of psychotherapy then involves a kind of reverse alchemy whereby anger that has soured into bitterness and hatred becomes once again simply anger—"the conscious response to an awareness of injustices suffered or losses and grievances sustained . . . [the anger] which involves self-love and awareness of the responsibility of making choices."[25] Like eleven-year-old Sarah's anger, which lives in the daylight of her relationships, or Tessie's anger, which sits comfortably side-by-side with self-love. Bernardez notes that when people are living under conditions of political oppression or terror, they often come not to know what they know and "have forgotten what they have forgotten." She also observes that anger silenced "contributes to the making of depression." And depression in women tends to begin at adolescence.

Perhaps women have forgotten girls. And not remembered this disconnection at adolescence. So that relationships between adolescent girls and women hold a key to the psychology and the politics of women's resistance.

When Anjli brought her paper on "To His Coy Mistress" to her English teacher, Mrs. Franklin, Nancy Franklin realized that she was hearing the poem in a way she had not heard it before—very differently from the way she had learned to listen in the course of her graduate training. Anjli had been asked to analyze the poem for tone; she was taking an advanced class taught simultaneously at several schools in the area. Nancy Franklin was one of the women pursuing the question: What does it mean to be a woman teaching girls, and it is to this group of women, in their year of their meeting, that she speaks about Anjli's paper and her decision to join Anjli's resistance.

Anjli, in the midst of writing her analysis—listening to the tone of the poem in her house late at night—suddenly begins writing in the first person as she takes in what she is hearing: the voice of an older man bent on overcoming a young woman's resistance ("Had we but world enough, and time, / This coyness, Lady, were no crime"). And Nancy Franklin, taking in Anjli's voice, feels the power of the poem anew and also the force of what Anjli is hearing. Anjli writes, her teacher recalls, "I am writing this paper and it is late at night, and I am terrified because this is such a morbid poem ("Thy beauty shall no more be found, / Nor, in thy marble vault, shall sound / My echoing song: then worms shall try / That long preserved virginity, / And your quaint honor turn to dust, / And into ashes all my lust."). This is such a frightening poem."

Anjli's paper was submitted to six teachers for cross-grading exercises, designed to insure consistency of standards. One woman, Franklin recalls, "actually wrote on the paper: 'She doesn't understand *carpe diem*. Why doesn't she know this term? This is not a college level paper.' " Another wrote, "She misreads Marvell's playfulness." And yet—Nancy Franklin

says, caught momentarily by the standards of her colleagues and then resisting their disconnection from Anjli and their dismissal of her reading—"this
paper was beautiful, And it made me see the poem in a new way." Sustaining
this connection, she draws out its implications for Anjli, for herself, and also
for society:

> This is a young girl; this is a seventeen-year-old, very innocent but very
> bright girl. Reading this, Lord knows, you go back and read that poem, at
> two o'clock in the morning. And she was terrified—the voice of an older
> man speaking to a young girl. And the comments she got on this paper. They
> all said: C−, you know, no good. "Doesn't know stanzaic patterns, missed
> all this playfulness, and *carpe diem, carpe diem.*" Now there's the educa-
> tional system at work. What did it tell her? Go underground; to survive, go
> underground, at least until you get out of this system. Or worse.[26]

Anjli read the graders' comments, discussed them with her teacher, remembered hearing about *carpe diem,* reread the poem, and, Nancy Franklin
writes, "found that indeed she could see the poem that way but more importantly, she could see it both ways." She knows that "she could rewrite the
paper now that she understands the way she was supposed to react saying
what she is supposed to say . . . 'If you were a guy,' she says, smiling, 'It
might be really funny.' " But Anjli also still cringes at the poem's morbid
images: "I don't think," she concludes, "a class full of girls could really
laugh at this."[27] What is puzzling, then, given Anjli's perspective, and also
potentially treacherous, is the position of the women graders; Anjli assumes
that she will be understood by girls, but she cannot assume such understanding from women.

At the intersection between political resistance and psychological resistance, at the time of adolescence, girls' psychological development becomes
indelibly political. If girls know what they know and bring themselves into
relationships, they will be in conflict with prevailing authorities. If girls do
not know what they know and take themselves out of relationship, they will
be in trouble with themselves. The ability of girls to tell it from both sides and
to see it both ways is not an illustration of relativism (the abandonment of an
absolute truth) but rather a demonstration of girls' understanding of relationship raised to a cultural level and a provisional solution to a difficult problem
of relationship: how to stay connected with themselves and with others, how
to keep in touch with themselves and with the world. As eleven-year-old
Tessie underscores the importance of voicing her argument with her mother,
so Anjli voices the disparity between how she reacts and how she is supposed
to react, what she says and what she is supposed to say, according to the authorities who correct and grade her. And Tessie's openness, at least in theory,
to her friend's hearing her mother's voice differently from the way she does,

corresponds to Anjli's generosity toward those who hear the poem differently: the guys and the graders. Women teaching girls, then, are faced with a series of intricate problems of relationship. Girls must learn the traditions that frame and structure the world they are entering, and they also must hold on to their own ways of hearing and seeing. How can women stay with girls and also teach cultural traditions? How can girls stay with women and also with themselves? What can women teach girls about living in a world that is still governed by men?

"What happens to girls when they get to that age?" Sharon Miller asks. A teacher of twelve-year-olds and the mother of a twelve-year-old daughter, she returns to what has been the riddle of female development—to Freud's question and the question posed by women therapists across the century: Why is it that girls, who seem "more intelligent and livelier than boys of the same age; [who] go out more to meet the external world and at the same time form stronger [connections with people]," seem to become less intelligent and less lively when they reach adolescence?[28] Freud observes that "the constitution will not adapt itself to its function without a struggle," and then goes on to talk about the function of women. Our research on girls' development has focused on elucidating the struggle, which is readily observed in girls at the time of adolescence.

Like girls in novels and poems written by women,[29] girls interviewed in contemporary school settings speak about taking themselves out of relationships as they approach adolescence: about "building a little shield," about "getting afraid to say when you're mad at somebody," about "losing confidence in myself. I was losing track of myself, really, and losing the kind of person I was."[30] Paradoxically, girls are taking themselves out of relationship for the sake of relationship and self-consciously letting go of themselves. This doubling of the psychological language augments the confusion girls experience at this time—the inability, in a way, to say what is happening, because the very words *self* and *relationship* have doubled in meaning, as if one psychology has been superimposed on another, causing girls to lose track of their own experience as they move into the larger world.[31] Lyn Brown, analyzing girls' narratives of relationships, notes that as girls approach adolescence they tend to withdraw authorization from their own experience and to replace realistic with inauthentic or idealized descriptions of relationships. Perhaps for this reason, girls who are developing well according to standard psychological measures and cultural yardsticks, are also

> engaging in difficult and sometimes painful personal battles around issues of voice and authorization, unsure of the accuracy of their own perceptions, afraid that speaking up will damage relationships or compromise their image in the eyes of others . . . showing signs of an impasse in their ability to act in the face of conflict.[32]

What happens to girls when they reach this age? "I think," Sharon Miller says, "they have let go of themselves. I think it is the unusual middle school girl who can say . . . if you don't like me the way I am, fine. Most girls can't say that because there is no one there." Why not? I ask her. I am thinking of the girls who are so resolute, so present at eleven. "Well, that's the question, you know; what happens to girls when they get to that age? Well, because that is the age when girls start identifying with adult women." And then, suddenly, seeing the circle closing, she says, hand rising, covering her mouth, "My God," as tears begin flowing, "And there is nothing there."[33]

Like a film running backward, women teaching girls arrive at the moments of their own resistance and come up against their own solutions to the problems of relationship that girls face. Then women may encounter their own reluctance to know what they know and come to the realization that such knowledge is contained in their body; and may discover that they have succumbed to the temptation to model perfection by trying to be perfect role models for girls and thus have taken themselves out of relationship with girls—in part to hide their imperfection, but also perhaps to keep girls from feeling their sadness and their anger. Women teaching girls, however, also may discover that they are harboring, within themselves, a girl who lives in her body, who is insistent on speaking, who intensely desires relationships and knowledge, and who, perhaps at the time of adolescence, went underground or was overwhelmed. It may be that adolescent girls are looking for this girl in women, and feeling her absence or her hidden presence. And it may be that women, in the name of being good women, have been modeling for girls her repudiation—teaching girls the necessity of a loss or renunciation, which girls question.

Perhaps there is a new cycle that, once beginning, will break up an old impasse in women's development and affect men as well. If women and girls can stay with one another at the time when girls reach adolescence, girls' playfulness and irreverence may tap the wellsprings of women's resistance. And women in turn, taking in girls' embodiment, their outspokenness and their courage, may encourage girls' desire for relationship and for knowledge and teach girls that they can say what they know and not be left all alone.

CODA

"Dear Kitty," Anne Frank writes on 6 January 1944, at the age of fourteen, in a passage from her diary that her father edited—in exactly the manner she predicts in the passage:

I have three things to confess to you today. . . . I *must* tell someone, and you are the best to tell, as I know that come what may you always keep a secret. . . . You know that I've grumbled a lot about Mummy, yet still tried to be nice to her again. Now it is suddenly clear to me what she lacks. Mummy herself has told us that she looked upon us more as her friends than her daughters; now that is all very fine of course, but still a friend can't take a mother's place. *I need my mother as an example which I can follow, I want to be able to respect her and though my mother is an example to me in most things she is precisely the kind of example that I do not want to follow.* I have the feeling that Margot thinks differently about these things and would never be able to understand what I've just told you. And Daddy avoids all arguments about Mummy.[34] (deleted passage is italicized)

"One Conclusion," Emma writes, beginning a new page in her journal,

One of the conclusions I come to is that many/most of the paintings/statues/ artwork of women I have seen is of women naked. A lot of the art of women that I saw was done by men. Maybe because the women posed. None of the girls I saw were naked. Maybe because artists like to have people pose naked, and they think women are better because they have more growth.

One question, Malka writes at the end of her second conversation with the Queen of Babylon, "Did these people, places, painted, sculpted, did they live? Did they live in the heart of the painter, sculptor?"

"Wouldn't there have been," Anna says irreverently—she has just finished writing a paper about the church and Galileo—"Wouldn't there have been a lot of animal stuff on Noah's ark after forty days?"

"I think I am trying," Rosie says, "to attach value to things. This is important. This is not important. Maybe order things more." What do you order them to, I ask, wondering what key she is tuning to, what standard she has in mind. And Rosie, the embodied saint, the underground woman, suddenly turns philosophical:

I don't know . . . but I guess I know that there should be an order, and I was trying to decide what that order was. Maybe that is part of what I am looking for . . . is an order to my life. This getting deep, philosophical.

I am listening to girls' questions—following girls' inquiry into relationships as it becomes more philosophical, more critical, and also more psychologically and politically dangerous. Emma's curiosity is edging toward men's feelings about women's bodies; Malka begins to trace the channels connecting men's hearts with cultural icons. If this inquiry continues, girls will find the line that connects the personal and the political, the line between the psychology of men and the cultural framework, and wonder how they fit in.

"I don't know," Rosie says, Socrates' plaint. "I guess I know," she follows, in rapid succession. She is observing how her mother spends her life, her time, asking in effect the same question that Malka asks the Queen of Babylon: "What are you doing?" And seeing what her mother has to say—whether her mother might come up with the Queen's funny answer: "Brushing my hair. I was interrupted this morning by news of a revolt," the answer that captures the doubling of women's lives and also speaks to girls' questions about what gives women pleasure and what women value and also about what power women have.

Rosie, the sharp-eyed adolescent, notices that her mother's "small study and bedroom are messy." She will have to create her own order of living, find some way to orchestrate her life. "I don't know . . . I know . . . you know . . . do you know? . . ." voices of the underground, speaking under the sign of repression, marking dissociations that are still tenuous, knowledge that is fragile, reaching out for connections that can sustain the promise that a secret underground one day will become a public resistance. Then a healthy resistance that is evident in girls at adolescence, rather than turning inward and becoming psychologically corrosive, can stay in the open air of relationships. And by remaining political, work to bring a new order of living into the world.

LINDA K. CHRISTIAN-SMITH

Chapter Eight

Voices of Resistance: Young Women Readers of Romance Fiction

I had made up my mind long before I reached the front door: if I had to give up swimming or Mark, I'd give up swimming any day.
                   —Janet Quin-Harkin, *California Girl*

It's just when you're reading you're in some other world, well, not really, physically, I mean, but you imagine you are. Sometimes I feel like I am the person going on dates, having loads of fun.
                   —Annie, a twelve-year-old white
                   middle-class romance fiction reader

Guys should be treatin' you good like in the books. Not bossin' you 'round and tryin' to hit on you all the time.
                   —Marge, a fourteen-year-old black
                   working-class romance reader

When Annie, Marge, and other young women read teen romance novels similar to Quin-Harkin's *California Girl*, they become parts of a fictional world where men give meaning and completeness to women's lives and women's

169

destinies are to tend heart and hearth. If this sounds somewhat anachronistic in these times of women's supposed independence and parity with men, one needs only to recall these late-twentieth-century truisms. Most women still earn less than men, many women clock in from nine to nine between paid work and housework, and marriage and baby carriage are still the social experiences having the most currency for women.[1] The past ten years of the Reagan and Bush administrations have done much to perpetuate conventional gender sentiments through their profamily policies and endorsement of traditional views of women associated with the New Right.[2] George Bush's veto of the 1990 Civil Rights Bill and his economic policies advantaging the rich continue the conservative legacy of Reaganism and the building of a conservative cultural and economic consensus. According to Hall, a key factor in building this consensus is tapping into the needs, fears, and desires of the public.[3] The New Right has been quite successful in articulating fears over women's growing independence and changes in family form and authority relations.[4]

However, the desires of many women for financial independence, political power, and more equitable relations with men represent countercurrents in this era of conservativism. The tensions and contradictions surrounding this struggle for popular consent are being played out in the national and local political arenas[5] and in the schools. Through their patterns of organization, instruction, and interactions, schools often attempt to "fix" students' gender, class, race, age, and sexual subjectivities into traditional patterns.[6] However, students, especially young women, often negotiate these practices and structures, accepting some, rejecting others, while trying to secure some influence over their schooling and futures.[7] These dynamics are quite apparent in young women's reading of teen romance novels. Through reading teen romances in schools, young women readers come to grips with many realities for women today and also attempt to refashion them through imagining other possibilities.

In this chapter, I discuss how middle- and working-class young women, ages twelve through fifteen, from diverse racial and ethnic backgrounds, construct their gender, class, racial, age, and sexual identities while reading adolescent romance fiction in school. I begin by providing a context for romance fiction in schools by linking the recent political events in the United States discussed above with the romance publishing industry.

THE POLITICS OF POPULAR FICTION

When young women read teen romance novels, they enter the world of a $500-million-a-year industry[8] whose stock in trade is fantasies of love, politics, and economics. As a popular culture form, teen romance fiction is the "area of negotiation" in the ongoing ideological struggle for young women's hearts and minds.[9] Teen romance fiction, like popular soap opera, pop music, and television, involves the shaping of consciousness as well as the occasion for reflection on fears, hopes, and dreams.[10] The rise of teen romance novels to the third most widely read young adult book[11] in only ten years[12] parallels the shift in the political climate of the United States to conservativism. I am not implying an outright conspiracy here. Rather, many segments of the culture industry, particularly publishing, are owned by multinational corporations[13] whose interests are politically conservative. These interests make their way into publishing through business practices and the content of books.[14]

In early 1980 Ronald Reagan became president of the United States, and, in the same year, the first new teen romance series, "Wildfire," published by Scholastic Books, appeared in the bookstores. The concept of romance fiction written for teens dates back to the 1940s and 1950s, when Betty Cavanna, Maureen Daly, and Rosamond du Jardin wrote books focusing on young women's first love experiences. The new romances have reappeared in the midst of several large-scale mergers within educational and trade publishing that have had the effect of endowing profit-and-loss sheets with a new importance.[15]Other changes are apparent. Editors in the old-fashioned sense are no longer key people. Rather, professional managers with business or legal backgrounds now occupy key decision-making positions. A consistent worry expressed by insiders in publishing[16] is that this business mentality may be narrowing the range of books published,[17] making it difficult for initially unprofitable but important books to be published. Teen romances are a response to dominant publishing interests that center on profitability and instant appeal.[18]

One way in which publishers today increase their profit margins is to cultivate constantly new reader markets and develop new books.[19] Harty notes that the schools have historically constituted a lucrative market for publishers.[20] According to *Publishers Weekly*, in 1984 the schools spent $695.6 million on books, making the schools the third largest account—surpassed only by general retailers and college bookstores. Although textbooks comprise the bulk of these sales, the trade division is growing steadily as more schools use these general interest books for instruction along with, or in place of, textbooks.[21] Teenage romance fiction is a case of publishers' developing new readers and books within a steady market. It is the product of school book-club Teenage Book Club (TAB) market research conducted by Scholastic Inc., a leader in the el-hi (elementary and high school) market, regarding which books were most frequently ordered by young women readers.[22]

Teen romance novels also appear as components of a highly lucrative segment of educational publishing, the Hi-Low market, which is comprised of books with "interesting" content and limited difficulty of reading[23] aimed at "reluctant readers." Reluctant readers are often students who may be able to read, but refuse to because they are disinterested in reading materials or have some actual reading difficulties.[24] Aulls suggests that reluctant readers can be best taught to read using Hi-Low materials.[25] Series romance fiction shares all the characteristics of many Hi-Lows, especially the differentiation of content on the basis of gender. For example, Scholastic's *Action* books feature mystery and adventure for boys and romance, dating, and problem novels for girls. The demand from teachers and librarians for reluctant-reader materials has increased in the wake of recent national debate about both the imputed difficulty of many students in learning to read, and their boredom with standard reading texts such as basals.[26]

However, the appearance of romance fiction has not been without controversy. Lanes notes that in her interviews with educators, parents, and librarians, general reactions ranged from annoyance to rage.[27] Romance fiction has been criticized for its "limited roles for females" and its depiction of "a narrow, little world" in which virtue is rewarded with the right boy's love.[28] The most vocal critic, the Council on Interracial Books for Children, claims that the books teach young women to put boys' interests above their own, encourage young women to compete against each other for boys, and depict the life of suburban white middle-class nuclear families.[29] Others identify the new romance fiction with the political ideology of the New Right.[30] Conservative elements have criticized the teen romances for promoting promiscuity through the sexual tension between girls and boys in the novels that stops at the first kiss. The novels keep readers excited and turned on sexually.[31] Still others have criticized the way in which romance fiction gets into the hands of young readers—primarily through school book clubs.[32]

Despite these controversies and adults' misgivings, teen romance fiction remains a force to be reckoned with: It is immensely popular with young women readers and represents an area of curriculum where students endeavor to have their voices heard.

THE RESEARCH CONTEXT

During an eight-month period in 1985–86, I studied teen romance-fiction readers in three schools in a large American midwestern city that I will call "Lakeview."[33] Once dominated by the automobile, farm-equipment, and alcoholic-beverage industries, the city and surrounding communities were left with the imprint of the economic crisis of the late 1970s.

Plant closings have transformed Lakeview from a smokestack blue-collar city to one of empty factories and service businesses.

Lakeview School District is a large district that draws students from the inner city and some of the outlying areas that were annexed to the city thirty years ago. My sites of research were Jefferson Middle School and Sherwood Park Middle School, two outlying 7–8 schools, and Kominsky Junior High School, an inner-city 7–9 school. At the time of the study, Lakeview was in the process of converting the junior high schools into middle schools. Jefferson and Sherwood Park each had about three hundred students. Sherwood Park's student population was mostly white. Like Sherwood Park, Jefferson was predominantly white, but had three Chinese students as well. Kominsky's seven-hundred-plus student body was about one-half white, one-quarter each Black and Hispanic, with a small Vietnamese and Asian Indian population. Both Jefferson and Sherwood Park split their students into three tracks (low, medium, and high) for reading instruction.[34] Reading placements were based on the results of the following: district-wide and individual-school standardized reading test scores, teacher recommendation, and students' previous grades. Kominsky and Sherwood Park also had an additional reading support service through the federally funded Chapter I program, which enrolled one-half and one-quarter, respectively, of their students.[35]

In order to study romance-fiction readers I used a variety of methods combining ethnography with survey research.[36] An initial sample of seventy-five young women from the three schools was assembled through interviews with teachers and librarians regarding who were heavy romance-fiction readers and by personal examination of school and classroom library checkout cards and book-club order forms.[37] A reading survey was given to all seventy-five young women.[38] From this survey, I was able to identify the heaviest romance-fiction readers, some twenty-nine young women, whom I interviewed individually and in small-group settings. These twenty-nine young women had five teachers for reading in the three schools. I observed these classes and interviewed these teachers. This chapter stems from the written reading survey of the seventy-five young women and from observation of, and interviews with, the twenty-nine young women and their five teachers.

ROMANCE NOVELS IN CLASSROOMS

My reading survey shows that at Jefferson and Sherwood Park, the novels tended to be read by white middle-class young women ages twelve through fifteen and, to a lesser degree, by Black, Hispanic, and Asian young women at all three schools.[39] At Jefferson and Sherwood Park, romance novels accounted for 36 percent of all books checked out from school libraries and ordered through book clubs, as compared to 25 percent at Kominsky. This is in keeping with recent Book Industry surveys that have placed romance fiction within the top three kinds of books that adolescents read, superseded by mystery and adventure books.[40] Another characteristic of readers concerns how readers were grouped for reading instruction. The twenty-nine heaviest readers were identified by school personnel as "reluctant" or "slow" readers and were tracked into remedial or low-ability reading classes.[41] In the three schools, the girls who most often read romance novels were also reluctant readers.

The twenty-nine young women's five reading teachers provided much insight into the complexity of teen romance fiction in schools. Three teachers were aware of the national controversy surrounding these books, and all felt some degree of apprehension regarding their use. The contradictory position of teachers is nicely illustrated by the observation of white middle-class Mrs. M. (Kominsky):

> I feel guilty about letting the girls order these books through TAB [a school book club]. I read a couple of them once. They are so simple and the characters in the novels are stereotypes. You know, Mom at home in her apron, Dad reading the paper with his feet up. But the girls seem to like the books, and the classroom sure is quiet when they're reading them.[42]

The romance-novel reading in these teachers' classrooms was the outcome of several factors. The teachers' overwhelming desire to see students reading and reasonably interested in books generated Mrs. K.'s idea that "any reading was better than no reading." Teachers were also under tremendous pressure from the administration to improve students' measured reading scores. For Chapter I teachers Mrs. K. and Mrs. M., those scores were key ingredients in retaining yearly federal funding of their programs and their jobs. All five teachers conceded the difficulty of keeping order in classrooms. Securing students' consent to read voluntarily made teachers' lives in the classroom "tolerable."

Most romance-novel reading occurred during independent study, which was in great abundance, as instruction was mostly organized around individual-learning models to provide for the specific needs and interests of each student. This was especially the case in Sherwood Park and Kominsky, where students read or worked on skill sheets. Student and teacher interactions were mostly limited to correcting skills sheets, updating reading folders, and answering procedural questions. Students mostly read privately and rarely shared their reading with their teachers or other students.[43]

Although most books were student selected, teachers attempted to influence book choice by categorizing books as "quality,"[44] award-winning books[45] or "fluff" books, like romances. Students did not automatically accept teachers' authority regarding book choice, as is illustrated by Mrs. B., a white middle-class Kominsky Chapter I teacher, and five of her students. As a strong advocate of "quality" teen literature, Mrs. B. crammed her room with an array of "quality" paperbacks, magazines, and newspapers. No romance fiction was to be found in this classroom library. The young women brought romance fiction from home or libraries and ordered them from mail-order book clubs. Mrs. B. more or less tolerated the romances in her classroom. This tolerance was the outcome of both pressure from the administration to show reading gains and protest from five young women.

Of all the teachers, Mrs. B. felt most apprehensive about granting any legitimacy to romance fiction. She fit the romances into her "quality literature" perspective by striking a bargain with her students: for every romance novel read, a student must read another type of book. The reality was that Mrs. B. hoped to draw the interest of the young women away from the romance fiction so that they would expand their reading to "quality" books. During weekly library visits, Mrs. B. exhorted students to "choose something you'll want to stick with." When students inquired into the reasons behind Mrs. B.'s dislike of romances, she neither offered any explanation nor encouraged any critical dialogue with romance-fiction readers about their reading.

Five of Mrs. B.'s students took matters into their own hands by championing romance-novel reading. Tina, a white working-class student, quoted Mrs. B. ("Read something interesting") to defend her choices. Tomeika and Jan, Black and white students from middle- and working-class backgrounds, respectively, supported their reading tastes by citing their mothers' devotion to the books. White middle-class Carol saw romance fiction as something truly pleasurable to read, in contrast to teacher-selected books: "I like Sweet Valley High [a line of romance novels] because the books Mrs. B. [my pseudonym] picks are so long and boring. . . . I read a story about a girl stranded on this island and how she survives. It was interesting, but doesn't have much to do with my life. Get real! How many girls are stranded on islands in 1985? At least with Sweet Valley the stories are fun and I learn a lot about boys." Finally, all five young women would continually languish over teacher-selected books, mutilating the pages and covers, and complaining how boring the books were. Or they would retire to the "book-nook" and covertly read their favorite romances, which they had stashed among the floor cushions.

READERS AND ROMANCES

Some young women were more avid readers than others, but the young women as a whole read an average of six romances a month at home and school.[46] However, these young women were not indiscriminate in their romance-fiction reading—that is, not just any romance novel would do. High on their lists were also romance-fiction lines such as Silhouette's "First Love" and "Blossom Valley," Scholastic's "Wildfire," and Bantam's "Sweet Dreams" and "Sweet Valley High." These novels were favored because they provided an easy and cheap way of securing books, through a book club. More important for Silhouette readers was the fact that Silhouette publishes a newletter soliciting letters from readers. The young women viewed the newsletter as important because, in the words of Val, a working-class Hispanic student at Kominsky, "They [Silhouette] care about what we want in books. I wrote once about a book I hated. I even got a letter back from Mrs. Jackson [an editor]. Funny thing, nobody ever asks us our opinions about nothing." That these opinion polls are part of Silhouette's sophisticated marketing program does not detract from the positive impact they had on these young women. The overall effect was to provide them with the experience of having their voices heard.

Why Young Women Read Romance Novels

In many ways, young women's reasons for reading romances compare with those of adult romance-fiction readers in Radway's 1984 study.[47] In both Radway's study and this one the reasons combined elements of fantasy, knowledge, and pleasure. The seventy-five young women felt that romance fiction offered the following things:[48]

1. Escape, a way to get away from problems at home and school
2. Better reading than dreary textbooks
3. Enjoyment and pleasure
4. A way to learn about romance and dating

The theme of escape from problems emerged over and over again, Mary Jo, a fourteen-year-old white middle-class student at Sherwood Park, commented that the romance novels portrayed the world as "I would like it to be." The happy resolution of family problems in the romances of Francine Pascal was especially appealing to twelve-year-old Carrie, a Black middle-class student at Kominsky. Carrie said: "In her books things get all mixed up like fights and other stuff, but basically people still love each other. I'd love to have a family like the Martins' [in *My First Love and Other Disasters*]. Sometimes when I read I kind of pretend that the family in the story is my family."

Precisely why romance-novel reading was highly valued in school is evident from the words of Claire, a white working-class student at Sherwood Park: "It's really a bore 'round here. Readin' Sweet Valley turns the worst day into something special." The books left readers with the same good feelings as meeting with their friends at lunch and in the halls, sustained them through an otherwise tedious school day. Romance-novel reading was often preferred to textbooks. Nancy, a white middle-class student at Jefferson, remarked: "I'll read Crosswinds any day. The stories are really interesting. . . . Social Studies? The book is so boring and who cares about a bunch of dates and battles."

Another aspect of the pleasure of the text was the positive feelings that came from identifying with romance-fiction heroines. Without exception, the heroine should be, according to Tomeika and Marge, both Black working-class Kominsky students, "pretty, smart, and popular." Being recognized as someone nice, intelligent, and funny was important to these young women. They were all aware of the social and academic significance of their placement in low-ability reading classes, and many of them felt that their teachers did not see them as intelligent or nice people. This desire to identify with a smart heroine coincided with the young women's desire to have teachers and other adults regard them as nice and capable, despite their academic placement.

Young women derived pleasure from imagining themselves as the heroines of romance novels. Through their reading, they lived out the specialness associated with being the object of a boy's affection. They viewed romantic relationships in fiction as very satisfying, with all minor misunderstandings eventually resolved. However, very few of the young women envisioned romance in everyday life as anything like romance fiction. Marge, a Black working-class student at Kominsky, claimed that most of the romances she read did not accurately portray romantic relationships as she encountered them in everyday life.[49] By the same token, Marge wished the boys she knew were more like the boys in the novels: "Treatin' you good. Not bossin' you 'round and tryin' to hit on you all the time." Marge further noted that girls would probably always have to "fight off" the unwanted attention of boys, but that it would be nice to dream it could be otherwise. The romance novels provided Marge with the dream of an ideal romance.

The romances gave the young women who were not dating, and some of the more shy young women, the opportunity to take romantic risks without consequences. Trina, a thirteen-year-old Chinese middle-class student at Jefferson, noted that "sometimes the way guys are in the books helps us girls understand them a lot better." This primer quality of romance fiction found favor with thirteen-year-old Marita, a working-class Hispanic Kominsky student. Marita's reading provided a valuable source of information about romance. Marita's family strictly controlled her whereabouts. Neither she nor her sisters were permitted to date until they were seventeen, and her older sisters were not open with her about their experiences. Marita depended on the romance novels for information.

The Book of Love

Readers' ideas about a good romance novel centered on structural characteristics and the heroine and hero.[50] The good romance novel has the following characteristics:

1. It is easy to read.
2. It does not drag.
3. Its heroine and hero are cute, popular, and nice, and have money.
4. It has a happy ending.
5. In it young women are strong and get the best of boys.

The young women placed a premium on the fact that the series romances contain about 150 to 175 action-packed pages of easy reading. Pat, a white middle-class student at Jefferson, explained that the novels "are sure easy to read. I know all the words and don't have to skip any of 'em." However, this preference for easy reading had unexpected consequences. Mrs. T., a white middle-class Jefferson reading teacher, saw a reciprocal, reinforcing relationship between the romances and the young women's status in the schools:

> Some of the girls show great impatience at reading books that are long. . . .
> That's why they like romance novels. Sure, they like to read about boys—
> that's all they have on their minds. But they do like anything that's easy and
> doesn't make them think. The romances are mindless drivel.

Young women also had definite ideas about what constituted an ideal heroine and hero. As noted earlier, according to Tomeika and May, Black working-class Kominsky students, the heroine should be "pretty, smart, and popular." The preference for a popular heroine was closely linked to these young women's personal desires to be liked by both sexes. Another priority was to be cherished and treated well by a nice boy. Those characteristics that helped heroines attract boys were precisely the ones they wished for in their own lives. The ideal hero had some similarities to the heroine. He should be "cute," "funny," "strong," "nice," "have money," and "come from a good home." While cuteness was certainly important, niceness and strength were indispensable. "Strength," for these young women, did not have to do with physical prowess, but rather stood for an array of attributes such as courage, initiative, and protectiveness. The young women were repelled by teenage versions of the "macho man" in books and everyday experience. As Karen, a white middle-class student at Sherwood Park, explained, "When I read a book, the guy has to be nice, he has to treat his girlfriend and everybody with respect." This notion of respect had much to do with the hero's being attuned to the heroine's needs and feelings. In these young women's real lives, there was the occasional boy who reminded them of the romance-novel hero, but mostly the boys they knew did not measure up to this ideal.

According to several young women, romance fiction should end happily, that is, the heroine and hero should have ironed out their difficulties and become once again a couple by the end of the story. Several of the older readers, who were romantically involved themselves, looked to romance fiction to provide in fantasy the hoped-for outcome of their own romances. Patty, a fifteen-year-old white working-class student at Kominsky, exemplifies this position: "It would be nice to think that Tommy and me would end up like Janine and Craig [the couple from the popular "Blossom Valley" series], you know, married with kids and having a nice home, car, and money." The saga of this fictional couple's romance, separation, and eventual marriage held out to this reader the possibility of living happily ever after.

The final quality of a good romance novel was that it had to have a heroine who is strong and assertive, especially toward boys. May, a Black working-class Kominsky student, strongly expressed this sentiment: "I've got no patience with girls who let boys walk all over them. Believe you me, no boy mess with me or he be sorry." Readers took pleasure in reading about heroines who "got the best of boys." Several readers mentioned Victoria Martin of *My First Love and Other Disasters* (by popular writer Francine Pascal) as a heroine whose courage and forthrightness they admired. This notion of "besting boys," "keeping them in line," was most often applied to situations where the heroine knew best, when the hero was treading on "female things" or trying to compel the heroine to do things against her beliefs.

So far I have indicated the fluid and often contradictory quality of these readers' interactions with texts where story-world and lived experience meet. An underlying theme is how readers' gender subjectivity is shaped through their reading. I will now discuss the dynamics at work during reading that help create the femininities of young working- and middle-class women, but also provide them with the occasion for pondering their social identities.

ALL I HAVE TO DO IS DREAM

Although readers' life experiences are important in constructing meaning when reading, the text still exerts a measure of control over those meanings. In this regard, Iser claims that part of the text's control happens through "blanks" or gaps in the text.[51] Many times the threads of the plot are suddenly broken off, as happens between chapters. Or they continue in unexpected directions. The blanks call for combining what has been previously read with readers' own life experiences and making predictions regarding further developments in the story. Although teen romance novels are not characterized by many unexpected twists and turns, they nevertheless require a certain amount of constitutive activity on the part of readers. When young women readers encounter blanks in romance texts that involve matters of femininity, readers are offered versions of femininity but are also given opportunities to think about them. In the case of teen romance-fiction readers, the blanks stimulate the analysis of relations between women and men, which I illustrate by recounting the readings by three young women of Marshall's *Against the Odds.*[52]

Annie, Marcy, and Nancy, three white middle-class eighth-grade students at Sherwood Park, all in Mrs. J.'s reading class, had recently read *Against the Odds.* This novel describes the struggles of four young women, Trina, Laurie, Joyce, and Marsha, who are among a group of twenty-five young women registering as new students at the all-male Whitman High School. This school's ninety-year history as an elite all-male college-preparatory institution is about to change under court-mandated affirmative action. The four young women have decided to attend Whitman because it has the strong math and computer-science curriculum their old school lacks. The young women are initially greeted with protest signs of "No Girls at Whitman High!" catcalling, and constant harassment. The young women confront the troublemakers and establish themselves as serious students. Trina in particular wins the respect, admiration, and affection of the most hard-boiled of all the boys, Chris Edwards. The novel ends with the vision of a romantically involved Trina and Chris and with the promise of a more gentle "battle of the sexes."

All the young women agreed that heroine Trina Singleton caused them to reflect on themselves. Nancy clearly expressed this in her comments on her favorite romance heroine: "That's gotta be Trina Singleton in *Against the Odds.* Trina is the kind of person I want to be 'cause she's not afraid to fight for her rights, while another girl might chicken out."

Against the Odds has certain blanks that invite completion as part of the story and characterization as they develop. At one point, Trina and her friends have a plan to revenge themselves for all they have endured and to put a stop to the harassment once and for all. Readers are left to contemplate what this plan might be for several pages, and even then it is only gradually unfolded. Annie filled the blanks in this manner:

A: It was fun trying to figure out what Trina and the other girls would do to get back at those boys. I thought that they would sneak into the boys' locker room and do something to their sports equipment. Marsha had the guts to do something like that.

LKCS: Was that something you might have done?

A: Are you kidding? No way! I'd never have the guts. Well, you'd have to do something, that's for sure. Hmm, I'd probably start a rumor about the guys or every time me and my friends would see them we would make like we were talking about them. They can't stand that!

Marcy's responses to the same passage also set up a conflict between who she is and who she would like to be:

M: I figured Trina and Laurie would come up with something fantastic. I never thought in a million years that they would stuff confetti drenched in cheap perfume into the boys' lockers.

LKCS: Would you do that, get even in this way?

M: Well, I'd like to do something like that, to get even with some of the boys in my math class who are real pains. But I'd get chicken and probably just fume.

LKCS: Can you tell me more?

M: It's kinda difficult, I mean, well, I guess I don't want to be seen as a girl who's too pushy with boys. You have to be careful about that. But then you can't let the boys push you around. I don't know.

The blanks allowed Annie and Marcy to imagine a course of action that trod a path between what was possible, given the story they had constructed, and what they thought would be possible, given their imagination and femininity. The way Annie filled in the blanks reveals that gender tensions exist and that young women are not passive victims. Her predicted plan and subsequent response show a view of femininity that allows for collective action against boys but sets limits on how forceful that action may be. Marcy adopts a position in relation to the text that sharpens a tension within her femininity when she admires the characters' plan, but expresses doubt as to her own ability to act in a similar manner. Like Annie, she refuses a discourse of female powerlessness and negotiates how assertive a women should be when it comes to men.

As the twenty-nine young women read their romance novels, they constructed a story that put on center stage their own hopes for, and fears of, romance and brought to bear their past and present positions within the school in becoming the subject of the romance text. Their school identities as reluctant readers, and their desire to be seen as capable, influenced their reading of the romances. Equally important was each young woman's ability to become the heroine and experience being an assertive and cherished girl. These constitute the contradictory and at times fragmenting gender positions young women construct in the course of their reading.

The young women's romance-novel reading had strong oppositional overtones, as previously indicated. Their identification with the assertive heroines and their pleasure derived from the romance novels fueled their attempts to continue their reading at all costs. The young women's vision of the romance novel as a vehicle for instilling a certain vitality into their reading classes, to make them less boring and more meaningful, was an attempt to have their voices heard and a bid to secure some power and control over one aspect of schooling. In Mrs. B.'s class, students introjected into the reading curriculum a text that operates on the fringes of accepted instructional materials, as evident in teachers' previous comments. These actions exemplify how some students negotiate the "given curriculum" in an attempt to win space for materials that have meaning in their lives.

With romance-novel reading as a symbol of their femininities, the young women brought a certain pleasure in their femininities into the classroom. McRobbie[53] claims that young women's pleasure has always been problematic in schools, whether it takes the form of flirting, wearing sexy clothes, or primping. Like Radway's Smithton readers,[54] the young women took pleasure in their ability to make sense of the novels and to articulate what these stories were about. This feeling of competence was not one they usually experienced in school. The young women's reading of romance fiction refuted in their own minds the judgments made by school personnel about their competence. The act of making meaning allowed them to refuse, if only momentarily, their identities as reluctant readers.

The young women constantly used the romance novels to escape temporarily the problems and unhappiness associated with school and general life difficulties. On the whole, the young women were barely passing their courses. Many experienced the strain and uncertainty of the downward economic trend in Lakeview. Their glimpses of an economy in trouble did not prevent many of the young women from dreaming of a secure and comfortable future to be achieved through a good marriage combined with their own employment. Although many of the young women were aware of the disjuncture between that world and their own, the novels provided the space for them to dream and construct reality as they would like it to be. The novels therefore played upon many young women's desires and yearnings for a different present and future.

Romance-fiction reading reinforces a version of gender relations based in heterosexuality. Readers identify with heroines and discursively become the heroine. This is evident in the comments of twelve-year-old Annie, a white middle-class student at Sherwood Park: "It's just when you're reading, you're in some other world, well, not really, physically, I mean, but you imagine you are. Sometimes I feel like I am the person going on dates, having loads of fun." Jenny, a fourteen-year-old Black middle-class student at Jefferson, describes the impact that one novel, Quin-Harkin's *Princess Amy*,[55] has had on her: "My favorite part is when the girl and the guy first kiss. That gives me a squishy feeling in my stomach, sorta like I'm actually there, being the girl that's gettin' kissed." These readers' endorsement of these relations between the sexes affirms traditional gender relations. The young women never disputed the desirability of heterosexual romance; they tried to capture it over and over in their reading of other romance fiction and wished for this specialness in their own lives. This was even the case when the young women's relationships with boys were fraught with conflicts to such a degree that the only satisfying romance they could imagine was one occurring in a novel.

How does this view fit with the strong assertive heroines the young women preferred to read about? In many ways, the young women's version of women's assertiveness was a bounded one, one constrained within traditional views. These young women could certainly "best" boys in everyday life, but the bottom line was that one could not be "too pushy," because this could destroy romantic prospects. The latter was clearly something the young women would not do, even when boys did not treat them well, as was the case with Marge, or in the "get even" fantasy of Annie. Hence, the young women's conception of the proper relationship between the sexes featured some assertiveness, along with staying in the good graces of boys.

Young women's romance-fiction reading is characterized by this tug-of-war between conventional femininity and more assertive modes. This tension was an important factor in shaping their class subjectivities, as seen in the young women's thoughts on their futures in the world of work and at home.

MATERIAL GIRLS

The twenty-nine young women's class positions were reinforced through their views on work, marriage, and children, which fed into their romance-fiction reading. Working for pay while in school was important for most of these young women, since it was the ticket to consuming, which in turn improved their chances for romance. Marriage, children, and careers were on the distant horizon. The young women's reading tapped into their desires for material things and centered the gender, class, and racial aspects of their identities around consumption.

Beautification with an eye to romance underlay the young women's wage work and consumption. The young women saw a direct relation between appearance, popularity, and romance. All the young women endorsed Trina's notion that "pretty girls get nice boyfriends." These beliefs were validated in their everyday lives. Patty, a white working-class Kominsky student, echoed the sentiments of many of the twenty-nine readers: "The prettiest and most popular girls here have their pick of the boys.'' These descriptions of the linkages between a girl's popularity and her beauty were similar to the way teen romance fiction depicts heroines.[56] The linking of beauty with romance not only motivated the young women's consumption, but also provided the reason for working for pay.

All the young women baby-sat and performed odd jobs to augment allowances or earn any spending money at all. Their earnings were spent on movies, fast food, records, and videos, with the greater part going for clothes and beauty products. With larger allowances, the white, Black, and Chinese middle-class readers baby-sat to buy, in white middle-class Claire's view, "little extras" or "something extravagant" that her allowance would not cover. For the white, Black, and Hispanic working-class young women, consumption was on a more limited scale. Pam, a white working-class Jefferson student, commented: "We've never had a lot of money to spend at home. After my dad lost his job, it was really bad. I bought most of my school clothes this year. This summer I baby-sat almost every night and mowed lawns in my neighborhood until my asthma got real bad." Pam was one example of an amazing entrepreneurship among the working-class young women to earn pocket money in the face of little or no spending money from parents. The young women in general had plans to continue working in high school in retail sales, clerical work, or the fast-food industry to have more spending money. They saw having a job as making the difference between doing without and having money to spend. This reality collided with the world of the teen romance novel.

Affluence and even luxury generally characterize the world of romance fiction. Although most of the heroines do casual work, their families are economically stable. This was a different world for the twenty-nine young women I spoke with. The working-class young women glimpsed this world as bystanders. The designer clothes and elaborate homes were not for them. Several middle-class young women saw this world slipping away. During the recent recession in Lakeview, many of these women's relatives, like Pam's father, had lost good, paying jobs and were unemployed or working for drastically reduced wages. Austerity hit the middle class as massive white-collar layoffs continued. These glimpses of an economy still in trouble did not prevent the young women from dreaming of a secure and comfortable future. The romances, with their economically secure world, allowed these young women to realize their dreams.

The young women's future plans included marriage, children, some further schooling, and work for pay.[57] Over half of the twenty-nine young women expected to marry before they were twenty and to work for a few years before having children. On the surface, they rejected the dominant vision projected by romance novels that married women are exclusively full-time mothers and housewives. White working-class Karen expressed the tensions surrounding these young women's futures: "Well, I'm gonna have to work for awhile to help out, but I want to be home taking care of my kids when they come." The working- and middle-class young women from two-paycheck families recognized the necessity of women in the work force. However, along with this realization was a strong longing for the more conventional roles depicted in romance fiction. This tension was an outcome of their dawning knowledge of the difficulty of juggling housework, children, and paid work. The young women's own considerable domestic responsibilities at home and their mothers' dawn-to-dusk work routines were sobering glimpses of what might be in store for them.

PLACES IN THE WORLD

There is considerable negotiation between students and teachers regarding romance fiction in the classrooms at Kominsky, Jefferson, and Sherwood Park. In the larger institutional context, state testing and pressures to demonstrate student growth in reading were factors in teachers' decisions to allow popular materials into the classroom. The five teachers also acknowledged that intensification of their work load, increasing numbers of students, and the immense amount of paper work for Chapter I teachers made it difficult to select materials carefully. Consequently, they strongly relied on the reputation of publishers. The selective rendering of experience in tradebooks and textbooks,[58] along with recent charges of censorship in school editions,[59] makes this reliance politically problematic. The "higher production quotas," increasing accountability, and intensification of teachers' work are expressions of capitalist practices and values within the schools.[60] Romance fiction represents another aspect of this mentality within the schools. Gitlin observes that symbolic relations are becoming steadily linked to politics and economics.[61] Consider the comments of Ron Buehl, "Sweet Dreams" editor, about marketing books in the way jeans are sold.[62] Teen romance novels not only sell millions, like jeans, but are commercials for consumer goods, like jeans and video games, that promote a way of life based upon conspicuous consumption. Teen romance fiction's promotion of a highly affluent style of life is out of reach for many of the twenty-nine readers and contradicts their current realities of families in economic trouble as the gap between the rich and poor has steadily widened during the Reagan and Bush administrations.[63]

Popular romance-fiction reading encapsulates the tug-of-war involved in securing consent to the new conservative political consensus. Romance reading is evidence of readers' desires along with their fears and resentment of the power of men and the subordination of women. Readers' preference for strong heroines and impatience with passive ones represents their desire to transcend current gender stereotypes and imagine a more assertive femininity, which, however, stops short of confrontation with boys. Through romance reading, readers transform gender and class relations. Men cherish and nurture women rather the other way around. This, together with readers' collective rejection of a macho masculinity, represents their partial overturning of one aspect of current traditional gender sentiments. These readers did not unilaterally accept romance fiction's depiction of married women's lives as primarily domestic. In these books, paid work was undertaken only out of economic necessity. Readers' "Horatia Alger" fantasy of feminine initiative represents the transformation of class relations by substituting breadwinning women for the June Cleavers of romance fiction. Along with this fantasy, there was a longing for a domestic life, one that emanates from these readers' dawning realization of the burdens represented by home and work. However, readers' final acceptance of romantic love and its power structure undercuts the political potential of these insights. Romance reading in no way altered the young women's present and future circumstances, but rather was deeply implicated in reconciling them to their places in the world.

Popular-romance reading also involves political actions around authority relations in schools. As Tina, Tomeika, Jan, and Carol wrested some control over their reading from Mrs. B., they de-centered the teacher's traditional authority on the question of reading choice. Their actions contested the power of teachers to decide what is best for students. In many ways, their actions here exemplified the assertive femininity that the young women constructed as they read. They were able to substitute this mode of femininity for the compliant femininity expected in the classroom. The struggles between these young women and their teacher were ultimately over whose gender and class meanings had legitimacy. However, their actions were contradictory in that they hardened the young women's opposition to "legitimate" texts and the official school knowledge they contain. Although the romance novels generated a high engagement with reading and provided readers with "really useful" gender knowledge, this knowledge did not count toward achieving academic success. The twenty-nine young women remained categorized as reluctant readers despite the rich and complex interpretations they made of romance fiction. Teachers did not interpret their reading as competent, because romance novels were not legitimate texts in teachers' eyes, despite student efforts to confer authority on them.[64] Although teachers and students compromised (as in the case of Mrs. B.), teachers still dispensed the rewards upon which academic success rests. There are few such rewards for teen romance readers.

Teachers' allowing readers to substitute romance novels for other instructional texts unwittingly contributed to the young women's opposition to the academic aspects of schooling. The absence of meaningful communication between students and teachers about their reading allowed many of the gender interpretations to remain in place. This practice militated against what is perhaps the most important aspect of learning from reading, that of making sense of books through discussion with others.[65] While the very championing of romance-novel reading momentarily empowered young women to assert a claim to a kind of schooling that would relate to their interests, it also had a dark side. Readers' resistances to the "official" curriculum set in motion the possibility that these young women might graduate with skills that qualify them only for low-skill, exploitative jobs, or that they might not graduate at all. In view of the movement of Lakeview toward a service economy featuring low-paying jobs, the limiting of these women to this kind of job seems likely. Service-sector industries are the dominant employers of women.[66] Romance reading prepared these twenty-nine Lakeview students for entering society as middle- and working-class women.

CONCLUSION

Popular romance-fiction reading exploits the many ideological strains that exist within society, and it represents the continuing struggle over women's places in the world. This fiction does not so much impose meanings on its readers, as construct readers' gender, class, racial, age, and sexual identities in complex ways. Volosinov has observed that language involves a "struggle over meaning."[67] As the study of teen romance-fiction demonstrates, this struggle is a political one that has long concerned feminists and other progressively minded individuals. Space does not permit a detailed account of the ways in which a political practice can be forged around popular texts.[68]

However, it is important that educators help students to locate the contradictions between popular fiction's version of social relations and their own lives as well as help them to develop the critical tools necessary to make deconstructive readings that unearth the political interests that shape the form and content of popular fiction.[69] This means moving from a definition of reading as an apolitical, internal, and individual activity to one of reading as a socially and historically situated political practice.[70] Many "reluctant readers" read in a solitary manner without opportunity to share with other readers their impressions of books. Collective reading groups and group writing of a romance novel are a few ways of transforming reading from a silent to a social activity. The teaching of reading today tends toward the use of fiction, especially in whole-language approaches. Often, readers do not read many expository materials or are not given adequate instruction in how to read them. This is a serious issue for reluctant readers, since expository materials are what Luke calls "the discourses of power," containing the socially valued knowledge.[71] Although fiction such as romance novels may give pleasure to readers, it will not help students secure diplomas, qualify for good paying jobs, and gain access to the dominant power structure.

The theory and practice of feminist pedagogy[72] and that of Freire's political literacy[73] approach represent points of departure for a "politics of reading."[74] This could involve teachers and readers discussing and writing about their everyday experiences of oppression within patriarchy, their moments of "breaking out," the feelings romance fiction brings to the fore, and the political and economic context of romance-fiction publishing. Politicizing text use is vital, since much of the hegemonic power of ruling elites in the United States is consolidated through written forms.[75] As the control of publishing is in the hands of large corporate interests, it is vital that political struggles continue to be directed toward the corporate sector and that alternative presses be supported. While this article shows the creative reconstruction of romance texts by readers, this fiction remains problematic for young women for developing their femininities from a range of characteristics rather than from those socially sanctioned.[76]

In some ways, the struggles of young women readers within their classrooms and the realm of meaning represent the kind of cultural politics that has long concerned feminists. The early feminist "politics of the personal" have made the personal a public political issue. Teen romances are about the public political aspects of what has been designated a personal set of relations. The first teen romance-novels provoked feminists to denounce the fiction's gender, class, and racial stereotyping.[77] Since these books are here to stay because of their profitability, feminists must continue to monitor the evolution of this genre and include teen romance-novels in their larger struggles over representation.

Although what I have briefly outlined above poses challenges for educators, there is much at stake here. For gender, class, race, age, and sexuality are not immutable categories in teen romance-fiction or anywhere else, but cultural constructs. Teen romance-fiction reading occurs at a time when young women begin to consider their places in the world. Through reading romances, young women readers come to grips with the world but also attempt to refashion that world, as well as their places in it.

MOST POPULAR BOOKS READ BY THE SEVENTY-FIVE GIRLS
(*IN ORDER OF POPULARITY*)

1. Pascal, Francine. *Perfect Summer,* Bantam's Sweet Valley High.
2. Harper, Elaine. *Love at First Sight,* Silhouette's Blossom Valley.
3. Harper, Elaine. *Turkey Trot,* Silhouette's Blossom Valley.

4. Conklin, Barbara. *P.S., I Love You,* Bantam's Sweet Dreams.
5. Pascal, Francine. *My First Love and Other Disasters,* Viking.
6. Tyler, Toby. *A Passing Game,* Silhouette's First Love.
7. Quin-Harkin, Janet. *California Girl,* Bantam's Sweet Dreams.
8. Marshall, Andrea. *Against the Odds,* Silhouette's First Love.
9. Conford, Ellen. *Seven Days to a Brand-New Me,* Atlantic.
10. Pevsner, Stella. *Cute Is a Four-Letter Word,* Archway.

R. W. CONNELL

Chapter Nine

Disruptions: Improper Masculinities and Schooling

A couple of decades ago a modest controversy broke out about masculinity and American schooling. The schools, Sexton argued in a widely-read book, were dominated by women and therefore imposed on boys a feminine culture.[1] Red-blooded "boy culture" was marginalized or suppressed, and therefore American males grew to manhood with difficulty in establishing true manliness. This concern was not original with Sexton. As Hantover has shown, the growth of the Boy Scout movement in the United States in the second decade of the century picked up middle-class anxieties about the feminization of boys and offered a kind of masculinizing medicine through Scouting.[2]

This now seems rather comic in the light of the feminist research of the last two decades, which has documented the actual power of men in the education system as in other institutions. The pendulum has swung far in the other direction, with emphasis on the silencing of women's voices in education and in culture more broadly.[3] There can be no honest doubt about the facts of the institutional power of men and the patriarchal character of the public culture.[4]

But this is not to say there are no questions to ask about men. To understand a system of power, one ought to look very closely at its beneficiaries. Indeed, I would argue that one of the cultural supports of men's power is the failure to ask questions about masculinity.

The surge of feminist research on education in the 1970s (epitomized in the remarkable 1975 report of the Australian Schools Commission, *Girls, Schools, and Society*) found conventional gender stereotypes spread blanket-like through textbooks, career counseling, teacher expectations, and selection processes. This was theorized as the transmission of an oppressive, restrictive "sex role" to girls. It followed that girls would be advantaged by modifying the sex role or even breaking out of it. This led easily to an educational strategy. A program of redress was required, to expand girls' occupational and intellectual horizons, affirm women's worth, and write women into the curriculum.

Almost all this discussion was about girls and their restrictive "sex role." By implication the boys were getting one too. But here the sex-role approach did not translate smoothly into educational reform. Since men are the privileged sex in current gender arrangements, it is not obvious that boys will be advantaged by teachers' efforts to change their "role." On the contrary, boys may resent and resist the attempt.

A puzzled literature on the "male sex role" in the 1970s scratched pretty hard to find ways by which men are disadvantaged or damaged by their sex role.[5] No convincing educational program ever came of it. Teachers grappling with issues of masculinity for boys are now reaching for new concepts.[6] The expectation now is that anyone working on these questions in schools faces a politicized and emotionally charged situation.

This is very much in accord with the development of research since the 1970s. More intensive research techniques, and more sophisticated theories of gender, have brought out two themes in particular. One is the importance of the institutional structure of education and the institutional practices of gender that children encounter in schools. Hansot and Tyack, in an illuminating historical paper, urge us to "think institutionally" about gender and schooling.[7] Thorne shows how situational is the segregation of the sexes in primary schools.[8] Messner shows how the formal structure of organized sport provides a temporary resolution for developmental problems of masculinity.[9] Kessler et al. point to the ways curricula and school organization separate out different kinds of femininity, and different kinds of masculinity, within the same school.[10] They introduce the idea of the "gender regime" of an institution such as a school, the established order of gender relations within it. A remarkable historical study by Heward of a second-echelon private school in England shows how a gender regime intended to produce a particular pattern of masculinity is produced in response to the class and gender strategies of the families who form the school's clientele.[11]

Close-focus historical work, interview research, and ethnography tend to find complexities and contradictions beneath the gender "stereotypes." Thus

Walker's 1987 paper on male youth culture in an inner-city school finds several peer groups positioned very differently in relation to the school's cult of competitive sport: some ethnically based peer groups competing through sport, others rejecting it or being marginalized by it.[12] From such research a concern has emerged about the different versions of masculinity to be found in a given cultural context, and the relations of dominance and subordination among them. This gives a new shape to the issue of the formation of masculinity. It is no longer adequate to see this as the absorption of a sex role. It must be seen as an active process of construction, occurring in a field of power relations that are often tense and contradictory, and often involving negotiation of alternative ways of being masculine.

This paper is an attempt to explore how this process works for certain outsiders. It examines the place of schooling in the lives of two groups of men who are in different ways distanced from the dominant models of masculinity: (a) a group of young unemployed working-class men, recently out of school, growing up in the face of structural unemployment and in the shadow of the prison system; (b) a group of men, mostly some years older and mostly from more affluent backgrounds, who are involved in "green' politics," that is, social action on environmental issues.

The first group was contacted mainly through an agency that is responsible for the welfare of unemployed youth and that seeks to place them in training programs. The young men concerned do not consciously reject the hegemonic model of masculinity in their milieu. But where the dominant model of working-class masculinity was built around a wage, a workplace, and the capacity to support a family, these young men *cannot* inhabit such a masculinity; this is ruled out by structural unemployment. They have, in various ways, constructed more fragmented masculinities, some violent and some more passively alienated.[13]

The second group was contacted mainly through organizations in the environmental movement. The men concerned have all been volunteers in "green" campaigns, several of them participating in the famous blockade in the early 1980s that saved the Franklin River from a hydroelectric scheme; some are paid workers in environmental organizations. In the Australian environmental movement there is a strong feminist presence. All these men, accordingly, have had a close encounter with feminism; most, indeed, have been under the necessity of dealing with feminist women on a daily basis. This has put them under strong pressure to adopt a countersexist politics. Several of them have gone on to a conscious attempt at reconstructing masculinity in the light of feminism.[14]

Research on schooling is usually confined to schooling, and thus has difficulty grasping where the school is located in a larger process. This paper is based on life-history interviews with adults that cover family, workplace, sexual relationships, friendships, and politics, in addition to schooling, as settings for the construction of masculinity.

The interviews became the basis of individual case studies, which in turn were grouped for the analysis of collective processes. The interviews were conducted in New South Wales, Australia, in 1985–87; all respondents were English-speaking and mostly of Anglo background.

Rather than following individual narratives, the approach taken in this paper is to identify key moments in the collective process of gender construction, the social dynamic in which masculinities are formed. In such moments the formation of the person, and the history of the educational institution, are simultaneously at issue.

GETTING INTO TROUBLE

Behind Mal Walton's high school is the bush, and at the edge of the bush are the school toilets. This is where Mal and his friends would gather:

> In high school [my friends] were real hoods[†] ["†" indicates an entry in the glossary] too. Like we used to hang down the back . . . we'd sit down there and smoke cigarettes and talk about women, get dirty books out, going through—what do you call it? I can't think of the word. Just the things you do at high school in the first year.

Mal had been placed in the bottom stream, and was evidently regarded by most of his teachers (though not all) as disruptive. The main reason he was in the bottom stream was that he could not read. He was arrested for theft at fifteen, in the year he left school. He has not had a lasting job in the six years since.

Harry the Eel (so called because of his fanatical devotion to the Parramatta football team "the Eels"), now twenty and about to become a father for the second time, used to practice his school smoking in the same fragrant setting:

> I was in a bit of trouble in the last four years of school. I got busted for—what was it? Second Form it was selling porno books. Third Form it was getting drunk at the school fete, and allegedly holding another bloke down and pouring Scotch down his throat—which we didn't do, he was hassling us for a drink. . . . They found him drunk and they said where did you get it? and he mentioned our names and Biff, straight into it. . . . Fourth Form, wasn't much happening in fourth form really, busted in the dunnies[†] having a smoke!

Eel started an apprenticeship, but his employer went broke and no one else would take over his training. Since then he has been on the dole, with casual jobs from time to time.

Eel hasn't been arrested, but his friend Jack Harley has. Jack is less of a tactician and fought every authority figure from his parents on. He thinks he was labeled a "troublemaker" at school because of an older cousin. He clashed early and often with teachers: "They bring me down, I'll bring them down." He was expelled from at least one school, disrupting his learning— "I never did any good at school." Eventually he assaulted a teacher. The court "took the teacher's word more than they took mine" and gave him a sentence in a juvenile detention center. Here he learned the techniques of burglary and car theft. About three years later he was doing six months in the big people's prison. At twenty-two he is on the dole, looking for a job to support his one-year-old child and his killer bull terrier.

These three young men come from laboring families, in Mal Walton's case from a very poor family. Their experience of school shows the relationship between the working class and education at its most alienating. What they meet in the school is an authority structure: specifically, the state and its powers of coercion. They are compelled to be at school, and once there—as they see it—they are ordered about arbitrarily by the teachers. The school is a relatively soft part of the state, but behind it stands the "hard" machinery of police, courts, and prisons. Push the school too far, and, like Jack Harley, one triggers an intervention by the enforcers.

Up against an authority structure, acts of resistance or defiance mean "getting into trouble." This is one of Jack Harley's commonest phrases and indicates how his actions are constantly defined in relation to institutional power. Fights with other boys, arguments with teachers, theft, poor learning, conflicts with parents, are all essentially the same. One can try to retreat beyond the routine reach of institutional power, as Mal Walton and his friends did in their idyllic moments in the toilet block on the edge of the bush. Yet even there, one will be "in trouble" when the authorities raid the retreat, as they did to Eel.

At the same time trouble has its attractions, and may be courted. Mal Walton, for instance, was caned a lot when he went to a Catholic primary school. So were his friends. In fact, he recalls, they fell into a competition to see who could get caned most. No one would win: "We just had big red hands." Why this competition? "Nothing to do; or probably proving that I was stronger than him or he was stronger than me." A violent discipline system invites competition in machismo.

More generally, the authority structure of the school becomes the antagonist against which one's masculinity is cut. Jack Harley, in the comment on teachers quoted above, articulated an ethic of revenge that defines a masculine pride common in his milieu. But he lacked the judgment to keep it symbolic. Teachers often put up with verbal aggression as part of their job, but they are hardly likely to stand still when physically attacked. So the courting of trouble calls out an institutional response, which may push an adolescent assertion of masculine pride toward an early-adult criminal career.

"Trouble" is both sexualized and gendered. Getting the "dirty books" out and "talking about women" are as essential a part of the peer group activity as smoking and complaining about teachers. In the mass high school system, sexuality is both omnipresent and illicit. To act or talk sexually becomes a breach of order, a form of "trouble," in itself. But at the same time it is a means of maintaining order—the order of patriarchy—via the subordination of women and the exaltation of one's maleness.

Patrick Vincent, currently on probation for car theft, succinctly explains why he liked being sent to a coeducational high school after being expelled from his boys-only church school: "Excellent, chicks everywhere, good perve."[†] He boasts that within a week all the girls in his class wanted to climb into his bed. The treatment of young women by these young men is often flatly exploitative.

KNOWING WHERE YOU STAND

To other boys, the hoods in the toilet may be objects of fear. Danny Taylor recalls his first year in an urban working-class high school. Despite being big for his age, he hated the physical contest:

> When the First Form[†] joins and all comes together from all different [primary] schools, there's this thing like sorting out who was the best fighter, who is the most toughest and aggressive boy in the form, and all the little mobs* and cliques develop. So it was like this pecking order stuff . . . and I was really frightened of this.

He did not enjoy high school until Form IV (about age sixteen), when "all the bullies left."

This is not peculiar to urban schools. Stewart Hardy, the son of a laboring family in the dry, flat country in the far west of New South Wales, makes the usual contrast between city and country but paints the same kind of picture:

> In the country . . . it was easier for us to get along with each other, although there was the usual dividing: the cool guys hang out together, and the cool girls hang out together, and there was the swots[†] and the wimps. . . . You knew where you stood, which group you belonged to.

Stewart and Danny joined the wimps and the swots, respectively. Both managed to use the education system to win social promotion (though in both cases limited) out of their class of origin.

The process of demarcating masculinities in secondary school has been noticed in ethnographies of working-class schools in Britain and Australia.[15] Willis's vivid picture of the "lads" and the "ear'oles" is justly celebrated. Such demarcation is not confined to working-class schools. A very similar sorting-out has been documented in a ruling-class private school, between the "bloods" (hearty, sporting) and the "Cyrils" (wimpish, academic).[16]

This suggests a typology of masculinities, even a marketplace of masculinities. To "know where you stand," in Stewart Hardy's phrase, seems to mean *choosing* a masculinity, the way one might choose a football team to root for.

It is important to recognize that differing masculinities are being produced in the same school context. But to picture this as a marketplace, a free choice of gender styles, would be misleading. These "choices" are strongly structured by relations of power.

In each of the cases mentioned, the differentiation of masculinities occurs in relation to a school curriculum that organizes knowledge hierarchically and sorts students into an academic hierarchy. By institutionalizing academic failure via competitive grading and streaming, the school forces differentiation on the boys. But masculinity is organized—on the macro scale—around social power. Social power in terms of access to higher education, entry to professions, command of communication, is being delivered by the school system to boys who are academic "successes." The reaction of the "failed" is likely to be a claim to other sources of power, even other definitions of masculinity. Sporting prowess, physical aggression, or sexual conquest may do.

Indeed, the reaction is often so strong that masculinity as such is claimed for the cool guys. Boys who follow an academic path are defined, conversely, as effeminate (the "Cyrils"). When this situation is reached, there is a *contest for hegemony* between rival versions of masculinity. The school, though it has set this contest up, may be highly ambivalent about the outcome. Many school administrations actively seek competitive sporting success as a source of prestige. The first-rate football team, or the school's swimming champions, may attract as much honor and indulgence from the staff as the academic elite.[17]

The differentiation of masculinities, then, is not simply a question of individual difference emerging or individual paths being chosen. It is a collective process, something that happens at the level of the institution and in the organization of peer group relationships.

Indeed, the relationship of any one boy to the differentiation of masculinities may change over time. Stewart Hardy remembers being terrified on his arrival at high school (and even before, with "horror tales" about high school circulating in his primary class). He and his friends responded by "clinging to each other for security" in a wimpish huddle in Form I. But then:

> Once I started getting used to the place and not so afraid of my own shadow, I felt here was my chance to develop a new identity. Now I can be a coolie, I can be tough. So I started to be a bit more belligerent. I started to get in with the gangs a bit, slag off[t] teachers behind their backs, and tell dirty jokes and stuff like that.

But it didn't last. After a while, as Stewart got older,

> I decided all that stuff was quite boring. It didn't really appeal to me, being a little shit any more, it didn't really suit my personality.

This was not just a matter of Stewart's "personality." His parents and his teachers put on more pressure for academic performance as the School Certificate (Form IV) approached. Indeed, his parents obliged him to stay on at school to Form VI, long after the "gangs" had left.

OVER THE HUMP

The labor market in modern capitalist economies is segmented and stratified in a number of dimensions. Perhaps the most powerful division in it is not any longer the blue-collar/white-collar divide, but the distinction between (a) a broad market for more or less unskilled general labor—whether manual or clerical—and (b) a set of credentialed labor markets for specific trades, semiprofessions, and professions. The public education system, as the main supplier of credentials (certificates, diplomas, degrees), is deeply implicated in this division. When Stewart Hardy's working-class parents ignored his protests and made him stay on in high school, they were pursuing a family strategy to get him over the hump between these two labor markets and into the world of credentialed labor.

For Stewart it was a rocky path. He resented the pressure, slacked off at school, got involved with a girlfriend, and did "miserably" at the Higher School Certificate (HSC). Soon after that, he ditched the girlfriend and got religion. But after he had been a while in the work force, his parents' pressure bore fruit, and he took himself to a technical college to have a second try at the HSC. This time he did so well that he qualified for university. He is now (aged twenty-four) doing a part-time arts degree and, at the same time, a computer training program organized by his employer, a big bank. He does not see computing as a career, but as a fallback: "If things get tight I can always go back to being a programmer, because there are always jobs for that." He may get into a career through his degree.

Stewart has got the message about qualifications, with a vengeance:

All the time I wasted before, I could have been at university getting a degree. Seven years out of school and I have absolutely no qualification at all. All I did was bum around and take whatever jobs came up.

The contrast with Mal Walton, Jack Harley, and Patrick Vincent is stark. They are glad of "whatever jobs come up" and expect to be at the mercy of such economic chances as far as they can see into the future. To them it isn't "time wasted," it is life.

Through the mechanism of educational credentials, Stewart Hardy has bought into a different construction of masculinity, in which the notion of a long-term career is central. A calculative attitude is taken toward one's own life. A passive and subordinated position in training programs is accepted in order to provide future protection from economic fluctuations. The life course is projected as if up a slope, with periods of achievement distinguished from plateaus of wasted time. The central themes of masculinity here are rationality and responsibility rather than pride and aggressiveness.

Young men from more privileged class backgrounds are likely to take this perspective from the start. Their families' collective practice is likely to be organized around credentials and careers from before they were born. For instance, I come from a family whose men have been in the professions—engineering, the church, medicine, education, law—for several generations. It never occurred to me that I would not go to university in my turn.

In such a milieu the practice of credentialing does not even require active consent, merely the nonoccurrence of a refusal. As Bill Lindeman, son of an administrator and an academic researcher, put it—

Because I'd had three siblings who'd gone ahead of me, so there was that sort of assumption there, that the opportunity was given to me to not question it, to not go to something else. And I didn't have strong interests: the strongest interest I had was surfing, in the Sixth Form. And there was nothing really to motivate me to go off and do anything else. So I went to Uni.

Here, very visibly, is a life course being constructed collectively and institutionally, through the education system and families' relationships to it. Of course, the young person has to do such things as sit in class and write exam answers: There is a personal practice involved. But to a marked degree it is a passive practice, following an external logic. The person's project is simply to become complicit in the functioning of an institutional system and the privileges it delivers. There is a painful contrast with the personal investments, and cost, involved in the hoods' doomed assaults on the same institutional system. One begins to feel the reason in all that anger.

DRY SCIENCES

What privileged young men find at the end of the educational conveyor belt is not necessarily to their taste. This becomes very clear in life histories from the environmental activists. Bill Lindeman went to university because there was nothing motivating him to go elsewhere. But after he had been there—and I hope it pleases his teachers—he began to think.

> When I chose science I chose zoology. My sister and my brother had done exactly the same and my other brother was doing physics, so we were all doing science. There was a strong analytical bent there. I chose life science because—that stemmed from my earlier childhood, enjoying natural places. It wasn't till I'd left Uni that I realized I was so bored with ninety-nine point nine percent of it. I just wasn't finding *nature* in laboratories, cutting up rats and dogfish. The vitality and change that you can learn from nature just isn't there. It was dry. I didn't relate it to the living world.

Bill's critique of the abstractness, the unlifelikeness, of biology is a familiar theme in critiques of other disciplines and of academic knowledge in general.[18] Bill's version is informed by his "green" politics. He began to resolve the problem in a research project involving long field trips to the Snowy Mountains, and then became deeply committed to environmental activism. In that context he also became concerned with the remaking of masculinity, though he has not specifically linked this theme back to his academic experience.

There is, nevertheless, a connection. The dry sciences of academic abstraction involve a particular institutionalization of masculinity. Masculinity shapes education, and education forms masculinity. This has become clear from work on the history and philosophy of science. It is not incidental that most of the people constructing Western science over the last four hundred years have been men. The view of the natural world that mainstream science embodies, the language and metaphors of scientific analysis—a discourse of uncovering, penetrating, controlling—have some of their deepest roots in the social relations between men and women. A different kind of knowledge could have been produced, and to some extent is produced, by people whose thinking is shaped by experience of a different location in gender relations. For instance, a science constructed by women might be more likely to use metaphors of wholeness than metaphors of analysis, seek cooperation with nature rather than domination over it.

Some early work in this vein implied that the structure of science reflected masculinity in general, that the attitude of abstraction and domination over nature was based on something intrinsic to being male. This argument would hardly apply to the relation of men to nature in central Australian aboriginal society, where the ethic of humans caring for the land and the land's "ownership" of the people is traditional.[19] Western science is, rather, based on a culturally specific version of masculinity. Indeed, we may see it as a class-specific version. There is a wide gap between technocratic masculinity as embodied in science and the hot, loud, messy masculinity of the "hoods."

Yet the version of masculinity to which Bill Lindeman is pointing is important, even crucially important, in the contemporary world. Winter and Robert some time ago noted the importance of the changing scale and structure of the capitalist economy for the dynamics of masculinity—a theme much ignored by "men's studies" literature since.[20] The dry sciences are connected, on the one hand, to administration, whose importance is obvious in a world of enormous state apparatuses and multinational corporations. On the other hand, they are connected to professionalism, which is a synthesis of knowledge, power, and economic privilege. Professionalism is central both to the application of developing technologies and to the social administration of modern mass populations.

In both respects the sciences are connected to power, and they represent an *institutionalized* version of the claim to power that is central in hegemonic masculinity. But this is not the crude assertion of personal force that is all the power someone like Jack Harley can mobilize. Rather it is the organized, collective power embodied in large institutions like companies, the state, and property markets. This is power that delivers economic and cultural advantage to the relatively small number of people who can operate this machinery. A man who can command this power has no need for riding leathers and engine noise to assert masculinity. His masculinity is asserted and amplified on an immensely greater scale by the society itself.

READING FEMINISM

The men in the study who are involved in countersexist politics, or who have adopted some feminist principles, have almost all read feminist books. Indeed, some say this is their main source of feminist ideas, alongside personal relationships with feminist women. In contrast, mass media seem to be the main source of information about feminism (more exactly, misinformation about feminism) among men who have *not* moved toward feminism.

Contemporary feminism is a highly literate political movement. The mobilization of the "second wave" was accompanied by a vast outpouring of writing: new books, new magazines, special issues of old journals, and so on.[21] Students and teachers made up a high proportion of activists. Writers like Simone de Beauvoir, Betty Friedan, and Mary Daly occupy a central place in modern feminism. The conflict of texts is central to the definition of its various factions and currents.[22] To become a feminist does not absolutely require a higher degree in literature, but it is certainly usual that someone consciously becoming feminist will read a lot.

Many people cannot read. This is true absolutely for Mal Walton, whose alienation from school is described above. He was tipped out into the labor market at fifteen unable to read a job advertisement. He is desperately disadvantaged by illiteracy, tries to conceal it from the employment service as well as from employers, and is currently asking his girlfriend to teach him to read. Illiteracy in first-world countries tends to be concentrated among poor and marginalized groups.[23] In a case like Mal's it is easy to see its class-driven connection with "getting into trouble," the war on school in which Mal's embattled masculinity was shaped.

More commonly in rich countries like the United States and Australia, young people do learn to read, in the sense that they can decode the letters and spell out the words, but do not put this skill to use for anything much beyond job advertisements and sports results. I think this is true for Eel and for Jack Harley. Patrick Vincent is in between, he can read reasonably well but has difficulty writing. None of these young men ever mention *ideas* they have got from print, only those that come from talk and television.

There is a level of *political literacy* where reading opens up new ideas, poses alternatives to existing reality, explains what forces are at work in the wider world. These young men have not entered this world. They are only likely to if there is a major politicization of the working class and a massive adult education initiative. Since the mass communication system that they are plugged into, commercial television, is totally opposed to radical reform, the strong likelihood is that they never will reach political literacy.

The men who do grapple with the textual politics of feminism are likely to be from privileged class backgrounds; Bill Lindeman's political literacy is an aspect of his easy insertion into higher education. Or they are men who, like Danny Taylor, have used the education system to escape a working-class milieu.

In neither case is the reading likely to be uplifting and enjoyable. The literature they are most likely to encounter, the "public face" of feminism, is—not to put too fine a point on it—hostile to men, and little is included to make distinctions between groups of men.[24] The reader is likely to encounter a lurid picture of men *en bloc* as rapists, batterers, pornographers, child abusers, militarists, exploiters—and women as victims. Titles like *Female Sexual Slavery, Women of Ideas and What Men Have Done to Them, Pornography: Men Possessing Women* set the tone. Young men who read much of this literature and take it seriously seem to have one major reaction: severe feelings of guilt. Barry Ryan sums it up:

> After university I was at the stage where I could understand academic literature, and I read some pretty heavy stuff, which made me feel terrible about being male for a long time.

Guilt is an emotion with social effects, but in this case they are likely to be disempowering rather than positive. A young man "feeling terrible about being male" will not easily join with other men in social action. Nor can he feel solidarity (except at some symbolic level) with women. Thus guilt implies that men's personalities must change but undermines the social conditions for changing them, an enterprise that requires substantial interpersonal support.

Nor is there any useful set of texts to turn to. In terms of what is widely available, there is little between popular feminism (which accuses men) and mass media (which ridicule feminism). A small literature of masculinity therapy exists, designed to assuage the guilt feelings of men affected by feminism.[25] This is almost as demobilizing as the guilt itself.

In such a situation, an educational effort in schools and tertiary institutions might bear rich fruit. Courses on sexual politics do exist at both levels. But they are few, especially in schools. Barry Ryan is the only one of the respondents to describe a school course of this kind, in a progressive private school:

> The teachers at that free school were the ones who decided to implement that sexism program and we [the students] were involved in it. I remember having to go and make a verbal submission. . . . We got this course together. I remember having all-male groups and the women having all-women groups, and talking about sexism, and that was basically it. We did a lot of discussion about sexism and how we communicated about women. I didn't learn that much in the course itself, it just taught me that it was something that I was going to have to think about. And so from then on I was always thinking about it.

On Barry's account the organizing framework of the course is "sexism," which would imply a focus on attitudes and perhaps a moralization of the issue.

Two respondents described meeting feminist content in tertiary courses, though not as focused as Barry's school course. Both had come back to education after a period in the work force, with a project of personal change in mind. This may explain why they were in courses dealing with such issues. Material on sexual politics is rare in tertiary courses with high proportions of male students.

REFLECTIONS

In this paper I have been trying to give some articulation to two "voices" that are at best muted, at worst silenced, in the discourse of patriarchy. The interviews show an aspect of the formation of masculinity that is more conflictual and more contradictory than the older accounts of sex role socialization implied. The school is not necessarily in harmony with other major "agencies" like the family or the workplace. It is not necessarily in harmony with itself. Some masculinities are formed by battering against the school's authority structure, others by smooth insertion into its academic pathways, others again by a tortuous negotiation of possibilities. Teachers' own characters and sexual politics are not brought into focus in these interviews, but they are no less complex than the sexual politics of the pupils.[26]

Educational institutions sometimes explicitly address themes of masculinity, and examples are documented in these interviews. They range from the countersexist course described by Barry Ryan to the organized sports mentioned by many of the respondents. In most of these life stories, sport (Eel is the obvious exception) does not have the significance, either as symbol or as practice, that has been suggested in some other studies of the making of masculinity.[27] It may be that choosing two groups that are in various ways distanced from mainstream versions of masculinity has found life stories in which sport is less important than usual. Or it may be that we need to reconsider the role of sport more generally. It is culturally conspicuous as an arena of masculinity; but mundane institutional processes may be more broadly significant in the shaping of personality as practical being in the world.[28] Only a diminishing minority of men continue to practice team sports after midadolescence.

In the long perspective, I would argue, it is the inexplicit, indirect effects of the way schools work that are crucial. A stark case is the way streaming and "failure" push groups of working-class boys toward alienation, and state authority provides them a perfect foil for the construction of a combative, dominance-focused masculinity. Equally clear is the role of the academic curriculum and its machinery of assessment and selection in institutionalizing a rationalized masculinity in professions and administration.

To put the point in more familiar language, the "hidden curriculum" in sexual politics is more powerful than the explicit curriculum. This creates a dilemma for people concerned with democratizing gender relations in the schools. What the school acknowledges as its activity in relation to gender, and may therefore be willing to discuss under the heading of "equal opportunity" or "antidiscrimination," is less significant than what it does not acknowledge. A change of awareness, a bringing-effects-to-light, must happen before the full spectrum of the school's influence can even be debated.

The intractable situation in schools has a lot in common with the difficulty of formulating a progressive sexual politics for heterosexual men in other forums. Despite promising beginnings, it has proved difficult to find or create a base for a consistent countersexist practice.[29] The contrast with the political mobilization of gay men in gay liberation, and more recently around AIDS issues, is striking. The structural problem is obvious. Heterosexual men are the dominant group in the gender order of contemporary society; therefore, propping up patriarchy, rather than demolishing it, will advantage them. In a quite basic way, trying to mobilize a countersexist politics is asking heterosexual men to act against their social interests.

Yet if recent research has shown anything, it is that heterosexual masculinity is not homogeneous; it is fissured, divergent, and stressed in many ways. The *possibility* of an educational politics of masculinity exists in these differences and tensions. Can this possibility be turned to practical account?

To the extent that learning depends on "interest," in the psychological sense, the omens are good. There is no lack of interest in questions of sexuality, gender, and sexual politics among boys and young men—as the topics of conversation in Mal Walton's toilet block illustrate. For many it is a matter of absorbing concern.[30]

At present the resources for responding to this interest are deployed in a way that makes them spectacularly difficult to use. Feminist textual politics are inaccessible to most men and require a teeth-gritting effort from the few who make contact. Courses on sexual politics are located mostly in higher education, which most men (like most women) do not reach. They are specifically located in sectors of higher education (such as humanities courses) not entered by most of the men who do become students. School-level equity programs concerned with gender are mostly targeted on girls, as might be expected given their "equal opportunity" rationale.

The first task, then, is simply to frame programs that stand a chance of reaching large numbers of boys. Given the importance of the academic curriculum and selection process in the shaping of masculinities, it would be self-defeating to rely mainly on "extracurricular" special-purpose programs such as sex education. As Yates has forcefully argued, countersexist action in schools must be concerned with mainstream curriculum and school organization. It is a question of an effort *across the curriculum*, much as language development is now conceived.[31] Thus, a school trying to examine and reflect on masculinity with its pupils will do so in relation to sport, in relation to science, in relation to art and literature, in relation to personal interaction in the peer group and between teachers and pupils, and in relation to the school's own institutional practices such as examining, streaming, and the exercise of authority.

Such an approach is in fact adopted in schools that have had some success in countersexist work in a coeducational situation, such as Hugh Myddleton Junior School in London:

> Monitoring the classroom interactions and the use of social space by boys in the school has led to a firm, if understated, affirmative action policy at the school. For example, the arrival of the new micro-computer equipment led to a decision to prohibit the boys from using it until the girls got a head start. In classrooms traditional girls' activities are validated by granting more space to their discussion and activities. The girls are encouraged to be vocally demonstrative. Boys are encouraged to dance, and a good music-in-the-nursery program has been developed. . . . Changed relations between kids and teachers have been encouraged because Richard [the principal] refuses to be the discipline ogre of the school. . . . A slow deliberate building of gains made over the last ten years has produced a consensus on sexism that we'd all like to see. It also shows what can be done by a male teacher when he puts effort into the issue seriously.[32]

We are still far from having a well-reasoned overall strategy in gender education within which the countercurrents in masculinity could find a clear voice. Perhaps that is too much to expect at present. But there are some more limited rationales on which teachers can act.

For one thing, the sources of information about sexuality and gender available to boys are often narrow and reactionary. It is an appropriate purpose for schools to introduce their pupils to the *whole* truth about an important area of their lives. That means introducing them to gay sexuality as well as straight, to the range of gender patterns across the world, to issues of rape and domestic violence as well as happy families. To do this requires prioritizing the experiences of those who are usually silenced or marginalized, especially women. This is not likely to be easy to do with many adolescent boys, but it is at least a coherent educational goal and one that may call on motives of curiosity and sympathy to expand horizons.

What this might mean is shown in Lees's splendid study of adolescent girls' experiences of sexuality. Lees argues for making "social education" the basis of sex education:

> Questions relating to the morality of sexual relations, domestic violence and the objectification of girls would be on the agenda. Instead of focusing purely on the mechanics of contraception, reasons for the fact that only a

third of sexually active teenagers actually use contraception would be critically examined . . . It is by challenging the terms on which girls participate in social life that boys and girls can be encouraged to see their relationships not in sexist stereotypical ways or as sex objects, but in terms of their human attributes.[33]

It is the inclusion of girls' and women's experiences of sexuality that gives the possibility of challenging sexist and abusive discourse among boys.

The life histories document a good many blocked paths, cases where the development of a patriarchal masculinity follows from a sense of being trapped, or where an attempt at reconstruction peters out in frustration, doubts, or confusion. In my teaching on issues of gender at university level, I have often seen men starting out with good will; then, confronted with the endless facts of gender inequality, and feeling themselves under an increasing fire of blame, turn away because they had no method for dealing with this and saw nothing but more blame and guilt coming down the pipeline.

Developing a sense of agency, a confidence in being able to accomplish something on these issues, is needed. Here cooperative work with feminist women is essential. Educators may get very useful cues from people working on problems about adult masculinity, such as counselors working with battering husbands and unionists taking countersexist action in workplaces.[34] Politics was once defined as ''slow boring through hard boards,'' and no one should expect quick results in this corner of sexual politics. But we now have enough leads, from practice and research, to make the effort worth undertaking.

GLOSSARY FOR OVERSEAS READERS

Hoods: Toughs, delinquents.

Dunnies: Outdoor toilets, so called from being traditionally painted a dun color.

Perve: The Male Gaze, looking at women as sex objects; or at women's underclothes, a couple having intercourse, etc.

Mob: Group (e.g., a flock of sheep, a peer group of people)— no overtone of Mafia.

Forms I-VI: The six years of high school in the New South Wales system. Form VI leads to the Higher School Certificate at matriculation level. Most working-class boys leave at Form IV.

Swots: Enthusiastic students, or simply those who ''succeed'' at academic work.

Slag off: To verbally abuse.

A BRIEF NOTE ON RESOURCES

Useful collections of readings (aimed at tertiary level) are A. Metclaf and M. Humphries, ed., *The Sexuality of Men* (London, Pluto Press, 1985); M. Kaufman, ed., *Beyond Patriarchy* (Toronto, Oxford Uni. Press, 1987); M. Kimmel and M. Messner, ed., *Men's Lives* (New York, Macmillan, 1989). I know of less at school level, but try *Boys Own: Boys, Sexism and Change* (Sydney, Inner City Education Centre, 1985) for Australia and J. Dryfoos, *Putting the Boys in the Picture* (Santa Cruz, CA, Network Publications, 1988) for the USA. An excellent contemporary analysis of the politics of masculinity is L. Segal, *Slow Motion* (London, Virago, 1990).

RICHARD A. FRIEND

Chapter Ten

Choices, Not Closets: Heterosexism and Homophobia in Schools

I'm 17 and a senior in high school. I'm not "out" to everyone at school, but I am to most of my friends and my folks. My parents and friends have been terrific. A lot of my friends' reaction was "oh, that figures." I'm not "out" at school because it is potentially dangerous. Dangerous because I might get beat up, it would make life tough for my friends, and because it would make it difficult to make new friends in some cases. The guys have it worse. A lot of people probably assumed that I'm gay for years, but I don't think a public declaration would be good. I often hear gay jokes at school and when the teacher doesn't say anything I find myself making a choice between silence and a response that would heighten any assumptions they might have. The sad thing is that many gay people end up laughing along with the jokes.

—Gail, personal communication,
27 July 1985

I'm 16 and I'm gay but I never felt comfortable in school. If they just had someone who knew, understood or even tried to understand

it would have helped. The subject was never
mentioned; nothing about homosexuality or
gays. It seemed as if it was bad, wrong or
against morals of everyday society. I thought
"Do I have a disease? Is it a sickness? How
did I catch it?" In time I realized it was O.K.
for me to be gay, but in school I had to be
straight and played a straight role. I left school
early every day because I was afraid of someone finding out. I wish someday the schools
would have a program to help young people
find the answers as to who they are and it's
O.K. to be gay.

—(Harold, personal communication,
27 July 1985)

INTRODUCTION

Gail and Harold are survivors. They each graduated high school. While
graduation is often the outcome used to measure success, school for these two
lesbian and gay youths was often a process of pain and struggle braided with
a tremendous amount of strength and courage. Their comments reflect the
conflicts and contradictions felt while participating in a system that attempted to silence their voices. Through the use of narratives, the voices of
lesbian, gay, bisexual, and heterosexual participants in public school will be
heard in this chapter in order to examine the nature of heterosexism in schooling and its impact on those within the system.

While schools can be described as potentially a site of extraordinary democracy, the processes and outcomes of schools deeply reproduce and promote the very social inequities they are said to equalize. Until recently,
however, serious discussion of how inequalities in terms of sexual orientation
are reproduced and sanctioned by schooling has been absent in the social
analyses of diversity, equity, and power in education.

This chapter provides an analysis of the nature of heterosexist silencing
in public schools and through the use of narratives attempts to de-silence the
experience of members who survive within the homophobic and heterosexist
cultures of schooling. As Grayson argues, "Homosexuality can no longer be
ignored as an educational equity issue."[1] By the very "perversity" of homophobic silencing, these voices could not reflect a random sampling. They
have been selected, instead, because of their poignancy and capacity to illustrate critical points of the analysis.

THE LAYERS OF SILENCING

Heterosexism and Homophobia: The Ideology of Silencing

Schools and families are two powerful social arenas where young people live and learn to make meaning out of their lives. Often these institutions work in tandem to cement the ideologies of heterosexism and fuel the terrors of homophobia, sedimented in the multiple layers of silence that results.

Heterosexism is defined as the belief that everyone is, or should be, heterosexual,[2] or what Lorde describes as "a belief in the inherent superiority of one pattern of loving over all others and thereby the right to dominance."[3] Based on this assumption of universal heterosexuality, or what Rich[4] calls "compulsory heterosexuality," a systematic set of institutional and cultural arrangements exist that reward and privilege people for being or appearing to be heterosexual, and establish potential punishments or lack of privilege for being or appearing to be homosexual. Heterosexism is prejudice against homosexuality that is maintained by a pervasive set of societal institutions that sanction and promote this ideology.[5]

The deep embeddedness of this ideology renders its appearance both subtle and pervasive. Within many aspects of schools' curricula, for example, the value of the superiority of heterosexuality over homosexuality is displayed. For an "innocent" example, consider figure 10.1, an illustration used in a physics text to teach the concept of positive and negative charges.[6] Adults and students typically do not question the heterosexist message inherent in this illustration.

From the assumption that everyone is, or should be, heterosexual and, therefore, heterosexuality's being imbued with greater value and privilege, feelings of fear and dislike toward homosexuality often result.[7] Homophobia is the fear and hatred of homosexuality in one's self and in others[8] and emerges as a result of heterosexism.[9] These feelings of fear and hatred create

FIGURE 10.1
A homophobic illustration used in a physics textbook to teach the concept of
positive and negative charge.

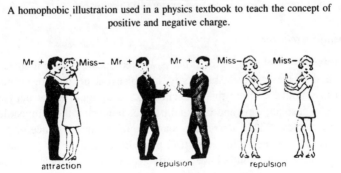

a discomfort that reinforces the attitude that "people should not be homosexual." For some people this discomfort and the associated set of attitudes and beliefs function to "legitimate" responses that may range from overt violence and harassment to a dismissal or discounting of the experiences of lesbian, gay, and bisexual people.

Heterosexism is not limited to schools, however. Family "cultures" typically participate as a layer in the silencing process. According to Krysial, "Gay people are the only minorities that do not have a parent as a role model."[10] Hunter and Schaecher report that "violence toward lesbian and gay people comes not only from strangers but very often from family as well."[11] One social worker told me that a gay youth he was working with shared that "growing up gay in my family is like being Jewish in a Nazi home." Most targets of hate crimes and prejudice can find support and understanding from their families. Targeted families may also provide their children the emotional and physical tools for managing and responding to oppression. This is usually *not* true for lesbian, gay, and bisexual youth, however. As Smith says, "Lesbians and gays are the only oppressed group that was born and raised by our oppressors."[12]

John said, "When I told my mother, she gave me $10.00 and told me I was on my own. That really hurt, I had always thought we were so close."[13] According to a sixteen-year-old lesbian:

> Her (my mother) first reaction was "You'd better go to the doctors about it!" This was followed by "How disgusting. Keep away from me." As if homosexuality was contagious. Now she thinks that just because I like girls, I must either hate men or want to be a man, (neither of which is true). She still doesn't understand as she still equates homosexuality with dirty old men screwing little boys up dark alleys.[14]

While oftentimes supported by families, heterosexism and homophobia are also shaped and reinforced in schools by two interrelated mechanisms of silencing—systematic exclusion and systematic inclusion.

Systematic Exclusion

Systematic exclusion is the process whereby positive role models, messages, and images about lesbian, gay, and bisexual people are publicly silenced in schools.[15] Often this silencing occurs by ignoring or denying the presence of lesbian, gay, and bisexual people, rendering them invisible. According to Rofes, "This across-the-board denial of the existence of gay and lesbian youth has been allowed to take place because their voices have been silenced and because adults have not effectively taken up their cause."[16]

Systematic exclusion occurs in several ways. When teachers interrupt racist or sexist name-calling in their classroom but do not intervene when homophobic comments are made (which is frequently the case),[17] there is a message of permission communicated in this silence. According to Dennis and Harlow,[18] when school officials fail to provide protection from peer harassment and violence, they are in violation of their duty in loco parentis to provide for students' safety during the day. Likewise, when issues related to sexual orientation are systematically left out of the curriculum, such as in health education or in English class (when discussing the work of James Baldwin, Virginia Woolf, Walt Whitman, or Gertrude Stein, for example), or when students spontaneously raise questions and offer a teachable moment (when they want to discuss the lesbian relationships they read about in the book *The Color Purple*), or when lesbian and gay teachers feel it is too risky to be open about their sexual orientations in the same ways that their heterosexual colleagues are open about their sexual orientations, systematic exclusion prevails.

The absence of openly lesbian, gay, or bisexual adults as role models is a powerful example of exclusion and can result in students' experiencing powerful contradictions. Many youth talk about the frustration and confusion they feel when they see teachers who are assumed or known to be lesbian or gay, hiding their sexual orientation in school. These adolescents understand and despair about the dangers—they live it too, feel cheated by the lost resource, and yet desperately, they also feel less alone.

The contradiction of strong but "closeted" role models is highlighted in the following testimony of a woman reflecting back on her experience in an all-girls high school.

I hated high school. It was a place to begin preparing and competing against other girls for admission to college. It was not a place to acknowledge, discover, or enhance our lives and heritage as women, let alone lesbians. How unfortunate, since there were so many strong, intelligent, sensitive women who taught there. Yet, there were few, if any, feminist role models or lesbian role models. We were learning how to "make it" in a man's world in a man's way. I was not "out" as a lesbian in high school. I didn't know I was one. The only lesbians that I knew were the gym teachers that we all gossiped about, yet, they commanded our respect and they received it. They were not "out" then. As I look back, these women both intrigued and intimidated me. Unfortunately the only role models that these women presented were ones of being strong women, but "in the closet". Therefore, that's what shaped my early unconscious picture of a lesbian and when I came to the realization that I was a lesbian, I was terrified. If there had been some acknowledgement of lesbian life and culture in high school, then I could have had choices and not closets. My education would have felt more honest, more relevant to me. I feel cheated! It's especially painful because I attended an all girl's high school which could have been a strong place to nurture my feelings and knowledge of women's history, feminism, lesbianism and other cultures. If education is to teach children about choices and how to make appropriate decisions, then any curriculum has to make room to present *all* possible ways to live a life.[19]

Even students who try to access information on their own are confronted with systematic silencing. In a workshop on heterosexism and homophobia for high school counselors, participants were asked to look at their offices for the presence of any messages regarding homosexuality and to consider what the absence of any messages might suggest to students. During the workshop, one counselor shared in writing what for him seems to represent potential clutter to a world in which he tries to maintain order:

> I have limited space in my small counseling office. I use that limited space to communicate to students that I am not too busy to see them. I keep my office uncluttered and as neat as possible. My office is filled with factual resource material: guide directories, files of information and sources of help. I am opposed to the use of slang terms. For example what is so "gay" about being homosexual? Does this mean all homosexuals are or should be happy? . . . Why is it so important to come out of the closet? Is self-disclosure a social benefit? If one exhibits himself before the public does this mean the public is expected to applaud? (personal written communication, 14 November 1990)

This counselor's questions highlight his conflict over seeing a connection between being available to students, having resource material, and facilitating a process whereby he helps students answer these questions for themselves.

Another common situation contributing to the difficulty students may face in getting information is that if the school library does have any books on homosexuality, they are frequently kept behind the reference desk. This systematically excludes information by making it inaccessible to students. Often the librarian's rationale is that these books are frequently stolen (students are too embarrassed to check them out). By keeping them off the shelves, however, a catch-22 is created, whereby students may need the books in order to begin to feel more comfortable with asking for the books. According to Whitlock,

> Finding books that present a positive view of gay and lesbian life can be very difficult for adolescents, even in large cities. If homosexuality is mentioned at all, it is typically presented with a strong homophobic bias. More absent still is any recognition of the many gay men and lesbians—of all

races, cultures and faiths—who have given us works of art, examples of heroism and courage or leadership in social movements. While the contributions people make in public life are more important than any single detail of personal life, learning about the homosexual orientation of poets like Walt Whitman or Audre Lorde, novelists like Willa Cather or James Baldwin, artists like Michelangelo, human rights leaders like Bayard Rustin or Dag Hammarskjold, playwrights like Lorraine Hansberry and pioneers in social welfare like Jane Addams could help shatter homophobic stereotypes.[20]

The systematic exclusion of information, resource materials, empathic support, and/or role models contributes to cementing the layers of silencing in schools.

Systematic Inclusion: Homosexuality as Pathology, Sexual Behavior, or Danger

The second, but interrelated, process that functions to institutionalize heterosexism in schools is systematic inclusion. When discussions regarding homosexuality do occur, they are consistently placed in a negative context. This results in the systematic inclusion of conversations about homosexuality only as pathology, only in regard to sexual behavior and/or framed as dangerous. An example from a health education text entitled *Masculinity and Femininity*, used in the Philadelphia public schools until recently (while no longer a text given to students, it is still available to teachers as a resource), highlights all three of these elements. Pictured is a sinister character lurking behind a tree outside of a school yard with the following caption:

> A male homosexual may wait patiently around a high school day after day, until he thinks he can safely approach and befriend a student. . . . If homosexuals can be so devious and careful, how can you avoid being trapped? Only your alertness can keep you out of a potentially dangerous situation.

While this example may appear extreme, it represents the type of negative messages that are sanctioned in schools when silence around homosexuality is broken in limited ways.

Another example of inclusion only as pathology or danger is when the only "official" conversations regarding homosexuality occur when discussing AIDS/HIV. Katie recalls that the only time homosexuality was ever formally addressed in school was in her junior year during an AIDS awareness day presentation given by a gay man. Katie said, "I was so excited. Wow, a gay person in the school. I sat in the chair where his jacket was. Wow, a real live homosexual's jacket and I was touching it" (personal communication, 20

November 1990). Limiting discussions about homosexuality to AIDS/HIV not only explicitly links homosexuality with danger and pathology, but also undermines effective AIDS/HIV prevention education.[21]

When the conversation does turn to homosexuality, it may focus only on sexual behavior. Homosexuality means sex; and heterosexuality equals love, family, and much more. According to one eighteen-year-old woman, "I am very happy being a lesbian but I just wish that society would accept us and gay men. I mean, honestly, why do they think it's a crime to love? They think we spend 24 hours a day in bed. Why?"[22]

In our society, sexual expression and sexual "privilege" in general are sanctioned only for adults; and in particular, for adults in a heterosexually monogamous marriage.[23] Adolescents grow up facing the challenge of identity formation in schools where, if sexuality is discussed at all, it is generally within the context of "the problems" of teen pregnancy, "the epidemic" of sexually transmitted diseases including AIDS/HIV, and/or "the horrors" of incest, rape, and other forms of sexual assault. This focus on the dangers of sexuality at the exclusion of conversations regarding the pleasure of sexuality,[24] particularly in sexuality education for adolescents,[25] contributes to the sex-negative, or erotophobic, climate whereby "sex is presumed guilty until proven innocent."[26] It is within this particular climate that adolescents are expected to crystallize their emerging sexual identities. It is no wonder, then, that adolescents in general, and lesbian, gay, or bisexual youths in particular, often experience their sexuality within a context of contradiction—a braiding of sexual pleasure with guilt, anxiety, and fear.

Ironically, while conversations regarding homosexuality may be limited to discussion of sexual behavior, the absent discourse of sexual pleasure prevails.[27] Rarely, if ever, would one find in a curriculum an example of sexual pleasures braided with sexual tension and conflict like in Ellen's (age fifteen) description.

> At the age of 8 I was playing mummy and daddy with a friend and we got into bed together. We became so involved in our enjoyment of touching each other that we forgot we were playing a game. Another friend was with us and when we asked her get into bed with us, she said what we were doing was bad and she went home crying. From then on, touching another girl in any sort of affectionate way seemed bad and wrong. But that didn't stop me from doing it.
>
> I had some really good experiences. One girl became my best friend. We spent the afternoon in my bedroom and had a great time. We kissed and cuddled and rubbed our bodies together and touched and masturbated and thoroughly enjoyed ourselves. My feelings were so over-powering. I loved her and she loved me. We felt what we were doing was pretty natural and

felt so good, but we were scared as hell if anyone might find us. I never saw her again after that week.

When I was 14, I was invited to stay with another friend. We stayed up late every night watching her video of 'Fame'. She was in love with Lee-Roy. God, it was awful. One night I had a backache and she opted to massage it for me. She practically tickled me to death, but she turned me on too. When we eventually went to bed together, I had to play as if I was Lee-Roy and she was my girlfriend. It was funny and a good laugh, but disgusting.[28]

This narrative is powerful not only as an account of lesbian sexuality so obviously missing in public discourse, but because it so poignantly expresses the apparent contradiction of intense pleasure and abandonment experienced within a context of danger and fear.

Systematic inclusion also operates through having one's adolescent experience "reframed" or "corrected" by a person in authority to fit with the predominant heterosexist ideology. Twenty-two-year-old Judy recounts: "I received very negative messages in junior high from a counselor. I told her I was attracted to female breasts. She said that was because I going to have them some day."[29]

Violence, or the threat of violence, for being or appearing to be lesbian or gay is part of the climate of schools supported by the process of systematic inclusion. While not interrupting homophobic name-calling may passively contribute to supporting heterosexism and homophobia, teachers can participate in supporting this ideology in more direct ways as well. The following testimony describes this process.

As a part of the (8th grade) Physical Education program there was a one-period "Hygiene" class each week which was conducted by one of our P.E. instructors. At some point in the year we reached the chapter in our textbooks where it became necessary for the instructor to talk with us about sex. The only thing I remember from that course is one of the boys making a joke about how homosexuals have sex and kidding with the instructor about how he knows the instructor would like to "get boned." Our sex educator became annoyed and said, "Yeah, you let some faggot try to stick his thing up my butt, I'd break his nose and then cut his joint off." The class broke out in hysterics and I joined them to hide my embarrassment and disgust with myself.[30]

While the teacher's comment may not have been intended to insult, harass, intimidate, or embarrass any students in his class, the effect was that he did embarrass and offend while at the same time giving tacit permission for anti-gay violence.

The systematic exclusion and silencing of accurate and affirmative messages regarding homosexuality, coupled with the systematic inclusion of negative and oppressive ideologies, reflects and reinforces heterosexist beliefs and attitudes in schools. The power of this hegemony is apparent when educators share their concerns regarding breaking the silence.

Breaking the Silence: Concerns of Educators

Resistance regarding breaking the silence, or not following the rules of systematic exclusion and inclusion, reflect the extent to which silence creates a cloud of mystification for students and educators. Teachers, in particular, express a fear of "unduly influencing" or "encouraging," a fear of "imposing values," of becoming individually "suspect," and the fears of backlash.

A common belief is that people are all born heterosexual and become influenced (usually by an adult homosexual) or "recruited" into homosexuality. This somehow translates into a concern among educators—if they *talk* about homosexuality, they may be *encouraging* it in their students. One educator, for example, participating in a workshop shared in writing her concern and personal conflict regarding combating homophobia. She had to grapple with the contradiction of being oppressed herself, wanting to be accepting while simultaneously wanting to "protect" children. Her conflict centers around not wanting to contribute to a system of oppression that she despises yet not being able to comfortably dismiss some of this system's messages that help to shape her world.

> I respect you for identifying your personal lifestyle. I understand your need to be accepted. I am willing to learn and understand. I accept you. However, I am afraid. I do not know why you are homosexual. Is it biological or environmental? Please don't try to influence my children. If they were to choose this lifestyle, I would never reject them. Because I am a member of a minority group in the U.S., I know first hand what it is like to be rejected. I have no right to be prejudiced against you. If I do this, I am perpetuating behavior that I detest. Thanks for the dialogue it helps me to understand. (personal communication, 28 August 1990)

Mystification clouds the fact that talking about sexual orientation in ways that acknowledge and affirm all people will only influence student's self-acceptance and their comfort with others who are similar to and different from themselves. Hidden behind the concern that talking about "it" will lead to "it" is the assumption that none of the students are lesbian, gay, or bisexual (and that having these conversations will make otherwise heterosexual students become homosexual, and that this would be bad); or that even if we could influence students' sexual orientation, that it would be better to develop heterosexual orientations than homosexual ones. Both of these assumptions reflect deeply the ideologies of heterosexism.

A second concern of educators about breaking the silence is that to do so is seen as ''imposing values'' and this is not considered to be the role of public education. To presume that discussing homosexuality in schools is to impose values, is not to notice that when we do *not* talk about the subject, we are also imposing a set of values. For example, schools' acceptance of prejudice against lesbian and gay people, according to Dennis and Harlow, ''bolsters the authority of privileged groups, legitimating prejudice and discrimination against any child who is a member of a racial, ethnic, or religious minority.''[31] The task for educators is to consider the school climate that they help to create and take responsibility for the outcomes that result from their value choices.

While there is often less stated resistance about reacting to homophobia in schools (intervening during a name-calling incident, for example), educators often express concern that if they act ''prophylactically,'' they themselves will become the targets of homophobic treatment. During a summer workshop, for example, one English teacher said, ''If I go back to my department and say, 'What about doing a unit on lesbian literature?' they're going to wonder 'Where in the hell was she this summer?'.'' Given the fact that sexual orientation is an invisible part of one's sexual identity, fear of suspicion rigidly reinforces the layers of silencing. As a white person, this teacher expressed no concern that her racial identity would be questioned when teaching about African American literature.

Fear of a backlash also motivates resistance to breaking the silence. The fear of opposition is strong—teachers fear their administrators, administrators fear parents, and so on. The fear of opposition alone often preempts the conversation. Fear that challenging heterosexism would lead to a charge of ''promoting homosexuality'' keeps many educators silent.[32] Within this oppressive climate educational professionals are called ''courageous'' or even ''subversive'' when they take a proactive stance in breaking the silence. This is why it is important to develop active community support and build alliances for these efforts from advocacy groups, unions, parents groups, alumni, and religious organizations even in the absence of active opposition.[33]

IMPACT ON STUDENTS: THE CONTRADICTIONS OF OPPRESSION AND RESISTANCE

For many students the texture and tone of schooling, with its potential violence and victimization, weave together a powerful and often contradictory pattern of experiences. Silencing and oppression may result in feelings of confusion, depression, and alienation. Students may react by dropping out, abusing drugs and alcohol, or committing suicide. However, it is as likely that within this context of oppressive silencing, lesbian and gay students develop strong sources of inner strength and a healthy sense of self and excel academically and socially. The evidence of oppression and resistance is only now accumulating.

Adolescence, as a developmental period with the goal of identity formation,[34] involves a great deal of social, psychological, biological, and cognitive changes.[35] Within this period of identity formation, adolescents are also coming to know themselves as sexual people. Given this developmental context, what is a homosexual? What is a heterosexual? We are told that many lesbian and gay people "recognize" their sexual orientation during preadolescent or teenage years.[36] Yet what does this mean?

Savin-Williams points out that, in general, adolescents are "more likely to experience cross orientation sexual contact than are adults" and "they are less likely to define themselves as homosexual individuals."[37] While "sexual orientation," defined as feelings of sexual attraction,[38] seems to be present from an early age[39] and perhaps at conception,[40] orientation does not correspond automatically with sexual behaviors or self-imposed identities.[41]

According to twenty-year-old Katie:

> It was in the summer of 9th grade while I was in basketball camp that I first remember being aware of my feelings of sexual attraction towards women. There was this one girl I played basketball with and I remember thinking "Wow. I want her to see me in a tank top. Wow. I want to kiss her." Throughout school though, I always had a boyfriend. By senior year I was finally putting a label to my feelings. I would be in the shower saying to myself, "I'm gay. I'm gay, I have to break up with Rob. I'm totally in love with Carol." By senior year I knew the word and finally applied it to myself based on what I was feeling, at least I did that in the shower. But 10 minutes later, while I was drying off, I would say "No, I'm not gay. I can't be. I have a boyfriend." (Katie, personal communication, 20 November 1990)

Katie's experience highlights the great potential for inconsistencies among sexual behavior, sexual orientation, and self-labeling as one's adolescent identity is forming.

Resonating Katie's experience, Savin-Williams writes:

> Given the complexity of whether one defines homosexuality by reference to orientation, behavior, or self-awareness and the fact that many teens experience a diversity of sexual behaviors and an emerging sexual identity over a period of years, a process which may not be completed until young adult-

hood, it is difficult to assess the prevalence of homosexual orientation among adolescents.[42]

Savin-Williams[43] stresses the importance of several empirically supported observations in understanding adolescent sexuality. First, not all homosexual adolescents are sexually active. Further, many homosexual adolescents are heterosexually active, while many heterosexual adolescents are homosexually active. Third, the fit between self-labeling and sexual behavior is often highly variable for adolescents. Finally, these factors evoke great stress and anxiety for adolescents of all sexual orientations.

Given estimates that approximately 10 percent of all adults identify themselves as exclusively or predominantly homosexual,[44] it can be estimated that in most public schools, with an average of thirty students per class, approximately three students in every class will grow up to identify themselves as lesbian or gay. This does not include the many others who will identify as bisexual or those whose cross-orientation sexual behaviors and feelings may cause themselves questions and/or concerns; or those whose gender-role behavior leaves others uncomfortable, and themselves anxious as a result. It is less important to focus on the prevalence of homosexuality or the impact heterosexism and homophobia has on lesbian and gay students, than it is to recognize the extent to which heterosexist silencing impacts on adolescents of all sexual orientations.

The homophobic fear and discomfort that emerges from and reinforces heterosexist arrangements and beliefs results in a range of overt behaviors. These may include anything from what may appear to be the "benign" silencing of ignoring, to the more pernicious levels of violence and harassment. Anti-lesbian and anti-gay violence is very prevalent in the United States and is on the rise.[45] Given that school-age youth are overrepresented among the perpetrators of anti-gay hate crimes,[46] for many youths who by choice or circumstance are identified as lesbian, gay, or bisexual in school, a great potential for victimization and harassment exists. According to a report released by the U.S. Department of Justice, lesbian and gay people are probably the most frequent victims of hate crimes, but the criminal justice system, like the rest of society, has not recognized the seriousness of this problem.[47] Comstock writes that "lesbian and gay crime victims report greater frequency of incidents in school settings than do victims of crime in general (25 percent, lesbian/gay; 9 percent, general)" and that "men experienced more violence in school settings than women (29 percent, men; 17 percent, women)," with people of color reporting more anti-gay and anti-lesbian violence in schools than whites.[48]

The harassment and violence runs a gamut from name-calling and egg tossing to homicide, and can be premeditated or reactionary. Given the pervasiveness of heterosexism in our culture, for some perpetrators, their motivation to engage in anti-lesbian and anti-gay violence need not be as much an expression of hatred "as it is a recreational option," framed as a rite of passage among males and seen as tacitly or overtly approved of by adults in their community,[49] these youth may reason that "if my church, parents and teachers are against homosexuality, what's the big deal with having a little fun."

In New York State, a broad survey of junior and senior high school students revealed that there is greater hostility toward lesbian and gay people than toward members of racial or ethnic minority groups.[50] Students also stated threats of anti-gay violence in the survey. Like the students surveyed, in writing about his personal feelings regarding homosexuality, eleventh grader Lamont says:

> The way I feel about gays. Personally I think gay men are very sick. He was born a man and should remain a man. His penis is to be used in a woman's vagina and not in a man's anus. I agree that they need to be shot. (personal communication, 16 June 1987)

Lamont was at least afforded the opportunity to explore the ramifications of these ideas in subsequent class discussion. This occurred because the teacher supported this type of dialogue.

Debrel describes the violence, the harassment, and the more typical lack of adult support that color his experience in high school.

> I hate attending school every day I just havnt gone to classes. Every where I go they use words, faggot, bitch, faggot Bitch, faggot motherfucker, sucking dick, stuff like that. Or trying to throw something to hit me, they hit on me, push me down. It's like one against a hundred. It's not like individuals its like everywhere I go in my school there is someone saying something to upset me. It happens mostly in the hall. Walk down the hall someone is try to grabe you or say they going get you. And in the classroom they would pick on me so bad I just get up and leave. Outside school some boys or young adult would try to rob me beat me up, or try to get me to do something I dont want to do—suck his pines that get me, very upset and mad when they approch me like that. There are sometime phyical violence. The teenage boys would try to beat me up because I am gay because I wont do things they want me to do. I get cussed very bad by students girls and boys sometimes my family. These are some of the word, I cant stand faggot, black bitch. I hate you faggot. I could be sitting in the class room some might shout out there that faggot and then the class will start laughing. The teacher won't say nothing about it but tell the class to be quiet thats about all. They will pretend like didn't here it. Like my English class they say things on the side but the teacher don't say nothing about it. . . . The at-

titude of my teacher is you got to go class pay them no mind. Science teacher, English teacher, Reading teacher, Math teacher all of them say the same thing and it make me sick to my stomach. Because they dont have to go through the problems every day, they dont know how it feel to be picked on every day.[51]

The most likely targets of the type of homophobic violence and public humiliation described by Debrel are adolescent males who are effeminate and sometimes females who are "overly" masculine.[52] When individuals, regardless of sexual orientation, fit the commonly believed stereotypes of gay and lesbian people, homophobic harassment is used to reinforce and enforce both heterosexism *and* sexism.

It is not by accident that those who are most frequently targeted are seen as violating expectations about how women and men "should be" or "should act." This is particularly true in explaining the greater discomfort with effeminate males as compared with masculine females. If, as a result of sexism, masculinity is valued more than femininity, often there is greater discomfort in response to a male who is seen as abandoning a position of power and authority. He can then be devalued for the "femaleness" in him and despised for the discomfort he is blamed for generating. Within this vein, it is argued, at least one can understand why "she would want to move up the ladder." In this way, homophobia enforces and reinforces both heterosexism and sexism. Pharr argues that homophobia is one of the fundamental roots of sexism.[53]

Not fitting what is considered the "appropriate" gender role is often framed by others as "flaunting" sexual behavior, therefore "justifying" a hostile response. This arrangement sets up powerful consequences for all students (especially males), warning them to *not* cross over the gender line. This line can be very tight and reflect specific behaviors, such as modes of dress or speech, but also types of expression and personality, such as sensitivity and emotionality. Martin and Hetrick explain further:

> Some people view simple openness and frankness about a homosexual orientation, regardless of the accompanying behavior, as "flaunting" and therefore as a hostile act. Others reserve that term for markedly deviant social behavior such as cross-dressing . . . (which) may be reactive behavior arising from one's minority position. In this case it becomes a means of coping with society's attitudes by exaggerating the behaviors expected by the society. When this is the case, it resembles the behavior of a black who shuffles or exaggerates stereotypical "black" behaviors in the presence of whites. Second, cross-dressing may reflect an acceptance of cultural attitudes toward homosexuality. That is, if a male is attracted to a male, then he is not masculine, and therefore must be feminine. If the young male accepts

this reasoning, he often feels that to be gay he must act feminine, and thus cross dresses. This later factor of cultural expectation also plays a role in the declarations of some young people, especially Black and Hispanic youth, that they are transsexuals.[54]

Others are targeted not because they necessarily fit some stereotype or "break the silence," but because they have been discovered by rumor or behavior to be gay or lesbian.[55] For many victims of homophobic targeting, the result is truancy or dropping out, drug and alcohol abuse, withdrawal from social activities, depression, and/or suicide.[56] Hippler reports that gay teenagers are three times more likely than nongay peers to become involved with substance abuse, and they are far more likely to run away from home or turn to prostitution.[57] Debrel, for example, dropped out of high school shortly after providing the above testimony, and his whereabouts are unknown. Harold, in the opening narrative, described leaving school early every day, and George, age seventeen, says:

> I play it as straight as I can, but it's hard. Like I go to all the parties and everything, but I have to get drunk. Drinking helps in playing it straight it also helps make it feel O.K. I would rather be drunk than alone. (personal communication, 24 November 1990)

Adolescents who may not be the direct targets of homophobic violence and harassment often expend considerable energy avoiding being discredited and targeted like the peers they witness.[58] Those who simply "observe" are deeply affected. Focusing on violence, Herek[59] explains, hate and bias crimes are particularly serious due to their potential victimization of an entire class of people, functioning, therefore, as a form of social control. Observing or being aware of the targeting of others, according to Herek, results in the fact that gay people "and heterosexuals alike may refrain from certain behaviors (e.g., men might not touch other men; women might not excel at tasks that require physical exertion) and avoid certain gestures or clothing styles because they fear being labeled as gay."[60]

For some lesbian and gay youths, heterosexism becomes internalized; feelings of self-doubt, self-hatred, and depression may emerge. According to Gonsiorik, "One of the greatest impediments to the mental health of gay and lesbian individuals is 'internalized homophobia.' "[61] The parents of twenty-year-old Robert W. Griffith have established a $500 memorial scholarship in the name of their son, who chose a warm, moonlit night in August of 1983 to end his life. He did not leave a note, but he left his diaries, which tell of the struggle Bobby had within himself about his homosexuality. This was how he "came out" to his parents.

Bobby is not alone. In a recent report on teen suicide by the U.S. Department of Health and Human Services, Gibson reports that gay youth are two to three times more likely to attempt suicide than other young people and may comprise up to 30 percent of completed youth suicides annually.[62] According to Remafedi, Farrow, and Deisher, approximately one-third of gay and bisexual youth they studied reported at least one intentional self-destructive act, and nearly half repeatedly attempted suicide.[63] An important predictor of self-harm, according to this study, was "gender noncomformity." The authors argue that "feminine or undifferentiated gender role may accentuate a gay adolescent's sense of 'differentness' and further exacerbate problems."[64] The extent to which femininity in males is seen as risk factor for suicide, suggests the powerful force of sexism and heterosexism on the lives of males in our culture.

It is important to note that not all youths crumble under the pressure of heterosexist arrangements and homophobic sentiments in schools. According to Gail, age eighteen:

> I never realized I was a lesbian until I was 17. I was madly in love with my best friend at school. She didn't speak to me decided she'd had enough of me. I sat with a gun pointed at my head. I mean, I was really far gone. I've done my wrists a couple of times. But I don't like pain and I don't like mess. Twice it was a very serious attempt, though. You know, like when you can't see a way out of what you're in and you want to end the way you're living— not your life. There's one thing about that—it's made me really anti-suicide. I don't want any bastard saying "Oh, she can't cope". I don't get depressed these days anyway.[65]

While Gail, for example, seriously considered suicide, she emerged from that process with a heightened degree of self-awareness and a strong commitment to survive. Savin-Williams stresses that theorists, educators, and practitioners should not assume that "tragedy" automatically results from living within an oppressive social context, when he writes:

> I affirm that in the United States gay men and lesbians have grown up in a homophobic culture, and I do not deny that this hatred has consequences. But to my knowledge, the causal link between external hatred and internal self-loathing has not been established . . . professionals may have lost contact with and thus distorted the lives of gay male and lesbian rank and file by emphasizing the negative in our history and culture. We may have lost sight of our resiliency and our joy.[66]

Students Who "Pass"

Most lesbian and gay youth opt for "passing" as heterosexual while in school,[67] and most self-identified lesbian and gay youth adjust fairly well while hiding their sexual orientation. Large numbers, however, are unable to manage the stress generated by being gay or lesbian in a homophobic school culture.[68] Given the frequency of "passing," what are the potential "costs" and "benefits" from this coping strategy? Remafedi[69] argues that healthy adolescent sexuality for lesbian and gay teens results from developing a positive lesbian or gay identity and self-affirming attitudes, along with the ability to adapt to and cope with a variety of social settings and contexts. This would be similar to developing a "bicultural" identity or "bilingual" fluency within a monocultural or "English only" preferred environment. In the opening narrative, Gail, for example, shares that while she is "out" to her family and close friends, she is not "out" at school. Like the Latino or Asian youth who must learn to "make it" in a racist world, Gail has learned to cope by knowing where it is safe to speak openly about herself and where she has to speak the "official language" of heterosexuality. The success of this coping strategy, as Remafedi[70] states, is contingent on the individual's resources for developing an affirmative lesbian or gay identity. Gail, for example, described the conflict she experiences in remaining silent and the sadness she feels for the gay people who end up laughing with the jokes. Again, this response reflects the contradictory nature of Gail's self-affirmation within the context of silence.

Stephanie, age eighteen, like Gail is "out" in some contexts yet chooses to "pass" in some respects given other parts of her life. She has a strong and clear lesbian identity and sense of pride, while also struggling with the costs of hiding at times. Stephanie chooses her battles wisely. While no longer denying or completely hiding her sexual orientation, last year was more difficult for her. She says:

> Last year was really bad. In a sense I was becoming a little homophobic because it was like a burden more than anything. Your sexuality was something you switched on and switched off. During the week you had to resort to being something else that you weren't on the weekends. And then on the weekends you're just like this flaming person. This year it's totally different. If somebody comes up at school and asks me, I wouldn't deny it. I would have denied it last year. This year there is still some stress with school because there are parts of my life I won't talk about. Or like with my college applications and my essay, there was some stress there because I was trying to decide whether I should come out in my application or whether I shouldn't. I decided to touch on it briefly, but I didn't completely come out. (personal communication, 24 November 1990)

According to Stephanie, she has had the resources of friends in a local lesbian, gay, and bisexual youth group, her girlfriend, a supportive psychologist, and God to help her develop an affirmative lesbian identity. She has built this within the context of determining for herself when it is safe to be "out" and when it is wiser not to be completely open.

For many lesbian, gay, and bisexual students who are closeted and have the "privilege" of being able to hide or pass, there can be a tremendous amount of energy and psychological cost spent in staying hidden.[71] Glenn has never had supportive resources like those that Stephanie described. He says,

> I accept who I am but I don't want others to know because I don't know how they will react. What good will it do to wear your homosexuality on your sleeve. In Nazi Germany were Jews any better off by wearing yellow stars or gays by wearing pink triangles? My relationships have been pretty superficial. I'm afraid that if they really knew me, they wouldn't be able to deal with it. It makes me wonder how much they really care about me. (personal communication, 13 November 1990)

According to Minton and McDonald, "In choosing to hide an essential part of the self, individuals are left with a gnawing feeling that they are really valued for what others expect them to be rather than for who they really are."[72] Compartmentalization can lead to feeling fragmented and contributes to the lack of authenticity in interpersonal relationships described by Glenn.

Like Glenn, while many adolescents may "know" that they are lesbian, gay, or bisexual, they are also keenly aware that the school environment is generally unsupportive and possibly actively hostile. Rather than risk the possible rejection and ridicule from their peers and teachers and possibly from their family, these students often choose to hide behind the assumption being made that they are heterosexual. If in the process of hiding, students also believe the prevailing heterosexist ideology that devalues homosexuality relative to heterosexuality, they are also learning to devalue themselves at the same time, experiencing what Neisen calls "shame due to heterosexism."[73]

A great deal of physical and psychological effort can be spent, therefore, in appearing to be heterosexual, out of the belief that if others were to suspect or find out about one's homosexuality, they would surely withdraw their socioemotional support.[74] This secrecy and deception, which can be a characteristic in hiding and keeping part of one's self from others, often creates the type of distance in interpersonal relationships described by Glenn—"if others really knew me, they would not want to be close to me." The type of low self-esteem that can result from this sort of internalized oppression often leads to interpersonal relationships that have very little genuine intimacy. Hunter and Schaecher[75] describe how, as a result of "fear of discovery," lesbian and gay youth become increasingly less comfortable engaging in school activities and begin to cut themselves off from others emotionally as well as physically. This may lead to poor grades, truancy, dropping out, and/or the failure to develop trusting relationships.[76]

Accommodation

In an effort to get by, and also to protect their cover, some lesbian and gay youth may accommodate to the homophobic environment by contributing to it. This may be accomplished by telling "fag" jokes or participating in the harassment of students who are identified as lesbian, gay, or bisexual. Troiden[77] argues that by attacking and ridiculing homosexuals, some lesbians and gay men distance themselves from their own homoerotic feelings. This type of behavior also deflects attention away from the individuals and may reinforce their status among their heterosexist peer group. The mental and physical health costs of such accommodation behavior, however, remain to be documented.

Heterosexual Overcompensation

Given the conditional self-acceptance associated with internalized oppression, there may be a perceived need to lead two mutually exclusive lives. One is the public life of heterosexuality. The other is a more secret and private lesbian or gay life. Some youth will actively seek out relationships with the other sex in attempts to have "the perfect cover up."[78] Troiden[79] describes this "heterosexual immersion" as adolescents' hope of curing their homosexual interests. According to Schneider and Tremble, heterosexual promiscuity may be a desperate attempt to affirm heterosexuality, for the gay adolescent; for straight youth it may "serve to ward off fears that they might be gay."[80] According to Regina, "I got pregnant when I was 15 because I knew my parents would have an easier time dealing with that than my lesbianism" (personal communication, 24 November 1990).

Overachievement

The "best little boy in the world" syndrome[81] is a mode of responding whereby students work to prove themselves to be exceptional. These may be the students who get themselves voted class president, or excel with some special academic, athletic, or artistic skill in an effort to gain peer acceptance. For some, this may reflect what Malyon[82] describes as compensation for feelings of inadequacy. For others, overcompensation and proving oneself may be a coping mechanism for responding to the environment, but not necessarily reflecting low self-esteem. In this way, they have both peer acceptance and are able to participate in activities that generate feelings of accomplishment and self-esteem. Katie says, for example, "I excelled in school. I was a perfectionist. But getting straight A's wasn't too hard for me'' (personal communication, 20 November 1990).

Rather than trying to be exceptional, others may try to be the exception. Yet this can be a double-bind process. In so doing, the student is saying, ''I may be lesbian [gay or bisexual], but I'm not one of 'them.' '' They identify with the dominant heterosexist culture and become the token lesbian, gay, or bisexual person. The stereotypes and heterosexist beliefs remain unchallenged. Although they received a great deal of resistance from leaders within the lesbian and gay communities, Kirk and Madsen [83] actually recommend this type of ''assimilationist'' approach to combating homophobia.

Confronting Oppression: Interrupting Heterosexism and
Building Self-Empowerment

Some students respond to homophobia and heterosexism through active resistance of many forms. Some refuse to accept the victimization and fight back physically and verbally. Glenn says, ''I was always a fighter. I talk back. When they slashed my tires, I slashed theirs'' (personal communication, 13 November 1990).

Others fight back legally, like Aaron Fricke,[84] who in court won his right to attend his high school prom with a same-sex date. Although eighteen-year-old Mary Jo Sullivan did not go through a highly publicized court battle like Aaron Fricke, she also went to her high school prom with her girlfriend. She says, ''Oh, I got some vicious looks, and there was a tussle with some boys on the dance floor . . . but I had gotten it approved by the administration before hand—I had planned it for a year and a half—so there wasn't a lot they could do.''[85]

A suburban Philadelphia youth was not so fortunate in his interactions with school administrators. After the youth had decided that he was willing to take the risk of bringing a same-sex date to his prom, the principal told him that he could not. The stated reason was that when the youth originally filled out the prom permission slip (which indicates who you will be attending the prom with, and that you agree to comply with various rules of conduct), he indicated he was bringing a female date.[86] Given the school climate, originally he did not feel safe in revealing who he really wanted to bring to the prom. Later, with the help of a teacher who was willing to advocate on his behalf with the administration, he felt the support necessary to take the risk of being honest and open. He was punished, however, for falsifying the permission form. This is an example of an individual who was penalized and rejected on the basis of problems created by the system's policies (stated and nonstated) themselves. This blaming-the-victim process is similar to what Herek[87] describes as a flaw in the government's policy of denying lesbian and gay people security clearances (they are seen as a risk, but the risk is created by the system that forces them to hide).

When his principal refused to support him, nineteen-year-old Shawn fought back by calling the police. He says,

> High school was an incredible mess for me. I grew up in a hick town where there was a lot of punk bashing and gay bashing. I was thrown over an ice rink, beaten up and faggot was always yelled in my face. My principal was afraid to do anything, so I called the police. I transferred from that school.[88]

As these examples illustrate, strength and courage are required in fighting oppression.

Dropping out may also be a form of active resistance. This can be considered as an attempt to keep oneself safe by removing oneself from a psychologically and physically dangerous environment.[89] In New York City, as a result of the great number of lesbian and gay youth who drop out, the Harvey Milk School, a separate public school for lesbian and gay youth, was founded.[90] Dennis and Harlow[91] describe this school as symbolizing both the rejection of gay teenagers by mainstream schools and the commitment of these teenagers to obtaining education free from discrimination. According to Whitlock,

> In the face of such constant homophobic abuse, it is hardly surprising that gay/lesbian youth are at high risk for truancy and dropping out. When this occurs administrators too often ignore the damage done to the young person's educational life, believing that if the student is gone, the problem is gone. Truancy and dropping out are taken as evidence that sexual minority youth are a particularly problematic population. Yet this behavior should more properly be seen as a coping strategy, born of desperation when authorities fail to provide a safe learning environment.[92]

Given the prevalence of dropping out, Project 10 was created in Los Angeles to prevent gay and lesbian youth from dropping out of Fairfax High School.[93]

Sharing similar concerns, in 1982 a well-known urban lesbian and gay task force began a strong advocacy campaign challenging the local school district to take an active stance against homophobia in public schools. As a result of this advocacy process, along with a team of professional educators and trainers, I was hired to develop and implement comprehensive staff training on the issues of sexism, racism, heterosexism, and handicapism. The purpose of equity training is to foster among educators an appreciation of the diversity of the school populations and to examine individual and collective responsibility for creating school climates that are ''fair''—in outcome as well as practice. Many of the examples and narratives in this text come from my experience in working with staff development projects of this type, as well as other equity training programs for a range of educational systems and agencies. Given the current social climate, the extent to which these programs even exist within public institutions reflects what can be described as "an act of courage" by the sponsoring school districts and agencies.

The process of responding to feeling or being treated as "different" can result in the development of several useful coping mechanisms, however. In challenging heterosexist notions, some students have the potential to deconstruct and then reconstruct their identity on their own terms. For many, this means reconstructing what it means to be gay, lesbian, or bisexual as positive and valuable, and framing the conflicts they have experienced as being associated with homophobia and heterosexism, not with their own homosexuality. Foucault[94] argues that one function of resistance is to gain self-empowerment by reconstructing the meaning of a homosexual identity—an attempt to control one's own sexual identity and one's destiny. Resistance for some lesbian, gay, and bisexual students may be a purposeful attempt to challenge and change the oppressive hegemony of heterosexist ideologies.

In writing about the "promise of lesbian and gay youth," Savin-Williams[95] describes a full-page editorial written in a prep school newspaper on 14 February 1987. Sloan Chase Wiesen wrote:

> There are no men, no women, no gays, no straights; there are only people who would be free to engage in the beautiful and harmless expression of romantic love to whomever they are drawn. Be yourself, whether that means being homosexual, bisexual, or heterosexual. If you are not yet sure what you are, that's fine too. Some people become aware of their sexuality as toddlers, some as pre-teens, some as teenagers, and even some as adults. So don't panic if you are still unsure, but never be afraid or ashamed to explore who you are and to be yourself. The only road to certain unhappiness is to pretend to be who you are not. Whatever your sexuality, you will find many others who are like you. Happy Valentine's Day.[96]

This senior high school student, with his ability to deconstruct the heterosexist messages he received and reconstruct the meaning of sexuality in positive and empowering ways is a clear example of the type of resistance to gain self-empowerment described by Foucault.[97] Sloan's gift was not only the self-empowerment he gained, but his willingness to share his learning with others. Two years after he wrote this Valentine's Day editorial, Sloan became a student of mine at the University of Pennsylvania. He continues to take risks and to share his learning with others.

Katie is also in the process of reconstructing her identity on terms that validate and affirm. She says,

Deep down inside I knew I was intelligent. I knew what I wanted to be. I knew I was a good person. Confusion about my sexuality muddled that for a while, but I'm coming to realize if I just act like myself, people have respect for me and I've internalized this. I know I'm still a good person. I used to take pride in secrecy and now I'm getting a flush of positive feedback for being honest and its clearing out all of the shit of the secrets. If everyone could come out in high school and gain all this strength think how they could excel. It's a shame it took me a couple of years to do this. If I had gotten this kind of support in high school. Somebody acknowledging my feelings and acknowledging them as something others feel as well—being told it's O.K. and not trying to change that—no one has said "you shouldn't feel that way." (personal communication, 20 November 1990)

Katie is not alone in experiencing the contradiction of powerful self-affirmation gained in response to an environment of oppression. It is seen clearly in the following twenty-year-old male's narrative as well. He says, "I love who I am and always will. Last week I was beaten up because I was gay. They may hurt me physically, but they can never scare me into a closet case."[98]

Kimmel says that in managing the potential crisis that being lesbian or gay means in our culture, "it may provide a perspective on major life crises and a sense of crisis competence that buffers the person against later crises.[99] The strength and resources that can result from tapping into one's source of personal power in this way, and learning strategies for taking care of oneself, can be a valuable lesson that many other students may not have the "privilege" to learn.

Nonlesbian, Nongay, and Nonbisexual Students

Homophobia and heterosexism also impact on students who are not lesbian, gay, or bisexual. As indicated before, the roots of hetero*sexism* are in sexism. If one of the purposes of sexism is to create a system where boys and girls grow up to be defined as "real" men and women, this definition includes being heterosexual. Boys who are "too sensitive" and girls who are "too independent" not only violate traditional gender-role expectations, but are also negatively stigmatized as homosexual. In this way, a homophobic label is used to enforce a sexist arrangement and functions to try to keep all students, heterosexual and homosexual alike, from violating what is expected of them in terms of gender-role behaviors. Herek[100] states, for example, that the social construction of heterosexual masculinity requires that, in order to be "a man" in American society, one must be homophobic.

Homophobia also functions to put limits on same-sex intimacy and bonding that may not be sexual. Intimacy and friendship of this kind begin to feel "too close for comfort" in the presence of homophobic feelings. As a result, trusting and intimate same-sex interpersonal relationships between heterosexual youth may be limited due to the barriers of homophobia.

Not only might the reinforcement of sexism by homophobia build barriers for women to their individual and collective power, but it also contributes to men's devaluing of women and those parts of themselves that are labeled "feminine." Sanday[101] extends this to argue that fraternity gang rapes are often an expression of collective male internalized homophobia. Not only does it represent an active hostility toward women aggressively acted out in bonding through a shared sense of "male entitlement," but it also allows men to be "sexual" with each other without becoming "suspect."

Homophobia also gives permission to heterosexual students for intolerance and violence against people with whom they may otherwise be close. They may actively hurt and alienate lesbian, gay, and bisexual peers and family members. And in doing so, homophobic persons lose the potential resources of a relationship when they behave in such a way that cuts the lesbian, gay, or bisexual person off. As Dennis and Harlow[102] explain, if a purpose of schooling is training in "citizenship," which is defined as habits of open-mindedness and critical inquiry, when prejudice and discrimination are encouraged, or at least not discouraged, in schools, poor lessons in citizenship result.

RECOMMENDATIONS

Silencing works to prevent the recommendations of lesbian, gay, and bisexual students for improving the school climate from being heard. Given safe space, lesbian, gay, and bisexual youth share many recommendations for creating schools filled with possibility. Schwartz[103] interviewed lesbian and gay youth in support groups across the country, who made many suggestions. Schwartz[104] provides the following three narratives. Brenda, age eighteen, says,

> There are kids in high school who are scared and don't know where to turn. There needs to be something in the educational system so they have a place to go. Also, teachers need to mention positive information in sexuality education classes. There needs to be more education in the schools. When people do studies on adolescents or write books, it is important to include lesbian and gay teens—we're always left out . . . we are there. Also, when you try to educate teachers, let them know to include us!

Ben, age eighteen, requests,

> In high school there should be posters which are supportive of gay people.
> Also, there should be support groups in high school. There needs to be a
> connection for gay kids in high school, because when you're not out, you're
> terrified.

Marc, age sixteen, says,

> At school there should be programs for counselors so they know how to help
> lesbian and gay teens. Also, the schools could have assemblies and have gay
> people come in and speak.

Eighteen-year-old Stephanie shared with me that if she could change schools,
she would

> take some of that football money and put it into the performing arts. Sex
> education would be more in depthly taught and homophobia and homosex-
> uality would definitely be addressed. If I could, I would change how people
> think about other people. To teachers, when you're in that room with that
> teacher, like they are always telling you, they're in control, and when they
> hear an argument or "faggot this" or some group being put down that's
> when they should step in and say "look I think you can find a more appro-
> priate word" or "look they're people too." While I'm not saying they
> should promote it, they should address it in a positive sense and if they do
> know somebody who is struggling be available for them—give resources,
> say "it's not that bad." (personal communication, 24 November 1990)

These recommendations are given by the lesbian, gay, and bisexual
youths who have found their voice in the safety of lesbian, gay and bisexual
youth groups. Given the nature of homophobia, however, those most silenced
must depend on their lesbian, gay, and bisexual sisters and brothers, as well
as heterosexual friends, to advocate on their behalf. What these narratives
suggest is the courage, the risk, and the power people who face silencing in
school experience.

CONCLUSIONS

Given that differences in race, social class, ethnicity, and sexual orientation do have important bearing on academic achievement and future success, it is important for professionals involved in the lives of students to be
aware of how these components of identity are shaped in the minds and lived
experiences of young people. While students may act out socially, experience
depression, rage, truancy, or even drop out, viewing the source of these prob-

lems as existing within the students rather than in the contexts in which they live their lives contributes to a process of blaming the victim. Given the heterosexism and homophobia in schools, it is clear that for lesbian, gay, and bisexual students, the tragedies they may experience do not center around being homosexual, but are a result of being hated or devalued or having who they are systematically silenced.

The layers of silencing may also contribute to focusing on the tragedies rather than the successes. The fact that many students emerge with such strength and power must not be over looked or minimized. More likely, students experience school in a paradoxical mix of empowerment and conflict. The challenge for educators, as well as social workers, psychologists, and anyone else concerned about youths, is to work to understand the socioemotional context in which students exist and provide resources for overcoming and dismantling the systems that lead to silencing and victimization while supporting resources that build equity. Fourteen-year-old Sally sums up the contradiction of developing strength in response to systematic silencing:

One teacher told me it was normal. Also, a hotline told me it was normal. Sometimes I get sick of hearing it's normal because if its normal, why do people make such a big deal out of it?[105]

Chapter Eleven

White Male Working-Class Youth: An Exploration of Relative Privilege and Loss

The 1970s and 1980s brought great change in the American class structure, change reflective of industrial reorganization and realignment since World War II. At the end of World War II, American corporations dominated world markets. The American steel industry was virtually the only major producer in the world, for example. By the 1960s, Germany, Japan, France, Italy, and Britain had rebuilt their steel industries, using the most advanced technology, and they became highly competitive with American industry. By the 1970s, American steel as an industry was in decline relative to that of other nations, and this pattern is repeated in a wide variety of industries, leading to large-scale factory closings and what has been heralded as "deindustrialization" and the "new economy."[1]

Accompanying deindustrialization in the 1970s was corporate restructuring—a strategy born in response to the "productivity crisis," or what became known as the "competitiveness problem."[2] Companies became "lean and mean," with all excess fat, usually in the form of employees, trimmed. Thus, slimmed down core firms and the gutting of the industrial wage-earning sector in the United States were the watchwords as America moved into the 1980s and 1990s.

These changes had large-scale impact on the nature of available jobs. Industrial jobs and entry-level jobs with core firms, which non-college-bound students previously had entered, were rapidly disappearing. Fortune 500 companies eliminated 3.1 million jobs between 1980 and 1987. Other analysts report that almost 2 million jobs were excised in manufacturing between 1979 and 1986, and 600,000 to 1.2 million middle-and upper-level executives lost jobs from 1983 to 1986. Indeed, the Department of Labor estimated that from 1980 through 1985, 11 million workers lost their jobs through plant closings and massive layoffs. Of these, 55 percent experienced downward mobility.[3]

The question arises, given corporate restructuring and deindustrialization, what kinds of positions will be available in the future? While predictions of the quality of new jobs awaiting youth vary, it is generally agreed that there will be a disproportionate number of opportunities in low-level positions relative to high-level ones. Based on the U.S. Bureau of Labor Statistics data, estimates are that there will be five hundred thousand to seven hundred thousand new and replacement jobs between 1982 and 1995 for the following positions: computer systems analysts, computer programmers, and electrical engineers. In contrast, estimates suggest that there will be between ten and fifteen million new and replacement jobs in the three traditional occupations—custodians, cashiers, and salesclerks. This represents from sixteen to thirty-two times the number of openings for the three high-level technical positions noted above. Job openings due to turnover, in particular, strongly favor the lowest paying occupations in the economy.[4] Michael Apple estimates that there will be more janitorial jobs—779,000—created between 1987 and 1995 than all the new computer service technicians and programmers, systems analysts, and computer operators combined.[5]

Until recently, the white male working class was relatively privileged in the economy in relation to African American men and women, and white women. While certainly not priveleged in comparison with middle-class white men, many working-class men have been enabled by labor union struggles to command good steady jobs with benefits in what Richard Edwards and others have called the "subordinate primary market."[6] This market segment is differentiated from both the independent primary markets and the secondary markets primarily by the presence of unions. It differs from the secondary market in that jobs in the secondary market, unlike those in the primary market, provide low pay and virtually no job security and movement in and out of them is common. Most importantly, work in the secondary market is not regular, and intermittent unemployment and periods of pervasive wagelessness among individuals is widespread. The majority of African American males and females, as well as most white women, are trapped in the secondary market sector.[7] Thus the position of white working-class males was, until recently, relatively privileged, by virtue of both their whiteness and their maleness.[8]

This position of relative privilege has been eroded, however, with deindustrialization and the weakening of labor unions in the 1970s and 1980s.[9] What, then, is happening to the white male working class? This chapter explores this issue by drawing upon data collected as part of a larger ethnography of white working-class youth in a high school located in a deindustrializing area in the northeastern United States. Given loss of relative privilege, what are the elements of experience and emerging voice among young white males? No longer able to count on the braiding of whiteness and maleness to secure privilege as they knew it, what, then are the voices of young men as this particular class fraction heads into the 1990s? How is the experience and voice of relative privilege, born of the intersection of whiteness and maleness, likely to be rearticulated as that relative privilege is eroded by both the economy and the collective struggles of white women, and of men and women of color?

It is not my intention here to address this complex set of issues in full. That would not be possible in the space of one chapter. Rather I will open up the discussion of white working-class male voice in the context of the new economy by focusing on two areas that emerged as exceptionally significant in the ethnography: (1) white male home/family identity and masculinist expression; and (2) expressed anger toward white women and men and women of color. As I will argue here, the two are linked. At the end of the chapter I will turn my attention to the possibility of white male involvement with the secular New Right. My intent here is to examine the voices of what has been seen as an exploited group under capitalism, and, at the same time, recognize that this group was a privileged one in relation to certain other groups. The "new" voice of the white working-class male reflects both this loss of relative privilege as well as consciousness associated with the struggles and position of the traditional proletariat.

FREEWAY

Data presented here were gathered as part of an ethnographic investigation of Freeway High. I spent the academic year 1985–1986 in the high school, acting as a participant observer for three days a week for an entire year. Data were gathered in classrooms, study halls, the cafeteria, and extracurricular activities and through in-depth interviews with over sixty juniors, virtually all teachers of juniors, the vice-principals, social workers, guidance counselors, and others. Data collection centered on the junior class, since this is a key point of decision, when PSATs, SATs, and so forth must be considered. In addition, this is the time when the bulk of a series of state tests must be taken if entrance to a four-year college is being considered.

The move to postindustrial society is particularly evident in Freeway due to the closing of Freeway Steel. The plant payroll in 1969 was at a record high of 168 million, topping 1968 by 14 million. The average daily employment was 18,500.

In the first seven months of 1971, layoffs at the Freeway Steel plant numbered four thousand, and decline continued into the 1980s. From 18,500 jobs in 1979, there were only 3,700 production and 600 supervisory workers left in 1983, and 3,600 on layoff. At the end of 1983 the plant closed. All that remains of close to twenty thousand workers are 370 bar mill workers.[10] A very high proportion of students at Freeway High had fathers, uncles, and/or grandfathers who worked in the plant or in one of the adjacent service industries ("gin mills" abounded, for example). In addition, many of the male teachers worked in the plant either before becoming teachers or during summers when they were off from college, being steered into these summer jobs by fathers who worked there. The town was intricately woven within the fabric of the plant in a number of ways. White sons simply assumed that they would follow their fathers' footsteps into the plant—into a possibly grueling, but definitely well paying and stable, job.

Examination of data gathered for the Standard Metropolitan Statistical Area, of which Freeway is a part (data for Freeway per se are not available), confirms a number of trends that are reflective of Barry Bluestone and Bennet Harrison's argument regarding deindustrialization. Occupational data for 1960–80 (the most recent data available to date) suggest that the most striking decreases in the area are found in the categories of "Precision, Production, Craft, and Repair" and "Operators, Fabricators, and Laborers." These two categories constitute virtually all the so-called blue-collar jobs. When combined, data suggest a relative decline of 22.3 percent in the "blue collar" category from 1960 to 1980. A look at some of the more detailed subcategories reveals more striking decline. Manufacturers, for example, have experienced an overall decline in the area of 35 percent between 1958 and 1982.

Data also suggest an increase in the "Technical, Sales, and Administrative Support" category. These occupations constitute 22.8 percent of the total in 1960 as compared with close to 31 percent in 1980, representing an increase of over one-third. Increases in "Service" and "Managerial and Professional Specialty" categories also reflect a shift away from industry and toward the availability of service occupations.[1]

The change in the distribution of occupations by gender needs to be clarified here as well. During this same time period, female employment increased 55 percent, while employment for men decreased 6 percent. For most occupations in the area, a net increase in employment during this period may be attributed mainly to the increase in employed women and a net decrease to a decrease in employed men.

Although the emerging economy has absorbed women at a faster rate than men, the proportion of full-time female workers is still lower than that of full-time male workers. Sixty-seven percent of male workers were full-time in 1980 as compared with only 43 percent of females. In addition, full-time female workers earned 56 percent of what full-time male workers earned in 1980, and women in sales have average incomes that are only 46 percent of the average income for men.[12] This is particularly important given that a growing number of positions in the Standard Metropolitan Statistical Area are in sales, and that these are filled disproportionately by women. Such trends are reflective of trends nationwide. Thus, the move toward postindustrial society has meant that a higher proportion of females is employed in the labor force relative to earlier years, but that females increasingly earn relatively lower wages than males. It also means, however, that many more men are earning far less money than they used to.

I will argue here that the desire for male-dominant families and expressed anger toward white women, and toward men and women of color, are linked to these economic realities. While both were certainly embedded within white working-class male culture historically, it is the loss of relative privilege under the new economy, coupled with these historically embedded sentiments, that fuels the white working class currently. Also, the New Right, a broader social movement, has provided a way of politicizing and consolidating these sentiments, thus lending them legitimacy within a larger sense.

DESIRE FOR MALE-DOMINANT FAMILIES

Previous investigators of the white working class have noted the sexism embedded within the identity of this class fraction. Paul Willis, J. C. Walker, and R. W. Connell have argued extensively that male white working-class identity is constructed partially in relation to that of the ideologically constructed identity of females.[13] For example, mental labor is not only less valued than manual labor, but it is less valued because it is seen as feminine. This encourages certain types of gender relations in the sense of separate spheres for males and females, the male sphere being superior. The "lads," for example, impose upon girlfriends an ideology of domesticity, "the patterns of homely and subcultural capacity and incapacity," all of which stress the restricted role of women.[14] The very form of the cultural affirmation of the male self and the particular form of the constructed female other affirm a certain form of male dominance, albeit coded in class terms.

In terms of male superiority, Freeway males exhibit the same virulent sexism uncovered in previous studies. This is particularly striking in light of the emerging identity of females. One or two boys exist somewhat outside these boundaries but basically white working-class males affirm a rather virulent form of assumed male superiority that involves the constructed identity of female not only as "other," but also as less than and, therefore, subject to male control. Discussions with males indicate that the vast majority speak of future wives and families in highly controlling and male-dominant terms. This contrasts sharply with the sentiments of females, a point to which I will return at a later point.

LW: You say you want more kids than your parents have. How many kids do you want?
Bob: Five.
LW: Who's going to take care of these kids?
Bob: My wife, hopefully. Unless she's working, too. . . . If she wants to work, we'd figure something out. Day-care center, something like that. I'd prefer if she didn't want to. I'd like to have her at home.
LW: Why?
Bob: I think it's up to the mother to do it [raise children; take care of the home]. I wouldn't want to have a baby-sitter raising my kids. Like, I think the principles should be taught by the parents, not by some baby-sitter.

. . .

LW: How about your life ten years from now; what do you think you'll be doing?
Rob: Probably be married. Couple of kids. . . .
LW: . . . Do you think your wife will work?
Rob: Hopefully she won't have to, 'cause I'll make enough money.
LW: Would you rather she didn't work?
Rob: Naw [Yes, I'd rather she didn't work].
LW: Women shouldn't work?
Rob: Housework.

. . .

Jim: Yes, I'd like to get married, like to get myself a nice house, with kids.
LW: . . . Who is going to be taking care of those kids?
Jim: Depends how rich I am. If I'm making a good salary, I assume that the wife, if she wanted to, would stay home and tend to the kids. If there was ever a chance when she wanted to go someplace, fine, I'd watch the kids. Nothing wrong with that. Equal responsibility because when you were consummating the marriage it was equal responsibility.
LW: So, you're willing to assume it?

Jim: Up to a certain point . . . Like if she says I'm going to go out and get a job and you take care of the kids, "You draw all day" [he wants to be a commercial artist]. "So, I draw; that's what's been supporting us for so many years." I mean, if she starts dictating to me . . . , there has to be a good discussion about the responsibilities.

. . . When both parents work, it's been proven that the amount of education they learn, it goes down the tubes, or they get involved in drugs. Half the kids who have drug problems, both of their parents work. If they are doing terribly in school, their parents work.

. . .

LW: When you get married, what will your wife be doing?
Lanny: Well, before we had any kids, she'd be working; but if we had kids, she wouldn't work; she'd be staying home, taking care of the kids.

. . .

Seth: I wouldn't mind my wife working as far as secretarial work or something like that. Whatever she wanted to do and she pursued as a career. If there was children around, I'd like her to be at home, so I'd like my job to compensate for just me working and my wife being at home.

. . .

LW: Do you think you wife would want to work?
Sam: I wouldn't want her to work.

. . .

LW: Let's say you did get married and have children, and your wife wanted to work.
Bill: It all depends on if I had a good job. If the financial situation is bad and she had to go to work, [then] she had to go to work.
LW: And if you got a good job?
Bill: She'd probably be a regular woman.
LW: Staying at home? Why is that a good thing?
Bill: I don't know if it's a good thing, but it'd probably be the normal thing.

Without question, most of the boys are envisioning family life in highly male-dominant terms. They see the possibility that their wives might work, but only out of "necessity," or, more likely, before children are born. They wish to see their own income sufficient to "support" a family; they expect to earn the "family wage," thus enabling their wives to assume the "normal" role of taking care of the home and children. Male students state that they would "help when they could," but they see children as basically the woman's responsibility, and they intend for their wives to be at home in a "regular" womanly fashion.

Only a handful of boys constructed a future other than that outlined above. Significantly, only one boy constructed a future in which his wife *should* work, although he does not talk about children. A few boys reflect the sentiment that marriage is a "ball and chain," and one boy said the high divorce rate makes marriage less than attractive. Both these latter themes are elaborated by the girls.

LW: What kind of person do you want to marry?
Vern: Someone who is fairly good-looking, but not too good looking so she'd be out, with other people screwing her up. Someone who don't mind what I'm doing, let me go out with the guys. I won't mind if she goes out with the girls either. I want her to have a job so she ain't home all the time. 'Cause a woman goes bonkers if she's at home all day. Give her a job and let her get out of the house.
. . . People tended to get married as soon as they got out of school, not as soon as, but a couple of years after. I think people nowadays don't want to get married until twenty, thirty.
LW: And that's because of what?
Vern: They've seen too many divorces.

It is noteworthy that Vern is the only boy to discuss divorce as an impediment to marriage. Almost every girl interviewed discusses divorce, and it is a topic of conversation within all female groupings. Despite Vern's relatively more open-minded attitude toward females, it is significant that he still envisions himself "allowing" his wife to work, and sees his role as one of controlling her time and space. He does not, for example, want her to be "too good-looking," because then she would be out, with "other people screwing her up." He also notes that he "does not mind" her going "out with the girls," and that he wants "her to have a job so she ain't home all the time." He therefore sees himself *giving permission* to his wife to have certain freedoms.

The boy below expresses the sentiment that marriage is a "ball and chain," and that he wants no part of it. Only a couple of boys expressed a similar sentiment or elaborated the theme of "freedom" associated with being single. Again, this is unlike the girls.

Tom: I don't want to get married; I don't want to have children. I want to be pretty much free. If I settle down with someone, it won't be through marriage.
LW: Why not?
Tom: Marriage is a ball and chain. Then marital problems come up, financial problems, whatever. I don't really want to get involved in the intense kind of problems between you and a spouse. . . . To me it's a joke.

LW: Tell me why you think that.
Tom: Well, I see a lot of people. I look at my father and mother. They don't get along, really.

The vast majority of boys at Freeway High intend to set up homes in which they exert control over their wives—in which they go out to work and their wives stay at home. Only a few question the institution of marriage, and only one begins to question a fundamental premise of patriarchy—that women's place is in the home and men's place is in the public sphere. As noted above, even this one boy sees himself controlling the actions of his wife. The white male voice, then, embodies a strong desire for male dominance in the home/family sphere as well as in the paid labor force. The assumption of privilege vis-à-vis women in the family comes through loud and clear.

Male supremacy as a key element of identity is borne out by classroom observations, where boys state positions similar to those stated above. Girls, although they challenge this position rather seriously on one level, do not tend to speak out against the boys in class, leaving the male voice a privileged one in the public arena. When the male vision is challenged, it is done so by male teachers, although not always for the most progressive of reasons. Overall there is a privileging of the young white male voice in the school—it tends not to be interrupted. Teachers do, at times, make an attempt to interrupt this voice, but this interruption is not sustained, and certainly not successful, as the following observations suggest:

Social Studies, 3 December 1985

MR. _____ : Why should women be educated? [A lot of chatter; many males saying they shouldn't be, or perhaps that they should be for secretarial science.]
MR. _____ : Look, you [the women] are better equipped to teach the children; you are better able to communicate with your husband if you are an educated woman. Also, today not everybody gets married. The better the education, the better the opportunity for a good job for both men and women.
MR. _____ : Women today probably need education more, because today in broken marriages and divorces, the women normally have the children.
BEN: But men have to pay child support—a hundred dollars a week. . . .
MR. _____ : Hey, you talk to many women, they don't get a penny from their former husbands. What about the guy who just got laid off from the steel plant—how are you going to pay a hundred dollars a week?

Ben talked to Mr. _____ after class and said his dad sends one hundred and twenty dollars a week for child support. Mr. _____ says, ''Great, but isn't it true that your mom has to wait for checks; sometimes some bounce;

so isn't it better that she has her own job?'' Ben says [rather sheepishly], "She works, too.''

Social Studies, 4 December 1985

MR. _____ : We were talking yesterday about whether it was a waste of time to educate women and we concluded that it wasn't. I concluded that it wasn't, and you agree if you want to get the right mark.
JIM: Who asked you?

Social Studies, 12 December 1985

[P. 103, of the text] Mr. _____ goes over the multiple-choice questions and asks students to answer.

MR. _____ : Question: Women are basically unwilling to assume positions in the business world. Agree or disagree?''
SAM: Agree.
MR. _____ : Why?
SAM: Because women want to raise children and get married.
MR. _____ : All women?
SAM: No, but most.
MR. _____ : Anyone disagree?
No disagreement

No doubt the "correct" answer to the question was "disagree," but there was no further discussion of the matter.

The point, again, is that males envision a future in which they inhabit the public sphere, and women the private. Men also expect to exert control over their wives in the private sphere. They intend to earn the "family wage," in return for which women will listen to them and take care of the home and children. Although, as I suggest below, females challenge this in their own envisioned future, they tend not to challenge it directly in the classroom. The affirmation of male superiority and envisioned control over women within white male working-class youth identity remains, therefore, largely uninterrupted in the public arena of the school.

The male voice regarding women contrasts sharply with that of the young women's own voice. Previous studies suggest that working-class high school females elaborate, at the level of their own identity, a private/public dichotomy that emphasized the centrality of the private and marginalizes the public. During adolescence, home/family life assumes a central position for girls, and wage labor a secondary position. As many studies have shown, working-class girls elaborate what Angela McRobbie calls an "ideology of romance," constructing a gender identity that serves, ultimately, to encourage women's second-class status in both the home and the workplace. Studies of McRobbie and Linda Valli, in particular, have been important in terms of our understanding of the way in which these processes work upon and through the identity of young women.[15]

This gender identity has serious implications for the position of women in both the family and the workplace, in the sense that it represents parameters within which struggles will take place. By defining domestic labor as primary, women reinforce what can be called the "domestic code," under which home or family becomes defined as women's place, and a public sphere of power and work, as men's place. The reality, of course, is that generations of working-class women have labored in the public sphere, and that labor also takes place in the home, albeit unpaid. Yet, as Karen Brodkin Sacks points out, "The Domestic Code has been a ruling set of concepts in that it did not have to do consistent battle with counterconcepts. It has also been a ruling concept in the sense that it explained an unbroken agreement among capitalists, public policymakers and later much of organized labor, that adequate pay for women was roughly 60 percent of what was adequate for men and need be nowhere near adequate to allow a woman to support a family or herself."[16]

Basically, the domestic code is articulated *for* women *by* Freeway men, and there is a certain privileging of this voice in the school. That is the code under which young white men of this class fraction would like their future wives to operate, placing themselves, as males, as the dominant head of family. Rather than struggle for any form of egalitarian relations between men and women, Freeway males are very clear that they would like male-dominant families under which women basically do as they are told.[17]

The most striking point about female identity in Freeway is that there is, unlike in the case of other, somewhat older, ethnographies of white working-class girls, little evidence of a marginalized wage-labor identity that would sustain the domestic code envisioned by males. The young women have, in fact, made the obtaining of wage labor a primary rather than secondary goal. Almost without exception, the girls desire to continue their education, and they are clear that they intend to do so in order to get their own life in order. It is worth noting that this is reminiscent of the voices of African American and African Caribbean females in studies of romance, marriage, and the future.[18]

In addition to stressing a wage-labor identity rather than marginalizing one, young Freeway women downplay a home/family identity. Although some assert that they wish to have some form of home/family identity, it is never asserted first, and it is asserted generally only as a possibility "later on," when their own job or career is "settled." Some of the girls reject totally the possibility of marriage and children; many others wish to wait "until

I am at least thirty," which is, to teenagers, a lifetime away. The primary point, however, is that they assert strongly that they must settle themselves first (go to school, get a job) before entering into family responsibilities; in other words, the construction of a home/family identity is secondary, rather than primary.

It is not my intention here to elaborate on female identity and the possible reasons why it takes the shape and form that it does. It is, however, pertinent to this discussion, in the sense that it sharply contradicts that identity developed *for women* by men. Males hope to establish male-dominant households—females intend to get on with their lives in, at least for the moment, rather individualistic terms, concentrating on establishing themselves in the public, rather than private, sphere. They intend to do this as a hedge against the very male-dominant homes Freeway boys wish to construct for themselves. As I will suggest below, this tension over the form of envisioned family life represents only a piece of a broader struggle related to the very definition of masculinity in this class fraction as a restructured economy takes hold. It is to this issue that I now turn.

FORMS OF EXPRESSED MASCULINITY

The male wage has been seen as key to understanding the establishment of patriarchal homes in working-class culture and as key to the male identity in general. As Paul Willis argues:

> Most importantly, perhaps, the (male) wage is still the golden key (mortgage, rent, household bills) to a personal household separate from parents and separate from work, from production. The home is the main living embodiment of the laborer's freedom and independence from capital—apart from wage labor, of course, which is the price for the independence of a separate home. But this price really does purchase something. The something is an area of privacy, security and protection from the aggression and exploitation of work, from the patriarchal dependencies of the parental home, from other vicissitudes of the work place. The separate home is still a universal working class objective and its promise of warmth and safety more than offsets the risk and coldness of work.[19]

Willis and others suggest that a "sense of being a man" acts as a hedge against the conventional order of class and status. The toughness and strength required to do working-class jobs both obscures its economic exploitation and can be the basis for some dignity and collective identity—a sense of pride in being able to do what middle-class "sissy" men cannot. Thus masculinist expression vis-à-vis the heaviness, difficulty, and dirtiness associated with traditional working-class jobs acts to value this form of labor above "paper pushing" work. Certain collectivist forms of masculinist expression grew up around working-class jobs and are embedded within the consciousness of male working-class culture.

Ray Raphael extends our understanding of the social construction of masculinity by noting that the manliness of manual labor can appear very attractive, particularly during adolescence, when masculinity and physicality are most closely linked in the male mind. In contrast, the absence of such labor can be experienced as a threat to constructed masculinity. Note the interview with Jimmy S. below:

> When I was sixteen, seventeen years old, I used to help out my dad in his men's clothing store. That was always an option for me, to go into the family business. There was money in it, at least some money, a successful business, but it had absolutely zero appeal.
>
> Part of the problem was style. I preferred jeans and sneakers, clothes that let you feel your own body. His customers all wore ties and jackets and pressed slacks and leather shoes with slick soles. To me, dressing like that was pointless. The shoes slipped on the ice or you fell in the mud. The jacket and slacks ripped when you bent down to pick something up. The tie flapped in your face when you ran or it got caught in the gears of some machine and choked you to death. The whole outfit functioned like some sort of strait jacket which was purposely designed to prevent any sort of physical activity. My dad's customers looked encased inside their own clothes. Emasculated, I wanted no part of it. I wanted to be out there in the world, active and alive and doing real physical things.
>
> I did alot of gazing out the window when I worked there, out through those sterilized mannequins he had on display to the brazen workmen who were always digging up the street. That was a whole other world: jackhammers, wheelbarrows, overalls, unshaven faces, sweat, muscles, it was definitely more manly. At that point in my life I would've easily chosen to wield a jackhammer rather than just stand around and wait on my dad's dandy customers."[20]

That this is associated with masculinist expression and not simply a class expression per se is highlighted by the fact that there is no equivalent romanticization of physicality within working-class female culture. As Allison Jones reminds us, physical labor for working-class women is seen as sheer drudgery—there is no point of romance with heavy and dirty jobs such as doing laundry, working in factories, and so forth, among women, as there is for men.[21]

It can be argued, therefore, that a restructured economy in which there is no longer a reliance upon traditional proletarian labor to the same extent signals a crisis in gender identity for the white working class male as much as it signals a lower standard of living. Forms of masculinist expression traditionally associated with the white working class are simply outmoded by a restructured economy. Pushing buttons or waiting on tables is not the same as wielding a jackhammer or heavy machinery in a steel plant. It is unlikely that a cult of manliness will envelop the service sector, particularly since both men and women occupy this sector. Also, since male identity is tied to supporting a family, the lower wages available to working-class men, in addition to forms of masculine expression appropriate for available jobs, will, by necessity, interact to encourage the production of a new male—a form of masculinist expression greatly at odds with that embedded within collectively based working-class male culture.

Where does this crisis in gender identity leave the white working-class male? As R. W. Connell and his associates remind us, there is no unitary form of masculinist expression. There are competing forms of masculinity, and the white working class must forge a new form in light of the phasing out of the old industrial order. Economic restructuring really does signal a crisis in gender identity for the white working-class male as much as it does a lower standard of living.

The male-dominant attitudes of the young men expressed in the previous section may be partially understood in these terms. It is arguably the case that they are asserting aggressively a resolution to this crisis by attempting to privilege themselves in the family regardless of the changes around them. Interestingly enough, their comments center on a home/family identity rather than on a workplace identity as was formerly the case.[22] They are asserting the right to male-dominant homes *in spite of the economy*—in spite of the phasing out of the old industrial order and their formerly relatively privileged place within it. Interestingly enough, of course, as young men center their identity struggle on the home and family, young women are centering their identity struggle on the workplace. The young women talk about their place in the work force and do not focus on the home. Young men, in contrast, talk about their place in the male-dominant home and do not discuss at any length their envisioned place in the work force. This reversal of sense of self in the home/family and public sphere can be seen as a struggle over gender forms and as a male assertion that they *will* still be in charge. The assertion of a more direct form of domination over women, in other words, domination not necessarily mediated through its cloak of labor dignity, contradicts young women's assertion that they wish to have more say over their own lives than their mothers and grandmothers did. A restructured economy is forcing the issue of gender definition in this class fraction. Young men are blurting out, "Dare anyone say I am not a man?" and are attempting to work through this crisis in gender identity by establishing direct domination over women in the home. Data from the ethnography in Freeway suggest that women are likely to challenge this.

ANGER

This crisis in gender identity, accompanied by the very real fact that the form of schooling offered these young men will not enable the vast majority of them to break into anything other than the contingent economy, leaves them quite bitter. This is coupled with perceptions that affirmative action has privileged white women and African American men and women and that their own devalued position can be, therefore, explained not only by Japanese cars but by laws that privilege others in what few good, stable positions are left. The anger seeps out in a variety of ways. As one student said to me in the middle of class, "If my mom ever tells me what to do, I'll punch her in the face, like this [slams one hand against the palm of the other, extremely brutally]."

This anger comes out most clearly with reference to people of color. While there has certainly always been racism in this class fraction, in part because capital used minority labor to break strikes, the anger expressed among young people in this study is particularly intense.

Freeway is a divided town, even though it is small, and African Americans and a small number of Arabs and Hispanics live largely on one side of the "tracks," and whites on the other, although there are whites living in a certain section of the predominantly minority side. Virtually no people of color live in the white area, which is not true of larger American cities, where one finds areas of considerable mix. Most of the African Americans live in a large public housing project located near the old steel plant. Most project residents receive welfare and have done so for a number of years. Much of the expressed racism plays itself out around "access" to females and, to some extent, drug use, as the examples below suggest.

Jim: The minorities are really bad into drugs. You're talking everything. Anything you want, you get from them. A prime example, the _____ ward of Freeway; about twenty years ago the _____ ward was predominantly white, my grandfather used to live there. Then Italians, Polish, the Irish people, everything was fine. The houses were maintained; there was a good standard of living. . . .
. . . The Blacks brought drugs. I'm not saying white people didn't have drugs; they had drugs, but to a certain extent. But drugs were like a social thing. But now you go down to the _____ ward; it amazing; it's a ghetto. Some of the houses are okay. They try to keep them up. Most of the homes are really, really terrible. They throw garbage on the front lawn; it's sickening. You talk to people in [surrounding suburbs]. Anywhere you talk to people, they tend to think the majority of our school is Black. They think you hang with Black people, listen to Black music.

. . . A few of them [Blacks] are starting to go into the _____ ward now [the white side], so they're moving around. My parents will be around there when that happens, but I'd like to be out of there.

. . .

LW: There's no fighting and stuff here [school], is there?
Clint: Yeah, a lot between Blacks and whites.
LW Who starts them?
Clint: Blacks.
LW: Do Blacks and whites hang out in the same place?
Clint: Some do; [the Blacks] live on the other side of town. . . . A lot of it [fights] starts with Blacks messing with white girls. That's how a lot of them start. Even if they [white guys] don't know the white girl, they don't like to see. . . .
LW: How do you feel about that yourself?
Clint: I don't like it. If I catch them [Blacks] near my sister, they'll get it. I don't like to see it like that. Most of them [my friends] see it that way [the same way he does].
LW: Do you think the girls encourage the attentions of these Black guys?
Clint: Naw. I think the Blacks just make themselves at home. They welcome themselves in.
LW: How about the other way around? White guys and Blacks girls?
Clint: There's a few that do. There's people that I know of, but no one I hang around with. I don't know many white kids that date Black girls.
Bill: Like my brother, he's in ninth grade. He's in trouble all the time. Last year he got jumped in school. . . . About his girlfriend. He don't like Blacks. They come up to her and go, "Nice ass," and all that shit. My brother don't like that when they call her "nice ass" and stuff like that. He got suspended for saying "fucking nigger"; but it's all right for a Black guy to go up to whites and say stuff like that ["nice ass"].
. . . Sometimes the principals aren't doing their job. Like when my brother told [the assistant principal] that something is going to happen, Mr. _____ just said, "Leave it alone, just turn your head."
. . . Like they [administrators] don't know when fights start in this school. Like there's this one guy's kid sister, a nigger [correction]—a Black guy—grabbed her ass. He hit him a couple of times. Did the principal know about? No!
LW: What if a white guy did that [grabbed the girl's ass]?
Bill: He'd probably have punched him. But a lot of it's 'cause they're Black.

Racial tension does exist within the school, and it reflects tension within the community and the society as a whole. It is clear that white boys attribute much of it to African Americans hustling white girls. This is the male perception, but I heard no such comment from any female in the school. White males view white females as their property and resent African-American males speaking to them in, at times, crude terms. However, it must be noted that white boys themselves might say "nice ass" to white girls, and so forth. It is the fact that Black males do it, and not that males do it, that is most offensive to white males. I never saw a white male go to the defense of a white female if she was being harassed by another white male. It is only when the male is Black that their apparently protectionist tendencies surface, indicating a deep racism that comes out over girls, in particular. White girls are considered "property" by white boys, as the above section suggests, and they resent Black intrusion onto their property. White males are intending to earn the "family wage," thus enabling them to establish male-dominant homes. This gives them, in their estimation, certain rights to white females, rights that Black males do not have. Not one girl voiced a complaint in this area. This is not to say that females are not racist, but it is not a central element of their identity in the same way as it is for boys at this age.

Observational data support the notion of racism among white youth. This is mainly directed toward African Americans, although, as the excerpts below indicate, racism surfaces with respect to Arabs as well. There is a small population of Yemenites who emigrated to Freeway to work in the mills, and this group is targeted to some extent also.

Social Studies, 26 November 1986*

SAM: Hey, Abdul, did you come from Arabia?
ABDUL: Yeah.
SAM: How did you get here?
ABDUL: I walked.
SAM: No, seriously, how'd you get here?
ABDUL: Boat.
SAM: Where'd you come from?
ABDUL: Saudi Arabia.
SAM: We don't want you. Why don't you go back.
[no comment]
TERRY: What city did you come from?
ABDUL: Yemen, if *you* ever heard of it.

. . .

Social Studies, 11 December 1986*

ED: Do you party, Nabil?
NABIL: Yeah.
PAUL: Nabil, the only thing you know how to play to polo on camels.
[Nabil ignores]

. . .

English, 2 October*

LW: [To Terry, who was hit by a car two days ago.] How are you?
TERRY: Look at me [sic] face. Ain't it cool? [He was all scraped up].
LW: What happened?
TERRY: Some stupid camel jockey ran me over in a big white car. Arabian dude.

Most of the virulent racism is directed toward African Americans, however. The word *nigger* flows freely from the lips of white males, and they treat African American females in the same way, if not worse, than they say African Americans treat white females. The following field notes, generated by Craig Centrie as part of the Freeway study, clarify this point.[23]

At the lunch table, 21 February 1986*
[discussion with Craig Centrie, research assistant]

PETE: Why is it [your leather bag] so big?
MIKE: So he can carry lots of stuff.
CC: I bought it because my passport would fit in it.
PETE: Passport: Wow—where are you from?
CC: Well I'm American now, but you need one to travel.
PETE: Can I see? (he pulls out his passport; everyone looks)
MIKE: This is my first time to ever see one. What are all those stamps?
CC: Those are admissions stamps so [you] can get in and out of countries.
MIKE: Look Pete. N_I_G_E_R_I_A [pronounced "Niggeria"] Yolanda [an African American female] should go there [everyone laughs].

. . .

In the lunchroom, 21 January 1986
Students [all white males at the table] joke about cafeteria food. They then begin to talk about Martin Luther King Day.

DAVE: I have a wet dream—about little white boys and little Black girls. [laughter]

. . .

In the lunchroom, 7 March 1986
Once again, in lunch, everyone complains about the food. Vern asked about a party he heard about. Everyone knew about it, but it wasn't clear where it would be. A kid walked past the table [of white boys].

CLINT: That's the motherfucker. I'll whop his ass. [The entire table goes "ou' ou' ou'."]
CC: What happened with those tickets, Pete? [some dance tickets had been stolen].

PETE: Nothing, but I'm pissed off at that nigger that blamed me.

Pete forgot how loud he was speaking and looked toward Yolanda [a Black female] to see if she reacted. But she hadn't heard the remark.

. . .

At the lunch table, 12 February 1986

MIKE: That nigger makes me sick.
PETE: Who?
MIKE: You know, Yolanda.
PETE: She's just right for you, man.
MIKE: Not me, maybe Clint.

. . .

At the lunch table, 12 February 1986
About two minutes later, Darcy [a Black female] calls me [CC] over. "What's your name?"

CC: Craig; what's yours?
DARCY: It's Darcy. Clint told me a lie. He said your name was Joe. Why don't you come to a party at Yolanda's house tonight?
YOLANDA: Why don't you just tell him you want him to come. [everyone laughs]
CLINT: Well, all right, they want you!
PETE: What do you think of Yolanda?
CC: She's a nice girl. What do you think?
PETE: She's a stuck-up nigger. Be sure to write that down.

. . .

[A group of males talk about themselves.] "We like to party all the time and get high!" [They call themselves "freaks" and "heads."] [about Blacks] "They are a group unto themselves. They are all bullshitters."

At the lunch table, 12 February 1986
Much of the time, students discussed the food. Vern talked about the Valentine's Day dance and began discussing getting stoned before the dance.

CC: Do you guys drink at the dance, too?
PETE: No, I don't know what they would do to us [everyone laughs]. There probably wouldn't be any more dances.

Yolanda and friends walk in. Yolanda and a friend were wearing exactly the same outfit.

CLINT: What are you two the fucking Gold Dust Twins?

YOLANDA: Shut the fuck up, 'boy' [everyone laughs].
PETE: Craig, they are nasty.
CC: What do you mean?
PETE: You don't understand Black people. They're yeach. They smell funny and they [got] hair under their arms.

Clint, Pete, Mike and Jack all make noises to denote disgust.

The males spend a great deal of time exhibiting disgust for racial minorities and, at the same time, asserting a protective stance over white females vis-à-vis African American males. They differentiate themselves from African American males and females in different ways, however. African American males are seen as over sexualized and intruding onto their property (white women). African American females, on the other hand, are treated as dirty and with simple disgust. Both are seen and interacted with largely in the sexual realm, however. The anger toward racial minorities comes through loud and clear.

CONCLUSION

I have, in this chapter, explored two areas of identity and voice among white working-class males. The particular curriculum to which these students are being exposed almost certainly guarantees that the vast majority of them will end up in the contingent work force, without security or benefits.[24] In addition, they will suffer a wage loss, relative to that which their fathers were able to command in the industrial economy. Indeed, recent data released by the Economic Policy Institute suggest that most American families are having to work longer hours, or have more family members work in the wage earning sector of the economy, just to keep family incomes from falling precipitously.[25] Declines associated with the state of working America, according to this report, are most keenly felt by young workers, ages 25–34, particularly those without college degrees. The young men in the study have, in fact, been the ones most devastated economically by the structural realignment of the economy.

Given the almost certain place of these young men in the contingent work force, coupled with their attempt to resolve the crisis in masculinity by establishing direct domination over women in the home, there is a distinct possibility that these men will, in the future, closely articulate with the secular New Right. It is likely that the New Right will be able to rearticulate smoothly the profamily rhetoric and racism expressed in the voices of the young men examined here.

Linda Gordon and Allen Hunter argue, for example, that antifeminism (read, assertion of male dominance) is now propelling a strong and growing New Right, a development which is not only a blacklash against women's and gay liberation movements, "but also a reassertion of patriarchal forms of family structure and male dominance.[26] Gordan and Hunter do not claim that the other issues have gone away. "Racism has not diminished as a political force, but it has been joined—and the whole right wing thereby strengthened—by a series of conservative campaigns defending the family, a restrictive and hypocritical sexual morality, and male dominance."[27] "It is possible to interpret even the campaign against school busing—a racist issue—as primarily an issue of the family. The loss of neighborhood schools is perceived as a threat to community, and therefore family stability—fears for children's safety and objections to the inaccessibility of their schools and teachers reflect both family love and parental desire for control."[28] Andrew Koplind argues that what is new about the New Right is its concentration on "profamily issues, and those who find that homosexuals, abortionists, and liberated women, make perfect targets of convenience for baffled and misled traditionalists."[29]

That the New Right will be able to consolidate the angry racism of Freeway males is highly likely as well. Michael Omi and Howard Winant have argued persuasively that while the agenda of the far right in America and racial supremacist groups will not attract a mass base, the New Right may very well be able to do so.

> The new right cannot simply defend patterns of racial inequality by demanding a return to segregation, for example, or by reviving simplistic notions of biological superiority/inferiority. As we have previously noted, the racial upheavals of the 1960s precluded a direct return to this form of racial logic. The new right objective, however, was to dismantle the political gains of racial minorities. Since these gains could not be reversed, they had to be *rearticulated*. The key device used by the new right in its effort to limit the political gains of racial minority movements has been "code words." These are phrases and symbols which refer to racial theories, but do not directly challenge popular democratic or egalitarian ideals (e.g., justice, equal opportunity).[30]

Omi and Winant suggest that the New Right is a powerful social movement that does not generally display overt racism. It does, however, rearticulate racial ideology by employing code words such as *maintenance of community*, or the ideology of the "family" in the case of the busing debates; arguing for "traditional" lifestyles and families, in the case of monitoring textbooks, and opposing multiculturalism; and emphasizing the well-worn notion of "reverse discrimination." On the issue of affirmative action, the New Right simply rearticulates the meaning of *fairness* and *equality* by arguing that the state has accommodated unfairly to special-interest groups such as minority groups at the expense of well-deserving white males.[31] Thus the New Right joins racist and sexist sentiments in its focus on the "traditional family" and reaffirms white-male supremacy.

The New Right agenda offers a powerful social movement with which white working-class males may ally in the future. With the demise of the traditional labor movement in the United States, and the rise of the New Right, it is possible to argue that if white working-class males see their identity as collective and articulate with a broader movement, it will be that of the New Right, which has the potential to consolidate the already existing sexism and racism in the male identity. While this racism and sexism is, at the moment, expressed largely individually, the New Right may well encourage these sentiments to become shared or felt as collective. It is, therefore, arguably the case that as these males mature, the New Right will be able, as a social movement, to offer shape and form to male working-class identity, thus changing the direction of working-class male politics from union politics to that of New Right politics.[32]

My point here is that the profamily rhetoric and coded racism of the New Right fit smoothly with the desire for male-dominant homes and expressed racism in the young white male working class. While there is still a certain privileging of the white male voice of racism and sexism in sites like schools, that privileging is unlikely to offset the real loss of privilege in the new economy. White male working-class voices are likely to become angrier and angrier. They are now expressed in a largely individualistic fashion but may soon be collectively expressed, given the very real match between voice in male youth identity and rightist social movement.[33]

ROBERT B. STEVENSON
JEANNE ELLSWORTH

Chapter Twelve

Dropouts and the Silencing of Critical Voices

INTRODUCTION

A common perception among both educators and the public is that students drop out of school because of personal deficiencies and/or family or cultural deprivation. Contributing to this perception is a research and policy agenda and a teacher and popular literature on school dropouts that have concentrated on the personal and demographic characteristics of the dropouts themselves. By focusing on students as the problem, this research and the literature it has spawned implies that schools bear little responsibility for students dropping out and therefore can take few actions to reduce the number of dropouts.

Contrary to this mainstream research agenda, the work of other researchers has revealed that the responses by schools to the problems of students at risk of dropping out play a crucial role in the decision to leave prior to graduation.[1] Rather than framing the problem solely in terms of students, this work has identified an interdependent relationship between school processes and the personal characteristics of dropouts. Those studies that have examined the perceptions of dropouts themselves have provided one source of evidence that the characteristics of the school contribute to the problem. For example, minority youth who have dropped out of urban schools have been reported as being highly critical of the school and "the contradictions between their academic learning and lived experiences."[2] In our own study, white dropouts from a working-class suburban school voiced strong criticisms not only of irrelevant curricula, but also of teachers, counselors, and administrators for their lack of caring and negative attitudes, and of school policies for their insensitivity to students' emerging adult status.[3]

These criticisms should have some impact on the perception of the nature of the dropout problem in terms of needed school reforms. Fine and Rosenberg argue, however, that the influence of these voices is severely limited because dropouts are perceived as deviant and therefore their perspectives are not worth consideration. This popular image of dropouts as deviant delegitimates their voices and therefore effectively silences their critique of schooling. Thus, the school remains protected from a serious analysis of its contribution to students dropping out.

In this chapter we examine the silencing of critiques of schooling by dropouts themselves. We begin by looking at the image of the dropout created by both the educational literature and the mass media and how this image deflects criticism of the school and any discussion of needed reforms in its policies and practices that might improve the retention of students until graduation. In contrast to this image, we discuss studies that have revealed the contribution of both the school and structural features of U.S. society to the problem of dropping out. We then report our own study, which suggested that, in contrast to urban minority dropouts, white working-class dropouts have internalized the image of personal deficiency and silenced themselves in voicing criticisms of the school.

IMAGES OF DROPOUTS

Wehlage and his colleagues describe how research on dropouts has been predominantly concerned since the 1960s with examining samples of dropouts in order to identify common personal and social characteristics. Such an exclusive focus, they argue, suggests that social characteristics cause students to leave school early and portrays dropouts as deviant or deficient with regard to their ability or disposition to cope with school. This agenda places the blame on the victim rather than the institution from which they have been excluded, either by choice or by pressure.

Similarly, the policy debate on the dropout problem usually revolves around national statistics describing the characteristics of those who leave high school before graduation. The use of such national data frames the issue exclusively in terms of student characteristics and thereby ignores the contribution of the school to the problem. Furthermore, the use of dropout rates in these statistics links the problem to particular populations and hides such facts as that "the total number of white dropouts is substantially greater than the total number of Blacks and Hispanics combined."[4] By seeking and identifying common characteristics, the diversity in the background and academic performance of students who drop out is ignored. Yet, on the other hand, although a disproportionate number of students from minority and economically poor backgrounds drop out of school, the problem is rarely addressed in terms of racial and class inequalities in schooling or in the broader society.

Typical of this orientation toward blaming the victim is the perspective articulated by leading officials in the federal Department of Education. Both the former assistant secretary of education for educational research and development in the Reagan administration, Chester Finn, and the present incumbent, Christopher Cross, have made public speeches pronouncing the futility of schools enacting reforms to accommodate "at-risk" students when what is really needed, they claim, is "a commitment to change values, to motivate students."[5] Secretary of Education Lauro Cavazos echoed a similar message when he announced that the lack of valuing of, and commitment to, education among Hispanic parents was to blame for the high rates of dropping out among Hispanic youth.[6]

This construction of the debate solely in terms of the social characteristics and home or cultural background of the dropouts is promulgated in the literature for educational practitioners. A cursory survey of the more popular teacher and administrator journals and publications (e.g., *Instructor, Learning, Principal*) revealed remarkably few articles on dropouts during the past seven years. The few articles that were published on the subject focused on the oppressive lives of dropouts and/or individual success stories. Even when school factors are cited, it is the students in those schools who are ultimately implicated in the dropout dilemma. For example, in a Phi Delta Kappa fastback series, in only two of seven profiles of dropouts are school-related factors presented as significant in the decision to leave school, and in both these cases the emphasis is on deviant behavior (e.g., drugs, gangs, violence) within the school.[7] More significant contributors to the dropout problem, the author suggests, are parents' lack of commitment to education and students' tardiness, lazy work habits, and low self-images.

The general public receives similar messages from popular literature and the mass media. One common message is that the phenomenon of dropping out is most prominently linked to dysfunctional aspects of dropouts' personal lives and family circumstances. This view emerges from the preponderance in popular publications of individual success stories, which invariably depict cases in which individuals have overcome such hardships as child abuse, homelessness, and drug abuse to return to or remain at school.[8] In other words, the implicit message conveyed by these stories is that individuals can rise above their circumstances, irrespective of how bad those circumstances are. Certainly the efforts of these individuals are laudable, as is the media attention to the positive aspect of the problem. However, the focus on their personal circumstances serves to deflect public attention away from questioning the role that school policies and practices might play in either failing to respond to or exacerbating the problems of youth in such dire situations.

This view is captured by a Boston school board member in commenting on his city's dropouts: "You can have the most state-of-the-art school in the world, but if a student is bringing a lot of baggage to school, he is not going to learn."[9] When "baggage" is blamed for a school's difficulties, the image is maintained that the sole source of dropouts' problems is their family circumstances.

Much of the publicity surrounding recent "get tough" and "carrot and stick" programs creates a similar image of the problem residing in individuals.[10] These programs, which attempt to encourage satisfactory attendance and/or grades by giving or withholding rewards perceived to be valued by adolescents, suggest that dropouts have deficiencies in their character that can be readily rectified by behavior modification approaches. For example, as of this writing, six states withhold driver's licenses from dropouts, and at least six others have proposed such legislation. Other state- or business-sponsored programs provide incentives, such as tuition-free college scholarships or cash contributions for educational expenses, for "at risk" students who remain in school and graduate with a high school diploma. Such programs can play a useful role in providing incentives to encourage and support some students who need more intermediate goals than the long-term prospect of economic rewards that are claimed to result from obtaining a high school diploma. However, as a single or primary strategy for reducing dropping out, they assume that the basic structure and practices of schools are sound and that students must be induced to stay in school irrespective of the quality of education and the kind of treatment they are receiving. In other words, it is acceptable for schools to remain the same, but young people must change and learn to "stick it out" regardless of whether their needs are being met. This notion was echoed in a recent television advertisement that defined the problem in terms of a lack of perseverance or commitment by portraying a young unemployed mother expressing both the wish that she had been tied to her chair in order to finish high school and her intention to do so with her own child.

THE CRITICAL VOICES OF URBAN MINORITY DROPOUTS

When we look at studies that have tried to unravel the causes of students dropping out, a more complex picture emerges. This picture includes a view of schools and larger structural features of our society as partners, along with student characteristics, in the problem. The interrelationship of school factors and personal and family circumstances has been vividly painted in the following words:

> If one comes from a low socio-economic background, which may signify various forms of family stress and personal difficulties, and if one is consistently discouraged by the school because of signals about academic inadequacies and failures, and if one seees the institution's discipline system as ineffective and unfair, but one has serious encounters with that discipline system, then it is not unreasonable to expect that one will become alienated and lose one's commitment to the goals of graduating from high school and pursuing more education.[11]

The above hypothesis is supported by the few studies that have examined the experiences and perspectives of dropouts themselves. Their voices have challenged the notion that schools do not contribute to the decision to quit. For example, African American and Hispanic dropouts from New York City high schools expressed powerful critiques of their schools.[12] Furthermore, discriminant analysis based on a battery of tests and surveys indicated that the attitudes of these dropouts did not fit the stereotypical image. In contrast to comparison subgroups of GED recipients and students who returned to school, dropouts were "relatively not depressed, . . . not conforming, and most willing to resist an unjust act by a teacher," while being "academically average" and "typical in attributions of success and failure."[13] Not only did the African American and Hispanic dropouts interviewed in the above study voice criticisms of educational institutions, but they also were critical of the lack of labor market opportunities for minorities even with a GED. Other studies have illuminated in more detail how these structural arrangements are perceived by minority students and influence their decision to leave school without a diploma. Ogbu,[14] for example, describes how a job ceiling and other racial barriers encountered by African Americans contradict the image of education as providing equality of opportunity and arguments for remaining in school until graduation. Castelike minorities, therefore, tend to blame the system for their educational (and employment) difficulties.

Yet the "tendency to label dropouts as incompetent in school because they possess characteristics identified as the products of deficient homes and cultural backgrounds"[15] means that their critiques are not recognized.[16] Thus, the criticism of schools as sites of unequal opportunities are silenced.

WHITE WORKING-CLASS DROPOUTS

The studies that have explored the factors leading to dropping out generally have been conducted in urban schools with high dropout rates and high proportions of minorities. Yet among low-income students, white students drop out more than minorities.[17] We were interested in comparing the reasons for dropping out provided by nonminorities with the explanations for minorities dropping out that were offered by the studies already cited. Of particular interest was the question: Do nonminority dropouts voice critiques of school policies and practices in attributing the blame for quitting school?

We interviewed twenty dropouts from an outer suburban school in a working-class community in a major city in New York state. All of them were white and had dropped out, or did not reenter after failing to graduate, during the 1987/88 school year. They were questioned about the factors that contributed to their decision to leave school and any changes that might have kept them in school. The school record and transcript of each dropout also was examined to determine the status of their academic problems.

Unlike the image of dropouts as coming from deficit homes, most of the dropouts lived with both parents, of whom at least one was employed, usually in a low-paid or semiskilled occupation. Some of their parents had college degrees, although a few also had dropped out of school. Thus, the demographic characteristics of our sample confirmed the finding from other studies[18] that students from a diversity of backgrounds drop out of school. Similarly, our interviews supported the argument advanced by the same researchers that a complex web of interrelated personal and school factors contribute to students' decision to drop out. This web tends to begin with a personal or family problem that the student finds interferes with his or her capacity to cope with the typical expectations and demands of school. The school's response, or lack of appropriate response, either exacerbates the problem or creates an additional problem for the student. For example, Alice was retained in grade four because of her reading difficulties (which she attributed to family problems), but that had the effect of isolating her from her friends, a situation that continued through later grades and eventually led to truancy. She claimed that this behavior resulted in her receiving a bad reputation among teachers, which in turn increased her desire to skip school. School policies on attendance prevented her from taking exams, which meant she received failing grades and therefore developed a serious credit deficiency problem.

Alice, like virtually all the dropouts we interviewed, criticized the school and identified specific personnel and policies (in her case, the attitude exhibited by many teachers and the retention and attendance policies) that contributed to her decision to drop out. A frequent criticism from many dropouts was a seeming lack of caring among teachers, administrators, and counselors. For example, Michelle commented that, upon returning to school after a two-month absence, she discovered that "I can't take any exams, I had detentions, and nobody cares. . . . My guidance counselor did nothing." So, instead of receiving offers of assistance to help with her problems and encouragement to remain in school, she was greeted with further obstacles. Other comments on school personnel included:

Bob: [there were] no sincere teachers, no high level of respect, . . . teachers don't care for its extra work for them . . . [they] don't research like they should about drugs and signals of children who need help.

Carol: Guidance conselors don't care, they just get you out [of their offices] no matter what.

Kevin: Their attitudes were negative, when you'd ask a question, they'd just blow it off

. . .

Interviewer: What was it you didn't like about those classes?

Fred: Teachers who thought they had it all, knew it all, knew what they were doing. Maybe they knew the subject but they didn't know kids.

Criticisms of curriculum and teaching practices focused on the irrelevance of subject matter and the boredom of classes and assigned work. For example:

Michael: [Courses were] irrelevant, a lot of stuff I didn't need to learn, I didn't think I would use it after school. They didn't get straight to the point about things.

Linda: They write it on the chalkboard, you copy it down and have a test on it next week.

Brad: [In] teaching about early America, they mislead students . . . the secrets of society should be exposed.

Other common complaints clustered around the school's policies, such as those relating to student behavior, discipline, and suspension. Policies such as being required to remain in the cafeteria during the whole lunch period made students feel as if they were regarded as irresponsible and untrustworthy. Sally, for example, said, "You can't leave the cafeteria at lunch, they watched us like hawks—no phone calls, no pop," while John added that "you can't do homework or study in the cafeteria, it felt like being in jail." This feeling apparently extended beyond the lunch period, as one dropout grumbled "it was ridiculous not to be able to walk the halls or leave a class without a pass." Roberta complained of the school in general "treating you like little kids, you couldn't clean your locker or talk to teachers during lunch." These comments illustrate how school policies might interfere with opportunities for students to develop attachments or a sense of belonging to the school.

Even more counterproductive, at least to these students, were the punishments for failure to abide by school policies. Often they exacerbated the very problem they were attempting to stop. As Bonnie stated, suspension for truancy was "like giving candy to a baby . . . first I skipped, then they kicked me out."

High schools, as organizations responsible for the welfare of a large and diverse number of adolescents, are confronted with a difficult task in establishing and enforcing rules for orderly and acceptable behavior. When these rules have the potential for exacerbating the problem, or creating additional problems for the student to which they are being applied, then the rules themselves, or their uniform and rigid application, need to be reexamined.

THE SELF-SILENCING OF CRITICAL VOICES

Despite the criticisms the dropouts in our study voiced of their school, nearly all of them ultimately reclaimed for themselves the blame for dropping out. We view this reclamation of blame as a self-silencing of personal criticisms of schooling and school processes.

This silencing of self seemed to grow from the tensions created by holding oppositional beliefs about school, oneself, and the relationship between the two. One such tension that surfaced was the dropouts' attempts to reconcile their lack of success with the fact that they viewed the school and its intentions as basically good. If Lois Weis is correct about the working class of the 1980s and 1990s increasingly accepting and "articulating some value for education,"[19] then the fact that these dropouts described their high school as essentially a good place should not be surprising. For some students, this tension of finding oneself in a good place but unable to succeed was transformed into a perception that they were not the right kind of person for school. For example, Marshall believed that "school wasn't for me, I don't have what it takes. I'm not dumb but I don't understand that kind of knowledge." Yet he felt that he should have been able to manage: "I should have got it."

Others alternated between blaming themselves and blaming their school, but eventually reclaimed for themselves the blame for their inability to graduate. Bob provides a compelling example of this phenomenon. He emphasized that "*I* never actually quit," and explained that when he returned to school after a long absence due to illness, his guidance counselor advised him to cut his losses and leave school for the remainder of the semester but then come back and complete the courses in summer school. Bob said he thought the plan was perfect, because his mother was unemployed at the time, so he felt he could help out by taking a job. However, when he showed up for summer school, he was informed that he couldn't enroll in the courses because he hadn't failed them. Bob believed that the counselor had lied to him and recalled losing his temper when learning of his predicament. Not surprisingly he offered a strong indictment of the school's counseling service.

Yet, when asked his main reason for leaving school, Bob mentioned the counseling incident but then began to blame himself: "I had no backbone and many problems resulting from having being raised in the standard broken home." In response to the next set of questions, he was again highly critical of the school:

> Teachers don't care, except for one or two. They have dry classes, and if you tried to talk to them—NO! Boring teachers don't care. . . . I hated simple classes and useless work; it didn't stimulate my intellect. There was no challenge, just book work. . . . You're set up for a world that isn't there, without the skills and knowledge needed to survive in the real world. You can only use their knowledge on tests.

Despite these strong criticisms of the academic program and the attitudes and competencies of teachers and counselors, he was unable or unwilling to blame his alienation on the school. Instead, he attributed his decision to drop out to defects in his own character, including "problems with my self-image, . . . and being sick from not wanting to go [to school]." Finally, Bob ended the interview and punctuated his self-criticism by saying that "*I* should have tried harder."

As students resort to their own deficiencies to explain their school failure, they delegitimate their own school critiques and help to maintain mainstream views of dropouts themselves, and not schools, as the major concern and focus for intervention. We explain this tendency of our dropouts to blame their quitting on personal deficiencies, rather than institutional deficiencies, as did the South Bronx dropouts studied by Fine, by suggesting that the white suburban dropouts we interviewed had internalized the popular media image of the dropout as incompetent or deviant. The critical question, however, is why do these nonminority dropouts internalize this image, when their minority counterparts reject it?

CLASS IDEOLOGY AND THE LACK OF A COLLECTIVE CONSCIOUSNESS

If dropouts are to reject the social construction of what a dropout represents, then they need to either possess a strong positive personal sense of identity or be able to draw upon a collective consciousness that serves to oppose the popular image. We will examine each of these possibilities in turn.

Most adolescents, by virtue of their stage of development, do not possess a strong sense of identity, but rather are in the process of identity formation. Adolescence is typically a period of self-exploration, including experimenting with different roles and searching for an identity that feels comfortable. Since the formation of an identity is in a state of flux, it is unlikely that any self-image will be sufficiently well-defined to counter a powerful and widely promulgated social image.

Part of the adolescent search for an identity is comparing oneself with peers and seeking an identity that is not deviant from collective adolescent norms. These collective norms reside in peer subcultures within the school. However, our dropouts were not a part of any such subculture in their school. First, they reported feeling isolated from their peers and unable to break into the tight memberships of the subcultural groups. So they had no peer-group attachment to aid in their identity formation. Second, as students, our dropouts saw most of their peers adjusting to the system, with few dropping out (the school's dropout rate was relatively low, at approximately 7 percent). Thus, these dropouts constituted a small group, and their inability to cope with school labeled them "unusual" or "deviant."

Interestingly, students who had participated in the high school's alternative program talked about the comarâderie in this program. This alternative involved one teacher who primarily worked with approximately twenty to twenty-five students who had their own separate space within the school and separate rules and policies. This structural arrangement and the students' comments suggest a sense of community that had the potential for the development of a subcultural group to which our dropouts might have become attached. However, the program served very few students at any one time, and the school's policy of returning students to the regular program after a year in the alternative resulted in the fragmentation of even this group as these students were dispersed among a wide range of classes. Although that was apparently not a deliberate strategy on the part of the school, the effect was to create a continually shifting population and thereby impede the potential development of a cohesive group that possessed a collective consciousness or group identity.

This situation is in contrast to the working-class "lads" described by Willis[20] who comprised a distinct, but minority, group that collectively formed an oppositional culture to that of the school.[21] Willis attributes this oppositional culture to conditions beyond the school that affect the social and economic mobility of the working class in England. In particular, the working class in industrial northern England did not subscribe to the notion that education could change their economic circumstances. The working-class parents in our outer suburban community, however, did apparently value the high school diploma as a necessary ticket to economic survival. This value was manifested in their usually strong objections to their son's or daughter's decision to quit school.

In the case of minorities, Ogbu has observed that youth receive mixed and conflicting messages from their parents. On the one hand, parents convey the value of education for economic survival and mobility, but on the other hand they acknowledge that discrimination in the labor market reduces their employment opportunities irrespective of educational qualifications. As a result, African American youth value education as the road out of poverty and associated social problems,[22] but they "tend to behave in ways that will not necessarily lead to school success. For example, they tend to be excessively tardy, lack serious attitude toward their schoolwork, and not to persevere in doing their schoolwork."[23]

Ogbu maintains that this paradoxical behavior seems to be part of an "evolved cultural pattern" characteristic of many Black communities.[24] Castelike minorities have collectively developed a structural explanation for the failure of education historically to help improve their circumstances. Their educational ambitions and struggle for equality of educational opportunity may have developed as a form of opposition to the dominant white society. They perceive their cultural and language differences not as barriers to be overcome but as "symbols of identity."[25] Therefore, Ogbu argues that these minorities develop a "cultural frame of reference [which] gives them both a sense of collective or social identity and a sense of self-worth."[26] Thus, this oppositional culture provides an alternative basis for the formation of an identity.

In contrast, our white dropouts obviously did not have a cultural history of racial discrimination. Furthermore, whiteness is usually not challenged other than as a dominant or oppressive force. The dominant white community, therefore, tends not to be confronted with the task of developing a well-defined or explicit cultural frame of reference. Consequently, white students in general are not likely to interpret their experience in light of their membership in a racial entity.

Furthermore, our dropouts belonged to the postindustrial working class in the United States, which has been described as "fractured": historically along regional racial and ethnic lines, and more recently by the displacement of industrial workers and the erosion of the labor union as a social and political collectivity.[27] Therefore, the working class has lost any form of collective consciousness that is distinctive from the dominant culture.[28] White working-class American youth have been reported as desiring a diploma for its economic utility because of the deindustrialization of the American economy and their resulting belief in the increase in importance of the high school diploma in the labor market.[29] Our dropouts could not explain their decision to leave school in terms of the economic irrelevance of a diploma. Given the working class's new educational aspirations, students could not draw on a cultural devaluing of education in attributing their lack of success to the unimportance of making an effort. In other words, it is no longer feasible for students to say: I didn't make the effort because I could get a job without a high school diploma. Similarly, in contrast to minorities, they could not claim that discrimination in the job market means that the possession of a diploma was of no economic use anyway. The white working class's cultural frame of reference tends to support rather than oppose schooling.

This notion of class ideology is rarely examined in U.S. schools. The image of the classless American society does not support serious consideration in the school curriculum of any class differences. While a working-class consciousness, although now fractured, has arisen in the workplace, as the history of labor unions illustrates, students are not located in the workplace but in schools. And schools generally deal uncritically, if at all, with workplace issues, such as labor history.[30] Neither the school nor the working-class culture provides a collective consciousness from which working-class youth can articulate a critique of schooling or explain their failure to succeed in school.

Without the working class having a clear oppositional identity, the culture of individualism, which already dominates the social fabric of white America, becomes a more powerful influence on the white working class as well. In the case of dropouts, since individualism means that everyone has an equal chance to succeed irrespective of their personal or family circumstances, failure can only be attributed to deficiencies in the individual. This ideology is, of course, consistent with the media image of dropouts.

Finally, these dropouts did not attend a school that lacked basic amenities, did not live in impoverished neighborhoods, and could not attach their failure to a collective history of unequal opportunities. In other words, the blame could not be located, as it could in the case of minority youth attending blighted inner-city schools, in the disadvantages experienced as a result of race or poverty. Therefore, the image of the dropout as deviant appeared, by a process of elimination, to be the only one that seemed to fit their situation.

CONCLUSION

In trying to sort out and articulate their decision to leave school, our dropouts were confronted with a split consciousness. On the one hand, they recognized that there were lots of problems with school and it didn't work out for them. Yet on the other hand, they felt they should have been able to cope, especially since most of their peers managed to cope. The resolution of this issue in terms of acceptance of the ultimate blame for their own failure to finish both emerges from and contributes to the image of the dropout as deviant. In other words, the dropouts had internalized the view that dropping out results from deficits in the student, even though their own experiences suggested that the school also was deficient. Their retreat into self-blame ultimately served to soften, counter, and delegitimate their strong and often cogent criticisms of teachers and teaching, curricula and counseling, administrative policies and practices, and school and social structures. Thus, the white working-class dropouts' critique of schools is silenced by themselves, and hence "the prevailing view that dropouts are deviant, lazy, or inadequate"[31] is reinforced.

Given that adolescents are unlikely to possess a strong personal sense of identity, a collective identity can provide an alternative basis for opposing this prevailing social image of the dropout. However, such an identity is unlikely to emerge "until the white working class in the U.S. reconstitute a class consciousness and identify with a collective rather than individual struggle to rise above their circumstances."[32] In the meantime, white working-class dropouts are likely to continue to blame themselves and maintain this self-imposed silence in regard to criticisms of the institutional arrangements and practices of schooling. Unfortunately, that response only deletes a potential voice from those who could take issue with the predominant view that schools do not contribute to the dropout problem. Yet it is time that the voices of dropouts are heard and accorded legitimacy by educators, since their critiques can suggest ways of shaping viable school responses to the needs of "at-risk" students.

MICHELE FOSTER

Chapter Thirteen

Resisting Racism: Personal Testimonies of African-American Teachers*

INTRODUCTION: MISSING VOICES

For the first six decades of this century, teaching was one of the few occupations open to Black college graduates, a condition that was captured in the oft-quoted phrase, "the only thing a college-educated Negro can do is teach or preach." Despite this fact, there is surprisingly little that chronicles the experiences of Black teachers. There are some biographies of famous Black educators who have made significant contributions to education, but these accounts do not encompass the experiences of thousands of Black teachers who, though not historically significant, nonetheless played an important role in education of Black children.[1] The voices of Black teachers are not adequately represented among first-person narrative accounts. Of sixty-five first-person teachers' narratives written in English in this century reviewed by this author, for instance, three were written by Black American teachers. Finally, though the anthropological and sociological literature is somewhat more inclusive, Black teachers appearing more frequently in this genre, except for a few balanced portrayals,[2] the typical representation of Black teachers is decidedly negative.[3]

One characteristic of the educational literature written about Black teachers between 1966 and the present is its almost singular focus on describing their relationship to maintaining the larger social order. Rarely do any of the accounts describe how Black teachers have actively resisted the status quo.

This chapter endeavors to fill this void. It focuses on the various individual and collective means by which Black teachers have resisted racism and thereby challenged the status quo. In so doing, it gives voice to nineteen Black teachers who, though not historically significant, are nonetheless considered exemplary by the Black communities they have served.

Chosen by "community nomination," a term coined and a method of sampling designed to capture the Black community's perspective of good teaching, these teachers worked anywhere from twenty-four to sixty-six years, in different regions of the United States, in both rural and urban settings.

Of the nineteen teachers, twelve spent their childhood years in communities where schools were segregated by law. Six grew up in communities where no laws required segregated schools, but where de facto segregation meant that schools were racially isolated, nonetheless. The remaining teacher spent half of her childhood in a segregated community before moving north with her family. Three-fourths of the teachers attended historically Black colleges, including three raised in the North who attended majority white elementary and secondary schools. All except one of those that attended predominantly white colleges, however, had spent their precollege years in segregated schools.

Whether raised in the North or in the South, however, all of the teachers were born, and most began their professional lives, during the era when separate but equal was the law of United States.[4] Five of the teachers, reared in the South, began their teaching careers in segregated southern schools, two of them in schools where they had once been students. Though two later relocated to the North and began teaching, three remained in the same school districts through the desegregation and postdesegregation years. Four of the teachers began their careers in schools where white students made up the majority, with the remaining ten having begun their careers in school systems that, though not legally segregated, nonetheless maintained racially imbalanced schools. Eight of the teachers have worked in the same district for two decades and are teaching their second generation of the same family.

INSTITUTIONAL BARRIERS: NORTH VERSUS SOUTH

Despite the fact that the teaching profession was open to Blacks, historians have amply documented that the careers of Black teachers have, nonetheless, been sharply circumscribed by racism. Over the years, Black teachers were paid less than white teachers, rarely hired except to instruct Black pupils, discriminated against by largely white unions, dismissed in large numbers following the *Brown v. Board of Education* decision, and denied access to teaching positions by legal and extralegal means.[5] Though the peculiarities of racism varied according to region, when compared to the material conditions of their white counterparts, those under which Black teachers have worked have been unique. In communities where laws mandated it, there was a clear and unambiguous pattern of segregation in schools. Teachers who began their careers in legally segregated communities were concentrated in separate schools; however, within these confines the range of teaching and administrative opportunities was open to them. Northern communities, where de jure segregation was absent, employed unofficial and more subtle practices to concentrate African American teachers in certain schools and restrict them from certain grade levels. The result was that northern and southern Black teachers resorted to different patterns of resistance, a fact borne out in these interviews.

RESISTING RACISM: SOUTHERN STYLE

One of many inequities in dual school systems was the discrepant per-pupil expenditures in white and Black public schools. Included in these expenditures were textbooks, teaching supplies, school library books, and other instructional supplies and salaries. In North Carolina, considered one of the most progressive southern states when it came to Black education, the per-pupil expenditures for Black students in 1939–40 were 72.6 percent of those for white students. Fourteen years later, the gap had been narrowed considerably, the per-pupil expenditure for Black students having reached 94.3 percent of the expenditure for white pupils.[6]

Of course these discrepancies were evident in differential salaries paid to Black and white teachers. In the 1928–29 school year, the salaries for white rural and urban North Carolina elementary school teachers were $724.38 and $1,181.27, respectively. Black elementary teachers who worked in rural areas, on the other hand, earned 57 percent of the salary of their white counterparts, while Black elementary teachers who worked in urban areas obtained 61 percent of the salary of urban white elementary school teachers. At the secondary level, the discrepancies were slightly less; Black high school teachers earned 72 percent of the salary received by white teachers.[7] In North Carolina in 1933, Black teachers were required by law to meet the same qualifications as whites for comparable certification. Yet this same law specified that whites possessing the same qualifications as Blacks were to receive 30 percent higher salaries. Salary differentials such as those in North Carolina were commonplace throughout the South.

In cooperation with the NAACP, Black teachers, through their respective state American Teachers Association, founded in 1902 as the National

Association of Teachers in Colored Schools, an organization of teachers from the twenty states that had separate schools for Blacks, and a counterpart to the all-white segregated National Education Association, fought to eliminate these discrepant salaries. In 1933, twenty-five hundred Black teachers met in Raleigh to listen to speakers and to voice their protest against the inequities in school funding, including teachers' salaries.[8]

Though it is not clear what resulted from this demonstration, a decade later, Black teachers were still not receiving salaries comparable to those of white teachers. Everett Dawkins,[9] who began teaching in Chatham County, a rural county less than fifty miles from Raleigh, recalls how he and his colleagues in the North Carolina Black Teachers Association, fought for salary equalization.

> When I started to work in 1943, two things that I look back on now, bother me quite a bit. Number one, teachers, period didn't make anything. I mean money, financially. It was like ninety dollars a month. A month. In addition to that Black teachers were not paid on the same rate as whites in North Carolina. So where we were getting like ninety, *they* were probably getting like 120 a month. But through the leadership of the North Carolina Teachers' Association, we were able to bring enough pressure to get the salaries at least equalized. The North Carolina Teachers Association was the Black teachers of North Carolina band together in an association. We had our own association called the North Carolina Teachers Association. They (the salaries) weren't very high, but at least they were equal. Everybody was making the same thing with the same certification. So that is one thing that has bothered me all these years. I feel like somewhere down the line somebody owes me some money.
>
> *Do you remember when you got your salaries equal?*
>
> It had to be about 1945 or 46, somewhere in that general area I can't pin it down as to date, but I do know that it was in the 40's. I'll put it that way. Somewhere between 43 and 50. You know I just feel like we got ch—well, I know the Black teachers got cheated in that respect. I don't have any real animosity with anybody, but it's just the fact that it seems to me that they were given a little more consideration, too, the fact that we were not paid on an equal basis.

As indicated above, salary differentials were not the only inequality in supposedly separate-but-equal dual school systems. Black teachers, especially those from rural counties, recalled that their schools had inferior physical plants and fewer supplies and materials than white schools. Lacking gymnasiums, students could only have physical education outside when the weather permitted. Black teachers in segregated southern schools never received teachers' manuals or other equipment and were responsible for purchasing their own schools materials. The books that Black students received were discarded from white schoolchildren and were often so badly torn that they were unusable.

Ella Jane, who began teaching in east Texas in 1955, spoke about the conditions she taught under for nine years before she was transfered to the previously all-white school after desegregation.

> In the Black schools, we only got—the textbooks that we got were the books that didn't have a space to write our names. They were torn out and the books came from the white schools after they were ready to put them in the trash. We didn't have teachers' editions. And in the year that our school burned down, I didn't even have textbooks. Not any kind. Our school, my high school burned down. Where I went to school, where I was working in 61 or 62 something like that, the school burned down. But the remainder of the school year I didn't have any textbooks. We didn't even get any more. We taught in the church. But the school did not furnish anything. You just managed on what you could find. You cut out stuff, you bought stuff. You bought your own construction paper, you bought your own glue, you bought your own Kleenex. You bought everything that you used. Maybe you would get a record player. For your class. But you'd have to get your own records. You just didn't have anything. You didn't have anything to work with. It was real hard. We didn't even have a gym. If we played ball, you had to play when the weather was good, and you had to play outside.

Echoing these sentiments, Bernadette Mosely talked about the conditions in one of the two segregated schools in Hampton, Virginia, in which she taught:

> Underwood was a very old school, whenever the temperature dropped below 30 or 32 degrees, we were cold. And there were times when the principal had to double up classes, it was so cold. Now how can you teach in a doubled up situation? It was just not ideal at all. I can remember one time the books were so worn out, I remember a first grade teacher in the faculty meeting at the end of school said, "Mr. Holmes I want to talk about these books that we have given these children." She said, "I don't even want to touch them myself. They're old and the state adoption has been passed." And everybody was talking out. He (the principal) said, "I'll tell you what you do." And at that school they had a coal furnace. And he said, "You go through them and all the old books that you think are not usable just stack them outside your room and I'll have the janitor bring them down here by the furnace room." You know two or three days after we got those books down there, the superintendent came in the school and made him take

everyone of those books back up into the classroom. "What's wrong with this? You can still read it."

Given these conditions, it may seem impossible that Black teachers would have been able to expose Black students to a rigorous curriculum or to educate them effectively. Though there are some documented exceptions,[10] the inferiority of segregated Black schools is a widely accepted fact. Detailed descriptions of Black schools in segregated southern school systems, and comparisons of the material conditions of Black and white schools, establish this point.[11] Inarguably, segregated schools were severely underfunded and lacking supplies and equipment. Though the schools lacked materially, it cannot unilaterally be assumed that the students enrolled in segregated schools were automatically deprived of challenging coursework.

In *Simple Justice*, the seminal history of the *Brown* decision, Kluger informs his readers that at two of the four Black schools in Topeka, "more of the teachers held master's degrees than at any of the white grade schools and their devotion to their work was exemplary." Kluger, profiling Mamie Luella Williams, who by community-wide agreement was Topeka's best Black teacher despite the all-Black schools in which she taught, describes her as "a master teacher."[12]

Accounts of competent Black teachers by white scholars are as rare as their recognition that, the material conditions of segregated schools notwithstanding, thousands of Black teachers were able to challenge their students intellectually and educate them effectively. Everett Dawkins, a retired teacher whose earlier narrative mentioned the struggle waged by members of the North Carolina Teachers Association to obtain equal salaries, who taught in a rural North Carolina School District for forty-one years, twenty-seven in segregated schools and fourteen in desegregated schools, is an example. While he agreed that segregation had a deleterious effect on the amount and quality of materials available to his county's Black public schools, Dawkins nonetheless was the first math teacher in his county to offer an advanced math course, which he taught to his students in the all-Black segregated high school.

> Everyone today says that Black kids can't do math, but in my little segregated school I had lots of kids who loved math and were good in it, too. Even though I had to teach a whole lot of subjects—because in all Black schools you had to be able to teach what they needed—math was my major and my favorite subject. So I decided that a lot of my students were ready for advanced math and I just started teaching it. It was the first advanced math class ever taught in the county. And, I taught it to Black kids for about

two years, before the school board found out and made me stop until the white high school could get the course going in their building. You know they couldn't stand that Black kids were gettin something their kids weren't gettin.

Though forced to comply with the school board's decision, Dawkins recognized the implementation and subsequent cancellation of the course as a political struggle over who was to control the content of Black education.

Controlling the education of Black children is a theme that surfaced repeatedly in the life histories of teachers who began teaching in legally segregated schools. Remembering the fight waged by the teachers and parents when Georgetown County tried to force a local Episcopal parochial school known for its quality courses and instruction to close, Miss Ruthie, an eighty-year-old South Carolina teacher who has taught at the school since 1938, describes how Black parents and teachers actively resisted the county's efforts to exercise control over their children's education:

> The county had just built a new school and they wanted all of us to go together to the new school. So we told them no. So they said that they were gonna see that this school closed down. My husband told them, "We'll see that it stays open." So that was the argument between the superintendent and us. So they stirred the people up telling them how they felt. They said if the children came here to school that when they finished here they couldn't go into public school for a higher education. And that's when the parents started to roll and we started keeping Columbia (the state capital) hopping. We got the Department of Education hopping. To answer the questions that they were putting out. We kept on going, but some of the parents, you know how they can frighten some off. The next year, the diocese said they couldn't support the school, but if we wanted to keep it open we could do it. They did everything they could to make us close the school. And we didn't. So then the diocese said if we wanted to keep it and the community wanted it we could do it without support and that's what we've been doing ever since.

Though Black teachers are often portrayed as middle-class individuals who invariably uphold the status quo,[13] there is evidence in these interviews that within segregated school systems, despite threats of retaliation, censure, and personal risks to themselves, Black teachers, sometimes individually and sometimes collectively with other teachers and parents, actively resisted racism and challenged an inequitable system by fighting for equal wages and more control over the education of Black children.

Everett Dawkins, a math major, refused a lucrative position with the federal government involving computers because of a promise made to his mother that he would serve his community as a teacher. Likewise, Miss Ruthie, mentioned earlier, attended Avery Institute, a school that, although it offered young Blacks "the best possible opportunities for self-culture, development, training and preparation for life's duties," also had a reputation for elitism. Despite this privileged background, she began teaching in "the rurals" living with the "little people" and has consistently stood with Black parents against the South Carolina Department of Education as it has tried to dismantle the local independent school, which since 1903 has provided an alternative to the substandard education offered in segregated schools, and to the discriminatory one now offered in the desegregated schools in the South Carolina Coastal Areas.[14]

RESISTING RACISM: NORTHERN STYLE

Irrespective of region, Black teachers have been victimized by racist hiring practices. Three teachers who began teaching in New England told of the subtle and not so subtle means northern school districts used to discriminate against Black teachers. Two teachers who relocated from the south to Hartford in the 1950s recalled how central office placement practices insured that Black teachers were to be assigned to some schools and not others.

After having taught for several years in Jacksonville, Florida, a certified high school English teacher was denied a position as a high school teacher in Hartford because of an unwritten policy banning Black teachers from teaching at the secondary level in all but a few racially isolated schools. Not until she became certified at the elementary level was this teacher able to secure a permanent position in the Hartford public schools. Another teacher, who moved to Hartford from West Virginia, told of the similar difficulties she encountered securing a position in Hartford.

> Then I came to Hartford. Did not get a job immediately. I applied. This was in 53. I applied each year that I went back to West Virginia, but they didn't have any openings, or they never called me. . . . I subbed at the Noah Webster School which was in the Northwest section of the city which was predominantly white—it was white. I was a long term sub for two months because the teacher there was on maternity leave. At the end of June the principal asked me what was I gonna do next year. I said I didn't know. She said, "Well, why don't you put your application in." I told her it had been in, So she called downtown and she said, "I want Bobbie here." They say, "We don't have an application." Course, I know where the application went. When I applied, it went in the waste basket. Because of the color of my skin. This was in 1953. I don't know how many Black teachers it might

have been, maybe six or seven in the city. I'm not sure of how many at the time, but there weren't that many Black teachers.

In Boston, prior to the 1974 desegregation order, Black teachers were severely underrepresented among the teaching force. Like in Hartford, those Black teachers who did manage to secure positions in Boston were isolated in specific schools. Jane Vanderall, who began teaching in Boston in the 1950s, explained what it was like for Black teachers in those years:

> At the time I started teaching, Black teachers were assigned to just that strip going from the South End into Roxbury, between, let me see, Tremont Street and Washington. You didn't get any choice. That's where you were sent and most of the Black teachers had a very hard time out of town (the area where Black teachers were assigned).

During the school desegregation suit, the Boston Teachers' Union went to court to try to preserve the privileged status of its largely white membership. Shrouding the issues in the cloak of seniority, they attempted to restrict further the number of Blacks entering their ranks.

Though local Black teachers' organizations existed in some large northern urban centers, there is little evidence in these interviews to suggest that these Black northern teachers worked collectively with other Black teachers within their school systems to challenge racism. In general, their challenges to the status quo seem to have been individual ones. Given the choice, some northern Black teachers, believing that taking positions in an all-white schools was not in the best interests of their Black students, staunchly opposed being transferred to predominantly white schools. Others, recognizing that their success might force white parents and students to confront their own feelings of superiority, when given the opportunity chose to desegregate all-white schools. Two teachers, both of whom came of age during the 1960s, explain their reasons for choosing to stay in urban Black schools. A high school English teacher, Pamela Owens, the 1981 California Teacher of the Year and the first Black to be so honored, spent three years on the state commission on the teaching profession and two years on the credentialing commission. Ten years later, still in great demand as a speaker to various civic, business, and professional groups, she has been beseiged with invitations to transfer to several of the more affluent white schools in the district. But Pam insists that, although she tells people that she will "do what I want to do," her reasons for staying are because she is "going to be where I *need* to be and where I can be of some good."

In the following passage Cheryl Thigpen, who began teaching in 1969, elaborates this view more fully. She begins by describing the financial incentives that encouraged teachers to enter urban schools without first assuring that they were actually committed to working with urban students.

> You know, in the beginning with the urban ed crisis, I've seen two things. One, I saw a lot of teachers who came into urban ed because of the fact that that was the time that the government was offering education loans, and you did not have to pay the loan back if you went into what they called a validated school. And a validated school was a school in which the children, a certain segment of the children are below the poverty level. So, a lot of teachers came into the urban schools because of that. They did not have to pay their student loans back. That was thing number one that I saw.

Contrasting her reasons for staying in urban schools with the more utilitarian reasons described earlier, she continues. Though she is able to articulate why she has elected to continue in her present position, she acknowledges a little-considered but alternate view that white children as well as Black benefit by the presence of Black teachers.

> But I always knew that I was there because that's where I wanted to be, because I felt that with the knowledge that I have, why am I going to pass it out to little white kids? Because they're going to make it in this world, and all the white folks out there, if they don't learn how to read or write, the white folks are still going to give those white kids jobs. So, I felt that I was too talented and I had too much to give to white children. I've always felt that way, whereas I have a friend who's in a white school, and she feels just the opposite of me. She feels that if Black teachers don't go into white schools, these kids won't know about Black people, and that Black people are capable of doing things such as teaching, which I agree with.

When Black teachers did press to be allowed to teach in desegregated settings, they sometimes met with organized resistance from the white community. Evelyn Taylor, who spent half of her childhood in a segregated southern school before moving north to complete her elementary and secondary education, spoke of the hostility and resistance encountered, and an unexpected source of support, when in 1960 she became the first Black teacher assigned to a California Bay area community:

> All right, so I got the job. But after I got the job, I was assigned to a school on this side of town and it was just horrible. I had been away that summer and when I came back I didn't know that all this stuff had gone on. They had called my house, "Nigger, nigger, nigger." They had held a what do you call it, a community meeting in the church and had all the people there. The principal came over to my house. . . . It was hard for either of them [her

husband or the principal] to tell me. There was even a dispute about the man who led this movement wearing his scouting uniform at that time. There was an article in the paper because you're not supposed to wear your uniform when you do—it was a mess. One of them told the principal that if I were permitted to teach here—and this is a shackey place over here—that I may want to live here. And at that time, there were no Blacks on this side of town. I knew that the whole community didn't want me. But I decided that OK, I'm just going to get through those gates that morning. I'm a teacher like everybody else. I'm trained and by golly, that's just the way it's going to be. But it was real good that the teachers at the school supported me.

In some cities, interdistrict programs have been used to achieve desegregation. Boston and St. Louis are two such cities. Believing that such programs benefit suburban districts at the expense of city districts, one teacher, who works in a city that participates in urban-suburban desegregation, commented that the programs in their communities subtly discriminate against Black teachers. Marcia Gray, the 1974 Missouri Biology Teacher of the Year, recalled how she and another Black science teacher were recruited to work in two suburbs participating in desegregation. After learning she was being hired to teach only Black students from the city, and white students in the lowest tracks, she declined. Unaware of her teaching assignment, the other teacher transferred to the suburbs only to find that all of the Black students were placed in one of her five classes. In keeping with the custom set during desegregation, these desegregated school districts are continuing but slightly altering the practice of siphoning off the most competent Black teachers from all-Black schools to desegregate the faculty and in this case enlisting them to teach undesirable suburban students.[15]

NORTH GOES SOUTH

Because of dual school systems, historically Black teachers were better represented among the teaching force in southern than in northern states. Desegregation, however, had a deep and lasting effect on the careers of many Black teachers. It is estimated that, between 1954 and 1979 in the seventeen southern and border states, approximately thirty-two thousand Black teachers were forced from their jobs.[16] In Kentucky, for example, the number of Black teachers declined by forty-one during the ten years between 1955 to 1965, even though an additional 401 teachers would have needed to be hired merely to keep pace with the increasing numbers of pupils. A study of 467 school districts revealed, moreover, that 127 of them had dismissed 462 African

American teachers, so that by 1970, the Black teacher-student ratio in the South was over twice that of the white student-teacher ratio.[17] Demotions, negative and unfair evaluations, outright dismissals, reassigning the most competent Black teachers to white schools were some the mechanisms employed by school districts to rid themselves of Black teachers. Concealed by these statistics are the stories of thousands of Black teachers, who were forced into stereotyped roles and whose careers were thwarted by desegregation. A math teacher from North Carolina recalled how he and another Black male teacher, neither of whom had ever played any kind of college athletics, were appointed coach and assistant coach of the football, basketball, and baseball teams in the newly integrated high school.

Discussing the integration of southern schools, Lamar Lancaster, a Chicago urban high school English teacher, whose two sisters have taught in Alabama for more than twenty-five years, observed that though schools in the South appear to have been more easily desegregated, the irony is that the schools are internally segregated. Speaking of the staffing patterns in his small hometown in Alabama, he remarked:

> Black teachers if they are in the school at all are teaching for the most part remedial courses that are all black. Very few blacks are teaching courses that you would value, literature, history or social studies. They are teaching remedial reading for blacks or home ec. Schools are all segregated within. In the one high school that so-called has all the wealthy kids—the city high school as such, they've got one black teacher. She teaches home ec or gym or something that. The one gym teacher—you know, a black guy teaches there, assistant coach. They don't want you to be coaches either down there, because sports is a big thing, you know football. You can be assistant coach, but very seldom do you see a white one there. That's the sort of thing I am talking about. They will push him out or find a reason to push him out or something. Well, initially especially, they didn't want any black principals down there and they trumped up charges against a lot of them and that sort of thing. And then the coaches. And it's not so subtle either.

Finally, the enduring racism experienced by Black teachers who teach in desegregated schools is captured in the narrative of Ella Jane, a teacher from a small east Texas town. After graduating from Prairie View A&M, she began teaching in 1955, first in the consolidated all-Black school. In 1964, summoned from her classroom to the superintendent's office, she was informed that she was to be one of only four Black teachers from a staff of twelve to be placed in the newly desegregated school. She remembered that day:

> I got in the car, left the school which was about eight miles out and came over to the administration building. I was sandwiched between a high school

principal on one side and one on the other and a secretary to the superintendent. And they carried me through the wringer. That's how I got here.
The questions they asked were ridiculous. They said, "Ella Jane, did you
know that we have to have some Black teachers?" And I said, "Yes." And
he said, "Did you know that you are going to be very fortunate because you
are going to be one of the Black teachers that we're going to hire?" And he
said, "You're the best teacher I have in the system, Black or white. I did not
have to tell you that and if you tell anyone I said that, I'm gonna tell 'em you
lied." He says, "Do you get my meaning?" And he said, "It should make
you feel very proud whether you do or not that you're going to be one the
ones who are retained." That's how that happened.

Continuing her narrative, Ella Jane explained how she and her cousin,
despite both possessing master's degrees, reported to school each day, but
neither of them was given a class. Instead, they sat in a classroom for half of
the school year without teaching a single student, because the white parents
were opposed to having them teach their children. Finally, in response to
white teachers' protests, Ella Jane and her cousin were assigned to teach remedial reading classes, composed of a dozen Black or poor white children,
established by the school board. For three years, they continued teaching remedial reading classes. During this entire period, the other teachers showed
their contempt for them and the Black students. Ella Jane speaks about how
they were treated:

We were just glorified students. Incidentally, I couldn't use the bathroom
with the teachers and everything. I would use the bathroom with the
students. I didn't eat with them (the other teachers). You know, they just
kind of treated me like dirt. We brought our Black students. The teachers,
the white teachers, would put the Black kids, this is the truth, on one side
and white ones on the other so they wouldn't touch, and so they wouldn't
mingle and that's the truth. This was starting in 64. This went on for a
long time.

As one of only two Black teachers now remaining in the small rural
school district desegregated for twenty-six years, Ella Jane has had to stand
virtually alone against institutional racism, resisting the school system's
effort to push her and confronting the individual racism of white colleagues
and parents.

Bernadette Mosely also recalled the hostility that, as members of the first
group to be transferred to a previously all-white school, she and other Black
teachers and the children encountered from the principal and his faculty.
Sometimes she had to intervene in order to protect Black students from excessively harsh treatment by white teachers, many of whom, she added, quit

rather than teach Black students. In addition to being ignored by white teachers, Black teachers in this school were systematically harassed by the principal. In the following excerpt, she describes two of many incidents and addresses the ways that African American teachers banded together to support each other:

> The principal was pretty nasty. The very first day of teaching, he or somebody had hired a Black teacher, at the last minute. The day before the teachers were to go. And she didn't know where the school was. He had given her some directions. And of course she got lost looking for the school. She got there and we were sitting in a meeting. And she came in quietly and he looked up and saw her and said, "I told you that you were supposed to be here by nine o'clock," in front of everybody. "If this is going to be your habit, maybe we ought to discuss your employment." It was terrible . . . We had a teacher who retired, from NASA, a Black teacher was teaching in another Black school that they were ready to get rid of and they had to place her, and they placed her at my school in the sixth grade. And so I don't know why he didn't like her. He was just on her all the time. I remember one afternoon after school I was trying to show her some methods I used. He had observed her social studies and he didn't like what she was doing. He had written up all this stuff on her and gave a copy of it on things that she could have been doing. And I said, "Yeah, there were a lot of things that you could do, but you were doing some things that I considered right." And then one day, he had antagonized this Black teacher so much that he had started sending for all the different supervisors to observe her. One of the elementary supervisors went in and she was Black and she didn't see anything wrong. So he was going over her head. He sent for another supervisor. But my point is that he made it so hard for that Black teacher that she didn't even wait 'til the end of year, she just walked out.

That Black teachers have encountered such unqualified racism in desegregated schools should not be surprising, for, as historians have amply documented, rarely have African-American teachers fared well in unitary school systems.[18]

A recent survey conducted by a leading Black periodical found that many Blacks now question the wisdom of desegregation. More than half felt that the quality of public school education for Black children had decreased in the past decade, with less than one-fourth responding that the quality of public school education for Black children had improved or remained the same. The respondents' rating of the quality of public school for white children was significantly different. Asked whether the quality of public school education for white students had improved, worsened, or remained the same, about one-third felt the quality had increased, less than 20 percent felt it had decreased, and almost a fourth felt there had been no change. Asked to assess whether the education of Black children had improved in the thirty-five years since schools were desegregated by court order, more than half felt that the education was the same or worse; almost 50 percent answered that the education Black children were receiving was worse, and less than 15 percent felt there had been no change. Finally, asked whether public school teachers had neglected the education of Black and white students in their particular communities and in the nation, the respondents were 2.5 times more likely to state that this was the case for Black students than for white students.[19] Conversations with Blacks who attended segregated schools reveal that they consider integration to have been a mixed blessing. While they acknowledge the improved material conditions that have resulted from desegregation, many complain that the gains in material resources do not compensate for the loss of community, the feeling of alienation, and the loss of pride that Black children now experience in white schools.[20]

Some Black legal and political analysts contend that the benefits that have accrued to Black children from desegregation have not offset the terrible toll exacted of them. Not only has the Black community suffered from the loss of Black professionals, but it has also suffered the loss of their accumulated wisdom about how, despite impoverished conditions, to educate Black children effectively.[21] Cruse and Bell both correctly note that none concerned with pushing *Brown* ever considered the pedagogical influence or the salutary effect of Black schoolteachers.

As these interviews have shown, in their own ways, all of these teachers have actively resisted racism. Though, because their battles have been waged on different terrains, their tactics have varied. Nonetheless, through their own encounters with racism these teachers have to come to understand, and are able to articulate, the difficulties and the complexities of developing in Black children the individual and collective resources needed for group advancement and self-fulfillment as they continue living in an unjust and racist society. Embedded in these interviews, moreover, is evidence that these teachers make a conscious effort to socialize Black children toward a "double consciousness" by cultivating in them individual resolution, mettle, moral strength, and clarity of purpose, while simultaneously developing strong racial pride and consciousness, a task they claim is now made more difficult for African Americans living in a racist society masked by a rhetoric of equal opportunity. Because in-depth analyses of these teachers' political awareness, teaching philosophy, and practice appear elsewhere, such analyses are not undertaken here.[22] The point being emphasized in this chapter is that, in contrast to depictions of Black teachers that portray them as individuals who invariably uphold the status quo, these teachers not only are aware of the institutional racism of American society, but throughout their careers have acted in ways that have challenged the existing social order. Scholars of decidedly different philosophical and theoretical orientations have called for communities to reclaim their histories through stories and narratives.[23] By failing to tell our own stories, we in the Black community have abetted white scholars who, in much the same way that they have promoted the myth of the culturally disadvantaged Black child, have by omission, distortion, and misinterpretation created the myth of the inadequate Black teacher. Not only are Black teachers more often characterized unfavorably than are white teachers, and as lacking the political awareness and resolve to challenge racism, but these negative characterizations diverge from the portrayals of Black teachers found in the essays, sociological studies, and autobiographies and narratives written by Blacks themselves or by authors allowing Blacks to tell their own stories. Though not scholarly analyses, these accounts portray Black teachers as individuals who not only forged productive relationships with their Black students, but who in their own ways have challenged the status quo.[24]

Though the larger story of Black teachers remains untold, these narratives are a starting point. Reclaiming our stories is essential in order to understand the resilience and strengths of Black communities and to incorporate what was best about the past into our communities and schools.

JODY COHEN

Chapter Fourteen

Constructing Race at an Urban High School: In Their Minds, Their Mouths, Their Hearts*

> *Conversation between an academic and an African-American high school student:*
>
> APPIAH:
> The truth is that there are no races. . . . What we miss through our obsession with the structure of relations of concept is, simply, reality.
> —Anthony Appiah "The Uncompleted Argument: DuBois and the Illusion of Race"
>
> VINNIE:
> It's still there. Color is a dead giveaway to who you are.
> —Group interview, 5/15/90

At an urban high school the student population is almost entirely African American; the nonteaching aides, too, are Black; the teaching staff is racially mixed; the administration is predominantly white. In the halls, Black athletes adorn posters with slogans of effort and triumph. However, African American Studies meets after school, during child-care and wage-earning hours, and carries no academic credit. A senior explains that Black students drop out because school is unrelated to their lives. Others add that cutting and acting out are ways that students express anger at what is not acknowledged in

289

school but permeates their daily lives. A young man offers, "[Schools] teach Black kids . . . to buy, but they don't teach [us] to create."

What is at issue here? Whites predominate in positions of power. The study of African-American culture is marginalized. African-American teenagers articulate concerns about an education that seems to leave them out. However, this is not willful neglect: Staff express commitment to the education of these young people. We confront not "sides" but contradictory realities. How might we make sense of "such moments of discontinuity and contradiction" to inform change?[1]

Multicultural education provides a framework for examining some of the contradictions in schools today. A buzzword vaguely and variously defined, multicultural education has been interpreted as assimilating students of color into the mainstream; improving intergroup relations; studying discrete cultural groups; promoting reform so that school programs reflect cultural diversity; and preparing students to challenge structural inequity.[2] The literature focuses on teachers' managing activities; scant attention is paid to a reconsideration of overall processes and content from a multicultural perspective.[3] With few exceptions, voices critical to this discussion—the voices of students themselves—go unheard.[4]

This essay suggests that young people's experiences, questions, and critiques of the meanings of race/ethnicity in our society are essential to developing multicultural education with consequences for their lives. In concert with young African Americans, students at the school described here, I will open a conversation about race and culture. In light of this talk, I will propose a reexamination of multicultural education.

How do we define race in the context of multiculturalism? Often we act as if racial categories were immutable facts. To the contrary, an examination of definitions over time and across communities suggests that race, like gender and class, is socially constructed and contested.[5] Schools operate as a crucial site for the enactment of racial meanings.[6] However, race is seldom addressed in schools. A public high school teacher can't recall the last time race was discussed at her school, despite racial tensions (personal communication). A seminar ending with a discussion of race stunned participants, long-term teachers in the system. Fine notes that there are too few Black teachers and that white teachers more often seem reluctant to raise "race and class contradictions in our society."[7]

If pedagogy is to address "the transformation of consciousness that takes place in the intersection of three agencies—the teacher, the learner and the knowledge they together produce,"[8] then education must invite genuine questions and multiple answers. Schools are uniquely positioned to provide opportunities to investigate race as a construct shaping our lives, as students and teachers bring rich, often contradictory, perspectives to this inquiry.[9]

Many of the young people I spoke with had already begun a process of in-quiry, as they tried on, discarded, and revisited images of race. I offer a window on their processes in the generation of knowledge.

Well outside the domain of the high school, academics from a range of disciplines seek to mine the meanings of race. Anthropologists interrogate the lives of culturally defined groups to reveal signifying patterns.[10] Psychologists investigate how race shapes and is shaped by personal and group identity development.[11] Critical educators situate race as a category of experience and oppression, as in the trilogy "class, race, and gender."[12] Literary post-structuralists set off "race" in quotation marks, metaphorically denoting its nonexistence as a thing-in-itself.[13] Like the teenagers we listen in on here, the literature represents multiple voices.

While this paper takes none of these disciplines as its own, it borrows from each to illuminate or provide counterpoint to the words of the young people who are the intended subjects here. In meshing the literature with the voices of African-American teenagers, I will construct a "theoretical fiction,"[14] a dialogue that *could* exist in our high schools.

RESEARCH AND/AS PEDAGOGY

Several recent studies use a deconstructive framework to examine pedagogies in antiracism and women's studies courses.[15] This essay examines high school students' conscious constructions of race; but the work began as research, becoming pedagogy only in the process, and the talk that constitutes data occurred outside the mainstream of classroom life.

Over six months, I spent time in a large urban high school in a working-class neighborhood. The student population is African American, a critical framework for engaging these young people's concerns. I am a white, female researcher/educator. Having entered a classroom to observe writing, I began to talk with students writing about issues of race. My colleague and her students were both curious and generous, so a series of individual and small-group interview sessions evolved. Student writings provided a springboard for investigating racial identities and politics.

Group sessions often began with a reading by the student writer. Texts included a dialogue, "Conversation (Two Brothers Talking): Revolution against a 'Nigger' mentality"; an I-Search paper on interracial relationships; proposed titles for a class newspaper; a guide for an interview with a board of education representative on African-American dropouts.

The situation differed from classroom teaching. As an unknown adult entering as researcher, I presented neither a familiar persona nor a predictable role. I had not yet earned trust; neither did I carry the authority of teacher as evaluator. My conversations with students lacked regularity and duration. On the other hand, students were free to participate or not. Perhaps risks were taken in the relative absence of classroom hierarchy. We had no curriculum to cover, and so we were free to pursue ideas and contradictions emerging from our discourse. Nonetheless, it was only later that I recast this research as pedagogy (during a conversation with Michelle Fine).

Lather suggests that as teachers we ask, "How can we position ourselves as less masters of truth and justice and more as creators of a space in which those directly involved can act and speak on their own behalf?"[16] This question resonates for us as researchers and writers as well. As I select and arrange these voices, I shave and shape their stories and my own. Nonetheless, my effort is to honor the integrity of their analyses. I am interested in these students' "creative process" as they construct race;[17] and in working toward "a pedagogy that would collapse the distinctions separating teaching, research, and art (and) might also have the power to guide transformation of the lived, social world."[18]

How do African-American teenagers enter into talk about race with each other and with a white researcher? Where does this talk go? Who talks, who listens, when is the talk comfortable or not, and why? These teenagers argue and laugh, agree and disagree with each other; they construct race differently in different contexts. Here are rich voices, partial voices, voices with much to teach as well as to learn. This essay will address "moments of rupture"[19] within public schooling by creating space and context for these voices, in concert with those of writers and scholars and with my own voice. Together we offer a mosaic of rich and suggestive possibilities for inquiry into race.

IDENTITY, DIFFERENCE, AND RACISM

These teenagers put forth no "party line" on race. We drew from diverse bodies of knowledge and experience to voice diverse theories. Later, sifting through data, I began to review our talk in terms of three broad discourses, overlapping strands often braided together, which I am calling "identity, difference, and racism."

Much of the early talk in group sessions revolved around issues of identity: How do you name and describe your racial or ethnic identity? How are African Americans unified and diverse as a racial/ethnic group? How do the contours of race shape the forging of personal identity?

Identity is often framed by difference, understood not as fact but as perspective. "What is not" defines the boundaries of "what is." Who is the same as I am, who is other, and according to what criteria? How are racial differences essential or constructed, and what do they mean in our lives?

In a world where difference connotes not equal, better/worse, having more/less power over resources, discourses of identity and difference are braided at many points with a discourse of racism, both interpersonal and structural, including talk about constructing race to deal with racism.

IDENTITY

Although identity development is not in the curriculum, teenagers continually formulate, act out, and revise identities.[20] Public education recognizes this developmental task by staffing schools with psychological personnel. But the ratio of students to trained staff makes meetings unlikely and discussion of real issues less likely still.[21] This may be compounded by racial difference between counselors and students.[22]

Interwoven with individual identity formation is the development of cultural identity, in our society closely linked with racial identity. "Strong and complex identification with one's culture and community are necessary not only for survival but also for a positive sense of self and for the making of an involved and active community member."[23] Schooling provides requisite information and affirmation for members of the dominant culture. Members of minority cultures, however, may find schooling irrelevant or even hostile to their development of cultural identities.[24]

Recently, attempts have been made to include images and information relevant to diverse populations. Some publishers have hired consultants to diversify textbook language and illustrations. In some districts "world history" courses that covered only the Western world now include the Third World. Some students study their cultures, using as resources both libraries and communities. However, identity development is a complex task, calling for more systematic, profound changes in schools.

Meanwhile, African-American teenagers are not simply recipients of education, but "create a culture of their own that is weighted with contradictions and ambivalence, promise and peril."[25] It is to this culture, enacted in a large, urban, African-American high school, that we now turn.

When I first asked, How do you name your racial identity, I assumed I was asking about language. Shavon, a usually reticent sophomore, spoke up right away: "I have Apache. My grandmother was white and her father was a Indian." Others named Cherokee as part of their racial identity. Hurston's ironic commentary, offered sixty years ago, provides counterpoint:

I am colored but I offer nothing in the way of extenuating circumstances except the fact that I am the only Negro in the United States whose grandfather on the mother's side was *not* an Indian chief.[26]

choose identity

From Shavon's perspective, is she offering an "extenuating circumstance" or highlighting the complexity of naming racial identity?

Vera, Aneesha, and Devon, seniors in a college-prep English class, launch readily into a discussion of racial identity. In describing their own identities, they explore language and the exercise of choice. Vera, an articulate and self-possessed young woman, begins:

> I name my racial identity because I have a lot of people in my family who are from Ghana in Africa and they are like my great-great-great grandmothers and grandfathers. I choose to call myself an African American because there's no such place as Black, there's no such place as Negro, and usually people tell their ethnicity from the place from which they came, like Italian-Americans.

Vera's analysis makes racial and ethnic identities synonymous and self-naming a matter of choice, and offers place as an identifying principle. Her logic is reminiscent of DuBois's ultimate displacement of (biological) race with race-as-civilization, a stance rife with contradictions.[27]

Devon implies other criteria for his self-naming: "I call myself Black because I really don't have any ties with Africa other than what I read, no family that I know of. They tell you that's where you came from but [pause] I just call myself Black." Vera analyses language as signifier, now distinguishing race and ethnicity, and problematizing the question:

> Calling yourself Black, I think that's automatically degrading because first of all that's what they want you to call yourself, and Black is an ugly color, and nobody is black, [Devon's] shirt is black, I'm brown, and there's no way to call a brown race, so I call myself an African. Even though the whole race is human, my ethnicity is African-American.

Gates, a literary theorist, draws on similar logic to contest the naming of racial identities in the interests of cordoning off the Other:

> Who has seen a black or red person, a white, yellow, or brown? These terms are arbitrary constructs, not reports of reality. But language is not only the medium of this often insidious tendency; it is its *sign*.[28]

Later, Vera revisits the nuances of color, irritated with a family friend who calls "white people beige and black people brown": "I said, What do you put down on an application, she said, Black, I said, Well then it doesn't matter what you say because they always gonna look at you and say, This is a Black woman." This contradiction in Vera's thinking—we exercise choice

seen as ethnicity

in naming our identities yet are passive recipients—may signify her struggle to construct an internal identity to meet the needs of the developing self and an external identity consistent with social realities.

Linda, a young woman identified by others as "the white girl" in school, states with some awkwardness: "Well, I think I'm Black, you know," and explains that her father is Black. In constructing racial identity models for counseling purposes, Helms uses this definition of *race:*

> a sub-group of people possessing a definite combination of physical characters, of genetic origin, the combination of which to varying degrees distinguishes the sub-group from other sub-groups of mankind [sic].[29]

Racial *identity* refers to "perceived" membership in a racial group,[31] but how does one distinguish the "definite" from the "perceived"? Linda, fair with hazel eyes and light silken hair, lacks the "combination of physical characters" that would label her "Black." Who is entitled to name Linda's race, and on what criteria? How does this naming shape her racial identity?

In spontaneous interactions, these teenagers offer diverse images of what African Americans are like. Young women critique the school rule barring students from wearing shorts: "Ain't no Black people wear shorts all the way up here!" (Damira's hand is on her hip. Everyone laughs; they begin a rendition of "Who Likes Short Shorts.") Terrance responds angrily to a debate over the class newspaper: "Why must our race always fight with each other? Why is our race so stubborn and narrow-minded?"

In discussion, underlying sociological questions emerge: What is the interplay between race and culture? How are stereotypes constituted? Now Terrance challenges his friend Kurt's characterization of Blacks as a group:

Kurt: I know a white kid named Mike with two Black parents, he act just as worse as us, I mean—

Terrance: Don't stereotype me, man.

Kurt: I ain't stereotyping you. I'm saying, he act like I do, he act just as bad as I do.

Anthropologists Abrahams and Szwed argue that stereotypical behaviors attributed to a group can often be mined for embedded cultural practices. In Black communities in the West Indies and the United States, "playing bad, playing black" is a public performance mode deemed admirable for males.[31] Even preschoolers learn to be community actors.[32] Kurt asserts this style of "acting bad" as Black character. His exchange with Terrance offers a glimpse of how group identity might be negotiated in a structured context.

For some, explicit learning about their cultural histories provides crucial foundations for identity development. No one mentions doing this learning in school. Ed reiterates a claim I heard often about rap:

[These groups] talk in their rap music about be yourself, they have a lot of words about your African-American heritage. Like about slavery times and what it was like. And about Egypt, and the pyramids. I love Black history. I've got tons of books on Black history at home. They say you have to know where you come from to know who you are.

Vera suggests that "cultural values" should be taught to young African Americans "cause half these people don't know who they are. . . . We need to redefine our values within our community." Devon argues that people should define their own values independent of race and community. Playwright August Wilson contends that we are never independent of race and culture: "You never transcend who you are. Black is not limiting. There's no idea in the world that is not contained by black life."[33] How are our identities shaped by context, and how are we free to shape both self and context? These teenagers are astute observers of tensions between individual and social context within the African American community. Yvonne voices the pressure she has felt since attending an all-Black school:

I had more trouble here getting along with people because it's like when you're in a mixed school nobody judge you for the way you look or what you wore, like here you gotta look a certain way just for people to like, to fit in. . . . See basically I keep to myself and everybody be like, she thinks she's too cute to be with anybody else.

Others nod. Rhomain, an incisive social critic, offers insight into the culturally condoned materialism that may feed a loss of self:

Black people grab for things that make them proud, so they'll grab for something material and place a great deal of emphasis and self-esteem on that, but if that material's taken away or lost it's like you've lost your insides.

Vinnie suggests the possibility of community as resource for individuality:

I think [people] are scared or hindered to be themselves for some reason, especially Black people, we have such a rich heritage and background that there should be no reason for all of us to be the same, we're so diverse.

Interestingly, these young men and women *do* speak in diverse voices, perhaps attesting to the shared context of an all-Black school where African-American teenagers may feel relative freedom to experiment with diverse selves, since they are not explicitly confronting the dominant culture of white

[handwritten: integrated schools => become more synchronized]

teens. In more racially integrated contexts, they might well react by synchro-
nizing voices and electing group styles, behaviors, and values in opposition
to those of the white mainstream.[34]

These young people talk about diversity within the African American
community in terms of the historical and current implications of skin color as
a signifier of power, particularly in the context of gender relations. The terms
are continually renegotiated. Kurt, a dark-skinned tenth-grade male, struggles with his own partial voices:

> Light-skinned is, I mean from the giddayup, it look good, I mean ain't noth-
> ing wrong with a dark-skinned sister, but light skin from the giddayup it
> looks good, I mean some people like lighter colors, some people like dark
> colors, I mean I don't know.

Rhomaine eschews personal aesthetic, offering a political framework:

> The way they depict Black people in sculptures and cartoons and movies—a
> lot of times it's been used to turn us against each other, because light-
> skinned Blacks never saw themselves in that negative imagery. Even though
> they were accepted in the Black community a lot of times, they saw them-
> selves more in a different perspective.

Tamika, the only woman in one group session and soft-spoken, claims
not to care about males' skin color. Kurt agrees emphatically, but trails off:
"I say it don't matter how they colored . . . if she light-skinned she light-
skinned, if she dark-skinned she dark-skinned, if she pitch-black, then
[pause] it depends." Finally, he describes what happens at the Easter parade:

> . . . So when the girls stepped to us, the majority of guys that got the girls
> were like Tamika's complexion [light-skinned] . . . so I'm saying, light-
> skinned must be, they must have some kinda, they must be more radiant or
> have some special beauty or something, I mean it looks good [pause] but I
> mean so does black or brown and all that.

Kurt voices multiple selves, exploring his access to different discourses on
the meaning of skin color. Given a context to continue his inquiry, he might
arrive at a stance; he might also position conflicting perceptions of skin color
in the larger framework of societal power relations.

DIFFERENCE

While *diversity* connotes variety, *difference* may imply dichotomy, even
disagreement. Who defines difference, on what criteria, and how are we—
grouped and separated by the boundaries of difference—affected?

[handwritten: Skin color factor]

Linda explains that her mother assured her she wasn't different: She could be anyone she wanted to be. She feels "the same" in white and Black communities. Although her brother is darker than she and in a mostly white school, "he don't feel different, he just feels mixed in like me." Difference then is a question of individual choice. She smiles shyly as she describes her own tastes in music and clothing as different from others' at school; para-doxically, she reiterates, "I'm not different, just blended in."

After our (one-to-one) interview, which is polite and awkward, I become aware that, like others at school, I have positioned Linda as white and so "same," which means I have positioned others as different, African Amer-ican, Other. I am faced with the heavy-handedness of my own narration. "By defining the other's difference, one is forced to take into account, or to ignore at one's peril, the shadow cast by the self."[35] Linda, whose birth mother is white and birth father and foster family, Black, perceives "blend" where I perceive distinction. When we name difference, distinguishing "not us" from "us," we frame identity. Difference (and so identity) is less a matter of fact than "a function of a specific interlocutionary situation . . . matters of strategy."[36]

Music may be the arena where these teenagers feel most invited to ex-plore racial identity and difference, to find themselves reflected in sound and imagery, to hear the sounds and images of others. Devon described music as a bridge between self and other, albeit not a bridge crossed by all:

> I know a lot of white kids who love rap, they grew up listening to rap cause they grew up around Black people, so that's what seems to be closing the gap. A lot of my [Black] friends tell me that what I listen to is noise, right, devil-worshipping crap, that's a quote, but . . . I chose to understand this thing, to read [white] lyrics, and therefore I have learned to like their music.

Interracial relationships remain a volatile topic among these young peo-ple, perhaps because of the intersection of race and gender issues shaped by societal power differentials. Several express concern that involvement with a white might alienate them from Blacks at school. Yvonne and Tamika de-scribe relationships that reframe difference. Yvonne begins with setting:

> The white people over there do not act white, they're more like Black peo-ple cause they live around Black people all their life, so it really wasn't no different. Like if [her boyfriend] was to come here, he would fit in with the Black people more than he'd fit with the white people.

Tamika talks about a friend's white boyfriend who "just fit in so well with everybody." Nevertheless, when I ask whether she ever forgets he is white,

Tamika and Yvonne respond, "You can't forget somebody's white!" Racial identity and difference are neither essential nor entirely fluid.

Damira too suggests that we construct difference in context. During a discussion of why only two of twenty-four students voted for *Black Underground* or *Black Times* as newspaper titles, she comments to me:

> You don't hear no white or Caucasian person saying "White Newspaper" or "White Something," so we know our color, I don't have to express it to everybody else, when they see me they'll know what color I am. Cause you don't see yourself as white such-and-such, . . . I'm proud of my color . . . but I don't want to put *Black Underground* . . . I (am) trying to broaden the issues.

Although African Americans, unlike most European Americans, are often not at liberty to forget race,[27] Damira may feel freer here than in a racially mixed environment to "broaden the issues." In 1903, W. E. B. DuBois struggled with the "double-consciousness" embedded in Damira's talk: "One feels ever his twoness—an American, a Negro; two souls, two thoughts, two unreconciled strivings; two warring ideals in one dark body."[38]

Hurston writes, "I feel most colored when I am thrown against a sharp white background."[39] Vinnie muses on his racially mixed elementary school: "I never put that much thought to race, because I wasn't just surrounded by all Black people and then, wham, white." In this light, identity and difference are created not by color alone but also by fit and contrast. Backdrop describes foreground.

Even an individual in a single encounter may voice contradictory perceptions of identity and difference. Kurt claims that race "makes no difference, I mean skin, we been through that . . . skin color is not what's happening." Later, he voices another perspective:

Kurt: I don't know, I never been white before.
JC: I never been Black before.
Kurt: I don't know how you feel and you don't know how I feel.

While most of these teenagers reject skin pigment as the barometer of identity and difference,[40] they grapple with complexities they are unable to resolve. During a discussion of historical criteria I ask, "But in *our* minds what would make somebody Black or white?" Kurt answers,

> In their mind, their mouth, their heart. You have to know 'em, you can't just walk up and say, Tamika, she look like she white, cause I mean Tamika can act like *too* Black, she could be Black and she just came out a real fair baby.

Given the opportunity, these teenagers challenge each other, using experience honed by humor to contest and build knowledge. Tamika claims she is Black because of "my attitude and how I think on things." Ed argues that Black people may "act white" in a white environment. Kurt agrees: You know how Valley girls talk, I know girls personally who went to nothing but white school all their life, they talk like, 'I'm like this and like that.' '' When Rhomaine contends that difference goes deeper, Kurt reflects on Mike, white child of Black parents:

> I mean he was accepted into the neighborhood cause of him, period, we don't kick that racial crap down the way, that's not right. He just came in and we treated him like, Yo you suck, and he's like, Yo you suck, we gonna roll it up. I mean he don't talk like, "I was going down the street." He like blended in. He still white and all, we know that, he just acts Black, like a Black person acts, or like I am and I'm Black.

Asked about a Black person who acts differently, Kurt reverts to color-based analysis: "Black is considered your skin color, and white is going by skin color, so you can be Black and born, raised and died in a white community and still be Black." While commitment to one idea may support a "right answer," contradictory ideas invite analysis, a higher order thinking skill necessary for moral development.[41]

Ogbu characterizes African-American teenagers as developing oppositional identities and norms in reaction to dominant white society.[42] While the teenagers I spoke with also note instances of opposition, many employ a strategy that reverses Ogbu's principle, as they struggle to thwart others' expectations of difference based on race. Vera (re)constructs an image of herself as white men's Other:

> When I was in the hospital, I had tonsillitis and my doctors used to come in there every day . . . and ask me what I'd be majoring in and stuff like that, and when they found out I had over a thousand on my SATs they acted a little different towards me. It was deep, because they expected me to say something like seven or eight hundred, and that's a stereotype right there that comes from, what can I say, a lack of exposure.

Are these professionals simply exercising the white privilege of "lack of exposure," or are they willing ignorance? "The resistance to finding out that the Other is the same springs out of the reluctance to admit that the same is Other."[43]

A young man reflects on "(d)ifference disliked as identity affirmed."[44]

> I'm driving home and a bunch of drunk white guys are yelling, "bunch of fucking niggers!" If it's a poorly dressed guy, I figure they're just saying it

because I'm dressed better. Me and my friends, with Puerto Ricans, we be saying, You going to Taco Bell or what? So I can relate to those white kids.

Through examination of his own assumptions of differences, he identifies momentarily with the white teens whose racism circumscribes his world. Is it possible to imagine a society where difference is not tantamount to oppression or at best tolerance, but offers the resource of diversity?

RACISM

The specific features of Blackness as cultural imagery are, almost by definition, those qualities which the dominant society has attempted to deny in itself, and it is the difference between Blackness and whiteness that defines, in many aspects, American cultural self-understanding.[45]

Field note, sixth-period English class:
The class is discussing medieval history as background to *Merchant of Venice*. The teacher has handed out a sheet of relevant terms, and someone asks for a description of the "Black Plague." A young woman calls out, "Why didn't they call it the 'White Plague.' "

In our society, where white skin buys privilege, difference is an entry to unequal positionings. It is difficult to imagine "separate but equal" as anything but a racist sham: "I understand your essential difference from me, and will make you live up to it with an imposed program of separate development."[46] We cannot explore identity and difference without bloodletting from the veins of racism coursing throughout.

Many of these teenagers struggle to construct dynamic identities grounded in awareness but not necessarily in reaction to white society,[47] grounded in a continuum of choices rather than in a single choice such as "racelessness."[49] Racism shapes these young people's experiences of the world. However, they are not passive but engaged in constructing racial identities *in action,* a self or selves that deal creatively with the challenges of being an African American in a racist society.

Although several tell of blatant, physically manifested instances of racism, most talk revolves around subtler, pervasive forms. Rhomaine, a mediocre student who shares impressive cultural knowledge, analyzes the structural racism in seemingly personal issues:

It's very deep-seated, if something happens in history you have to go back to it and find out. Like Vinnie said, hundreds of Black women were used by white men, so white men have a very deep-seated fear that erupts if they ever see a Black man with a white woman . . . because they feel that the Black men would do the same thing that they did. . . . [Also] our standards of beauty in this country are white . . . we've been under that so long, upset with being that which we see, that a lot of people hate themselves, they'll go out looking for an interracial thing or to have children, mix with other races. So it's a lot more into the psyche and into the heart that people think it is, it's not just simple.

Damira and Kathy also probe structural racism, complicated by issues of gender. An all-female group debates Black women's opportunities in the working world. Damira's metaphor for satisfying quotas provides ironic commentary on the racism and sexism of this ostensible "equalizer":

[When an employer hires a black woman] they killed two minorities, you a woman, there they go, they killed that minority, and you Black, they killed another one. Then they don't got nobody on their shoulders, Oh you don't hire women, you don't hire Black people. They killed it right there, the two minorities.

Kathy describes difficulties faced by Black women in a racist society.[49]

In a lot of Black home situations you have mostly the mother . . . and then the mother have a older girl and then she have younger children, and so [the girl's] childhood is usually taken up by the children. . . . And when your parent isn't home and you gotta make decisions for yourself and you make the wrong decision, and then, you know, you making decisions, you feel, I'm grown cause I do everything my mom should be doing anyway.

Kathy's analysis is laced with frustration. She argues that after pregnancy a young woman should not stay home on welfare but "go ahead . . . strive to do more for yourself." Kathy's own "aspirations" provide a basis for her critique of societally imposed constraints and of the "cultural practices" of peers.[50]

Much of the discourse on racism revolves around interpersonal tensions sometimes read as manifestations of structural racism. A young woman captures these tensions compellingly:

Mostly it's older people. . . . Well maybe the young whites just don't talk about you, maybe they got it in their minds, Nigger nigger nigger. What they're saying is they're your friend, but they thinking, Nigger nigger nigger.

In racially mixed contexts, these youngsters strive to imagine identity, difference, and racism as experienced by their European American counterparts. Vera recalls the complexities of racial dynamics at a predominantly white summer program:

> A lot of my white girlfriends used to hang out in my room cause they're like, Vera's the life of the party, cause they never saw anybody act fun yet when they themselves would be around them, and you know it was just fun for me to be around them. . . . They couldn't say certain things around me because they didn't want to offend me . . . and white people always have that problem, I sympathize with them about that too because they're always trying to, they watch what they say so carefully because they're afraid that it may be sort of prejudiced.

Aneesha jumps in, "They're like, 'I'm not prejudiced, no I'm not!' Everybody in this world has some ounce of prejudice." Vera, Aneesha, and Devon have all been treated as if "you're different from all the others." Devon explains, "When [whites] try to hide the fact that you are Black, and I mean *you know* that you are, they're gonna say stuff that's gonna supposedly offend your average Black person." In such mixed contexts, these teenagers may draw their racial identities in bolder strokes.

The racism described by these young African Americans is full of subtle contradictions, requiring acute attentiveness. While Vera enjoys her role in the (white) group, she examines carefully the racial tension felt and perhaps faced by her young white friends. Recalling her roommate, Vera muses, "She was kind of uptight, you could tell, but I sorta let her know, you could loosen up some, I'm not gonna hurt you or anything. They so afraid of you in a way," then, "But you know, we have to give them a reason to feel that way too." White fear, Vera's power to defuse it, and her notion that Blacks may be implicated in this fear seem symptomatic of the labyrinthian nature of relationships in the 1990s.

Black parents have long taken into account the "functional value of racial socialization" based on perceived social realities.[51] African American adolescents may critique their parents' "powerlessness,"[52] yet as they forge separate identities they too act in light of cultural realities. In "How It Feels to Be Colored Me," Hurston deconstructs the title: " 'Compared to what? As of when? Who is asking? In what context? For what purpose? With what interests and presuppositions.' "[53] Similarly, these teenagers construct identities in the plural, given the plural realities of daily life in school and community, with peers, authorities, and families.

In Fordham's study, Black teenagers confront a mismatch between a school culture that rewards competition and individual achievement and a community culture that values cooperation and group advancement. Her analysis foregrounds the invention of "racelessness" as a means of obviating

the need for racial identity as a Black American to her identity as an American, hoping that a raceless persona will mitigate the harsh treatment and severe limitations in the opportunity structure that are likely to confront her as
a Black American.[54]

The African Americans I spoke with—who attend a school demograph-
ically similar to Fordham's and some of whom are successful by conventional
measures—offer a range of strategies for constructing race to cope with racism. While they too struggle with "severe limitations in the opportunity
structure," their constructions of race are compellingly complex, including,
but not limited to, strategic use of the appearance of "racelessness." Aneesha's narrative, in which her phone manner clearly fooled a prospective employer into assuming she was white, evokes appreciative, pained laughter.
Her tone is laced with irony:

> When I got there [the employer] looked at me like, who is this. I said, Hello,
> my name is Aneesha Haskins, I'm here for the job interview. She said, Are
> you the young lady I spoke to yesterday? I said, Yes I am. She said, You are
> very well spoken. [Group laughter] I said, I know! [More group laughter]

Aneesha explains that sometimes life demands that "you change your roles"
but this does not mean "forgetting who you are." She refuses to play victim,
to give up self-consciousness and choice, as a raceless persona would require;
neither is she willing to forego a job opportunity.

Like students and professionals whom Fordham quotes at length, Vera
has been called "white" by members of the low-income Black community
where she grew up. She describes feeling "stuck in the middle" between
Black English vernacular, used with friends, and "a certain way that you talk
when you're talking to somebody of authority." Vera articulates awareness of
both the institutionalized racism in the "design of ghettos" and the internalized racism described by Woodson, whom she quotes: "If there's not a back
door [African Americans] will make one, because they know their place."
Rather than submerging her developing identity, Vera seeks to expand what it
means to be an African American; her struggle highlights the conflict and
creativity required to construct race in a racist society.

The civil rights movement may represent to these youngsters a naive attempt to (re)construct race relations through denial of difference. Vera, Aneesha, and Devon agree that a color-blind society is "a baseless dream." They
shake their heads at "Martin Luther King—us all grabbing hands and singing
songs—after they sing [whites and Blacks] will wind up fighting anyway, you
know." I ask what the dream is now, and Devon shrugs: "You adjust." He
describes dinner with a white friend, a mayor's son:

Devon: It was like, [the family] were waiting for me to like, you know, they
were like testing me, I was sitting there eating and they're—

Aneesha: Waiting for you to evict [spit out] something.
Devon: Yeah. They're waiting for you to make a mistake or something. But I just look at them, I act normal, I just act like myself and so they were impressed by that . . . I mean, try to speak clearly and all so they would understand, then I'd come home to my mom and speak a little more loosely.

Devon's narration positions him as young educator of a white family, requiring on-the-spot analysis of identity, difference, and racism. Later, he is educated by the racism of a white schoolmate who calls him "oreo": "I said I would take charge now, nobody would lead me around like that."

Aneesha urges Vera to tell "the watermelon story," in which she is the educator of white peers, a role about which she expresses ambivalence:

It was me and my two Black friends, we were in front, and the special fruit for the day was watermelon. And the one white girl behind me—you could tell the whole group got quiet when she came—tapped me on my shoulder and asked me how the watermelon tastes. I said, How would I know, I'm in line just like you are, and I said it nice and calm and everything. I said, I don't even eat watermelon, why didn't you ask one of your friends in back of you. . . . And then I just went on about my business. I think she probably learned something from that, because I don't eat watermelon, and if I would eat watermelon I wouldn't eat it there.

Vera's narrative takes us back to Hurston's deconstructive questions: Who wants to know, and for what purpose? Even in the retelling, she says she doesn't *eat* watermelon, not that she doesn't *like* it. The complexities of the decision not to eat watermelon expose the density of our cultural constructs. Vera's "nice and calm" tone, emerging through metaphorically gritted teeth, contrasts with Rhomaine's explicit language of anger:

The Legions of Fury, that's what I call all 40 million of Black people in this country, the hate had built up so much and the resentment because of what happened to us . . . I don't think white people understand the pressure or the anger or the right to be angry. So that's why I say, Legions of Fury, we have to create now.

Later, Rhomaine's suddenly wistful tone reveals another self: "I would love, I was telling Vinnie this, I wouldn't want my color to make a difference in anything I did [pause] but my color is how I [am] perceived." Rhomaine is not Fordham's "raceless" student: Graduation is his sole symbol of academic success, and he sees himself headed for an uncertain future. He more nearly fits Helms's developmental category "emersion," in his positive, political identification with Black/African culture.[55] But his sudden voicing of a wish to act in a color-neutral setting evokes the possibility of a world where color dimensions but need not dominate who we are.

Rhomaine's friend Vinnie struggles to reconcile his certainty that "the world will never be equal" with his hope for "more harmony in the future." In a final exchange:

JC: How do you feel about, I'm a white researcher asking this stuff?
Vinnie: I didn't look at you as someone different, I mean, I'm pretty open-minded, unless you want to bring out the racial thing . . .
JC: I guess I am.
Vinnie: But I'm saying it's good for all people to talk about race because I think knowledge is the only way that we can get along . . . if we just got to know people as people . . . because *in the dark world (we're) the same, we all die, we're all born.* [my emphasis]

Through engaging in talk and constructing knowledge, can we move *in this world* toward equity in diversity, harmony in difference?

RACE AND SCHOOLS

In these conversations, African American teenagers share experiences, theories, and questions about the meanings of race/ethnicity, as they live, learn, and construct what is and what could be. Such talk suggests starting points for education that affirms and explores cultural diversity. As we reconsider multicultural education, both students' roles in reforming schooling and our understandings of such categories as race/ethnicity must be interrogated. Not only are students authorities on their own experiences, but they also bring critical insight to the complexities of race/ethnicity. Further, student's problematizing of the reified category of race suggests that schools go beyond transmitting knowledge about cultural groups to study race, gender, and class as dynamic, interacting social constructs.

It is beyond the scope of this essay to talk globally about multicultural curriculum building. Instead, I offer a series of practice-based images emerging from the conversations opened in these pages. Let us imagine such talks as a springboard for structured, school-based planning teams of staff, parents, students, and community members, for the purpose of generating a multicultural curriculum. Let us further suppose the experientially based discourses of identity, difference, and racism to be proposed by such a team as thematic cores for interdisciplinary courses of study. What might a series of related thematics look like?

The study of racial/ethnic *identity* could generate student inquiry into their own racial and cultural identities, through critical readings of recorded versions of history as well as through "readings" of their homes and communities. The disciplines of psychology and sociology raise critical questions: How is the identity development of the individual shaped by his or her racial/ethnic group identity, and how do individuals shape group identity? Literature that explores these themes, as well as expressive modes that engender group identity, such as music, cuisine, and folklore, could be interrogated. Students could use knowledge of groups' identities to generate and analyze "cultural and epistemological statements."[56]

An investigation of *difference* in a global context may find intellectual roots in ethnology, the study of similarities and differences among cultures. An organizing question might guide inquiry: How do differences reflect essential qualities and/or social constructions? Students could use their own experiences and questions to do critical readings of texts often judged "too difficult," texts by anthropologists, educators, literary theorists, and scientists that propose diverse and often contradictory theories of difference. Lived experiences also provide contexts for inquiry, such as observations and interviews with members of one's own and other's groups. An examination of discourses used by diverse cultural groups focuses the study of language on difference, interrupting the unproblematized teaching of "standard English."[57]

An interdisciplinary study of *racism* might begin with students using their lives and the media to generate questions about the history and psychology of racism, and about how to challenge racism in our society and our lives. An organizing question might seek models for constructing identity and difference without recourse to racism. Students could conduct research in libraries, theaters, the mass media, and communities, and could share findings and take actions in and beyond their schools.

The teenagers whose words fill these pages are engaged with issues of race and culture, gender and social class, as they strive to make meaning in their lives. By dealing with these issues only tangentially, or as if transmitting a "body of knowledge," schools consign their curricula to a marginal position in many young people's lives. The images of multicultural practice offered here represent one set of possibilities for how schools might facilitate students' struggles with these issues. Such images need to be developed by school-based teams of instructional leaders, teachers, nonteaching staff, and parents engaged—with students—in constructing and implementing a multicultural curriculum.

However, the diverse and even conflicting agendas that often divide those whose voices are crucial to this project may pose daunting obstacles to such conversations. Indeed, these constituencies may not *want* to communicate with one another. The essay concludes with suggestions of structural supports to facilitate open lines of communication.

Because of the lack of training in multicultural education, administrators' and teachers' years of experience do not necessarily translate into expertise with these issues. On a district-wide level, instructional leadership might address cultural concerns by investigating current thinking on a key issue. Principals in an urban district are studying Afrocentric education; such a group might offer new perspectives on district guidelines and school-based multicultural programs.

Educational change movements are emphasizing teacher empowerment through school-based reforms. A restructuring initiative aimed at comprehensive high schools includes a seminar where teachers explore the implications of cultural diversity for their schools and classrooms. As teachers reflect on practice, they generate questions and learn to facilitate student inquiry. As "mediators of culture,"[58] teachers also need contexts to explore these issues collaboratively, within and across disciplines, in such units as "houses" or "charter schools." They need to reexamine not only processes of teaching and learning, but also their own racial and cultural identities and perhaps privilege,[59] and their relationships with colleagues and students of similar and different backgrounds.[60]

Nonteaching staff, parents, and other community adults also provide crucial resources, as "collaborators, sources of critical information, innovators [and] critics."[61] These adults must be offered legitimated positions of influence and opportunities to investigate educational agendas.

Constructing racial/cultural identities in a racist, culture-biased society is a demanding task, one in which democratic schooling must play a key role, particularly if we recognize that equality of treatment does not guarantee equality of opportunity. Education that invites students to construct cultural knowledge should affirm all of our lived experiences, and engage students in designing their own educations through conscious study and construction of the world we live in.

WILLIAM G. TIERNEY

Chapter Fifteen

The College Experience of Native Americans: A Critical Analysis

---

The literature on the Native American[1] experience in postsecondary institutions is generally relegated to footnotes in books about other minorities in the United States.[2] Further, what little information exists pertains to statistical summaries about where Indian students go to college, their rates of participation, leave-taking, and the like. In many respects, Native Americans are invisible in academe; researchers neither study them nor do institutions devise specific strategies to encourage Indian students to attend, to participate, and to graduate.

Yet "invisibility" is a social construct. Simply stated, those students who are Native American are not invisible to themselves, to their parents, to their tribes. Although national surveys may provide faulty data that reduces an Indian student to an asterisk, the Indian student does not perceive his or her experience in that manner.

How do Indian students perceive academe? What are the challenges that await Indian students when they enter college? How we interpret those experiences depends upon the theoretical frameworks from which we operate. Accordingly, in this chapter I undertake two tasks. First, I make the invisible visible. Through the case history of one Indian student we hear of some of the struggles he has encountered as a student at a mainstream community college. Second, I offer two contrasting frameworks—a model of social integration and a critical perspective—for interpreting the student's experience. I argue that Indian students are invisible because of assimilationist attitudes based on the widely utilized social integration model. I conclude with the implications for this interpretation, and I raise issues for further research.

A VOICE

On a cold, clear February morning Delbert Thunderwolf (a pseudonym) and I sat down with one another for the third time in eighteen months. He is a thirty-one-year-old community college student who is an American Indian from the upper Midwest. He is majoring in business. Delbert is a tall man, over six feet, and has the frame of a runner. He grew up "in my mother's house and in some other relatives' families," throughout his adolescence. Although he was born on the reservation, he moved to a city near the reservation until he left the area for college. He attended a boarding school for high school; when he finished school he worked for about six months and then chose to go to college.

Delbert is one of the individuals I interviewed for a two-year research project concerning the recruitment and retention of Native American students to two- and four-year colleges and universities. By the end of the project I had interviewed over two hundred individuals—other Indian students such as Delbert, as well as faculty, staff, and administrators at eleven institutions.

The first time I spoke with Delbert he had recently arrived at the public community college, and he discussed his reasons for going to college. He said:

> I attended Southwestern Indian Polytechnic Institute for two semesters, but I drank myself out of there. I was drunk for a long time. I sobered up four years ago, and in that time I had a chance to reevaluate my educational needs. I worked as assistant manager in a clothing and feed store here in town. I started seeing a bunch of people around me with college educations and they were going for what they wanted. And me, I couldn't do that on $5.50 an hour. I hurt myself physically on the job twice, and I said, "This is dumb." At first I was afraid to come back to college. I was afraid I wouldn't make it. It took a lot to do it, and I'm glad I did. I'm still afraid, though.

When I met with Delbert the second time, he spoke about the other Indian students at the public community college.

> Some students come here and it's hard for them to get adjusted. A lot of them, they have fifth, sixth, sometimes third grade, reading levels because the reservation schools aren't any good. Some of these reservations here are

so big that it's hard to change that philosophy that you've got to be by your mom and dad in order to survive. They come off the res. and they don't have the survival instinct for the big city.

I think white people think education is good, but Indian people often have a different view. I know what you're going to say—that education provides jobs and skills. It's true. That's why I'm here. But a lot of these kids, their parents, they see education as something that draws students away from who they are.

And then there's the obstacles. There's no money. You go from one financial aid office and get told to go somewhere and then somewhere else. You give up. You can't figure out the papers and you wind up thinking you're dumb. So you leave. I've seen a lot of them leave. . . . They go home. I try to explain to them, "What are you going to do? What are you gaining for yourself inside?" There's never no answers. They just go home.

Delbert expects to graduate soon. During our final interview he reflected on college and expanded on his thoughts about education.

Drugs and alcohol are a terrible problem. I've seen students leave like I did. They sort of drink themselves out of the place. But sometimes I think that's not the problem. I think somewhere you have to give Indian people a different view of why they are here, what education is, so they can help keep the focus on why they want to stay in school.

A lot of teachers might know a lot about business or accounting, but they don't know anything about Indians or what it's like to be away from home. One problem for students is that they don't find people to help. . . . No one tells Indian students to go after their dream.

I would like to take all of my instructors and lead them through my life. Show them what it's like to come off the reservation. They would see how Indian people hold onto each other real fast in order to hold the old ways together. They'd see how much trouble it is to make the decision to leave home and come to school, how Indian people love staying around and being on the reservation, at home. How it's really a struggle to come here. I would love to have my instructors see that. Just to have them see the bonding that takes place. They'd see us right.

I would like to tell them that education shouldn't try and make me into something I'm not. That's what I learned when I wasn't here. Who I am. And when I learned that, then I could come back here. I sort of walked away for a while and then came back. It's one of the best gifts I've ever had. But a lot of us just walk away.

CONTEXTUALIZING INDIAN VOICES

How are we to interpret the comments of Delbert Thunderwolf? The purpose in listening to him is surely not to call upon one student's voice to highlight how all American Indian students perceive higher education, as if Delbert were a symbolic "Everyman." Although their population is undeniably smaller than other cadres of postsecondary students, such as Anglos and African Americans (see table 15.1), in some respects the Native American student population is more diverse than any other student group.

In addition to traditionally conceived variables pertaining to college students, such as male/female, urban/rural, parents who attended college and those who did not, and the like, we also need to think of Indian students according to additional variables, such as where they grew up—on a reservation or off—what role tribal language played in their lives, and how traditional or nontraditional they are according to Indian mores.

According to more common notions of college going, for example, Delbert Thunderwolf might be described as an adult male whose parents did not attend college and who grew up in a city. Yet because he is a Native American, some would say it is also pertinent to find out how much time he spent on a reservation (very little), whether he speaks a tribal language (he does not), and if he is "traditional" in the sense that he partakes of American Indian ceremonies and rituals (he does to a certain extent).

Consequently, Delbert's voice should be interpreted as nothing more than what it is—one voice among many. Indeed, he has several voices of his own, such as the autobiographical voice and that of someone caught between

TABLE 15.1
Racial and Ethnic Enrollment Data from Institutions of Higher Education, 1968–1984

Year	Total (in thousands)	Percentage						
		White	Minority	Black	Hispanic	Asian	American Indian	Alien
1968	4,820	90.7	9.3	6.0	Other	3.5		—
1970	4,966	89.4	10.6	6.9	Other	3.7		—
1972	5,531	87.7	12.3	8.3	Other	4.0		—
1974	5,639	86.5	13.5	9.0	Other	4.5		—
1976	10,986	82.6	15.4	9.4	3.5	1.8	.7	2.0
1978	11,231	81.9	15.9	9.4	3.7	2.1	.7	2.2
1980	12,087	81.4	16.1	9.2	3.9	2.4	.7	2.5
1982	12,388	80.7	16.6	8.9	4.2	2.8	.7	2.7
1984	12,162	80.3	17.0	8.8	4.3	3.1	.7	2.7

Source: 1968–1974 U.S. Department of Education, "Racial and Ethnic Enrollment Data from Institutions of Higher Education," biennial, as reported in *Statistical Abstract of the United States 1986,* 106th edition, U.S. Department of Commerce, Bureau of Census, table 259, page 153.
1976–1984: U.S. Department of Education, National Center for Education Statistics, "Fall Enrollment in Colleges and Universities" surveys, as reported in *Digest of Education Statistics 1986–87* and *Digest of Education Statistics 1980.*

two worlds. Yet his comments also are echoed by other students involved in this study who spoke of similar dilemmas when they attended college.[3] Delbert's voice, then, is both unique and representative; his perceptions and reactions to the world are unique to himself, yet they also are situated within a tribal culture that is shared with other American Indians.

My objective here is to utilize Delbert's comments to highlight the differences between two theoretical perspectives on minority college-going and participation, which in turn influences the actions and policies we take in academe pertaining to minority students. Prior to discussing these perspectives, however, it will be helpful to contextualize his voice. What do we know about Native American participation in academe? Where do Indian students go to college, and what happens to them when they enter?

College-Going Patterns

As noted at the outset of this chapter, there is a notable lack of research and information about Native American participation in higher education. We do know that the history of American Indian participation in general, and in higher education in particular, has revolved around notions of assimilation and cultural genocide. Since 1617, when King James sought to establish a "college for the Children of the Infidels," Euro-Americans have persistently sought to remake Native Americans in the image of the white man—to "civilize" and assimilate the "savages." Dartmouth College, William and Mary, and Princeton University, among others, began as institutions with explicit mission statements to educate Indian people and "civilize" them. Yet native peoples have steadfastly struggled to preserve their cultural integrity. The college campus, then, has historically been a stage for this cross-cultural drama.[4] And again, because American Indians are a small percentage in the overall framework of college participation, few studies or books have documented the educational struggles native peoples have faced, or the manner in which they have met these challenges.

Even surveys that include Native Americans as part of their studies note the concerns the researchers have in utilizing data on Native Americans. Astin, for example, commented in *Minorities in American Higher Education* that the size of the sample of Native Americans "was often so small as to raise serious questions about the reliability of the results."[5] Judith Fries recently completed a report specifically about Native Americans in higher education for the Center for Education Statistics. She, too, noted, "Most sample surveys are either too small to produce reliable estimates for American Indians, or Indians are grouped into an 'other' category."[6]

What we do know is that the composite population of Native Americans is economically poorer, experiences more unemployment, and is less formally well-educated than the national average.[7] A greater percentage of the population live in rural areas than the rest of the country, where access to postsecondary institutions is more difficult.[8] By all accounts the Native American population of the United States is becoming increasingly youthful. Current estimates place the total population of Native Americans as slightly less than two million. Between 1970 and 1980, the number of Indians between the ages of eighteen and twenty-four increased from 96,000 to 234,000. The average age of the population is sixteen.[9]

Several different surveys suggest that less than 60 percent of those students who are ninth graders will eventually graduate from high school.[10] Eighty-five percent of those students who enter a postsecondary institution will not receive a four-year degree (see table 15.2). Only one-third of those who graduate from high school will go on to college. Well over half of the college-going population will attend a two-year institution, compared to a third of the Anglo college-going cohort.[11]

Native Americans are among the smallest of student populations on four-year campuses; as of 1986 only seven four-year institutions had over five hundred American Indians in attendance. Those institutions that enroll a predominantly Native American population are essentially tribally controlled colleges—most of which are located on Indian reservations. In sum, if one hundred students enter the ninth grade, sixty of them will graduate from high school and about twenty will enter academe. Of those twenty students, about three will receive a four-year degree.

The challenge now turns to how we might interpret this data. How might we locate Delbert Thunderwolf's comments and perceptions of academe, given the generalized context of Native Americans in postsecondary education? To answer these questions I turn to two theoretical formulations that afford competing interpretations of Delbert's comments.

TABLE 15.2

Percentage Enrollment of Racial/Ethnic Groups by Type of Institution, 1986–1987

Institution	Black	American Indian	Asian American	Hispanic	White	Nonresident Alien
2-Year Public	40.6	54.3	44.7	56.3	36.9	23.4
2-Year Private	3.7	3.9	0.8	2.3	2.4	1.8
4-Year Public	39.2	34.3	41.4	31.2	42.3	42.9
4-Year Private	16.5	7.5	13.1	10.2	18.4	31.9
TOTAL	100.0	100.0	100.0	100.0	100.0	100.0

*Source:*Unpublished data: National Center for Education Statistics, Integrated Postsecondary Education Data Systems (1986–87).

TWO PERSPECTIVES OF COLLEGE GOING AND LEAVING

Social Integration

The manner in which researchers have conceptualized minority participation in education is in keeping with much of the current research on student
development and attrition.[12] An abundance of Durkheimian "social facts"
have been discovered that have led to different hypotheses. Researchers, for
example, believe that parental education, individual motivation, age of student, and socioeconomic status (SES) are important factors in determining
college participation and retention.[13] The implications of such research, obviously, are that if a student's parents went to college, or if a student is "motivated," or if a student is of a traditional age, then it is more likely the
student will attend and persist in postsecondary education.

Vincent Tinto has synthesized previous research efforts pertaining to student attrition and posited his own theory of student leave-taking. Tinto's
work is important for a discussion of Native American students for at least
three reasons. First, his work has gained wide respect amongst researchers in
academe. Tinto's formula is the most popular model to describe college participation and departure. Second, he has struggled to take into account the
cultural contexts in which students reside, and in doing so, he had laid to rest
the more harmful psychological assumptions that have tended to "blame the
victim" for school departure. Third, based on extensive quantitative analyses, Tinto persuasively argues in his recent book, *Leaving College,* that most
students do not leave college because they have "failed." He states, "Leaving has little to do with the inability to meet the formal academic requirements of college persistence. The majority of student institutional departures
are voluntary in character."[14] As we shall see, such a finding is of key importance when we consider Delbert Thunderwolf's comments; first, however,
I elaborate on Tinto's model.

The scaffolding for Tinto's model rests on two ideas: (a) Van Gennep's
rituals of passage and (b) Durkheim's theory about suicide, anomie, and the
need for social integration. To summarize these two concepts, Van Gennep
assumed that the members of a society underwent a variety of rituals throughout their lives that moved them from one stage to another—from childhood
to adolescence, from adolescence to adulthood—and so on. Durkheim pos-
tulated that the cause of suicide in society was due to the lack of an individual's integration with larger societal structures such as the church, the state,
and the family.

Basically, Tinto argues that college life implies a passage from one stage
to another and that college-going depends upon how well the college can

integrate the student into the social and academic life of the institution. He comments that the model "argues that some degree of social and intellectual integration must exist as a condition for continued persistence."[15]

Although Tinto does not directly discuss Native Americans in his book, the implications are far-reaching, given the strength of Native American culture, their "roots," and the different cultural values they presumably have from the culture of the mainstream institutions they attend. Indeed, the implicit assumption is that Native Americans will need to undergo a cultural suicide of sorts in order to avoid an intellectual suicide. As Tinto notes, "to become fully incorporated into the life of the college, they have to socially as well as physically disassociate themselves from the communities of the past. Their persistence in college depends upon their becoming departers from their former communities."[16] The implication is that Indian students must depart from their culture if they are to succeed at the "ritual" of college.

To summarize the pertinent points of Tinto's theory of social integration for Native Americans, I offer five axioms:

1. Postsecondary institutions are ritualized situations that symbolize movement from one stage of life to another.
2. The movement from one stage of life to another necessitates leaving a previous state and moving into another.
3. Success in postsecondary education demands that the individual become successfully integrated into the new society's mores.
4. A postsecondary institution serves to synthesize, reproduce, and integrate its members toward similar goals.
5. A postsecondary institution must develop effective and efficient policies to insure that the initiates will become academically and socially integrated.

In the next section I will take issue with the axioms that have been outlined, and I will suggest an alternative way we might think of Native American participation in postsecondary education.

A Critical Perspective

Tinto's work is a significant contribution to understanding the problems of retention. He has demonstrated how colleges and universities often differ dramatically from the communities that students leave. Certainly, the problems a Native American student encounters upon entering the culture of a mainstream organization demonstrates on a grand scale what Tinto seeks to explain.

In advancing a critical agenda, however, I argue that our theoretical propositions need to do more than causally explain why particular groups of students encounter difficulty when they enter a postsecondary institution. Theory needs to explain not only what is (the understood reality of a situation) but also what *could* be. With regard to student participation in postsecondary education, we need to develop theoretical horizons that do not call upon a unitary synthesis of what we want students to become, but rather allow for the multiple voices that exist among students to be heard. Peter McLaren is worth quoting at length with regard to where the inquiry needs to go:

> We need to further develop a language of representation and a language of hope which together will allow the subaltern to speak outside the terms and frames of reference provided by the colonizer, whether or not the colonizer in this case happens to be the teacher, the researcher, or the administrator. We need a language of analysis and hope that . . . does not prevent minorities and the excluded to speak their narratives of liberation and desire. . . . The project of critical pedagogy is positioned against a pedantic cult of singularity in which moral authority and theoretical assurance are arrived at unproblematically without regard to the repressed narratives and suffering of the historically disenfranchised.[17]

Most would agree that Native Americans have been "historically disenfranchised" in American society. From various histories of Native Americans[18] or from investigations of the current economic conditions of Native Americans,[19] consistent policies of discrimination against tribal peoples become readily apparent. What should be done to end discriminatory practices and to promote strategies that will allow for the conditions wherein American Indians "speak their [own] narratives of liberation and desire?"

From the perspective advanced here, each of the underlying assumptions of Tinto's framework must be brought into question. Tinto's model is one of integration, yet he never questions what such a focus will do to those whose values and culture are different from the norm. Or rather, Tinto highlights what will happen—those who do not integrate will depart—and he creates a framework based on integration. What are the consequences of such a view? I am suggesting that Tinto's overreliance on an integrative model of persistence offers potentially harmful consequences for minority students in general, and Indian students in particular. The anthropologist Ray McDermott is helpful here. He says:

> There is a preoccupation among us: Because we claim to offer good education to all and because many minority people seem to reject it, we are plagued with the question—"What is it with them, anyway?" Or, "What is their situation that school seems to go so badly?"[20]

What McDermott and I are arguing is that we need to step back and ask more primary questions about the nature of college-going. We need to ask how failure is arranged and institutionalized in colleges and universities. From this perspective, the inherent assumptions of Tinto's model must be brought into question. What follows is an analysis of the five axioms of Tinto's formulation; I utilize the scaffolding of critical theory and the commentary of Delbert Thunderwolf to offer an alternative framework for thinking of minority student participation in academe.

College as Ritual/Choice. Postsecondary institutions may be ritualized situations, as Tinto suggests, but they do not fit the framework of anthropological rituals, for the simple reason that, with regard to American Indian students, one culture is trying to integrate another culture into its system. Van Gennep's "rituals of passage" were never conceived as acts perpetrated on one culture by another. Van Gennep's rituals also were not choice options; everyone underwent the ritual. Yet with regard to Delbert, he did need to make a choice. His first decision was to undergo the "ritual" of college, but he then chose to leave, and then he chose to return. The ritual system in which he was involved—the public community college—was not of his own culture, but of the mainstream culture.

Further, as the Spindlers' have effectively argued, when we think of traditional cultures and rituals of passage we do not find the concept of "dropout," and we do not discover adolescents choosing whether to undergo the ritual. The Spindlers offer examples from the Hutterites in North America and the Arunta of Australia to point out how mainstream American society differs from traditional societies. To be sure, education is a form of initiation, and all societies struggle to educate their young. But with the Arunta and others, the Spindlers argue, "all of the initiates succeed, none fail, in this intensive, compressive school. To fail would mean at least that one could not be an Arunta, and usually this must mean death . . . social death."[21] Van Gennep's rituals in a traditional society are managed to produce success. To fail to initiate the young into society is unthinkable; the continuity of culture would be destroyed, and society would disintegrate. There are no dropouts. Yet in American society, education does produce dropouts, and success is not assured, especially for American Indian students.

With regard to Delbert, we hear that he believed college was a mixed opportunity, a good and bad choice. He went to an institution, dropped out, worked, and realized that he needed to go back to college when he saw people who had college degrees. "They were going from what they wanted," said Delbert, "and I couldn't do that on $5.50 an hour." In Delbert's eyes, then, college offered the ability to make choices about his life that he otherwise could not have. Delbert viewed college as an avenue that would enhance his economic potential.

Yet he also saw colleges as a harmful and difficult choice. He commented that Indian parents "see education as something that draws students away from who they are." He wanted his teachers to "see how much trouble it is to make the decision to leave home and come to school . . . how it's really a struggle to come here." From a critical perspective, then, the ritual of college is a decision for Indian students that forces them to choose between the world of their tribe and that of academe.

College as Leave-Taking. This assumption follows naturally from the previous argument. If one accepts that individuals exist in developmental patterns, then initiation rituals can be seen as moving initiates from one stage to the next. The problem with such a view when we apply it to college again is highlighted when we think of the Native American experience.

Initiation rituals are not predicated on the belief that the initiates must leave their previous culture and accept a new one. Indeed, initiation rituals exist to provide individuals with more knowledge about the culture in which they reside. Mainstream institutions, however, are based on the assumption that all students, including minority students, not only must leave a developmental stage, but implicitly also must depart from their own cultures as they assume the mantle of adulthood. "There is an assured and assumed continuity," the Spindlers' comment about the rituals of the Hutterites. "The system is self-sustaining."[22] Yet the system we have in place in colleges and universities is not culturally self-sustaining for minority students; instead, it is based on the belief that for success to occur, cultural disruption must take place.

Delbert pointed out how difficult the cultural disruption was for his friends. "It's hard for them to get adjusted," he said. Delbert argued that "education shouldn't try and make me into something I'm not." Delbert resisted cultural disruption, and he implied that the only way he was able to succeed in college was first to understand who he was as an Indian. "I sort of walked away for a while and then came back," he commented. "It's one of the best gifts I've ever had." Although Delbert was able to avoid assimilation, he stated what the national figures confirm: "A lot of us just walk away."

Postsecondary Success. From an integrationist model, when one succeeds in academe, one has adopted the new culture's mores and become integrated. I am not suggesting that integration is bad or harmful. However, to adopt a model predicted on integration and not to attempt to define what one means by the term underscores the problems that will arise for those not in the mainstream. By not delineating what he means by *integration*, Tinto leaves the term open for self-definition. And those in power in academe will define integration the way it has traditionally been done. As we know, in the case of

American Indians, integration has been a code word for assimilation. Assimilation has meant the loss of their culture.

One difference between an integrationist and a critical analysis comes with Delbert's comment about education. He acknowledged that "education provides jobs and skills." But he also went on to state that Indian people did not necessarily see education only in that manner; he argued that "somewhere you have to give Indian people a different view of why they are here, what education is." His point was that education in mainstream institutions was alienating and foreign for Indian students and that alternative venues needed to be created.

According to the model of social integration described above, one would agree with Delbert's comment that education caused cultural disruption. College is a ritualized situation that makes students into new people. To the extent that students do not engage in the process, the social integrationist would argue, they are at risk of dropping out. Success or failure in college turns on how an individual and the family interprets the educational process. Because education "draws students away from who they are," it has the potential of being interpreted as a positive, negative, or neutral influence. A social integrationist might see the influence as positive, or at least neutral; nonetheless, the influence exists.

Within the context of Delbert's comments, however, we see that drawing "students away from who they are" was perceived as negative, harmful. Presumably, Delbert viewed education in terms of integration, and integration was seen as a form of assimilation. A critical perspective acknowledges how the two "worlds"—that of the institution and that from which Delbert comes—are different. The educational process is seen as trying to remake people into something different from who they are, and such attempts are viewed in a negative light.

Postsecondary Goals. We are led to believe that the goals of education will be similar for all. In one light, one cannot argue with such an assumption. All students need to be equipped with the intellectual and vocational skills necessary to function in the twenty-first century. Yet Pottinger succinctly elaborates the dilemma for Native Americans: "Few individuals wish to be handicapped by inadequate preparation for the 'real world,' a real world which demands skills relevant to the latest advances in technology. But how does one achieve this competence without losing touch with one's heritage?"[23]

The integrative framework that Tinto proposes implicitly demands that students choose: either maintain your culture and risk economic and social problems, or eschew your culture and gain a college degree and all the benefits that will be forthcoming. Framed in this manner, if we return to the data of Native American participation in academe, we see that they have overwhelmingly chosen their culture rather than to undergo the initiation rituals of an oppositional culture in a mainstream institution.[24]

Yet, one is hard-pressed to look upon nonparticipation or attrition from postsecondary education as a "success" if the consequences are a student's inability to earn an income or take control of her or his life. I am suggesting that we ought to investigate how organizational participants might develop strategies framed by a concern for redefining the parameters of the organization. Rather than assimilate minorities into the organization, we need to shift our emphases so that alternative discourses can be heard. Henry Giroux defines such an educational strategy as "border pedagogy":

> Students must engage knowledge as a border-crosser, as a person moving in and out of borders constructed around coordinates of difference and power. These are not only physical borders, they are cultural borders historically constructed and socially organized within maps of rules and regulations that limit and enable particular identities, individual capacities, and social forms. In this case, students cross over into borders of meaning, maps of knowledge, social relations, and values that are increasingly being negotiated and rewritten as the codes and regulations which organize them become destabilized and reshaped.[25]

Giroux means more than simply that students should be able to understand their own cultures and also exist in others. He does not mean to imply that students' cognitive capacities are like different television channels with which they can flip back and forth depending upon their desire. Nor does he intend to suggest that educators should be concerned merely with creating the conditions whereupon Native Americans or any other minority may appropriate the dominant discourse. Rather, the implications of a critical approach for postsecondary organizations necessitate redefining how we think, and hence act, in the organizational world.

The Role of Colleges. Delbert spoke about the "obstacles" Indian students face, with an example about financial aid. He said, "You go from one financial aid office and get told to go somewhere else. . . . You give up." A social integrationist will see Delbert's comments as identifying organizational barriers to be overcome. The assumption is that the organization is ineffective and policies need to be developed so that the organization will become more efficient. On the one hand the organization must provide more assistance, so that students are not lost and do not "give up." On the other hand, Indian students must be taught to learn the process, so that they can successfully navigate the bureaucratic waters.

In some respects the critical response is problematic. Student departure from college may be viewed as a point of resistance. In effect, Indian students reject the cultural requisites that the organization places upon them. Rather than seeing them as victims, a critical theorist might view such an action as a form of cultural integrity and strength. Indian students reject being assimilated into mainstream society, and the only avenue for their rejection is to depart.

The problem turns, for the critical theorist, on the consequences of departure. Delbert commented that he asked students when they leave, "What are you going to do," and he found, "There's never no answers." The point is not that cultural resistance is wrong or futile, but surely there are organizational responses other than the assumption that students must become integrated into the mainstream culture. Critical theorists, however, have yet to operationalize such a response, but clues about how one might act arise with a comment by Delbert.

He commented that most whites "don't understand," and that he wanted "to lead them through [his] life." His hope was that in doing so, his instructors would "see right." Again, the integrationist model assumes that the purpose of "seeing right" is to create a more effective system so that students will successfully undergo the rituals of transition.

Delbert, however, was not speaking about "seeing right" in order for Indian students to become assimilated to the ways of the mainstream. Indeed, he referred again to the need to resist the mainstream. "Education shouldn't try to make me into something I'm not," said Delbert. "That's what I learned when I wasn't here. . . . Who I am." Yet Delbert's time away from school involved alcohol abuse and a job that he did not find particularly challenging; it was the spiritual and ceremonial learning activities with his people that forced him to think about "who he was," which in turn enabled him to return to school. One wonders what kinds of activities minority students must undergo to maintain their identity and grasp the tools that a college education offers.

I am suggesting that organizations need to be constructed where minority students' lives are celebrated and affirmed throughout the culture of the institution. The point is not simply to have a Native American studies center or a course or two devoted to native peoples. Minority students need institutions that create the conditions where the students not only celebrate their own histories but also are helped to examine critically how their lives are shaped and molded by society's forces.[26] Such a theoretical suggestion has implications for virtually all areas of the organization—from how we organize student affairs, to the manner in which we construct knowledge, from the role of assessment, to the role of the college president.

The emphasis of a critical analysis shifts away from what strategies those in power can develop to help those not in power, to analyzing how power exists in the organization, and given how power operates, to developing strategies that seek to transform those relations. All organizational participants will be encouraged to come to terms with how they may reconstruct and transform the organization's culture. As opposed to a rhetoric of what mainstream organizations will *do* for Native Americans—a top-down managerial approach—the struggle is to develop strategies and policies that emerge from a vision of working *with* Native Americans toward a participatory goal of emancipation and empowerment.

CONCLUSION

I have offered two different theoretical constructs that have direct implications for Native American participation in academe. Tinto's model of social integration offers a wealth of explanatory evidence about why individuals do not persist and what strategies institutional participants might develop to help them persist.

Critical theory offers an alternative lens with which to analyze Native American college-going patterns. I provided a critique of social integration and argued that a Durkheimian model of college as a ritual of passage has two conceptual flaws. First, anthropologists who subscribe to the notion of rituals of transition have never defined rituals as individual choices that move people from one culture to another, but rather have defined them as stages of human development. Second, a model based on an implicit understanding of integration will inevitably subscribe to cultural assumptions that pertain to mainstream culture and deny or overwhelm alternative interpretations of other cultures.

Delbert Thunderwolf's perceptions of his experiences afforded an opportunity to think about Native American involvement in academe and to contrast the two perspectives. Participants in an academic world that subscribe to a model of cultural integration will not hear Delbert's words in a manner similar to how the critical theorist hears them. In effect, Delbert's voice is not heard. Yet for critical theorists, "seeing right" or "hearing right" is not enough; the question before us must be: If our theoretical notions enable us to hear Delbert's voice, then what must we do? What are the implications for action? These are the questions that now await us.

CAMERON McCARTHY

Chapter Sixteen

Beyond the Poverty of Theory in Race Relations: Nonsynchrony and Social Difference in Education

Contemporary curriculum researchers are still very much prone to see racial antagonism as a kind of deposit or disease that is triggered into existence by some deeper flaw of character or of society. In this sense, both mainstream and racial conceptualizations of racial inequality can be described as "essentialist" and "reductionist," in that they effectively eliminate the "noise" of multidimensionality, historical variability, and subjectivity from their explanations of educational differences.[1] Let me clarify what I mean by essentialism and reductionism. By essentialism I refer to the tendency in current liberal and neo-Marxist writing on race and gender to treat social groups as stable or homogeneous entities. Racial groups such as "Asians," "Hispanics," or "Blacks" are therefore discussed as though members of these groups possessed some "unique" or innate set of characteristics that set them apart from "whites." Feminist theorists such as Theresa DeLauretis have critiqued dominant tendencies in mainstream research to define gender differences in terms of transcendental essences. She maintains that differences in the political and cultural behavior of women and men are determined by social and historical contingencies and not some essentialist checklist of innate, biological or primordial characteristics.[2] As I will show later in my essay, essentialism significantly inhibits a dynamic understanding of race relations and race-based politics in education and society. Reductionist strategies, on the other hand, tend to locate the "source" of racial differences in schooling in a single variable or cause. Current approaches to racial inequality therefore tend to rely too heavily on linear, monocausal models or explanations that retreat from the exploration of the political, cultural, and economic contexts in which racial groups encounter each other in schools and society. Cortes points to these limitations in his examination of current approaches to racial inequality in education:

> Some analyses [of racial differences in education] have relied too heavily on single-cause explanations. Group educational differentials have been attributed, at various times, to language difference, to cultural conflict, to discriminatory instruments (such as I.Q. tests), or to the cultural insensitivity of educators. Yet as surely as one of these has been posited as "the," or at least "the principal," cause of group achievement differentials, then other situations are discovered in which these factors exist, and yet group achievement differentials do not occur. . . . There has been a tendency to decontextualize explanations. That is, explanations about the relationship between sociocultural factors and educational achievement often posit causation without consideration of the context in which these factors operate.[3]

As Cortes points out, without an examination of institutional and social context, it is difficult to understand how racial inequality operates in education. Current mainstream and radical conceptual frameworks do not effectively capture the heterogeneous and variable nature of race relations in either the school setting or society. Theoretical and practical insights that could be gained from a more relational and synthetic method of analyzing racial domination in education—one that attempts to show in detail the links between social structures (whether they be economic, political, or ideological) and what real people, such as teachers and students, do—have been forfeited.

Despite these limitations, however, the mainstream and radical educational literature on race relations in schooling has pointed us in some very important directions. For instance, we now know where some of the most significant tensions, stresses, and gaps in our current research on social difference and inequality are. I believe that it is precisely these gaps, stresses, tensions, and discontinuities that must be explored if researchers are to begin to develop a more adequate account of the operation of racial inequality in education and society.

In the first part of this essay, I will examine three areas that I consider crucial points of difference and tension between and within mainstream and radical approaches to racial inequality in the curriculum and educational literature. These areas can be summarized as follows: (a) the structure-culture distinction, (b) macro- versus micro- theoretical and methodological perspectives on race, and (c) the issue of historical variability versus essentialism in the designation of racial categories.

In the second part of this paper, I will make the case for an alternative approach to racial inequality, what I shall call a *nonsynchronous theory* of race relations in schooling and society. In advancing the position of nonsynchrony, I will argue against essentialist and reductionist or single-cause explanations of the persistence of racial inequality in education that are currently being offered in both the mainstream and the radical curriculum and educational literature. Instead, I will direct attention to the complex and contradictory nature of race relations in the institutional life of social organizations such as schools.

Let us first look at the principal tensions within mainstream and radical accounts of racial inequality.

AREAS OF TENSION IN RACE AND CURRICULUM RESEARCH

Structure versus Culture

Radical school critics such as Gilroy and Henriques maintain that liberal educational theorists place a great deal of emphasis on "values" as the site of the social motivation for the maintenance and persistence of racial inequality.[4] This emphasis on values as a central explanatory variable in liberal theories of racial inequality should not be dismissed out of hand. The primary theoretical and practical merit of this liberal position resides in the fact that it seeks to restore human agency to the project of evaluating the relationship between social difference and education. Thus, for liberal theorists in their examination of racial antagonism in schooling, it is the active agency and subjectivities of students and teachers that really matter and that can make a difference in race relations.

In a related sense, liberal researchers also recognize the cultural role of education in initiating the social neophyte into dominant values, traditions, and rituals of "stratification."[5] But liberal pluralist researchers conceptualize racial values as emanating from a coherent Cartesian individual subject. When groups or social collectivities are invoked in liberal frameworks on racial inequality, they are specified in terms of aggregates of individuals. The problem here, as I have indicated elsewhere, is that such an emphasis on individual agency also results in the undertheorization of the effectiveness of social and economic structures in the determination of racial inequality.[6]

This tension between structure and agency is also powerfully expressed within radical discourses. Neo-Marxists insist that racial domination must, in part, be understood in the context of capitalism's elaboration of macrostructures, and not simply in terms of individual preferences. They draw our attention to the fact that racial domination is deeply implicated in the

fundamental organization of specific human societies, as well as in the evolution of capitalism as a world system. In this way, we come to understand
race as a profoundly social category. Racial domination is thus conceptualized at the level of social collectivities and their differential and conflictual
relationships to the means of production. This alerts us to the powerful connections among racial domination and economic inequality, differential material resources and capacities, and unequal access to social and political
institutions such as schools.

But recent Marxist cultural criticism has sought to raise other issues
concerning social difference and inequality in American education.[7] These
issues—of identity, subjectivity, culture, language, and agency—direct attention to the informal curriculum of schools and the subcultural practices of
school youth. This theoretical development has taken place partly in response
to the early work of radical school critics, such as Bowles and Gintis, who
tended to subordinate agency, meaning, and subjectivity to economic structures (for example, the workplace) exogenous to the school.[8] Writers such as
Apple and Wexler contend that previous neo-Marxist emphasis on economic
structures focuses attention on only one part of the puzzle in our investigation
of racial inequality.[9] In a similar manner, liberal emphasis on social and cultural values as the primary site of racial antagonism provides us with only a
partial understanding of the way in which racial dynamics operate. Marxist
cultural theorists have therefore attempted to transcend the binary opposition
of structure versus culture entailed in previous neo-Marxist and liberal theories by offering a more interactive view of the central contradictions in capitalist society. However, to the extent that some critical curriculum and
educational theorists have attempted to incorporate these more interactive
perspectives into their examination of the relationship between schooling and
inequality, these efforts have been directed almost exclusively toward understanding the dynamics of class, not race.

Macro- versus Microperspectives

There is a further bifurcation in the curriculum and educational literature
on race: Mainstream theorists have tended to focus more directly on mic-
rolevel classroom variables, while radical theorists have offered macroper-
spectives on racial inequality that have privileged areas outside the school,
such as the economy and the labor process. Radical school critics have generally specified structural relations at such a high level of abstraction (the
level of the mode of production) that all human agency evaporates from their
analysis of society. This abstract approach is also residually present in more
recent critical curriculum studies of social difference and inequality in the
institutional settings of schools.[10] These more culturalist theorists have ar-

gued that race is linked to other social dynamics, such as class and gender, in a system of multiple determinations. Sarup has quite persuasively argued that these "additive" models of inequality have simply failed to capture the degree of nuance, variability, discontinuity, and multiplicity of histories and "realities" that exist in the school setting.[11] In a similar manner, both Omi and Winant and Burawoy have pointed to the fact that the intersection of race and class can lead, for example, to the augmentation or diminution of racial solidarity, depending on the contingencies and variables in the local setting such as the school.[12] All of this points toward the need for theoretical and practical work articulated at what Hall calls the "middle range."[13] That is to say, it is important that radical theorists begin to specify more directly the ways in which race operates in the local context of schools.

Let me be clear about what is at issue here. I believe that the radical intuition that racial inequality is implicated and must be understood in the context of the development of capitalism's macrostructures is basically correct if it takes seriously the relatively autonomous workings of the state. On the other hand, unqualified liberal emphasis on individual motivation and rational action as the terms of reference for "normal" behavior locates racism in idiosyncratic, arbitrary, and abnormal attitudes and actions. This requires us to abandon materialist explanations of racial antagonism and seek recourse in differential psychology and so on. The burden and responsibility for the oppression of racial minorities are squarely placed on the shoulders of these irrational or "authoritarian personalities."[14] Liberal theorists' reliance on attitudinal models also limits our understanding of social changes in the area of race relations. Within these frameworks, change and transformation of oppressive race relations are made conditional upon the institutional reformation of irrational and intolerant individuals and their return to the observance of rational norms that guide the society and its institutions. Needless to say, historical evidence and the very persistence of racial inequality in schools and society go against the grain of this thesis and the programmatic responses it has precipitated. It is therefore not enough, as neo-Marxist theorists rightly point out, to talk about changing attitudes without addressing the structural and institutional impediments that exist in education and society to the mobility and maneuverability of racially marginalized groups.

The Issue of History

Though both the macrological and the micrological perspectives that underpin radical and liberal formulations give us a general map of racial logics, they do not tell us how movement is orchestrated or realized along the grid of race relations. That is, neither current liberal nor neo-Marxist theories of schooling inform us about the historical trajectory of racial discourse and the struggles over such racial discourse within specific institutions such as education. There is indeed a tendency within mainstream and radical frameworks to treat racial definitions ("Black," "white," etc.) as immutable, *a priori* categories. Racial categories such as Black and white are taken for granted within the popular common sense as well as in the writings of scholars in the curriculum field. Associated with this tendency are tacit or explicit propositions about the origins of races and racism. Mainstream theorists identify the origin of the races in physical and psychological traits, geography, climate, patterns of ancient migrations, and so on.[15] Radical theorists, on the other hand, link race and racism to the specific event of the emergence of capitalism and its "need" to rationalize the superexploitation of African slave labor and the segmented division of the labor market.[16] The major methodological problem of all of these "origins" arguments is that they presume the eternal existence of racial distinctions and incorporate them into the analysis of racial antagonism as though such distinctions were functional social categories that have remained stable throughout history. In both mainstream and radical writings, then, "race" is historically given. (After all, says our common sense, "we know who Black people and white people are merely by observation and inspection.") The historical variability associated with racial categories and the social purposes that racial distinctions serve are consequently undertheorized.

But as Omi and Winant have argued, race is preeminently a "social historical concept."[17] For example, it is only through developed social practices and the particular elaboration of historical and material relations in the United States that "white consciousness," with its associated category "white people," emerged. Likewise, it is only through similar historical and social practices that racial "others"—who in reality have varying economic and social positions—emerged under the definition of "Black," "Asian," "Latino," and so on. In this sense, racial categories and "the meaning of race and the definitions of specific racial groups have varied significantly over time and between different societies."[18] A few examples are useful in helping to illustrate the instability and variability of racial categories.

In the United States, the racial classification "white" evolved with the consolidation of slavery in the seventeenth century. Euro-American settlers of various "ancestries" (Dutch, English, and so forth) claimed a common identity in relation to exploited and enslaved African peoples. As Winthrop Jordan observes:

> From the first, then, vis-à-vis "Negro," the concept embedded in the term *Christian* seems to have conveyed much of the idea and feeling of "we" against "they": to be *Christian* was to be civilized rather than barbarous, English rather than African, white rather than black. The term *Christian*

itself proved to have remarkable elasticity, for by the end of the seventeenth century it was being used to define a species of slavery which had altogether lost any connection with explicit religious difference. In the Virginia code of 1705, for example, the term sounded much more like a definition of race than of religion: "And for a further christian care and usage of all christian servants, Be it also enacted, *by the authority aforesaid, and it is hereby enacted,* That no negroes, mulattos, or Indians, although christians, or Jews, Moors, Mahometans, or other infidels, shall, at any time, purchase any christian servant, nor any other, except of their own complexion, or such as are declared slaves by this act." By this time "Christianity" had somehow become intimately linked with "complexion". . . . Most suggestive of all, there seems to have been something of a shift during the seventeenth century in the terminology which Englishmen in the colonies applied to themselves. From the initially most common term *Christian,* at mid-century there was a marked shift toward "English" and "free." After about 1680, taking the colonies as a whole, a new term appeared—"white."[19]

It is through these same practices of inclusion and exclusion that the "others" of colonial America—the enslaved African peoples—were defined as "Negro" or "Black." Thus, the racial category "Negro" redefined and homogenized the plural identities of disparate African people whose "ethnic origins" were Ibo, Yoruba, Fulani, and so on.

Racial categories also vary contemporaneously between societies. For example, while the racial designation "Black' in the United States refers only to people of African descent, in England, oppressed Asian and African Caribbean minorities have appropriated "Black" as a counterhegemonic identity. In Latin America, racial categories are used and appropriated with a higher degree of flexibility than in the United States. Omi and Winant, drawing on the work of cultural anthropologist Marvin Harris, foreground this variability and discontinuity in race relations in Latin America:

By contrast [to the United States], a striking feature of race relations in the lowland areas of Latin America since the abolition of slavery has been the relative absence of sharply defined racial groupings. No such rigid descent rule characterizes racial identity in many Latin American societies. Brazil, for example, has historically had less rigid conceptions of race, and thus a variety of "intermediate" racial categories exist. Indeed, as Harris notes, "One of the most striking consequences of the Brazilian system of racial identification is that parents and children and even brothers and sisters are frequently accepted as representatives of quite opposite racial types." Such a possibility is incomprehensible within the logic of racial categories in the U.S.[20]

Social practices of racial classification are elaborated and contested throughout society and within given institutions by personal and collective action. In this way racial definitions are reproduced and transformed. Historically, education has been a principal site for the reproduction and elaboration of racial meaning and racial identities. An examination of the career of racial discourses within the overall trajectory of curriculum and educational theories and practices rapidly disabuses us of the notion that education is a "neutral" or "innocent" institution with respect to racial struggles.[21] An investigation of the genealogy of racial discourses in education would, for example, take us through these domains:

1. Colonial/plantation America's education laws that prohibited the education of Black Americans, such as the eighteenth-century statutes of South Carolina and other states[22]
2. Jim Crow educational policies in the North and the South that segregated and concentrated Blacks and other minorities into inferior schools[23]
3. Mental measurement and human intelligence theories—from the laboratory of cranium estimates to the anthropological and biological theories of racial difference in the work of the likes of Morton and Gobineau, and the genetics-based theories of race and intelligence of Eysenck and Kamin and Jensen[24]
4. Curriculum theories of social efficiency, differential psychology, and cultural deprivation that labeled Black youth as "underachievers," and have labeled Black families and Black communities as "defective" and "dysfunctional"
5. Liberal and progressive-inspired educational programs such as Head Start, compensatory education, and multicultural programs that have been aimed at helping to close the educational and cultural gap between Black and white youth

At every historical juncture of the racialization of dominant educational institutions in the United States, African Americans and other racial minorities have contested and have sought to redefine hegemonic conceptions of racial differences in "intelligence" and "achievement" and the curriculum strategies of inclusion and exclusion and selection that these commonsense racial theories have undergirded. Over the years, this cultural resistance has been mobilized on two principal fronts. On the one hand, since the period of Reconstruction, African Americans have conducted what Gramsci would call a "war of maneuver" outside the "trenches" of dominant universities, schools, and other educational centers by establishing parallel and alternative institutions of learning.[25] While it is true that these institutions have not always been directed toward transformative projects, Black educational institutions have provided a material basis for the nurturance of Black intellectual and cultural autonomy.[26]

Simultaneous with the elaboration of alternative institutions, African Americans and other minorities have conducted a "war of position" in the courts and the schools for equality of access to education.[27] These struggles have also been enlarged to include insurgent challenges over a redefinition of dominant university academic programs. These challenges have directly influenced the emergence of the "new" disciplines of ethnic studies, women's studies, and so on, that have helped to broaden the range of knowledge and interests in the university setting.

Education has played a central role in the drama of struggles over racial identities and meaning in the United States. But any historical account of the racialization of American education must avoid the easy familiarity of linear narrative. The reproduction of hegemonic racial meanings, the persistence of racial inequality, and the mobilization of minority resistance to dominant educational institutions have not proceeded in a straightforward, coherent, or predictable way. A systematic exploration of the history of race relations in education does, however, lead us to a recognition of the agency of oppressed minorities, the fluidity and complexity of social dynamics, and the many-sided character of minority/majority relations in education.

The tensions and silences within mainstream and radical approaches to racial inequality discussed here underscore the need for a more relational and contextual approach to the operation of racial differences in schooling. Such an approach would allow us to understand better the complex operation of racial logics in education and would help us to explore more adequately the vital links that exist between racial inequality and other dynamics—such as class and gender—operating in the school setting.

In the next section, I will present two related alternative approaches— the theories of *parallelism* and *nonsynchrony*—that will directly address the conceptually difficult but intriguing issues concerning (a) the structuring and formation of racial difference in education, and (b) the intersection of race, class, and gender dynamics in the institutional setting of schools. I will also report and discuss ethnographic examples of nonsynchrony in race relations in schooling from the work of Grant, Nkomo, and Spring.[28]

NONSYNCHRONY AND PARALLELISM: LINKING RACE TO GENDER AND CLASS DYNAMICS IN EDUCATION

Racial inequality is indeed a complex, many-sided phenomenon that embraces both structural and cultural characteristics. But exactly how does racial difference operate in education? How are the "widely disparate circumstances of individual and group racial identities" intertwined and mediated in the formal and informal practices of social institutions such as schools?[29]

How do educational institutions "integrate" the macro- and microdynamics of difference? One of the most significant contributions to an understanding of these difficult questions regarding the operation of racial inequality has been advanced by Apple and Weis in what they call the "parallelist position."[30] In this approach, the authors argued that it was more helpful to conceptualize the social formation in terms of interlocking spheres of economy, politics, and culture. Apple and Weis claimed further that dynamic relations of race, class, and gender interact with each other in complex ways, but that each is necessary for the mutual reproduction of the others. It is impossible in this essay to give these arguments the thorough treatment that they deserve—more extensive discussion is presented elsewhere.[31] But let me say here that perhaps the most significant contribution the parallelist approach offered was that it introduced into the sociology of curriculum accounts a new way of understanding causation with respect to racial antagonism. These proponents of parallelism suggested that causal processes related to racial antagonism should no longer be located in a single theoretical space, namely, the structural properties of "the" economy. Causal influences on racial antagonism were conceptualized as coming from a "plurality" of processes operating simultaneously within the economic, cultural, and political spheres of society. The parallelist approach therefore problematized the elements of positivistic causal linearity that residually percolated within radical accounts of race and curriculum. In this sense, too, proponents avoided the tendency toward single-cause explanations of racial inequality so dominant among adherents of mainstream neo-correlational paradigms of educational research. Instead, these theorists pointed us toward the plurality of liabilities that handicap minority youth as raced, classed, and gendered social subjects. Apple and Weis presented this more integrated model in the following manner:

> Education is not a stable enterprise dominated by consensus, but instead is riven with ideological conflicts. These political, cultural, and economic conflicts are dynamic. They are in something like constant motion, each often acting on the others and each stemming from structurally generated antagonisms, compromises, and struggles. In the context of our increased general understanding of the relationships between culture and the formation of, and/or resistance to ideological hegemony, what does this mean for the more specific problem of ideology and education?
>
> First, rather than a unidimensional theory in which economic form is determinate, society is conceived of as being made up of three interrelated spheres—economic, cultural/ideological, and political.
>
> Second, we need to be cautious about assuming that ideologies are only ideas held in one's head. They are better thought of less as things than as social processes. Nor are ideologies linear configurations, simple pro-

cesses that all necessarily work in the same direction or reinforce each other. . . . A number of elements or dynamics are usually present at the same time in any one instance. This is important. Ideological form is *not* reducible to class. Processes of gender, age, and race enter directly into the ideological moment. . . . It is actually out of the articulation with, clash among, or contradictions among and within, say class, race, and sex that ideologies are lived in one's day-to-day life.[32]

Apple and Weis also criticized the tendency of mainstream and radical theorists to bifurcate society into separate domains of structure and culture.[33] They argued that such arbitrary bifurcation directly helped to consolidate tendencies toward essentialism (single-cause explanations) in contemporary thinking about race. Researchers often "locate the fundamental elements of race, not surprisingly, on their homeground."[34] For neo-Marxists, then, it is necessary first to understand the class basis of racial inequality; and for liberal theorists, cultural and social values and prejudices are the primary sources of racial antagonism. In contrast, Apple and Weis contended that race is not a "category" or a "thing-in-itself," but a vital social process that is integrally linked to other social processes and dynamics operating in education and society.[35] The proposition that "each sphere of social life is constituted of dynamics of class, race, and gender" had broad theoretical and practical merit.[36] For example, it highlighted the fact that it is impossible to understand fully the problem of the phenomenally high school-dropout rate among Black and Hispanic youth without taking into account the lived experience of race, class, and gender oppressions in U.S. urban centers and the ways in which the intersections of these social dynamics work to systematically "disqualify" inner-city minority youth in educational institutions and in the job market. In a similar manner, a theoretical emphasis on gender dynamics helped to complement our understanding of the unequal division of labor in schools and society and directed our attention to the way in which capitalism uses patriarchal relations to depress the wage scale and the social value of women's labor.

In advancing the parallelist position, Apple and Weis therefore presented us with a theory of *overdetermination* in which the unequal processes and outcomes of teaching and learning and of schooling in general are produced by constant interactions among three dynamics (race, gender, and class) and in three spheres (economic, political, and cultural). In significant ways it represented a major advance over the "single group" and single variable studies that had hitherto dominated the study of race relations in education.

But the parallelist approach to the analysis of social difference, while rejecting much of the reductionism and essentialism of earlier neo-Marxist structuralism, offers an "additive" model of the intersection of race, class, and gender that does not address issues of contradiction and tension in schooling in any systematic way. Neither does it address the "mix" of contingencies, interests, desires, needs, differential assets, and capacities that exist in local settings such as schools. Thus, it does not offer us a clear enough insight into the specificity or directionality of effects of the intersection of race, class, and gender in education.

In contrast to the parallelist theorists' emphasis on reciprocity and mutuality of effects, I will argue, as does Hicks, that the intersection of race, class, and gender in the institutional setting of the school is systematically *contradictory* or *nonsynchronous* and can lead to the augmentation or diminution of the effect of race, or for that matter any other of these variables operating in the school environment.[37] Since the terms *contradiction* and *nonsynchrony* are central to the arguments about the operation of racial inequality and antagonism in education, it is important that I specify their meanings.

I use the term *contradiction* here and throughout in two senses. First, the use of *contradiction* is associated with a deconstructive project that is central to my discussion of racial inequality in this essay. I therefore draw attention to moments of rupture, discontinuity, and structural silence in existing school practices and the social relations that define minority/majority encounters in education. For example, those moments of discontinuity and contradiction are articulated in the gap between the ostensible objective of efficiency in school policies such as tracking and their unintended effects of marginalizing a large number of minority youth from an academic curriculum. Although educational administrators and teachers readily point to the "fairness" of existing normative rules and criteria for assigning students to high/low academic tracks in school, the application of such normative rules (grades, standardized tests, etc.) procedurally constrains Black access to genuine equality of opportunity in education. At the same time these rules benefit white middle-class youth, who have a clear advantage with respect to instructional opportunities, teacher time, and material resources such as computers.[38] In all-Black schools, similar structural advantages can accrue to Black middle-class students vis-à-vis their working-class counterparts, as Rist discovered.[39] These "built-in" discontinuities exist as structuring principles in everyday pedagogical and curriculum practices and profoundly influence minority encounters with whites in education.

There is also a second, more positive, application of the term *contradiction*. In this more Hegelian usage of the concept, I wish to suggest that it is precisely these discontinuities in minority/majority experiences in schooling that can provoke or motivate qualitative change and forward motion in social relations between Blacks and whites. In this sense, I maintain that a genuine exploration of these contradictions in minority/majority education can help to lay the basis for meaningful race-relations reform.

The concept of *nonsynchrony* also highlights the issue of contradiction, but more specifically summarizes the vast differences in interests, needs, desires, and identity that separate different minority groups from each other and from majority whites in educational settings. Like Hall, I believe that it is necessary to offer theoretical arguments at a more conjunctural or middle level if we are to get a better handle on the way these dynamics operate in schools.[40] Such an emphasis on nonsynchrony in the institutional context would help us to specify these dynamics of race and gender in a manner that would allow for an understanding of the multivocal, multiaccented nature of human subjectivity and the genuinely polysemic nature of minority/majority relations in education and society.[41]

By invoking the concepts of contradiction and nonsynchrony, I wish to advance the position that individuals or groups, in their relation to economic, political, and cultural institutions such as schools, do *not* share identical consciousness and express the same interests, needs, or desires "at the same point in time."[42] In this connection, I also attach great importance to the organizing principles of selection, inclusion, and exclusion. These principles operate in ways that affect how marginalized minority youth are positioned in dominant social and educational policies and agendas. Schooling in this sense constitutes a site for the production of politics. The politics of difference is a critical dimension of the way in which nonsynchrony operates in the material context of the school and can be regarded as the expression of "culturally sanctioned, rational responses to struggles over scarce [or unequal] resources."[43] As we will see, students (and teachers) tend to be rewarded and sanctioned differently according to the resources and assets they are able to mobilize inside the school and in the community. This capacity to mobilize resources and to exploit the unequal reward system and symbolic rituals of schooling varies considerably according to the race, gender, and class backgrounds of minority and majority students. White middle-class male students therefore come into schools with clear social and economic advantages and in turn often have these advantages confirmed and augmented by the unequal curriculum and pedagogical practices of schooling. However, this process is not simple, and the production of inequality in school is a highly contradictory and nonsynchronous phenomenon—one that does not guarantee nice, clean, or definitive outcomes for embattled minority and majority school actors.

But exactly how does nonsynchrony work in practice? What are the "rules of the game" that govern the production of inequality in the school setting? And how does inequality in educational institutions become specifically classed, gendered, or raced?

There are four types of relations that govern the nonsynchronous interactions of raced, classed, and gendered minority and majority actors in the school setting. These relations can be specified as follows:

1. *Relations of competition:* These include competition for access to educational institutions, credentials, instructional opportunity, financial and technical resources, and so on.
2. *Relations of exploitation:* The school mediates the economy's demands for different types of labor in its preparation of school youth for the labor force.
3. *Relations of domination:* Power in schooling is highly stratified and is expressed in terms of hierarchy of relations and structures—administration to teacher, teacher to student, and so forth. The school also mediates demands for symbolic control and legitimation from a racial and patriarchal state.
4. *Relations of cultural selection:* This is the totalizing principle of "difference" that organizes meaning and identity formation in school life. This organizing principle is expressed in terms of cultural strategies or rules of inclusion/exclusion or in-group/out-group that determine whose knowledge gets into the curriculum, and that also determine the pedagogical practices of ability grouping, diagnosing, and marking of school youth. These relations also help to define the terms under which endogenous competition for credentials, resources, and status can take place in the school. It should be noted that there is considerable overlap between and among the relations of cultural selection and the other relations of competition, exploitation, and domination operating in the everyday practices of minority and majority school actors.

In the school setting, each of these four types of relations interacts with, defines, and is defined by the others in an uneven and decentered manner. For example, the principles of cultural selection embodied in codes of dress, behavior, and so forth, which help to determine the assignment of minority youth to low-ability groups, also help to position these youth in respect to power (domination) relations with majority peers and adults.[44] Cultural selection therefore influences minority access to instructional opportunity as well as access to opportunities for leadership and status in the classroom and in the school.[45] In a similar manner, relations of cultural selection help to regulate endogenous competition for credentials and resources, thereby constraining minority and majority students to a differential structure of "choices" with respect to the job market and ultimately to the differential exploitation of their labor power by employers. Of course, the reverse is also true, in that teachers' and administrators' perceptions of the structure of opportunities for minorities (exploitation relations) can have a significant impact on the processes of cultural selection of minority and majority students to ability groups and curricular tracks in schooling.[46] By virtue of the daily operation of these four types of relations—of competition, exploitation, domination, and cultural selection—and their complex interaction with dynamics of race, class, and gender, schooling is a nonsynchronous situation or context. In this nonsynchronous context, racial dynamics constantly shape and are in turn shaped by the other forms of structuring, namely, gender and class.[47]

The concept of nonsynchrony begins to get at the complexity of causal motion and effects "on the ground," as it were. It also raises questions about the nature, exercise, and multiple determination of power within that middle ground of everyday practices in schooling.[48] The fact is that, as Hicks suggests, dynamic relations of race, class, and gender do not unproblematically reproduce each other.[49] These relations are complex and often have contradictory effects in institutional settings. The intersection of race, class, and gender at the local level of schooling can lead to interruptions, discontinuities, augmentations, or diminutions of the original effects of any one of these dynamics. Thus, for example, while schooling in a racist society like the United States is by definition a "racist institution," its racial character might not be the dominant variable shaping conflict over inequality in every schooling situation.[50] That is to say that (a) the particular mix of history, subjectivities, interests, and capacities that minority and majority actors bring to the institutional context, and (b) the way in which these actors negotiate and "settle" the rules of the game (the relations of competition, exploitation, domination, and cultural selection) will determine the dominant character and directionality of effects in the specific school setting.

Such a "dominant" character refers to the relations along which "endogenous differences" in the school are principally articulated. These dominant relations thus constitute an "articulating principle," pulling the entire ensemble of relations in the school setting into a "unity" or focus for conflict.[51] Such an articulating principle may be race, class, or gender. For instance, it can be argued that a sex-dominant situation exists within American university education with respect to struggles over women's studies and the very status of women in academe itself. Gender has been the articulating principle that has sharpened our focus on issues around the fundamental white male privilege operating in the university system with respect to the differentiated organization of curricular knowledge, unequal patterns of selection and appointment to tenure-track faculty positions, unequal relations between male professors and female students, and so on. The issue of gender has had multiplier effects, illuminating flash points of difference across a

340 *Beyond Silenced Voices*

FIGURE 16.1
An example of a *Sex-Dominant Situation*

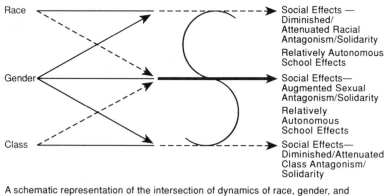

A schematic representation of the intersection of dynamics of race, gender, and class in Schooling (S), in which gender is responsible for the most powerful effects in the school setting.
Solid lines indicate autonomous effects
Bold lines indicate augmented effects.
Broken lines indicate attenuated/relatively autonomous or diminished effects.

range of traditional male-dominated disciplines. Sexual antagonism within academe has focused our attention on the *modus operandi* of the university and its relations of competition, exploitation, domination, and cultural selection. But the powerful impact of sexual antagonism within the university has also had the effect of masking racial antagonism and or determining the political terms on which racial conflicts may be fought. (One should hasten to note that the opposite was true in the 1960s, when the balance of forces of contestation tended toward the prominence of racial difference as the articulating principle for conflicts over inequality in education.) Issues of minority failure and the underrepresentation of minorities at every level within the tertiary section of American education continue to be peripheral to the dominant Anglocentric agenda in the university system. Figure 16.1 illustrates the interaction of race, gender, and class relations in a sex-dominant situation. In this model of nonsynchrony, relations of sexual antagonism and solidarity are augmented, while race and class relations are diminished. The principal sources of conflict, mobilization, and countermobilization within given educational institutions may then be around issues concerning gender relations: sexual harassment, women's studies, new codes of conduct within the university with regards to relations between the sexes, and so forth. This might not necessarily mean that issues around race are totally ignored. Indeed, one result might be that issues concerning minority women and their interests and aspirations would become more directly strategic and pivotal in the overall effort to secure reform in race relations in education—a situation in which it could be said that race-relations struggles in education benefited from a highly augmented focus on issues concerning gender. (Clearly the reverse was true in the 1960s.)

Within the current sociological and educational literature, there are a number of practical examples of the contradictory effects of the intersection of race, class, and gender in settings inside and outside schools that can help to illustrate the nonsynchronous model I have outlined.

The work of researchers such as Omi and Winant and Sarup directs our attention to the issues of nonsynchrony and contradiction in minority/majority relations in education and society and suggests not only their complexity but the impossibility of predicting the effects of these dynamic relations in any formulaic way based on a monolithic view of race.[52] In their discussion of educational and political institutions, Omi and Winant and Sarup have emphasized the fact that racial and sexual antagonisms can, at times, cut at right angles to class solidarity. The work of Marable and Spring focuses our attention in the opposite direction by pointing to the way in which class antagonisms have tended to undermine racial solidarity among minority groups involved in mainstream institutions.[53] For instance, Marable and Spring argue that since the civil rights gains of the 1960s, there has been a powerful socioeconomic and cultural division within the African American community. This has been principally expressed in terms of the evolution of an upwardly mobile Black middle class that has sought to distance itself in social, educational, and political terms from an increasingly impoverished Black underclass. Spring contends that such class antagonism operates as a determining variable in critical relationships between the Black community and mainstream educational institutions. As we shall see, such class antagonism also influences, and is vitally influenced by, the endogenous relations of differentiation already existing within the school setting.

As a case in point, Spring reports on a longitudinal study of the class dynamics operating within a Black suburban community ("Black Suburbia") and the way in which these dynamics get expressed in the relationship of Black students and their parents to the school system.[54] Spring's account begins in the mid 1960s, when a Black professional middle-class (PMC) population moved into a midwestern suburb formerly populated predominantly by whites. The new residents of Black Suburbia quickly embraced the predominantly white-administered school system. As the constituents of the "new" middle class in the district, Black PMC parents and their children readily granted legitimacy to the existing relations of differentiation (cultural selection, competition, and so forth) operating in the schools in exchange for access to "quality education." They saw the schools as guarantors of continued upward mobility for their children. According to Spring:

A study of the community [Black Suburbia] in the late 1960s showed the
mobility concerns and educational aspirations of the new black population. . . . The study found that both the middle-aged and young middle-
class black residents had high expectations of upward mobility and believed
that *quality* schools were a major element in *quality* community. The population group labeled ''New, Middle-Aged, Black Middle-Class Residents''
were earning more than $10,000 a year and were employed as managers,
proprietors, and professionals. This group was found to have an ''extraor-
dinarily high degree'' of expectations for continuing upward mobility and
concern about the quality of schools.[55]

The term *quality school* indeed summarized an ideological and strategic
trade-off or ''settlement'' that was tacitly implicated in the overwhelming
Black PMC support for the white-administered school system. But this settlement between the school system and its new PMC patrons was soon to be
imperiled by a change in the demographic and cultural milieu of the Black
Suburbia community and its schools. And both the expectations of upward
mobility and the high educational aspirations of the Black PMC residents
who had arrived in the late 1960s were, by the 1970s, ''threatened by the
rapid influx of a poor black population.''[56] This influx of low-income Blacks
dramatically altered the social class composition of Black Suburbia: ''Between 1970 and 1973 the percentage of children from welfare families increased . . . from 16 to 51 percent. In other words, the migration of
upwardly mobile middle-class blacks was followed by the rapid migration of
black welfare families.''[57]

Teachers responded negatively to the entrance of increased numbers of
low-income Black students into the school system, and the ''standard of education'' in Black Suburbia schools declined:

One of the first things to happen was that the educational expectations of the
mainly white teachers and administrators in the school system began to fall.
This seemed to be caused by the assumption of the white school staff that
the blacks moving into the community were not interested in education and
would create major problems in the school system.[58]

These developments precipitated a crisis of legitimacy in the school system's relations to its Black constituents. However, the racial response of the
school system to the increasing numbers of Black students was not met or
challenged by a united front among the Black residents of Black Suburbia.
Indeed, class antagonism between the more affluent Blacks and the lower-
class Black residents intensified both in the schools and in the community.
PMC Black students blamed the lower-class students for the sharp decline in
educational standards in the schools. They complained that the teachers were

incapable of controlling the "rowdies"—a code word for low-income Black students. This class antagonism spilled over into the community. Many Black PMC parents expressed the fear that their children would be corrupted by the "rowdy-culture" of welfare kids who "were organized into natural street groupings," as one parent put it.[59] As class antagonism intensified, the more affluent Black parents took the further step of withdrawing their children from the public schools and sending them to private institutions. To put the matter directly, Black PMC parents lost confidence in the public schools because they perceived teachers as having failed to control the "corrupting" influence of low-income students, whom these parents blamed, along with their teachers, for the declining standard of education.

From the perspective of these PMC Black residents, the Black Suburbia school system had failed to deliver on its side of a tacit agreement, and Black students stood to suffer in competitive relations for credentials and long-term futures in the labor market. According to Spring's account, the racially motivated strategies of cultural selection that existed in the Black Suburbia schools had, as a response to the influx of low-income students, now come full circle to handicap Black middle-class youth as well. But ultimately, in this highly provocative racial situation, the response of the residents of Black Suburbia to their school system was highly contradictory and nonsynchronous. Racial dynamics and identity were clearly subverted by class interests and the powerful socioeconomic divides that existed among Blacks in this midwestern community. To say the least, the interests of Black PMC residents and their low-income counterparts diverged. Resulting class antagonism undermined racial solidarity among Black residents and weakened their collective ability to negotiate with the white-administered school system or challenge the racial basis of the poor-quality education that the public schools were offering to their children.

Another example gets us closer to the nonsynchronous dynamics of unequal social relations in a number of classrooms in the United States. Based on findings from a study of "face-to-face interactions" in six desegregated elementary school classrooms in a midwestern industrial city, Linda Grant concludes that "Black females' experiences in desegregated schools . . . differ from those of other race-gender groups and cannot be fully understood . . . by extrapolating from the research on females or research on blacks."[60] Grant conducted detailed observations of the classrooms of six teachers (all women, three Blacks and three whites) at the two schools, Ridgeley and Glendon, involved in her two-year study.[61] Some 40 percent of the 139 students in the first-grade classrooms studied were Black. Among other things, Grant found that strategies of evaluation and cultural selection (tracking, ability grouping, and so forth) varied considerably according to "race-gender group" (Black males, Black females, white females, and white males). For instance, Black females were more likely than any other race-gender group to be labeled "non-academic."[62] This was particularly true of the evaluations by white teachers:

> White teachers, however, gave more attention to non-academic criteria. In fact, they made proportionally fewer comments of an academic nature about black girls than any other race-gender group. [For example,] assessments of black females contrasted markedly with these teachers' assessments of white males, for which academic criteria predominated.[63]

While teachers identified both Black and white females as more mature and "helpful" than their male counterparts, white girls were more likely to be labeled as "cognitively mature and ready for school."[64] In contrast, Black girls were labeled as "socially mature," and Grant contends that teachers exploited this "social maturity." Teachers' strategies of cultural selection also had an impact on domination relations of teacher to student and student to student in these first-grade classrooms. Thus, teachers tended to deploy Black girls as "go-betweens" when they wanted to communicate rules and convey messages informally to Black boys.[65] Race-gender group differences were also reproduced in terms of the first graders' access to instructional opportunity, as well as in the students' informal relations and orientation to teachers in the Ridgeley and Glendon elementary schools:

> Although generally compliant with teachers' rules, black females were less tied to teachers than white girls were and approached them only when they had a specific need to do so. White girls spent more time with teachers, prolonging questions into chats about personal issues. Black girls' contacts were briefer, more task related, and often on behalf of a peer rather than self.[66]

Black males were even less likely than Black females—or any other race-gender group—to have extended chats with teachers. And relations between Black males and their female teachers were defined by mutual estrangement. Indeed, Grant suggests in another article based on the same data that these teachers were afraid of or "threatened" by their Black male students. Nevertheless, teachers tended to identify at least one Black male in each class whom they singled out as an academic achiever or a "superstar."[67] In none of the six elementary school classrooms that Grant studied was any of the Black girls singled out as a high academic achiever.[68] Instead, Grant maintains, Black girls were typified as "average achievers" and assigned to "average" or "below average" track placements and ability groups.

Ultimately, the effects of the processes of cultural selection that existed in the classrooms that Grant observed were nonsynchronous. Teachers did not relate to their Black students or white students in any consistent or monolithic way. Gender differences powerfully influenced and modified the differential ways in which teachers evaluated, assessed, diagnosed, labeled, and tracked Black and white students. The influence of gender on the racial response of teachers to their students was particularly evident in the case of Black females. In significant ways, teachers emphasized the social, caring, and nurturing qualities of the Black females in their first-grade classrooms. In subtle ways, teachers encouraged "black girls to pursue social contacts, rather than press towards high academic achievement."[69] Consequently, Grant concludes that desegregated education at the elementary schools she studied had unintended negative (racial) costs for all Black children. The processes of cultural selection that operated in the desegregated classrooms she observed worked to the disadvantage of Black children with respect to competition for instructional opportunity, teacher time, and resources in these schools. Grant also suggests that existing processes of cultural differentiation not only served to constrain the structure of educational opportunity available to Black students within the school setting, but also helped to structure their incorporation into exploitation relations from the very start of their school careers. For Black females these costs were particularly severe and were determined strongly by gender. This meant that Black girls' experiences in the six desegregated classrooms were systematically nonsynchronous or qualitatively different from those of Black boys or any other race-gender group:

> The emphasis on black girls' social rather than academic skills, which occurs particularly in white-teacher classrooms, might point to a hidden cost of desegregation for black girls. Although they are usually the top students in black classes, they lose this stature to white children in desegregated rooms. Their development seems to become less balanced, with emphasis on social skills. . . . Black girls' everyday schooling experiences seem more likely to nudge them toward stereotypical roles of black women than toward [academic] alternatives. These include serving others and maintaining peaceable ties among diverse persons rather than developing one's own skills.[70]

CONCLUSION

The findings of curriculum and educational researchers such as Grant and Spring help to illustrate and clarify the complex workings of racial logics in the highly differentiated environment that exists in school settings.[71] By drawing attention to contradiction and nonsynchrony in educational processes of cultural selection, competition, exploitation, and domination, these critical researchers directly challenge mainstream single-group studies of inequality in schooling that have tended to isolate the variable of race from gender

and class. Instead, the work of Grant and others underscores the need to examine the historical specificity and variability of race and its nonsynchronous
interaction with forms of class and gender structuration in education. Monolithic theories of racial inequality suppress such an understanding of these
complexities and treat racial groups as biological and cultural "unities."[72]

The nonsynchronous approach to the study of inequality in schooling
alerts us to the fact that different race-class-gender groups not only have qualitatively different experiences in schools, but actually exist in constitutive
tension, often engage in active competition with each other, receive different
forms of rewards, sanctions, and evaluation, and are ultimately structured
into differential futures. The critical theoretical and practical task, then, as
Hall suggests, is one of "radically decoding" the specific relations and nuances of particular historical and institutional contexts:

> One needs to know how different groups were inserted historically, and the
> relations which have tended to erode and transform, or to preserve these dis-
> tinctions through time—not simply as residues and traces of previous
> modes, but as active structuring principles of the present society. Racial cat-
> egories *alone* will *not* provide or explain these.[73]

The work of Grant, Spring, and Sarup has furthered our understanding
of the complex workings of race and other dynamics in educational
institutions.[74] Their findings are also important in helping us to deconstruct
the multiple determination of power in the school setting and the way in
which such micropolitics can undermine the viability of conventional approaches to curriculum reform. What is abundantly clear is that monolithic or
homogeneous strategies of curriculum reform that attempt to ignore or avoid
the contradictions of race, class, and gender at the institutional level will be
of limited usefulness to minority youth. At the same time, though, new approaches to race-relations reform in education must begin with a more sophisticated and robust conceptualization of the dynamic relations between
minority and majority actors in the school setting. In this regard, efforts to
get beyond essentialism, reductionism, and dogmatism in current theories of
race relations in education would constitute a very good place to start.

Notes

INTRODUCTION

1. bell hooks, *Talking Back: Thinking Feminist, Thinking Black* (Boston: South End Press, 1989), 78.

CHAPTER 1

1. R. Mickelson and M. L. Oliver, "The Demographic Fallacy of the Black Academic: Does Quality Rise to the Top?" in *College in Black and White: Black Students on Black and White Campuses,* eds. W. Allen, E. Epps, and N. Haniff (Albany: SUNY Press, 1991a); R. Mickelson and M. L. Oliver, "Making the Short List: Black Faculty in Higher Education," in *The Racial Crisis in Higher Education: Problems and Solutions,* P. Altbach and K. Lomotey, (Albany: SUNY Press, 1991b). The absolute number of African American Ph.D.'s awarded each year in this country as well as the proportion of total degrees granted to Blacks, declined between 1975 and 1985; see M. W. Hirschorn, "Doctorates Earned by Blacks Declined 26.5 Pct. in Decade," *Chronicle of Higher Education* 35(3 February, 1988): A1, and G. E. Thomas, "Black Students in U.S. Graduate and Professional Schools in the 1980's: A National and Institutional Assessment," *Harvard Educational Review* 57(3, 1987): 261–282. According to the U.S. Department of Education, 1,253 Blacks received Ph.D.'s in 1975 (3.8 percent of the total awarded), as compared to 1,154 in 1985 (3.5 percent of all new doctorates). Moreover, the rates at which African Americans received bachelor's and master's degrees also declined during this period. The decrease is most dramatic at the master's level where proportions of total degrees awarded to African Americans dropped from 6.6 percent in 1975 to 4.9 percent in 1985 (National Center for Educational Statistics, Digest of Educational Statistics, [Washington, D.C.: United States Government Printing Office, 1988]). Because more than one-half of all doctorates awarded to Blacks are in education, the actual pool of potential faculty for academic positions in the physical and natural sciences, the humanities, and the social sciences

is actually smaller than the data initially suggest. Unfortunately, an analysis of the factors which contribute to the narrowing academic pipeline for minorities is beyond the scope of this essay.

2. Clearly there is a gender crisis in higher education as well. Women work disproportionately in the lower ranks of the academic hierarchy. While we recognize the importance of gender discrimination, especially for women of color, we will focus on the racial crisis in higher education in this essay.

3. The following discussion draws heavily on the excellent biography of Just by Kenneth R. Manning, *Black Apollo of Science: The Life of Ernest Everett Just* (New York: Oxford University Press, 1983). A general account of the exclusion of early Black scholars is found in M. R. Winston, "Through the Back Door: Academic Racism and the Negro Scholar in Historical Perspective," *Daedelus* 100 (1971). J. J. Casso and G. D. Roman, *Chicanos in Higher Education,* (Albuquerque: University of New Mexico Press, 1975) provide an overview of similar phenomena among Chicanos in academia.

4. R. Manning, *Black Apollo of Science:* 227.

5. M. de la Luz Reyes and J. Halcon, "Racism in Academia: The Old Wolf Revisited," *Harvard Educational Review* 58(3): 299–314.

6. R. Clark, phone interview with first author (15 June, 1990).

7. R. Clark, *Family Life and School Achievement* (Chicago: University of Chicago Press, 1986). J. McCurdy, "Cal. Jury Awards $1-Million to Teacher Who Charged Racism in Tenure Denial," *Chronicle of Higher Education* (25 April, 1990): All; C. McGraw, "Jury Awards Black Professor $1 Million in Bias Suit Against College," *Los Angeles Times,* 29 March, 1990: B1.

8. R. Clark, phone interview with first author (15 June, 1990); J. McCurdy, "Cal. Jury Awards $1-Million."

9. J. M. Brodie and E. Wiley, III, "The Campus Wide Trauma of Discrimination Litigation," *Black Issues in Higher Education* 7(14, 1990): 1; B. Lee and G. La Noei, *Academics in Court* (New York: Simon and Schuster, 1987).

10. H. Edwards, *Black Students* (New York: Free Press, 1970); J. Prager, "Equal Opportunity and Affirmative Action: The Rise of New Social Understandings," *Research in Law, Deviance, and Social Control* 4(1982): 191–218.

11. There are three ways that preferential treatment in hiring can come about. The first is involuntary and has its origins in section 706 (g) of Title VII of the Civil Rights Act. If the courts find that the respondent has intentionally engaged in unlawful employment practices, the court may enjoin the respondent from further discrimination and order such remedial action as may be appropriate. This may involve gender and/or racial quotas, and in addition to occurring in less than 5 percent of the preferential treatment cases, exists only when a court finds an employer guilty of inten-

tional discriminatory employment practices. The second type of preferential treatment, and most common, is voluntary affirmative action where an employer without a prior court finding of guilt, sets up a voluntary affirmative action program that favors protected groups. The third instance is that of federal contractors who are required by law to engage in affirmative action. It is important to understand what affirmative action guidelines are:

> An affirmative action program is a set of specific and result-oriented procedures to which a contractor commits to supply every *good-faith effort* [authors' italics]. The objective of those procedures plus such efforts is equal employment opportunity. An acceptable affirmative action program must include an analysis of areas within which the contractor is deficient in the utilization of minority groups and women, and further, goals and timetables to which the contractor's good-faith efforts must be directed to correct the deficiencies and thus to increase materially the utilization of minorities and women at all levels and in all segments of the work force where deficiencies exist (Revised Order No. 4, Office of Federal Contract Compliance Programs, U.S. Department of Labor, 1978).

Affirmative action guidelines are *good-faith efforts,* not race/gender quotas cast in concrete, as many critics of preferential policies would have us believe. Technically, the Civil Rights Act only prohibits discrimination. Executive orders give rise to affirmative action guidelines. As such, affirmative action, as we know it, could be wiped out by an executive order from George Bush (S. Nkomo, personal communication with first author, 10 September, 1990). The legal essence of affirmative action consists primarily of court opinions. The authors wish to thank Stella Nkomo for her help in both clarifying these issues and providing definitions of the types of preferential policies relevant to our discussion.

12. J. Fleming, G. R. Gil, and D. H. Swinton, *The Case for Affirmative Action for Blacks in Higher Education* (Washington, D.C.: Howard University Press, 1978); N. Smelser and R. Content, *The Changing Academic Market Place* (Berkeley: University of California Press, 1980).

13. Adams v. Califano, Civil Action No. 3095-70, U.S. District Court, Washington, D.C., 1971.

14. J. H. Braddock, II, and J. M. McPartland, "How Minorities Continue to be Excluded from Equal Employment Opportunities: Research on Labor Market and Institutional Barriers," *Journal of Social Issues* 43(1987): 5–40; J. H. Braddock, II, and J. M. McPartland, "Social Science Evidence and Affirmative Action Policies," *Journal of Social Issues* 43(1987): 133–144.

15. Braddock and McPartland, "How Minorities Continue to Be Excluded," 18.

16. Ibid., 12.

17. James Coverdill, "Personal Contacts, the Recruitment Efforts of Firms, and Labor Market Outcomes," (unpublished doctoral dissertation, Northwestern University, 1991.)

18. Braddock, II and McPartland, "How Minorities Continue to Be Excluded," 27–29.

19. Smelser and Content, *The Changing Academic Market Place.*

20. N. Glazer, *Affirmative Discrimination* (New York: Basic Books, 1978); G. C. Loury, "Beyond Civil Rights," in *The State of Black America,* ed. J. D. Williams. (New York: National Urban League, 1986): 163–74; J. Sowell, *Affirmative Action Reconsidered: Was It Necessary in Academia?* (Washington, D.C.: American Enterprise Institute, 1975); S. Steele, "A Negative Vote on Affirmative Action," *New York Times Magazine,* 13 May, 1990, 46; S. Steele, *The Content of Their Character* (New York: Harper, 1990).

21. D. M. Gilford and J. Snyder, *Women and Minority Ph.D.s in the 1970's: A Data Book* (Washington, D.C.: National Research Council, 1977); J. Duster, "The Structure of Privilege and Its Universe of Discourse," *The American Sociologist* 11 (1976): 73–78.

22. W. H. Exum, "Climbing the Crystal Stair: Values, Affirmative Action, and Minority Faculty," *Social Problems* 30(1983): 393.

23. T. Caplow and R. McGee, *The Academic Marketplace,* (New York: Basic Books, 1958); Smelser and Content, *The Changing Academic Market Place.*

24. T. Caplow and R. McGee, *The Academic Marketplace,* 120.

25. R. Turner, "Sponsored and Contest Mobility and the School System," *American Sociological Review* 25(1960): 855–67.

26. Smelser and Content, *The Changing Academic Market Place,* 27.

27. D. Davidson, "The Furious Passage of the Black Graduate Student," in J. Ladner, *The Death of White Sociology,* in ed. J. Ladner. (New York: Vintage, 1973).

28. Gilford and Snyder, *Women and Minority Ph.D.'s.*

29. G. E. Thomas, "Black Students in U.S. Graduate and Professional Schools in the 1980s: A National and Institutional Assessment," *Harvard Educational Review* 57(3, 1987): 261–82.

30. W. R. Allen, A. Haddad, and M. Kirkland, *Preliminary Report. Graduate and Professional Survey* (Ann Arbor, Mich: National Study of Black College Students, University of Michigan, 1982); W. R. Allen, E. G. Epps, and N. A. Haniff, eds., *College in Black and White: Black Students on Black and White Campuses* (Albany: SUNY Press, in press).

31. Allen, Epps, and Haniff, eds., *College in Black and White.*

32. For a complete description of our data, creation of variables, statistical procedures used to conduct the analyses, see Mickelson and Oliver "The Demographic Fallacy of the Black Academic," and Mickelson and Oliver, "Making the Short List."

33. Comparing grades across institutions is always difficult for researchers who seek a reliable indicator of performance. Used as the sole indicator of graduate students' quality across institutions, GPA might be problematic. But because grades are only one of the elements that constitute the quality index, we believe that the measure is sufficiently reliable to test our hypotheses.

34. Because the students in the NSBCS sample range from first-year graduate students to those in the process of writing a dissertation, it would be inappropriate to demand that first-year students meet the same standards in our measure of quality as fourth- or fifth-year students. Therefore we used a sliding scale that takes into account the natural history, the development, and the maturation of students in graduate school.

35. A complete description of the variable is available upon request from the authors.

36. D. Gottfredson, "Black and White Differences in the Educational Attainment Process," *American Sociological Review* 46(1981): 448–472.

37. Braddock and McPartland, "Social Science Evidence."

38. M. Omi, "The 'New' Racism: Contemporary Racial Ideologies," paper presented at the annual meetings of the American Sociological Association, Washington, D.C., 1990.

39. Loury, *Beyond Civil Rights;* J. Sowell, *Preferential Policies: An International Perspective* (New York: William Morrow, 1990).

40. Steele, "A Negative Vote on Affirmative Action."

41. T. F. Pettigrew and J. Martin, "Shaping the Organizational Context for Black American Inclusion," *Journal of Social Issues* 43(1987): 41–78.

42. C. Ray and R. Mickelson, "Restructuring Students for Restructured Work: The Economy, School Reform, and Noncollege Bound Youth," *Sociology of Education* 65(3, 1992).

43. Pettigrew and Martin, "Shaping the Organizational Context."

44. M. Spence, *Market Signaling: Information Transfer in Hiring and Related Processes* (Cambridge, Mass: Harvard University Press, 1973); M. Spence, "Job Market Signaling," *Quarterly Journal of Economics* 87(1973): 355–74; Coverdill, "Personal Contacts"; Braddock and McPartland, "Social Science Evidence and Affirmative Action Policies."

45. Coverdill, "Personal Contacts".

46. R. Alvarez, "Comment" (on Hernandez, Strauss, and Driver, "The Misplaced Emphasis on Opportunity for Minorities and Women in Sociology"), *The American Sociologist* 8(1973): 124.

CHAPTER 2

1. Jeannie Oakes, *Keeping Track: How Schools Structure Inequality* (New Haven: Yale University Press, 1985).

2. See, for example, Lois Weis, ed., *Class, Race, and Gender in American Education* (Albany: State University of New York Press, 1988); Ann Bastian, et al., *Choosing Equality: The Case for Democratic Schooling* (New York: New World Foundation, 1985); and Carl A. Grant and Christine Sleeter, "Race, Class, and Gender in Educational Research: An Argument for Integrative Analysis," *Review of Educational Research* 56(1986): 195–211.

3. I have referred to gifted education as the "new meritocracy" (Mara Sapon-Shevin, "Giftedness as a Social Construct," *Teachers College Record* 89(1, Fall 1987): 45) Michelle Fine refers to the "justice of unjust outcomes" (Michelle Fine, "Expert Testimony for Englewood School District Case, in Massachusetts Advocacy Center, *Locked In/Locked Out: Tracking and Placement Practices in Boston Public Schools* (Boston: Massachusetts Advocacy Center, 1990). June 1987); and Jeannie Oakes has described ability grouping as "the most legitimate basis for differentiation (Jeannie Oakes, "Tracking in Mathematics and Science Education: A Structural Contribution to Unequal Schooling," in Lois Weis, ed., *Class, Race, and Gender in American Education*, 119.)

4. See, for example, Mara Sapon-Shevin and Mayer Shevin, "Issues for Parents: Implications of the "Gifted Label," in Roberta M. Felker, ed., *A Parent's Guide to the Education of Preschool Gifted Children* (Washington, D.C.: Council of State Directors of Programs for the Gifted and the National Association of State Boards of Education, 1982).

5. Mihaly Csikszentmihalyi and Rick E. Robinson, "Culture, Time, and the Development of Talent," in Robert J. Sternberg and Janet E. Davidson, eds., *Conceptions of Giftedness* (New York: Cambridge University Press, 1986), 266.

6. Steven Selden, "The Use of Biology to Legitimate Inequality: The Eugenics Movement within the High School Biology Textbook, 1914–1949", in Walter Secada, ed., *Equity in Education* (New York: Falmer Press, 1989), 118–45.

7. See, for example, B. Farber, *Mental Retardation: Its Social Context and Social Consequences* (Boston: Houghton Mifflin, 1968); Steven A. Gelb, "From Moral Imbecility to Maladaptive Behavior: The Social Construction of Educable Mental Retardation," paper presented at the annual meeting of the American Educational Research Association, San Francisco, April 1986.

8. S. Marland, *Education of the Gifted and Talented* (U.S. Commission of Education, 92d Congress, 2d Session, Washington, D.C.: United States Copyright and Printing Office, 1972. [Commonly known as the Marland Report.]

9. Alfred Gitelson, Judge, County of Los Angeles Superior Court Case 822854, cited in *Gifted and Talented Education 1989–1990*, Grand Forks Public Schools.

10. Marland, *Education of the Gifted and Talented.*

11. James J. Gallagher and Patricia Weiss, *The Education of Gifted and Talented Students: A History and Prospectus* (Washington, D.C.: Council for Basic Education, 1979), 1.

12. Kerry Freedman, "Dilemmas of Equity in Art Education: Ideologies of Individualism and Cultural Capital," in Walter Secada, ed., *Equity in Education* (New York: Falmer Press), 110.

13. Gallagher and Weiss, *Education of Gifted and Talented Students,* 30.

14. Ibid., 32–33.

15. James T. Webb, Elizabeth A. Meckstroth, and Stephanie S. Tolan, *Guiding the Gifted Child: A Practical Source for Parents and Teachers* (Columbus, Ohio: Ohio Psychology, 1982), 26.

16. Virginia Ehrlich, *Gifted Children: A Guide for Parents and Teachers* (Englewood Cliffs, N.J.: Prentice-Hall, 1982), 33–34.

17. Mara Sapon-Shevin, "Explaining Giftedness to Parents: Why it Matters What Professionals Say," *Roeper Review* 9(3, 1987), 180–84.

18. Stephanie S. Tolan, "Parents and 'Professionals': A Question of Priorities," *Roeper Review* 9(3, 1987), 185.

19. Heritage Foundation, "The Crisis: Washington Shares the Blame," *The Heritage Foundation Backgrounder* (Washington, D.C.: Heritage Foundation, 1984).

20. Freedman, "Dilemmas of Equity in Art Education," 110.

21. David Fetterman, *Excellence and Equality: A Qualitatively Different Perspective on Gifted and Talented Education* (Albany: State University of New York Press, 1988), 1.

22. Ibid., 5.

23. Ibid., 123.

24. Ibid., 127.

25. Sapon-Shevin, "Giftedness as a Social Construct."

26. Ehrlich, *Gifted Children,* 167.

27. Michael Apple, *Education and Power* (Boston: Routledge & Kegan Paul, 1982), 40.

28. Michelle Fine, "De-Institutionalizing Educational Inequity," in Council of Chief State School Officers, ed., *At Risk Youth: Policy and Research* (New York: Harcourt Brace Jovanovich, 1988), 110.

29. M. Sapon-Shevin, "Gifted Education in the Deskilling of Regular Classroom Teachers," *Journal of Teacher Education* 41(1, 1990): 39–48; M. Sapon-Shevin, *Playing Favorites: Gifted Education and Disruption of Community* (forthcoming from SUNY Press).

30. Massachusetts Advocacy Center, *Locked In/Locked Out*.

31. Ibid., v.

32. Boston Latin School, "A Response to *Locked In/Locked Out: Tracking and Placement in Boston Public Schools* (Boston: Boston Latin School, 1990).

33. Christine LaCerva, "Curriculum and the Inner City Classroom: Sexuality and Social Change," in James Sears, ed., *Sexuality and the Curriculum* (New York: Teachers College Press, in press).

34. John Dewey, *The School and Society* (Chicago: University of Chicago Press, 1989), 3.

35. Fine, "De-institutionalizing Educational Inequity," 111–13.

36. Ibid., 112.

CHAPTER 3

1. This brief historical account of testing and minorities does not attempt to discuss the broader matter of how standardized testing developed in the United States and in Europe. For a more detailed history of standardized testing, see Walter Haney, "Testing Reasoning and Reasoning about Testing," *Review of Educational Research* 54(4, 1984): 597–654.

2. Richard Kluger, *Simple Justice: The History of Brown v. Board of Education and Black America's Struggle for Equality* (New York: Vintage Books, 1977).

3. Carl Brigham, *A Study of American Intelligence* (Princeton, N.J.: Princeton University Press, 1923). Brigham recanted his racist interpretation of the WWI army test scores as early as 1930. See Stephen J. Gould, *The Mismeasure of Man* (New York: Norton, 1981), for a discussion.

4. Joint Center for Political Studies. *Visions of a Better Way: A Black Appraisal of Public Schooling.* (Washington, D.C.: Joint Center for Political Studies, 1989).

5. Gould, *Mismeasure of Man;* Kluger, *Simple Justice.*

6. L. M. Terman. (Ed) *Intelligence Tests and School Reorganization* (Yonkers-on-Hudson, NY: World Book Company, 1922). Paul D. Chapman. *Schools as Sorters: Lewis M. Terman and the Intelligence Testing Movement, 1890–1930*, Ph.D. dissertation, Stanford University, 1980. Univ. Microfilms No. 80-11615.

7. Paul D. Chapman. *Schools as Sorters,* 103–4.

8. David A. Goslin, *Teachers and Testing* (New York: Russell Sage Foundation, 1967), 20.

9. Jeannie Oakes, *Keeping Track: How Schools Structure Inequality* (New Haven, Conn.: Yale University Press, 1985).

10. Gould, *Mismeasure of Man,* 96–97.

11. James S. Coleman, E. Q. Campbell, C. J. Hobson, J. McPartland, A. M. Mood, F. D. Weinfield, and R. L. York, *Equality of Educational Opportunity* (Washington, D.C.: U.S. Government Printing Office, 1966), as summarized in Robert L. Linn, "Ability Testing: Individual Differences, Prediction, and Differential Prediction," in *Ability Testing: Uses, Consequences, and Controversies, Part Two.* Edited by A. K. Wigdor and W. R. Garner. (Washington, D.C.: National Academy Press, 1982, pp. 365–66.

12. Fred E. Crossland, *Minority Access to College: A Report to the Ford Foundation* (New York: Schocken Books, 1971), 58.

13. In this introduction to mathematical concepts concerning testing, I largely avoid mathematical formulas and omit discussion of more complex issues such as sample versus population measures, and the concept of statistical significance.

14. Arthur R. Jensen, *Bias in Mental Testing* (New York: Free Press, 1980), 98.

15. National Commission on Testing and Public Policy. *From Gatekeeper to Gateway: Transforming Testing in America* (Chestnut Hill, Mass.: National Commission on Testing and Public Policy, 1990)

16. Walt Haney, George Madaus, and Amelia Kreitzer, "Charms Talismanic; Testing Teachers for the Improvement of American Education," *Review of Research in Education* 14(1987): 169–238. Though in general Black Americans, Hispanic Americans, Asian Americans, and American Indians have been shown, on the average, to score lower than whites on a wide range of standardized tests, as noted in the literature cited above, the magnitudes of differences vary for different minority groups, as we illustrate later in this chapter.

17. C. P. Backer, quoted in Daniel J. Kevles, *In the Name of Eugenics: Genetics and the Uses of Human Heredity* (Berkeley: University of California Press, 1986), 171. See also Mary Jo Bane and Christopher Jencks, "Five Myths about Your IQ," in *The IQ Controversy,* ed. N. J. Block and G. Dworkin (New York: Pantheon, 1976), 325–38).

18. Ina V. S. Mullis, Eugene H. Owen, and Gary W. Phillips. *Accelerating Academic Achievement: A Summary of Findings from Twenty Years of NAEP* (Princeton, N.J.: National Assessment of Educational Progress, Educational Testing Service, September, 1990), 39.

19. Mullis, Owen, and Phillips, report that from 1971 to 1988 the average Black-white gap narrowed 33 points for seventeen-year-olds, 21 points for thirteen-year-olds and 16 points for nine-year-olds (*Accelerating Academic Achievement*, 42). They do not report standard deviations of NAEP scores, but given standard deviations of 35, 37, and 41 for these three age (or grade) levels reported in Langer, Applebee, Mullis, and Foertsch, the decreases amount, respectively, to 94, 57, and 37 percent of a standard deviation of the 1988 scores. According to Langer, Applebee, Mullis, and Foertsch, the average reading proficiency gap between Blacks and whites has thus been reduced to about two-thirds of a standard deviation at all three grade levels. (Judith A. Langer, Arthur A. Applebee, Ina V. S. Mullis, and Mary A. Foertsch, *Learning to Read in Our Nation's Schools: Instruction and Achievement in 1988 at Grades 4, 8, and 12* (Princeton, N.J.: National Assessment of Educational Progress, Educational Testing Service, 19-R-02, 1990).

20. Gerald David Jaynes and Robin M. Williams, *A Common Destiny: Blacks and American Society* (Washington, D.C.: National Academy Press, 1990), 349–352, discuss the possibilities that school desegregation and compensatory education programs may be the causes of the decreasing Black-white achievement gap revealed by the NAEP results.

21. Jaynes and Williams, *A Common Destiny*.

22. Joel Spring, *The Sorting Machine: National Educational Policy Since 1945* (New York: David McKay, 1976), 218.

23. Lois Weis, Eleanor Farrar, and Hugh Petrie. *Dropouts from School: Issues, Dilemma, and Solutions* (Albany: State University of New York Press, 1989).

24. Thomas D. Snyder, *Digest of Education Statistics* (Washington, D.C.: U.S. Government Printing Office, 1987), 86. With regard to use of such census data to estimate dropout rates, Jaynes and Williams (*A Common Destiny*) note that it is difficult to reconcile estimates from Bureau of the Census surveys indicating rates of young Black high school completion of around 75 percent with other reports that high school dropout rates among Blacks are as high as 50 percent. They suggest that part of the explanation for the discrepancy may be that young high school dropouts are less likely to be reached in census surveys and thus such surveys may underestimate current dropout rates.

25. Amelia Kreitzer, George Madaus, and Walt Haney, "Competency Testing and Dropouts," in Weis, Farrar, and Petrie, eds., *Dropouts from School*, 129–52.

26. John E. Cawthorne, *"Tough" Graduation Standards and "Good" Kids*. Chestnut Hill, Mass.: Boston College, Center for the Study of Testing, Evaluation and Educational Policy, 1990.

27. Elinor Woods and Walt Haney, *Does Vocational Education Make a Difference: A Review of Previous Research and Reanalyses of National Longitudinal Data Sets* Cambridge, Mass.: Huron Institute, 1981.

28. National Commission on Testing and Public Policy, *From Gatekeeper to Gateway;* and Oakes, *Keeping Track.*

29. John T. Grasso and John R. Shea, *Vocational Education and Training: Impact on Youth* (Berkeley, Calif.: Carnegie Council on Policy Studies in Higher Education, 1979), 6.

30. Oakes, *Keeping Track.*

31. These consequences are obvious because, in order to select 40 percent of a group on a test whose scores are normally distributed (and standardized tests are typically created so as to yield normal distributions of scores), it is necessary to set a cutoff score at about one-quarter of a standard deviation about the mean of the entire group. Since, given the circumstances described above, the mean of nonminorities will be slightly higher than the mean for all, this will have the consequence of selecting somewhat more than 40 percent of the nonminorities. However, this cutscore would be at least one full standard deviation above the mean of nonminorities, and only about 16 percent of scores fall higher than one standard deviation above the mean for that group.

32. Jaynes and Williams, *A Common Destiny.*

33. Lyle V. Jones, "The Influence on Mathematics Test Scores, by Ethnicity and Sex, of Prior Achievement and High School Mathematics Courses," *Journal for Research in Mathematics Education* 18(3, 1987): 180–86. Lyle V. Jones, Nancy W. Burton, and Ernest C. Jr Davenport, "Monitoring the Mathematics Achievement of Black Students," *Journal for Research in Mathematics Education* 15(2, 1984): 154–64.

34. Analyzing NAEP data from 1976, Jones, Burton, and Davenport showed that access to advanced courses varies not just within schools also between schools. Students in schools with more than 80 percent white student populations took, on average, a half year of math more than students in schools that were less than 50 percent white ("Monitoring Mathematics Achievement," 162).

35. Christopher Jencks, Michael Smith, Henry Acland, Mary Jo Bane, David Cohen, Herbert Gintis, Barbara Heyns, and Stephen Michelson, *Inequality: A Reassessment of the Effect of Family and Schooling in America* (New York: Basic Books, 1972).

36. This quote is from page 3 of the 1979 court decision on the Larry P. case. For more discussion of these court cases and others concerning educational testing, see Haney, "Testing Reasoning."

37. George F. Madaus, Peter W. Airasian, and Thomas Kellaghan, *School Effectiveness: A Reassessment of the Evidence* (New York: McGraw-Hill, 1980), 116–18.

38. R. L. Williams, D. Mosby, and V. Hinson, *Critical Issues in Achievement Testing of Children from Diverse Educational Backgrounds* (Washington, D.C.: U.S.

Office of Education, 1976. Joan Bollenbacher, "The Testing Scene: Chaos and Controversy," in *Testing in the Public Interest: Proceedings of the 1976 ETS Invitational Conference* (Princeton, N.J.: Educational Testing Service, 1976).

39. Leonard Baird, "What Graduate and Professional School Students Think about Admissions Tests," *Measurement in Education* 7(3, 1977): 1–7. In noting these survey results, it is worth pointing out that not all surveys have shown tests to be viewed negatively by minority individuals. In a survey of students in North Carolina and Louisiana, for example, it was revealed that most Black students viewed those states' competency tests as fair and needed. Rodney J. Reed., *School and College Competency Testing Programs: Perceptions and Effects on the Black Students in Louisiana and North Carolina* (Atlanta, Ga.: Southern Education Foundation, 1987).

40. Ronald Flaugher, "The Many Definitions of Test Bias," *American Psychologist* 33(7) (July 1978): 671–79.

41. For the purposes of this chapter, the following discussion of test validity and bias is highly abbreviated. More detailed treatments may be found in A. Anastasi, *Psychological Testing* (New York: Macmillan, 1988). Robert L. Linn, "Ability Testing: Individual Differences, Prediction, and Differential Prediction, in *Ability Testing: Uses, Consequences, and Controversies, Part II*, ed. A. K. Wigdor and W. R. Garner (Washington, D.C.: National Academy Press, 1982) and A. K. Wigdor and W. R. Garner, eds., *Ability Testing: Uses, Consequences, and Controversies.* (Washington, D.C.: National Academy Press, 1982).

42. Thomas Donlon, *The College Board Technical Handbook for the Scholastic Aptitude Test and Achievement Tests* (New York: College Entrance Examination Board, 1984), 142.

43. Warren W. Willingham, Charles Lewis, Rick Morgan, and Leonard Ramist, *Predicting College Grades: An Analysis of Institutional Trends over Two Decades* (Princeton, N.J.: Educational Testing Service, 1990).

44. L. M. Terman, *The Intelligence of School Children, How Children Differ in Ability. The Use of Mental Tests in School Grading and the Proper Education of Exceptional Children* (Boston: Houghton, Mifflin, 1919) as reported in Peter Archer, *A Comparison of Teacher Judgements of Pupils and the Results of Standardised Tests*, Ph.D. dissertation, University College Cork, Ireland, 1979.

45. Linn, "Ability Testing," 335–88. Joseph D. Matarazzo, *Wechsler's Measurement and Appraisal of Adult Intelligence*, 5th ed. (Baltimore, Md.: Williams & Wilkins, 1972), 280–84.

46. Lee J. Cronbach, *Essentials of Psychological Testing* (New York: Harper & Row, 1961), 115.

47. A variety of studies have shown that the correlation between height and weight is in the range of 0.70–0.80. This means that height "explains" about half of

the variance in weight (0.70 squared is 0.49). In contrast, as noted in the text, test scores tend to explain only about one-quarter of the variance in grade point average.

48. C. Michael Pfeifer, Jr., and William E. Sedlacek, "The Validity of Academic Predictors for Black and White Students at a Predominantly White University," *Journal of Educational Measurement* 8(4, 1971): 253–61.

49. Donlon, *College Board Technical Handbook.*

50. Hunter M. Breland, *Population Validity and College Entrance Measures,* CEEB Research Memorandum 79-08 (New York: College Entrance Examination Board, 1979). Richard P. Duran, *Hispanics' Education and Background: Predictors of College Achievement* (New York: College Entrance Examination Board, 1983).

51. Boyd B. McCandless, Albert Roberts, and Thomas Starnes, "Teachers' Marks, Achievement Test Scores, and Aptitude Relations with Respect to Class, Race, and Sex," *Journal of Educational Psychology* 63(2, 1972): 153–59.

52. See Haney, *Testing Reasoning,* for a discussion.

53. The classic example of this problem is illustrated in Anscombe's quartet of four data sets, each having the same means and standard deviations on X and Y and the exact same correlation and regression relations between the two variables, but very different other relations between the two variables (e.g., non-linear relations). Edward R. Tufte, *The Visual Display of Quantitative Information* (Cheshire, Conn.: Graphics Press, 1983).

54. Jensen, *Bias in Mental Testing,* 515.

55. Linn, "Ability Testing," 384–85; Donlon, *College Board Technical Handbook,* 155–59.

56. Robert L. Thorndike, "Concepts of culture-fairness," *Journal of Educational Measurement* 8(2, 1971): 63–70.

57. Ibid., 67.

58. Ibid., 63.

59. It is worth noting that in much of the literature on decision consistency, people talk about positives, and negatives rather than passes and failures. However, since the term *positive* is used in somewhat contrary ways in some of this literature, and because it is normal to speak of passing and failing tests, we use "passes" instead of "positives" and "failures" instead of "negatives."

60. Nancy Cole, "Bias in Selection," *Journal of Educational Measurement* 10 (1973): 237–55.

61. Nancy Petersen and Melvin Novick, "An Evaluation of Some Models for Culture-fair Selection," *Journal of Educational Measurement* 13(1, 1976): 3–31.

62. Melvin Novick and D. Ellis, "Equal Opportunity in Educational and Employment Selection," *American Psychologist* 32(5, 1976): 306–20.

63. Jensen, *Bias in Mental Testing*, 454.

64. Donlon, *College Board Technical Handbook*, 141, 162–63. While data reported in the Donlon *Handbook* indicates that relatively small proportions of College Board members have conducted studies through the Board's Validity Study Service, surveys of college admissions officials indicate that around 45 to 50 percent of public four-year colleges report conducting or commissioning predictive validity studies. (AACRAO/College Board survey results cited in James Crouse and Dale Trusheim. *The Case Against the SAT* (Chicago: University of Chicago Press, 1988), 41–42.

65. Rodney Skager, "On the Use and Importance of Tests of Ability in Admission to Postsecondary Education," in Wigdor and Garner, *Ability Testing*, 286–314.

66. Donlon, *College Board Technical Handbook*, 143.

67. McCandless, Roberts, and Starnes, "Teachers' Marks."

68. Crouse and Trusheim, *The Case against the SAT*.

69. R. D. Goldman, D. E. Schmidt, B. N. Hewitt, and R. Fisher, "Grading Practices in Different Major Fields," *American Educational Research Journal* 11(1974): 343–57. R. D. Goldman and R. E. Slaughter, "Why College Grade Point Average is Difficult to Predict," *Journal of Educational Psychology* 68(1976): 9–12. Howard Kirschenbaum, Sidney B. Simon, and Rodney W. Napier, *Wad-ja-get? The Grading Game in American Education* (New York: Hart, 1971).

70. Walter Haney, "Testing Reasoning."

71. McCandless, Roberts, and Starnes, "Teachers' Marks." William L. Goodwin and James R. Sanders, *An Exploratory Study of the Effect of Selected Variables on Teacher Expectation of Pupil Success*, paper presented at the annual meeting of the American Educational Research Association. Los Angeles, 5–8 February 1969. Ray C. Rist, "Student Social Class and Teacher Expectations: The Self Fulfilling Prophecy in Ghetto Education," *Harvard Educational Review* 40(1970): 411–412.

72. Timothy Z. Keith, "Time Spent on Homework and High School Grades: A Large-sample Path Analysis," *Journal of Educational Psychology* 74(2, 1982): 248–53.

73. Jeremy D. Finn, "Expectations and the Educational Environment," *Review of Educational Research* 42(3, 1972): 387–410.

74. Lloyd G. Humphreys and Thomas Taber, "Postdiction Study of the Graduate Record Examination and Eight Semesters of College Grades," *Journal of Educational Measurement* 10(3, 1973): 179–84.

75. Keith, "Time Spent on Homework."

76. Alexander Astin. "Open Admissions and Programs for the Disadvantaged," *Journal of Higher Education* 42(1971): 620–47.

77. Jensen, *Bias in Mental Testing,* 46.

CHAPTER 4

*This paper appeared in *Harvard Educational Review,* vol. 58, no. 1, February 1988.

1. M. Focault, *The History of Sexuality,* vol. 1 (New York: Vintage Books, 1980).

2. The research reported in this article represents one component of a year-long ethnographic investigation of students and dropouts at a comprehensive public high school in New York City. Funded by the W. T. Grant Foundation, the research was designed to investigate how public urban high schools produce dropout rates in excess of 50 percent. The methods employed over the year included: in-school observations four days/week during the fall, and one to two days/week during the spring; regular (daily) attendance in a hygiene course for twelfth graders; an archival analysis of more than twelve hundred students who compose the 1978–79 cohort of incoming ninth graders; interviews with approximately fifty-five recent and long-term dropouts; analysis of fictional and autobiographical writings by students; a survey distributed to a subsample of the cohort population; and visits to proprietary schools, programs for Graduate Equivalency Diplomas, naval recruitment sites, and a public high school for pregnant and parenting teens. The methods and preliminary results of the ethnography are detailed in M. Fine, "Why Urban Adolescents Drop Into and Out of High School," *Teachers' College Record* 87(1986); 393–409.

3. L. Harris, *Public Attitudes about Sex Education, Family Planning, and Abortion in the United States* (New York: Louis Harris & Associates, 1985).

4. B. Kantrowitz, M. Hager, S. Winger, G. Carroll, G. Raine, D. Witherspoon, J. Huck, and S. Doherty, "Kids and Contraceptives," *Newsweek,* 16 February 1987, 54–65; J. Leo, "Sex and Schools," *Time,* 24 November 1986, 54–63.

5. G. Bauer, *The Family: Preserving America's Future* (Washington, D.C.: U.S. Department of Education, 1986).

6. Leo, "Sex and Schools," 54.

7. C. Smith-Rosenberg, "Sex as Symbol in Victorian Purity: An Ethnohistorical Analysis of Jacksonian America," *American Journal of Sociology* 84(1978): 212–247.

8. C. MacKinnon, "Complicity: An Introduction to Andrea Dworkin's 'Abortion,' Chapter 3, 'Right-Wing Women'," *Law and Inequality* 1(1983): 89–94.

9. W. Fisher, D. Byrne, and L. White, "Emotional Barriers to Contraception," in D. Byrne and W. Fisher, eds., *Adolescents, Sex, and Contraception* (Hillsdale, N.J.: Erlbaum, 1983), 207–39.

10. Fisher, Byrne, and White, "Emotional Barriers to Contraception."

11. C. Vance, *Pleasure and Danger* (Boston: Routledge and Kegan Paul, 1984).

12. G. Rubin, "Thinking Sex: Notes for a Radical Theory of the Politics of Sex," in C. Vance, ed., *Pleasure and Danger* (Boston: Routledge & Kegan Paul, 1984).

13. A. Lorde, "Uses of the Erotic: The Erotic as Power," paper presented at the Fourth Berkshire Conference on the History of Women, Mt. Holyoke College, August 1980.

14. "Koop's AIDS Stand Assailed," *New York Times*, March 1987, A25.

15. A. Snitow, C. Stansell, and S. Thompson, eds., *Powers of Desire* (New York: Monthly Review Press, 1983).

16. N. Freudenberg, "The Politics of Sex," *Health PAC Bulletin* (New York: Health PAC, 1987).

17. C. Golden, "Diversity and Variability in Lesbian Identities," paper presented at Lesbian Psychologies Conference of the Association of Women in Psychology, March 1984; R. Petcheskey, *Abortion and Woman's Choice* (New York: Longman, 1984); S. Thompson, "Search for Tomorrow: On Feminism and the Reconstruction of Teen Romance," in Snitow, Stansell, and Thompson, *Powers of Desire*.

18. P. Brown, "The Swedish Approach to Sex Education and Adolescent Pregnancy: Some Impressions," *Family Planning Perspectives* 15, 2(1983): 88.

19. Brown, "The Swedish Approach to Sex Education and Adolescent Pregnancy," 93.

20. Philadelphia School District, "Sex Education Curriculum," draft (1986); New York City Board of Education, *Family Living Curriculum Including Sex Education Grades K through 12* (New York City: Board of Education, Division of Curriculum and Instruction, 1984).

21. P. Boffrey, "Reagan to Back AIDS Plan Urging Youths to Avoid Sex," *New York Times*, 27 February 1987, A14; "Chicago School Clinic is Sued Over Birth Control Materials," *New York Times*, 16 October 1986, A24; M. Dowd, "Bid to Update Sex Education Confronts Resistance in City," *New York Times*, 16 April 1986, A1; J. Perlez, "On Teaching About Sex," *New York Times*, 24 June 1986, C1; J. Perlez, "School Chief to Ask Mandatory Sex Education," *New York Times*, 24 September 1986 A36; L. Rohter, "School Workers Shown AIDS Film," *New York Times*, 29 October 1985, B3.

22. This information is derived from personal communications with former and present employees of major urban school districts who have chosen to remain anonymous.

23. Personal communication.

24. L. Irigaray, "When Our Lips Speak Together," *Signs* 6, 69(1980); H. Cixous, "Castration or Decapitation," *Signs* 7, 41(1981): 55.

25. C. Burke, "Introduction to Luce Irigaray's 'When Our Lips Speak Together', " *Signs* 6(1980): 66–68.

26. O. Espin, "Cultural and Historical Influences on Sexuality in Hispanic/Latina Women: Implications for Psychotherapy," in C. Vance, ed., *Pleasure and Danger,* 149–64; B. Omolade, "Hearts of Darkness," in Snitow, Stansell, and Thompson, *Powers of Desire,* 350–67.

27. J. Benjamin, "Master and Slave: The Fantasy of Erotic Domination," in Snitow, Stansell, and Thompson, *Powers of Desire,* 280–99.

28. For a counterexample, see G. Kelly, *Learning about Sex* (Woodbury, N.Y.: Barron's Educational Series, 1986).

29. Fine, "Why Urban Adolescents Drop Into and Out of High School."

30. Fine, "Silencing in Public School," *Language Arts* 64(1987): 157–74.

31. M. Green, "In Search of a Critical Pedagogy," *Harvard Educational Review* 56(1986): 427–41; N. Noddings, "Fidelity in Teaching, Teacher Education, and Research for Teaching," *Harvard Educational Review* 56(1986): 496–510.

32. New York City Board of Education, *Family Living Curriculum Including Sex Education Grades K–12.*

33. Fine, "Silencing in Public School''; Foucault, *The History of Sexuality.*

34. Leo, "Sex and Schools."

35. G. S. Hall, "Education and the Social Hygiene Movement," *Social Hygiene* 1(December 1914): 29–35.

36. M. Imber, "Towards a Theory of Educational Origins: The Genesis of Sex Education," *Educational Theory* 34(1984): 275–86; B. Strong, "Ideas of the Early Sex Education Movement in America, 1890–1920," *History of Education Quarterly* 12(1972): 129–61.

37. M. Bigelow, *Sex Education* (New York: Macmillan, 1921).

38. B. Ehrenreich, E. Hess, and G. Jacobs, *Remaking of Love* (Garden City, N.Y.: Anchor Press, 1986).

39. J. Weeks, *Sexuality and Its Discontents* (London: Routledge & Kegan Paul, 1984).

40. O. Espin, "Cultural and Historical Influences on Sexuality"; Golden, "Diversity and Variability in Lesbian Identities"; Omolade, "Hearts of Darkness."

41. Weeks, *Sexuality and Its Discontents.*

42. MacKinnon, "Complicity."

43. Petchesky, *Abortion and Woman's Choice.*

44. Foucault, *The History of Sexuality;* Irigaray, "When Our Lips Speak Together;" Rubin, "Thinking Sex."

45. Benjamin, "Master and Slave"; Rubin, "Thinking Sex"; Weeks, *Sexuality and Its Discontents.*

46. Rubin, "Thinking Sex."

47. R. Weitz, "What Price Independence? Social Reactions to Lesbians, Spinsters, Widows, and Nuns," in J. Freeman, ed., *Women: A Feminist Perspective,* 3d ed. (Palo Alto, Calif.: Mayfield, 1984).

48. J. Leo, "Sex and Schools;" Harris, *Public Attitudes.*

49. Leo, "Sex and Schools."

50. P. Scales, "Sex Education and the Prevention of Teenage Pregnancy: An Overview of Policies and Programs in the United States," in T. Ooms, ed., *Teenage Pregnancy in a Family Context: Implications for Policy* (Philadelphia: Temple University Press, 1981).

51. J. Hottois and N. Milner, *The Sex Education Controversy* (Lexington, Mass.: Lexington Books, 1975); P. Scales, "Sex Education."

52. D. Kirby and P. Scales, "An Analysis of State Guidelines for Sex Education Instruction in Public Schools," *Family Relations* (April 1981): 229–37.

53. F. Sonnenstein and K. Pittman, "The Availability of Sex Education in Large City School Districts," *Family Planning Perspectives* 16, 1 (1984): 19–25.

54. D. Kirby, *School-based Health Clinics: An Emerging Approach to Improving Adolescent Health and Addressing Teenage Pregnancy* (Washington, D.C.: Center for Population Options, 1985).

55. Freudenberg, "The Politics of Sex Education."

56. Benedetto, "AIDS Studies Become Part of the Curricula," *USA Today,* 23 January, 1987, D1.

57. P. Kirby, *School-based Health Clinics''*; Public/Private Ventures, *Summer Training and Education Program* (Philadelphia: Public/Private Ventures, 1987).

58. M. Zelnick and Y. Kim, "Sex Education and Its Association with Teenage Sexual Activity, Pregnancy, and Contraceptive Use," *Family Planning Perspectives* 14, 3 (1982): 117–26.

59. L. Zabin, M. Hirsch, E. Smith, R. Streett, and J. Hardy, "Evaluation of a Pregnancy Prevention Program for Urban Teenagers," *Family Planning Perspectives* 18, 3(1986): 119–26.

60. D. Dawson, "The Effects of Sex Education on Adolescent Behavior," *Family Planning Perspectives* 18(1986) 162–70; W. Marsiglio and F. Mott, "The Impact of Sex Education on Sexual Activity, Contraceptive Use, and Premarital Pregnancy among American Teenagers," *Family Perspectives* 18, 4(1986): 151–62; D. Kirby, *School-Based Health Clinics."*

61. E. Jones, J. Forrest, N. Goldman, S. Henshaw, R. Lincoln, J. Rosoff, C. Westoff, and D. Wulf, "Teenage Pregnancy in Developed Countries," *Family Planning Perspectives* 17, 1(1985): 55–63.

62. J. Dryfoos, "A Time for New Thinking about Teenage Pregnancy," *American Journal of Public Health* 75(1985): 13–14; J. Dryfoos, "School-Based Health Clinics: A New Approach to Preventing Adolescent Pregnancy?", *Family Planning Perspectives* 17, 2(1985): 70–85; National Research Council, *Risking the Future: Adolescent Sexuality, Pregnancy and Childbearing,* vol. 1(Washington, D.C.: National Academy Press, 1987).

63. Kirby, *School-Based Health Clinics.*

64. Kirby, *School-Based Health Clinics.*

65. Leo, "Sex and Schools."

66. A Torres and J. Forrest, "Family Planning Clinic Services in the United States, 1983," *Family Planning Perspectives* 17, 1(1985): 30–35.

67. Reproductive Freedom Project, *Parental Consent Laws on Abortion: Their Catastrophic Impact on Teenagers* (New York: American Civil Liberties Union, 1986).

68. Reproductive Freedom Project, *Parental Consent Laws on Abortion.*

69. Reproductive Freedom Project, *Parental Consent Laws on Abortion.*

70. Reproductive Freedom Project, *Parental Consent Laws on Abortion.*

71. V. Cartoof and L. Klerman, "Parental Consent for Abortion: Impact on Massachusetts Law, *American Journal of Public Health* 76(1986): 397–400.

72. S. Melton and N. Russon, "Adolescent Abortion," *American Psychologist* 42(1987): 69–83; Reproductive Freedom Project, *Parental Consent Laws on Abortion.*

73. Leo, "Sex and Schools."

74. Harris, *Public Attitudes.*

75. Benedetto, "AIDS Studies Become Part of Curricula."

76. Zabin et al., "Evaluation of a Pregnancy Prevention Program."

77. St. Paul Maternity and Infant Care Project, *Health Services Project Description* (St. Paul, Minn.: St. Paul Maternity and Infant Care Project, 1985).

78. Petchesky, *Abortion and Woman's Choice.*

79. J. Dryfoos, "A Time for New Thinking"; Dryfoos, "School-Based Health Clinics"; Kirby, *School-Based Health Clinics;* Select Committee on Children, Youth, and Families, *Teen Pregnancy: What is Being Done? A State-By-State Look* (Washington, D.C.: U.S. Government Printing Office, 1986).

80. National Research Council, *Risking the Future.*

81. J. Dryfoos, "A Time for New Thinking"; Dryfoos, "School-Based Health Clinics."

82. Weinbaum, personal communication, 1986.

83. Weinbaum, paraphrased personal communication, 1986.

84. D. Polit, J. Kahn, and D. Stevens, *Final Impacts from Project Redirection* (New York: Manpower Development Research Center, 1985).

85. M. Burt, M. Kimmich, J. Goldmuntz, and F. Sonnenstein, *Helping Pregnant Adolescent: Outcomes and Costs of Service Delivery, Final Report on the Evaluation of Adolescent Pregnancy Programs* (Washington, D.C.: Urban Institute, 1984).

86. Fine, "Why Urban Adolescents Drop Into and Out of High School"; Weinbaum, personal Communication, 1987.

87. Hispanic Policy Development Project, *1980 High School Sophomores from Poverty Backgrounds: Whites, Blacks, Hispanics Look at School and Adult Responsibilities,* vol. 1, no. 2 (New York: Hispanic Policy Development Project, 1987).

88. Children's Defense Fund, *Preventing Adolescent Pregnancy: What Schools Can Do* (Washington, D.C.: Children's Defense Fund, 1986).

89. Fine, "Why Urban Adolescents Drop Into and Out of High School."

90. Jones, et al., "Teenage Pregnancy in Developed Countries."

91. Fine, "Why Urban Adolescents Drop Into and Out of High School."

CHAPTER 5

*This paper is reprinted from *Harvard Educational Review,* vol. 56, no. 1, February 1986. Discussions at the Symposium on "Minority Languages in Academic Research and Educational Policy" held in Sandbjerg Slot, Denmark, April 1985, contributed to the ideas in the paper. I would like to express my appreciation to the participants at the Symposium and to Safder Alladina, Jan Curtis, David Dolson, Norm Gold, Monica Heller, Dennis Parker, Verity Saifullah Khan, and Tove Skutnabb-Kangas for comments on earlier drafts. I would also like to acknowledge the financial support of the Social Sciences and Humanities Research Council (Grant No. 431-79-0003) which made possible participation in the Sandbjerg Slot symposium.

1. C. Jusenius and V. L. Duarte, *Hispanics and Jobs: Barriers to Progress* (Washington, D.C.: National Commission for Employment Policy, 1982).

2. The Education of All Handicapped Children Act of 1975 (Public Law 94–142) guarantees to all handicapped children in the United States the right to a free public education, to an individualized education program (IEP), to due process, to education in the least segregated environment, and to assessment procedures that are multidimensional and nonculturally discriminatory.

3. A. A. Ortiz and J. R. Yates, "Incidence of Exceptionality among Hispanics: Implications for Manpower Planning," *NABE Journal* 7(1983): 41–54.

4. J. Cummins, *Bilingualism and Special Education: Issues in Assessment and Pedagogy* (Clevedon, England: Multilingual Matters, and San Diego: College Hill Press, 1984); J. U. Ogbu, *Minority Education and Caste* (New York: Academic Press, 1978).

5. Cummins, *Bilingualism and Special Education.*

6. T. Skutnabb-Kangas, *Bilingualism or Not: The Education of Minorities* (Clevedon, England: Multilingual Matters, 1984).

7. S. G. Schneider, *Resolution, Reaction, or Reform: The 1974 Bilingual Education Act* (New York: Las Americas, 1976).

8. For a discussion of the implications of Canadian French immersion programs for the education of minority students, see California State Department of Education, *Studies on Immersion Education: A Collection for United States Educators* (Sacramento: California State Department of Education, 1984).

9. K. A. Baker and A. A. de Kanter, *Effectiveness of Bilingual Education: A Review of the Literature* (Washington, D.C.: U.S. Department of Education, Office of Planning and Budget, 1981); J. Cummins, *Heritage Language Education: A Literature Review* (Toronto: Ministry of Education, 1983); Cumins, *Bilingualism and Special Education;* Skutnabb-Kangas, *Bilingualism or Not.*

10. J. Cummins, "Linguistic Interdependence and the Educational Development of Bilingual Children," *Review of Educational Research* 49(1979): 222–51; Cummins, *Heritage Language Education;* Cumins, *Bilingualism and Special Education.*

11. Cummins, *Bilingualism and Special Education;* B. McLaughlin, *Second Language Acquisition in Childhood: Vol. 2. School-Age Children* (Hillsdale, N.J.: Erlbaum, 1985).

12. Ogbu, *Minority Education and Caste;* L. Wong-Fillmore, "The Language Learner as an Individual: Implications of Research on Individual Differences for the ESL Teacher," in M. A. Clarke and J. Handscombe, eds., *On TESOL '82: Pacific Perspectives on Language Learning and Teaching* (Washington, D.C.: TESOL, 1983), 157–71.

13. J. Fishman, *Bilingual Education: An International Sociological Perspective* (Rowley, Mass.: Newbury House, 1980); Ogbu, *Minority Education and Caste;* C. B. Paulston, *Bilingual Education: Theories and Issues* (Rowley, Mass.: Newbury House, 1980).

14. Wong-Fillmore, "The Language Learner as an Individual."

15. R. Troike, "Research Evidence for the Effectiveness of Bilingual Education," *NABE Journal* 3(1978): 13–24.

16. Ogbu, *Minority Education and Caste.*

17. Cummins, *Bilingualism and Special Education.*

18. Ogbu, *Minority Education and Caste.*

19. R. Feuerstein, *The Dynamic Assessment of Retarded Performers: The Learning Potential Assessment Device, Theory, Instruments, and Techniques* (Baltimore: University Park Press, 1979).

20. C. Mullard. "The Social Dynamic of Migrant Groups: From Progressive to Transformative Policy in Education," paper presented at the OECD Conference on Educational Policies and Minority Social Groups, Paris, 1985.

21. Ogbu, *Minority Education and Caste.*

22. S. B. Heath, *Ways with Words* (Cambridge: Cambridge University Press, 1983); Wong-Fillmore, "The Language Learner as an Individual.

23. J. U. Ogbu and M. E. Matute Bianchi, "Understanding Sociocultural Factors: Knowledge, Identity, and School Adjustment," in California State Department of Education, ed. *Sociocultural Factors and Minority Student Achievement* (Sacramento: California State Department of Education, in press).

24. Ogbu, for example, has distinguished between "caste," "immigrant," and "autonomous" minority groups. Caste groups are similar to what has been termed "dominated" groups in the present framework and are the only category of minority

groups that tends to fail academically. Immigrant groups have usually come voluntarily to the host society for economic reasons and, unlike caste minorities, have not internalized negative attributions of the dominant group. Ogbu gives Chinese and Japanese groups as examples of "immigrant" minorities. The cultural resources that permit some minority groups to resist discrimination and internalization of negative attributions are still a matter of debate and speculation. The final category distinguished by Ogbu is that of "autonomous" groups, who hold a distinct cultural identity but are not subordinated economically or politically to the dominant group (for example, Jews and Mormons in the United States). See Ogbu, *Minority Education and Caste;* Ogbu and Bianchi, "Understanding Sociocultural Factors."

Failure to take account of these differences among minority groups both in patterns of academic performance and in sociohistorical relationships to the dominant group has contributed to the confused state of policymaking with respect to language minority students. The bilingual education policy, for example, has been based on the implicit assumption that the linguistic mismatch hypothosis was valid for all language minority students, and consequently, the same types of intervention were necessary and appropriate for all students. Clearly, this assumption is open to question.

25. J. Cummins, "Functional Language Proficiency in Context: Classroom Participation as an Interactive Process," in W. J. Tikunoff, ed., *Compatibility of the SBIS Features with Other Research on Instruction for LEP Students* (San Francisco: Far West Laboratory, 1983), 109–31; W. J. Tikunoff, "Five Significant Bilingual Instructional Features," in Tikunoff, *Compatibility of the SBIS Features,* 5–18.

26. There is no contradiction in postulating student empowerment as both a mediating and an outcome variable. For example, cognitive abilities clearly have the same status in that they contribute to students' school success and can also be regarded as an outcome of schooling.

27. Cumins, *Bilingualism and Special Education;* Skutnabb-Kangas, *Bilingualism or Not.*

28. Cummins, *Heritage Language Education;* Cumins, *Bilingualism and Special Education.*

29. A. D. Cohen and M. Swain, "Bilingual Education: The Immersion Model in the North American Context," in J. E. Alatis and K. Twaddell, eds., *English as a Second Language in Bilingual Education* (Washington, D.C.: TESOL, 1976): 55–64.

30. Skutnabb-Kangas, *Bilingualism or Not.*

31. J. Campos and B. Keatinge, *The Carpinteria Preschool Program: Title VII Second Year Evaluation Report* (Washington, D.C.: Department of Education, 1984); Cummins, *Heritage Language Education;* P. Rosier and W. Holm, *The Rock Point Experience: A Longitudinal Study of a Navajo School* (Washington, D.C.: Center for Applied Linguistics, 1980).

32. K. H. Au and C. Jordan, "Teaching Reading to Hawaiian Children: Finding a Culturally Appropriate Solution," in *Culture and the Bilingual Classroom: Studies in Classroom Ethnography* (Rowley, Mass.: Newbury House, 1981).

33. The terms *additive bilingualism* and *subtractive bilingualism* were coined by Lambert to refer to the proficient bilingualism associated with positive cognitive outcomes, on the one hand, and the limited bilingualism often associated with negative outcomes, on the other. See W. E. Lambert, "Culture and Language as Factors in Learning and Education," in A. Wolfgang, ed., *Education and Immigrant Students* (Toronto: Ontario Institute for Studies in Education, 1975), 55–83.

34. K. Hakuta and R. M. Diaz, "The Relationship between Degree of Bilingualism and Cognitive Ability: A Critical Discussion and Some New Longitudinal Data," in K. E. Nelson, ed., *Children's Language 5* (Hillsdale, N.J.: Erlbaum, 1985), 319–45; B. McLaughlin, "Early Bilingualism: Methodological and Theoretical Issues," in M. Paradis and Y. Lebrun, eds., *Early Bilingualism and Child Development* (Lisse; Netherlands: Swets & Zeitlinger, 1984), 19–46.

35. PACs were established in some states to provide an institutional structure for minority parents' involvement in educational decision making with respect to bilingual programs. In California, for example, a majority of PAC members for any state-funded program was required to be from the program target group. The school plan for use of program funds required signed PAC approval.

36. J. Curtis, "Bilingual Education in Calistoga: Not a Happy Ending," report submitted to the Instituto de Lengua y Cultura, Elmira, N.Y., 1984.

37. Wong-Fillmore, "The Language Learner as an Individual."

38. Cumins, *Bilingualism and Special Education*.

39. J. Tizard, W. N. Schofield, and J. Hewison, "Collaboration between Teachers and Parents in Assisting Children's Reading," *British Journal of Educational Psychology* 52(1982): 1–15.

40. C. S. Beers and J. W. Beers, "Early Identification of Learning Disabilities: Facts and Fallacies," *Elementary School Journal* 81 (1980): 67–76; G.S. Coles, "The Learning Disabilities Test Battery: Empirical and Social Issues," *Harvard Educational Review* 48(1978): 313–40; Cumins, *Bilingualism and Special Education*.

41. D. K. Ramphal, *An Analysis of Reading Instruction of West-Indian Creole-Speaking Students*, Ph.D. dissertation, Ontario Institute for Studies in Education, 1983.

42. D. H. Graves, *Writing: Teachers and Children at Work* (Exeter, N.H.: Heinemann Educational Books, 1983), 99–103.

43. D. Barnes, *From Communication to Curriculum* (New York: Penguin, 1976); E. Wells, "Language, Learning, and the Curriculum," in G. Wells, ed., *Language, Learning, and Education* (Bristol, England: Centre for the Study of Language and Communication, University of Bristol, 1982), 205–26.

44. P. Freire, *Pedagogy of the Oppressed* (New York: Seabury, 1970); P. Freire, *Education for Critical Consciousness* (New York: Seabury, 1973).

45. Cumins, *Bilingualism and Special Education;* E. Wells, "Language, Learning, and the Curriculum." This "reciprocal interaction" model incorporates proposals about the relation between language and learning made by a variety of investigators, most notably in the Bullock Report, and by Barnes, Lindfors, and Wells. Its application with respect to the promotion of literacy conforms closely to psycholinguistic approaches to reading and to the recent emphasis on encouraging expressive writing from the earliest grades. Students' microcomputing networks such as the *Computer Chronicles Newswire* represented a particularly promising application of reciprocal interaction model of pedagogy. See Bullock Report, *A Language for Life* [Report of the Committee of Inquiry appointed by The Secretary of State for Education and Science under the chairmanship of Sir Alan Bullock] (London: HMSO, 1975); Barnes, *From Communication to Curriculum;* J. W. Lindfors, *Children's Language and Learning* (Englewood Cliffs, N.J.: Prentice-Hall, 1980); G. Wells, "Language, Learning, and the Curriculum"; K. S. Goodman and Y. M. Goodman, "Learning about Psycholinguistic Process by Analyzing and Reading," *Harvard Educational Review* 47(1977): 317–33; D. Holdaway, *The Foundations of Literacy* (Sydney, Australia: Ashton Scholastic, 1979); F. Smith, *Understanding Reading,* 2d ed. (New York: Holt Rinehart & Winston, 1978); C. Chomsky, "Write Now, Read Later," in C. Cazden, ed., *Language in Early Childhood Education,* 2d ed. (Washington, D.C.: National Association for the Education of Young Children, 1981), 141–49; M. E. Giacobbe, "Who Says Children Can't Write the First Week?" in R. D. Walshe, ed., *Donald Graves in Australia: "Children Want to Write"* (Exeter, N.H.: Heinemann Educational Books, 1982), 99–103; Graves, *Writing: Teachers and Children at Work;* C. A. Temple, R. G. Nathan, and N. A. Burris, *The Beginnings of Writing* (Boston: Allyn & Bacon, 1982); and H. Mehan, B. Miller-Souviney, and M. M. Riel, "Research Currents: Knowledge of Text Editing and Control of Literary Skills," *Language Arts* 65(1984): 154–59.

46. Bullock Report, *A Language for Life.*

47. Wong-Fillmore, "The Language Learner as an Individual."

48. J. Cummins, M. Aguilar, L. Bascunan, S. Fiorucci, R. Sanaoui, and S. Basman, *Literacy Development in Heritage Language Programs* (Toronto: National Heritage Language Resource Unit, in press).

49. C. Daiute, *Writing and Computers* (Reading, Mass.: Addison-Wesley, 1985).

50. H. Mehan, A. Hertweck, and J. L. Meihls, *Handicapping the Handicapped: Decision Making in Students' Educational Careers* (Palo Alto: Stanford University, in press).

51. R. Rueda and J. R. Mercer, "Predictive Analysis of Decision Making with Language Minority Handicapped Children," paper presented at the BUENO Center 3rd Annual Symposium on Bilingual Education, Denver, 1985.

52. Cumins, *Bilingualism and Special Education.*

53. For a detailed discussion of delegitimization strategies in antiracist education, see Mullard, *The Social Dynamics of Migrant Groups.*

54. C. B. Cazden, "The ESL Teacher as Advocate," plenary presentation, TESOL conference, New York, 1985.

55. Clearly, the presence of processing difficulties that are rooted in neurological causes is not being denied for either monolingual or bilingual children. However, in the case of children from dominated minorities, the proportion of disabilities that are neurological in origin is likely to represent only a small fraction of those that derive from educational and social conditions.

56. Campos and Keatinge, *The Carpinteria Preschool Program,* 17.

57. E. Hernandez-Chavez, M. Burt, and H. Dulay, *The Bilingual Syntax Measure* (New York: Psychological Corporation, 1976).

58. Campos and Keatinge, *The Carpinteria Preschool Program.*

59. Campos and Keatinge, *The Carpinteria Preschool Program,* 41

60. Campos and Keatinge, *The Carpinteria Preschool Program.*

61. Campos and Keatinge, *The Carpinteria Preschool Program,* 41.

62. Although for pedagogy the resistance to sharing control with students goes beyond majority/minority group relations, the same elements are present. If the curriculum is not predetermined and presequenced, and the students are generating their own knowledge in a critical and creative way, then the reproduction of the societal structure cannot be guaranteed—hence the reluctance to liberate students from instructional dependence.

CHAPTER 6

*This paper is reprinted from *Harvard Educational Review,* vol. 58, no. 3, August 1988.

1. L. Delpit, "Skills and Other Dilemmas of a Progressive Black Educator," *Harvard Educational Review* 56, 4(1986): 379–85.

2. Delpit, "Skills and Other Dilemmas."

3. Such a discussion, limited as it is by space constraints, must treat the intersection of class and race somewhat simplistically. For the sake of clarity, however, let me define a few terms: *Black* is used herein to refer to those who share some or all aspects of "core Black culture," that is, the mainstream of Black America—neither those who have entered the ranks of the bourgeoisie nor those who are participants in the disenfranchised underworld. *Middle-class* is used broadly to refer to the predom-

inantly white American "mainstream." There are, of course, non-white people who also fit into this category; at issue is their cultural identification, not necessarily the color of their skin. (I must add that there are other non-white people, as well as poor white people, who have indicated to me that their perspectives are similar to those attributed herein to Black people.) See J. Gwaltney, *Drylongso* (New York: Vintage Books, 1980).

4. *Multicultural Britain: "Crosstalk,"* National Centre of Industrial Language Training, Commission for Racial Equality, London, John Twitchin, Producer.

5. M. W. Apple, *Ideology and Curriculum* (Boston: Routledge & Kegan Paul, 1979).

6. Gwaltney, *Drylongso.*

7. E. Siddle, "A Critical Assessment of the Natural Process Approach to Teaching Writing," qualifying paper, Harvard University, 1986.

8. Delpit, "Skills and Other Dilemmas."

9. E. Siddle, "The Effect of Intervention Strategies on the Revisions Ninth Graders Make in a Narrative Essay," Ph.D. dissertation, Harvard University, 1988.

10. S. B. Heath, *Ways with Words* (Cambridge: Cambridge University Press, 1983).

11. C. F. Snow, A. Arlman-Rup, Y. Hassing, J. Josbe, J. Josten, and J. Vorster, "Mother's Speech in Three Social Classes," *Journal of Psycholinguistic Research* 5 (1976): 1–20.

12. Heath, *Way with Words.*

13. I would like to thank Michele Foster, who is presently planning a more in-depth treatment of the subject, for her astute clarification of the idea.

14. The colons [::] refer to elongated vowels. M. Foster, " 'It's Cookin' Now': An Ethnographic Study of the Teaching Style of a Successful Black Teacher in an Urban Community College," Ph.D. dissertation, Harvard University, 1987.

15. The colons [::] refer to elongated vowels. M. Foster, " 'It's Cookin' Now.' "

16. Bernstein makes a similar point when he proposes that different educational frames cannot be successfully institutionalized in the lower levels of education until there are fundamental changes at the post-secondary levels. See B. Bernstein, "Class and Pedagogies: Visible and Invisible," in ed., B. Bernstein, *Class, Codes, and Control,* vol. 3 (Boston: Routledge & Kegan Paul, 1975).

17. J. Britton, T. Burgess, N. Martin, A. McLeod, and H. Rosen, *The Development of Writing Abilities* (London: Macmillan Education for the Schools Council, and Urbana, Ill.: National Council of Teachers of English, 1975/1977).

18. C. Cazden, "The Myth of Autonomous Text," paper presented at the Third International Conference on Thinking, Hawaii, 1987.

19. G. C. Massey, M. V. Scott, and S. M. Dornbusch, "Racism without Racists: Institutional Racism in Urban Schools," *The Black Scholar* 7, 3(1975): 2–11.

CHAPTER 7

*An earlier version of this essay was presented as the Tanner Lecture on Human Values at the University of Michigan on 16 March 1990 and published in the *Michigan Quarterly Review,* Fall 1990. The research which underlies this paper was encouraged and supported by Joan Lipsitz and the Lilly Endowment, by Steven Minter and the Cleveland Foundation, by Judith Simpson and the Gund Foundation, by Lawrence Cremin, Marion Faldet, Linda Fitzgerald and the Spencer Foundation, by the American Association of University Women, by Benjamin Barber and the Walt Whitman Center at Rutgers University, and also by Leah Rhys, principal of the Laurel School in Cleveland, Ohio, Virginia Kahn, founder of the Atrium School in Watertown, Massachusetts, and Patricia Graham, dean of the Harvard Graduate School of Education. I am deeply grateful to the girls who participated in these projects and to the women who have accompanied me most closely on this journey—Lyn Mikel Brown and Annie Rogers—the two psychologists I refer to in the paper, and also Judy Dorney and Patricia Flanders-Hall, who took the lead in the project on Women Teaching Girls, and the teachers and psychologists who participated in the retreats. Normi Noel added theater to the Writing, Outing, and Theater Club, Kristin Linklater taught me about the embodiment of voice, and Tina Packer, artistic director of Shakespeare and Company, stimulated my thinking.

1. The quotations from the eleven-year-old girls are taken from the girls' journals and also from my journal. The Theater, Writing, and Outing Club is part of the project "Strengthening Healthy Resistance and Courage in Girls" being conducted by Annie Rogers and myself, together with Normi Noel, in public and private schools in the Boston area. Among the sixth-grade girls at the Atrium School, a private coeducational elementary school, there is some diversity in cultural background and family composition; cultures represented in this group of girls include North American Protestant, Jewish, and Hispanic/Latina. The women involved in this project are also somewhat culturally diverse (North American, Canadian, Catholic, Jewish, and Protestant). The absence of Black girls in this particular Theater, Writing, and Outing Club is a clear limitation and not characteristic of the public school Theater, Writing, and Outing Club, which is part of the ongoing Harvard Project.

2. Sigmund Freud, *The Interpretation of Dreams,* 1899/1900. Vols. 4 and 5 of *The Standard Edition of the Complete Psychological Works of Sigmund Freud* (London: Hogarth Press, 1955). See also *The Complete Letters of Sigmund Freud to Wilhelm Fleiss: 1887–1904* (Cambridge: Harvard University Press, 1985).

3. Carol Gilligan, *In a Different Voice: Psychological Theory and Women's Development* (Cambridge: Harvard University Press, 1982); "Prologue" and "Teaching Shakespeare's Sister: Notes from the Underground of Female Adolescence," in Gilligan, Lyons, and Hanmer (Eds.), *Making Connections* (Cambridge: Harvard University Press, 1990); Carol Gilligan, Lyn Mikel Brown, and Annie Rogers, "Psyche Embedded: A Place for Body, Relationships, and Culture in Personality Theory," in A. I. Rabin et al. (Eds.), *Studying Persons and Lives* (New York: Springer, 1990).

4. Virginia Woolf, *Three Guineas* (San Diego: Harcourt Brace Jovanovich, 1938), 6.

5. Anne Frank, *The Diary of Anne Frank, The Critical Edition* (New York: Doubleday, 1989), 678.

6. Aristophanes, *Lysistrata/The Acharnians/The Clouds* (London: Penguin Books, 1973), 180–81.

7. Ibid., 93.

8. Ibid., 93.

9. Ibid., 142.

10. Virginia Woolf, *To the Lighthouse* (New York: Harcourt, Brace, 1927), 300.

11. Anna's quotations are taken from interviews conducted over the course of a five-year study of girls' development at the Laurel School in Cleveland, Ohio. Papers from the project, which involved girls and women who were diverse in racial as well as economic background, were presented at the Harvard-Laurel Conference on "The Psychology of Women and the Education of Girls," held in Cleveland, April 1990, and are being prepared for publication by Harvard University Press.

12. Tessie was one of ten eleven-year-old girls living in a suburb of Boston and interviewed by Sharry Langdale in 1981 as part of the Project on the Psychology of Women and The Development of Girls conducted at Harvard University.

13. This analysis was carried out by Lisa Marie Kulpinski, a graduate student in the Human Development and Psychology Program at Harvard University, and reported in her paper "Adolescence: Hitting a Fork in the Road," 1990.

14. Frank, *The Diary of Anne Frank*, 545.

15. Glen Elder and Avshalom Caspi, "Studying Lives in a Changing Society: Sociological and Personological Explorations," in A. Rabin et al. *Studying Persons and Lives* 226–28. See also Anne Peterson, "Adolescent Development," *Annual Review of Psychology* 39 (1988): 583–607.

16. Woolf, *Three Guineas*, 113.

17. Jorie Graham, *Erosion* (Princeton, N.J.: Princeton University Press, 1983), 16–21.

18. Toni Morrison, *The Bluest Eye* (New York: Pocket Books, 1970), 53.

19. Frank, *The Diary of Anne Frank*, 557.

20. Sophocles, *Oedipus the King*. In the more literal Loeb Classics translation, this line reads "How could the soil thy father eared so long / Endure to bear in silence such a wrong" (Cambridge: Harvard University Press, 1912), 113. In the text, for purposes of clarity, I have cited Fitzgerald's freer translation.

21. Dianne Argyris and Judy Dorney, graduate students in the Human Development and Psychology Program at Harvard University, compiled and analyzed the girls' thoughts and feelings about the Laurel School honor code, and this work was the basis for the presentation to the faculty.

22. Madeline R. Grumet, *Bitter Milk: Women and Teaching* (Amherst: University of Massachusetts Press, 1988), 58, 25. See also Jane Roland Martin, *Reclaiming a Conversation* (New Haven: Yale University Press, 1985).

23. Aristophanes, *Lysistrata/The Archanians/The Clouds*, 212.

24. Sara Ruddick, *Maternal Thinking: Toward a Politics of Peace* (Boston: Beacon Press, 1989), 227–230.

25. Teresa Bernardez, "Women and Anger: Cultural Prohibitions and the Feminine Ideal," Stone Center Working Paper Series, No. 31 (Wellesley, Mass.: Wellesley College, 1988), 5. See also Jean Baker Miller, *Toward a New Psychology of Women* (Boston: Beacon Press, 1976) for a discussion of women and anger and the roots of anger in women's political oppression.

26. Quotations taken from the taped transcript of the Women Teaching Girls project, Harvard-Laurel retreat, February 1990.

27. Nancy S. Franklin, "Teachers' Tales of Empowerment: A Story from an English Teacher," paper presented at the Harvard/Laurel Conference on the Psychology of Women and the Education of Girls, 6 April 1990, Cleveland, Ohio. Conference papers are being prepared for publication by Harvard University Press.

28. Freud, "Femininity," in *New Introductory Lectures on Psycho-Analysis,* Lecture 33, [1932] 1933, in Vol. 10 of *The Standard Edition*, 117, and also "The Transformations of Puberty," in *Three Essays on the Theory of Sexuality,* 1905, vol. 7 of *The Standard Edition*. See also Karen Horney, "The Flight from Womanhood," *International Journal of Psychoanalysis* 7(1926): 324–39; Clara M. Thompson, "Adolescence" and other papers in *Interpersonal Psychoanalysis* (New York: Basic Books, 1964); and Jean Baker Miller, "The Development of Women's Sense of Self," (Wellesley, Mass.: Wellesley College, 1984). Stone Center Working Paper Series, No. 12.

29. See for example, Charlotte Bronte, *Jane Eyre;* Toni Morrison, *The Bluest Eye;* Jamaica Kincaid, *Annie John;* Carson McCullers, *The Member of the Wedding;* Margaret Atwood, *Cat's Eye;* and also Michelle Cliff, "Claiming an Identity They

Taught Me to Despise." in *The Land of Look Behind;* and Sharon Olds, "Time-Travel," in *Satan Says.*

30. Lyn Mikel Brown, "A Problem of Vision: The Development of Voice and Relational Knowledge in Girls Ages 7 to 16," *Women's Studies Quarterly,* in press.

31. For a fuller discussion of this phenomenon, see Gilligan, *In a Different Voice* and "Teaching Shakespeare's Sister," and Lori Stern, "Disavowing the Self in Female Adolescence: A Case Study Analysis," Ed.D. dissertation; Harvard University, 1990. See also Jean Baker Miller, "Connections, Disconnections, and Violations," *Work in Progress No. 33,* Stone Center Working Paper Series (Wellesley, Mass.: Wellesley College, 1988).

32. Lyn Mikel Brown and Carol Gilligan, "Meeting at the Crossroads: The Psychology of Women and The Development of Girls," paper presented at the Harvard/ Laurel Conference on the Psychology of Women and the Education of Girls, 5 April 1990, Cleveland, Ohio, and submitted for publication.

33. Quotations taken from the taped transcript of the Women Teaching Girls Project, Harvard-Laurel Retreat, October 1989.

34. Frank, *The Diary of Anne Frank,* 440.

CHAPTER 8

1. See Karin Stallard, Barbara Ehrenreich, and Holly Sklar, eds., *Poverty in the American Dream* (Boston: South End Press, 1983).

2. See Allan Hunter, "Why Did Reagan Win? Ideology or Economics?" *Socialist Review* 79 (1985): 29–41.

3. Stuart Hall, "Authoritarian Populism: A Reply," *New Left Review* 151 (1985): 115–24.

4. Refer to Allan Hunter, "Virtue with a Vengeance: The Pro-family Politics of the New Right," unpublished doctoral dissertation, Department of Sociology, Brandeis University, Waltham, Mass., 1984.

5. See Tony Vellela, *New Voices* (Boston: South End Press, 1988).

6. Jean Anyon, "Intersections of Gender and Class," in *Gender, Class, and Education,* ed. Stephen Walker and Len Barton (London: Falmer Press, 1983); Linda K. Christian-Smith, "Gender, Popular Culture, and Curriculum," *Curriculum Inquiry* 17 (1987): 365–406; Lois Weis, ed., *Class, Race, and Gender in American Education* (Albany, N.Y.: SUNY Press).

7. See Gaby Weiner, *Just a Bunch of Girls* (Milton Keynes, Eng.: Open University Press, 1985); Linda Valli, *Becoming Clerical Workers* (Boston: Routledge & Kegan Paul, 1986).

8. Market Facts, *1983 Consumer Research Study on Reading and Book Purchasing: Focus on Juveniles* (New York: Book Industry Study Group, 1984).

9. These qualities of popular culture are discussed in Tony Bennett, Colin Mercer, and Janet Wollacott, eds., *Popular Culture and Social Relations* (Milton Keynes, Eng.: Open University Press, 1986); Henry A. Giroux, Roger Simon, and Contributors, eds., *Popular Culture and Critical Pedagogy* (Granby, Mass.: Bergin & Garvey, 1989); Leslie Roman and Linda K. Christian-Smith, eds., *Becoming Feminine: The Politics of Popular Culture* (New York: Falmer Press, 1988).

10. Roman and Christian-Smith, *Becoming Feminine.*

11. Market Facts, *1983 Consumer Research Study.*

12. Refer to Linda K. Christian-Smith, *Becoming a Woman through Romance* (New York: Routledge, 1990), for a more detailed history of teen romance fiction.

13. For an extend discussion of this topic, see Michael W. Apple and Linda K. Christian-Smith, *The Politics of the Textbook* (New York: Routledge, 1991).

14. This point is developed at greater length in Linda K. Christian-Smith, "The English Curriculum and Current Trends in Publishing," *English Journal* 75 (1986): 55–57.

15. Louis Coser, Charles Kadushin, and Walter Powell, *Books: The Culture and Commerce of Publishing* (New York: Basic Books, 1982).

16. Joseph Turow, *Getting Books to Children* (Chicago: American Library Association, 1978).

17. Christian-Smith, "Gender, Popular Culture, and Curriculum."

18. Walter Retan, "The Changing Economics of Book Publishing," *Top of the News* 38 (1982): 233–35.

19. Leonard Shatzkin, *In Cold Type* (New York: Houghton Mifflin, 1982).

20. Sheila Harty, *Hucksters in the Classroom* (New York: Center for Responsive Law, 1979).

21. The growing implementation of a literature-based curriculum for reading instruction lends an added urgency to the critical examination of romance fiction and its use in schools.

22. Selma Lanes, "Here Come the Blockbusters—Teen Books Go Big Time," *Interracial Books for Children Bulletin* 12 (1981): 5–7.

23. Readability, or the difficulty of reading writing, is most often estimated through sentence length and word length. A number of the Hi-Low's that I have analyzed using readability measures are written at the fourth- to fifth-grade level. Pub-

lishers routinely estimate readability and print it in terms of grade level on the copyright page of their books.

24. Wayne Otto, Charles W. Peters, and Nathanial Peters, *Reading Problems: A Multidisciplinary Perspective* (Reading, Mass.: Addison-Wesley, 1977), 313.

25. Mark Aulls, *Developmental and Remedial Reading in the Middle Grades* (Boston: Allyn & Bacon, 1978).

26. Rudolph Flesch, *Why Johnny Still Can't Read* (New York: Harper & Row, 1981); The National Commission on Excellence in Education, *A Nation at Risk* (Washington, D.C.: U.S. Government Printing Office, 1983).

27. Lanes, "Here Come the Blockbusters."

28. Ibid.

29. Brett Harvey, "Wildfire: Tame but Deadly," *Interracial Books for Children Bulletin* 12 (1981): 8–10.

30. A more thorough discussion is contained in Christian-Smith, *Becoming a Woman through Romance.*

31. Christine T. Madsen, "Teen Novels: What Kind of Values Do They Promote?" *The Christian Science Monitor,* 17 December, 1981: B14–B17.

32. Pamela Pollack, "The Business of Popularity," *School Library Journal* 28 (1981): 25–28.

33. All names are fictitious.

34. The outlying schools tracked students in math, science, and language arts as well. Most of the girls in my sample were tracked together, so they interacted with one another across a range of subject areas.

35. In 1965, Congress passed the Elementary and Secondary Education Act known as "Title I" (now "Chapter I") as part of its "War on Poverty." Chapter I's focus was improving the reading and mathematics knowledge of the poor and educationally disadvantaged. Although Chapter I funding has been severely curtailed of late, it still remains the major form of compensatory education within many urban school districts.

36. For a detailed discussion of the methodology and issues surrounding interpretive research, see Christian-Smith, *Becoming a Woman through Romance.*

37. I focus exclusively on school because access to homes was difficult.

38. Refer to Christian-Smith, *Becoming a Woman through Romance,* for the reading survey and a discussion of survey research.

39. There are very few romance novels in which characters are not white. Tracy West's *Promises* (New York: Silhouette, 1986) features Black main characters. However, the novel has no specifically Black cultural dimensions.

40. Market Facts, *1983 Consumer Research Study.*

41. In the three schools, most of the heavy romance novel readers identified by the selection tools and staff happened to be students identified by school personnel as reluctant readers. No "skilled" readers were found in the initial sample of seventy-five girls and the final sample of twenty-nine girls. While librarians and teachers acknowledged that some skilled readers read teen romances, they read them neither exclusively nor with the frequency of the twenty-nine readers.

42. All pauses and hesitations have been omitted.

43. There was very little communication between readers within the classrooms observed or outside of school on the topic of the teen romances.

44. Mrs. B. characterized "quality literature" as a superbly told story, rich characters, and a concise "literary" style. She did not view book quality as connected to the way women were represented.

45. The major adolescent book awards in the United States are the American Library Association's Notable Books, the Laura Ingalls Wilder Award, the Newberry Award, and the National Book Award.

46. The findings of the 1983 Consumer Research Study on Reading and Book Purchasing by the Book Study Group found that the average reader read 24.9 books for leisure or work over a six-month period.

47. Janice Radway, *Reading the Romance* (Chapel Hill, N.C.: University of North Carolina Press, 1984).

48. A close textual analysis of a sample of teen romance fiction is contained in Christian-Smith, *Becoming a Woman through Romance.*

49. I was not able to fully account for the formation of the racial identity of the young women of color through romance reading because of racial tensions in the schools that preceded and continued during the time of the study. For further discussion, refer to Christian-Smith, *Becoming a Woman through Romance.*

50. For a comparison to adult romance novel readers, see Radway, *Reading the Romance.*

51. Wolfgang Iser, *The Implied Readers: Patterns of Communication in Prose Fiction from Bunyan to Beckett* (Baltimore, Md.: The Johns Hopkins University Press, 1974).

52. Andrea Marshall, *Against the Odds* (New York: Silhouette, 1985).

53. Angela McRobbie, *Jackie: An Ideology of Adolescent Femininity*. (Stencilled Occasional Paper, the Centre for Contemporary Cultural Studies, Birmingham England, 1978).

54. Radway, *Reading the Romance*.

55. Janet Quin-Harkin, *Princess Amy* (New York: Bantam Books, 1981).

56. For a discussion of this topic, see Christian-Smith, *Becoming a Woman through Romance*.

57. Their plans beyond high school included technical college, beauty school, and training in computers.

58. Christian-Smith, "Gender, Popular Culture, and Curriculum," and Joel Taxel, "The American Revolution in Children's Fiction: An Analysis of Historical Meaning and Narrative Structure," *Curriculum Inquiry*, 14 (1984): 7–55.

59. Anne Bridgman, "A.L.A. Study of Book-Club Alterations Prompts Shifts in Policy," *Education Week*, 12 September 1982, 6–7.

60. Michael W. Apple, *Ideology and Curriculum* (Boston: Routledge & Kegan Paul, 1979).

61. Todd Gitlin, "Television's Screens: Hegemony in Transition," in *Cultural and Economic Reproduction in Education*, ed. Michael W. Apple (Boston: Routledge & Kegan Paul, 1982), 202–46.

62. Pamela Pollack, "The Business of Popularity," 25–28.

63. Randy Albelda, Elaine McCrate, Edwin Melendez, and June Lapidus, *Mink Coats Don't Trickle Down* (Boston: South End Press, 1990).

64. See Linda K. Christian-Smith, "Power, Knowledge, and Curriculum: Constructing Femininity in Adolescent Romance Novels," in *Language, Authority and Criticism*, ed. Suzanne de Castell, Allan Luke, and Carmen Luke (London: Falmer Press, 1989), 17–31.

65. Unlike Radway's readers in *Reading the Romance*, the twenty-nine girls did not exchange books or share their reading.

66. Roger Keeran, "AFL-CIO Report: Service Sector," *Economic Notes* 53 (October 1985): 4.

67. Valdimir N. Volosinvov, *Marxism and the Philosophy of Language* (New York: Seminar Press, 1973).

68. Refer to Christian-Smith, *Becoming a Woman through Romance*.

69. Ibid.

70. On a critical perspective on reading, see Allan Luke and Carolyn D. Baker, *Towards a Critical Sociology of Reading Pedagogy* (Amsterdam: John Benjamins, 1990).

71. Ibid.

72. Nancy Schniedewind, "Teaching Feminist Process," *Women's Studies Quarterly* 15 (1987): 15–31.

73. Paolo Freire and Donaldo Macedo, *Reading the Word and the World* (Granby, Mass.: Bergin & Garvey, 1987).

74. In calling for a combination of approaches, I acknowledge the different traditions represented by feminist pedagogy and political literacy.

75. Refer to Apple and Christian-Smith, *The Politics of the Textbook*.

76. See Christian-Smith, *Becoming a Woman through Romance*.

77. Brett Harvey, "How Far Can You go in a Teen Romance?" *The Village Voice*, 10–16 February, 1982: 48–49.

CHAPTER 9

*An earlier version of this paper was published in *Oxford Review of Education*, whose permission to republish passages is acknowledged. My thanks to the men who were interviewed, both for their time and for their willingness to tackle difficult issues. Norm Radican and Pip Martin did most of the interviews. The project was funded by the Australian Research Grants Committee with supplementary grants from Macquarie University. My thinking on these issues has been particularly influenced by Gary Dowsett. I am also indebted to Lin Walker's thinking about working-class girls and schooling.

1. P. Sexton, *The Feminized Male: Classrooms, White Collars, and the Decisions of Manliness* (New York: Random House, 1969).

2. J. P. Hantover, "The Boy Scouts and the Validation of Masculinity," *Journal of Social Issues* 34 (1) (1978): 184–95.

3. A. Rich, *On Lies, Secrets, and Silence* (New York: Norton, 1979).

4. R. W. Connell, *Gender and Power* (Stanford: Stanford University Press, 1987); B. B. Hess and M. M. Ferree, *Analyzing Gender* (Newbury Park, California: Sage, 1987).

5. T. Carrigan, R. W. Connell, and J. Lee, "Toward a New Sociology of Masculinity," *Theory and Society* 14 (5) (1985): 551–604.

6. G. W. Dowsett, *Boys Own* (Sydney: Inner City Education Centre, 1985); C. Thompson, "Education and Masculinity," in A. O. Carelli, ed., *Sex Equity in Education* (Springfield, Illinois: Thomas, 1988), 47–54.

7. E. Hansot and D. Tyack, "Gender in Public Schools: Thinking Institutionally," *Signs* 13 (4) (1988): 741–60.

8. B. Thorne, "Girls and Boys Together . . . But Mostly Apart: Gender Arrangements in Elementary Schools," in *Relationships and Development*, ed. W. W. Hartup and Z. Rubin (Hillsdale, Erlbaum, 1986), 167–84.

9. M. Messner, "Boyhood, Organized Sports, and the Construction of Masculinities," *Journal of Contemporary Ethnography* 18 (4) (1990): 416–44.

10. S. Kessler, D. J. Ashenton, R. W. Connell, and G. W. Dowsett, "Gender Relations in Secondary Schooling" *Sociology of Education* 58 (1) (1985): 34–48.

11. C. Heward, *Making a Man of Him* (London: Routledge, 1988).

12. J. C. Walker, *Louts and Legends* (Sydney: Allen & Unwin, 1988).

13. M. Donaldson, "Labouring Men: Love, Sex and Strife," *Australian and New Zealand Journal of Sociology* 23 (3) (1987): 165–84. R. W. Connell, "Live Fast and Die Young: The Construction of Masculinity among Young Working-Class Men on the Margin of the Labour Market," submitted for publication.

14. R. W. Connell, "Remaking Masculinity in the Context of the Environmental Movement," *Gender and Society,* 4 (4), in press.

15. D. H. Hargreaves, *Social Relations in a Secondary School* (London: Routledge & Kegan Paul, 1967); P. Willis, *Learning to Labour* (Farnborough, England: Saxon House, 1977); J. C. Walker, *Louts and Legends.*

16. R. W. Connell, *Teachers' Work* (Sydney: Allen & Unwin, 1985).

17. R. W. Connell, "An Iron Man: The Body and Some Contradictions of Hegemonic Masculinity," in *Sport, Men, and the Gender Order: Critical Feminist Perspectives* M. A. Messner and D. F. Sabo, eds. (Champaign, Illinois: Human Kinetics Books, 1990).

18. P. Lafitte, *The Person in Psychology* (London: Routledge & Kegan Paul, 1957); L. Johnson, *Free U.* (Sydney: Free University, 1968); A. Rich, *On Lies, Secrets, and Silence.*

19. K. Maddock, *The Australian Aborigines,* 2d ed. (Ringwood: Australia: Penguin, 1982): 29–36.

20. M. F. Winter and E. R. Robert, "Male Dominance, Late Capitalism, and the Growth of Instrumental Reason," *Berkeley Journal of Sociology* 24 (25) (1980): 249–80.

21. C. Ehrlich, "The Woman Book Industry," *American Journal of Sociology* 78 (1973): 1031–44.

22. H. Eisenstein, *Contemporary Feminist Thought* (London: Unwin Paperbacks, 1984); L. Segal, *Is the Future Female?* (London: Virago, 1987).

23. C. St. J. Hunter and D. Harman, *Adult Illiteracy in the United States* (New York: McGraw-Hill, 1979).

24. L. Segal, *Is the Future Female?*

25. H. Goldberg, *The Inner Male* (New York: Signet, 1987); W. Farrell, *Why Men Are the Way They Are* (New York: Berkeley, 1988).

26. R. W. Connell, *Teachers' Work*.

27. M. Messner, "Boyhood, Organized Sports, and the Construction of Masculinities"; R. W. Connell, "An Iron Man."

28. R. W. Connell, *Gender and Power*.

29. A. Tolson, *The Limits of Masculinity* (London: Tavistock, 1977); J. Snodgrass, *For Men against Sexism* (Albion, CA.: Times Change Press, 1977).

30. D. C. Holland and M. A. Eisenhart, *Educated in Romance* (Chicago: University of Chicago Press, 1990).

31. L. Yates, "The Theory and Practice of Counter-Sexist Education in Schools," *Discourse* 3 (2) (1983): 33–44.

32. G. W. Dowsett, *Boys Own*.

33. S. Lees, *Losing Out: Sexuality and Adolescent Girls* (London: Hutchinson, 1986): 149–50.

34. J. Ptacek, "Why Do Men Batter Their Wives?" in *Feminist Perspectives on Wife Abuse*, ed. K. Yllo and M. Bograd (Newbury Park, California: Sage, 1988), 133–57; D. Adams, "Treatment Models of Men Who Batter: A Profeminist Analysis" in Yllo and Bograd, *Feminist Perspectives on Wife Abuse*, 176–99; S. Gray, "Sharing the Shop Floor," in *Beyond Patriarchy*, ed. M. Kaufman (Toronto: Oxford University Press, 1987).

CHAPTER 10

1. D. A. Grayson, "Emerging Equity Issues Related to Homosexuality in Education," *Peabody Journal of Education* 64 (1989): 132–45.

2. R. A. Friend, "The Individual and Social Psychology of Aging: Clinical Implications for Lesbians and Gay Men," *Journal of Homosexuality* 14 (1/2) (1987):

307–31. R. A. Friend, "Sexual Identity and Human Diversity: Implications for Nursing Practice," *Holistic Nursing Practice* 1 (4) (1987): 21–41. R. A. Friend, "Older Lesbian and Gay People: Responding to Homophobia," *Marriage and Family Review* 14 (3/4) (1989): 241–63. R. A. Friend, "Older Lesbian and Gay People: A Theory of Successful Aging," *Journal of Homosexuality* 20 (3/4) (1990): 91–110.

3. A. Lorde, "I Am Your Sister: Black Women Organizing across Sexualities," in *The Psychopathology of Everyday Racism and Sexism*, ed. L. Fulani (New York: Haworth, 1988), 26.

4. A. Rich, "Compulsory Heterosexuality and Lesbian Existence," *Signs: Journal of Women in Culture and Society* 5 (8) (1980): 3–32.

5. J. H. Neisen, "Heterosexism: Redefining Homophobia for the 1990's," *Journal of Gay and Lesbian Psychotherapy* 1, (3) (1990): 21–35.

6. From H. Warren, *Talking about School* (London: London Gay Teenage Group, 1984), 24.

7. Friend, "Individual and Social Psychology of Aging." Friend, "Sexual Identity and Human Diversity." Friend, "Older Lesbian and Gay People Responding to Homophobia." Friend, "Older Lesbian and Gay People: A Theory of Successful Aging."

8. G. Weinberg, *Society and the Healthy Homosexual* (New York: St. Martin's, 1972).

9. Friend, "The Individual and Social Psychology of Aging." Friend, "Sexual Identity and Human Diversity." Friend, "Older Lesbian and Gay People: Responding to Homophobia." Friend, "Older Lesbian and Gay People: A Theory of Successful Aging." Neisen, "Heterosexism."

10. G. J. Krysial, "A Very Silent and Gay Minority," *The School Counselor* 34 (4) (1987): 304–7.

11. J. Hunter and R. Schaecher, "Stresses on Lesbian and Gay Adolescents in Schools," *Social Work in Education* 9 (3) (1987): 180–190.

12. A. J. Smith, "From Stigma to Paradigm: The Uses of Difference," paper presented at the third North American Anti-Homophobia Educators Conference—Challenging Oppression: Creating Multicultural Communities, sponsored by the Campaign to End Homophobia, Chicago, 6 July 1991.

13. John, personal communication, 30 November 1990.

14. L. Trenchard, ed., *Talking about Young Lesbians* (London: London Gay Teenage Group, 1984), 10.

15. Grayson, "Emerging Equity Issues."

16. E. Rofes, "Opening Up the Classroom Closet: Responding to the Educational Needs of Gay and Lesbian Youth," *Harvard Educational Review* 59 (1989): 444–53.

17. L. Gordon, "What Do We Say When We Hear 'Faggot'?" *Interracial Books for Children Bulletin* 14 (3/4) (1983): 25–27.

18. D. I. Dennis and R. E. Harlow, "Gay Youth and the Right to Education," *Yale Law and Policy Review* 4 (1986): 446–78.

19. Written testimony to the Philadelphia Board of Education, 15 September 1986, 4 October 1986, 10 November 1986.

20. K. Whitlock, *Bridges to Respect* (Philadelphia: American Friends Service Committee, 1988), 16.

21. Ibid.

22. Trenchard, *Talking about Young Lesbians*, 12.

23. J. C. Gonsiorek, "Mental Health Issues of Gay and Lesbian Adolescents," *Journal of Adolescent Health Care* 9 (1988): 114–22. G. Rubin, "Thinking Sex: Notes for a Radical Theory of the Politics of Sexuality," in *Pleasure and Danger: Exploring Female Sexuality,* ed. C. S. Vance (Boston: Routledge & Kegan Paul, 1984), 267–319.

24. C. S. Vance, "Pleasure and Danger: Toward a Politics of Sexuality," in *Pleasure and Danger,* ed. Vance, 1–27.

25. M. Fine, "Sexuality, Schooling, and Adolescent Females: The Missing Discourse of Desire," *Harvard Educational Review* 58 (1988): 29–53.

26. Rubin, "Thinking Sex."

27. Fine, "Sexuality, Schooling, and Adolescent Females."

28. Trenchard, *Talking about Young Lesbians,* 31.

29. L. B. Schwartz, "Adolescent and Young Adult Sexuality: A Study of Self-identified Lesbian and Gay Youth," Ph.D. diss., University of Pennsylvania, 1990, 241.

30. Written testimony to the Philadelphia Board of Education, 15 September 1986, 4 October 1986, 10 November 1986.

31. Dennis and Harlow, "Gay Youth and the Right to Education," 475.

32. D. Tartagni, "Counseling Gays in a School Setting," *The School Counselor* 26 (1978): 26–32. Hunter and Schaecher, "Stresses."

33. Whitlock, *Bridges to Respect.* Warren, *Talking about School.*

34. E. Erikson, *Childhood and Society* (New York: Norton, 1963).

35. E. S. Hetrick and D. A. Martin, "Developmental Issues and Their Resolution for Gay and Lesbian Adolescents," *Journal of Homosexuality* 14 (1/2) (1987): 25–43.

36. E. Coleman, "Developmental Stages of the Coming Out Process," *Journal of Homosexuality* 7 (1981/82):31–43. D. A. Martin, "Learning to Hide: The Socialization of the Gay Adolescent," *Adolescent Psychiatry* 10 (1982): 52–65. G. J. McDonald, "Individual Differences in the Coming Out Process for Gay Men: Implications for Theoretical Models," *Journal of Homosexuality* 8 (1982): 47–60. Whitlock, *Bridges to Respect.*

37. R. C. Savin-Williams, *Gay and Lesbian Youth: Expressions of Identity* (New York: Hemisphere, 1990), 3.

38. Friend, "Older Lesbian and Gay People: A Theory of Successful Aging." Savin-Williams, *Gay and Lesbian Youth.*

39. J. Money and A. Ehrhardt, *Man and Woman, Boy and Girl* (Baltimore: Johns Hopkins Press 1972). J. Money, *Lovemaps* (New York: Irvington, 1988). W. Stayton, "A Theory of Sexual Orientation: The Universe as a Turn On," *Topics in Clinical Nursing* 1 (3) (1980): 1–7.

40. R. C. Savin-Williams, "An Ethological Perspective on Homosexuality during Adolescence," *Journal of Adolescent Research* 2 (1987): 283–302.

41. Savin-Williams, *Gay and Lesbian Youth.*

42. Ibid., 5.

43. Ibid.

44. A. Kinsey, W. Pomeroy, and C. Martin, *Sexual Behavior in the Human Male* (Philadelphia: Saunders, 1948). A. P. Bell and M. S. Weinberg, *Homosexualities* (New York: Simon & Schuster, 1978). J. Marmor, *Homosexual Behavior: A Modern Reappraisal* (New York: Basic Books, 1980).

45. G. M. Herek, "Hate Crimes against Lesbians and Gay Men: Issues for Research and Policy," *American Psychologist* 44 (1989): 948–55.

46. Ibid.

47. G. D. Comstock, *Violence against Lesbians and Gay Men* (New York: Columbia University Press, 1991), 52.

48. Ibid., 76.

49. P. Finn and T. McNeil, "The Response of the Criminal Justice System to Bias Crime: An Exploratory Review," contract report submitted to the National

Institute of Justice, U.S. Department of Justice, 7 October 1987. (Available from Abt Associates, Inc., 55 Wheeler St., Cambridge, MA 02138-1168.)

50. Governor's Task Force on Bias-Related Violence, *Final Report*, 1988. (Available from Division of Human Rights, 55 West 125th St., New York, NY 10027.)

51. Written testimony, 30 September 1983.

52. D. A. Martin and E. S. Hetrick, "The Stigmatization of the Gay and Lesbian Adolescent," *Journal of Homosexuality* 15 (1/2) (1988): 163–83). J. T. Sears, "The Impact of Gender and Race on Growing Up Lesbian and Gay in the South," *NWSA Journal* 1 (3) (Spring 1989): 422–57.

53. S. Pharr, *Homophobia: A Weapon of Sexism* (Inverness, CA: Chardon Press, 1988).

54. Martin and Hetrick, "Stigmatization," 176–77.

55. Ibid.

56. Martin, "Learning to Hide." Martin and Hetrick, "Stigmatization." Gonsiorek, "Mental Health Issues." Hunter and Schaecher, "Stresses." Rofes, "Opening Up the Classroom Closet."

57. M. Hippler, "The Problem and Promise of Gay Youth," *The Advocate*, 16 September 1986, 42–47, 55–57.

58. Martin and Hetrick, "Stigmatization."

59. Herek, "Hate Crimes."

60. Ibid., 943.

61. Gonsiorek, "Mental Health Issues," 117.

62. P. Gibson, "Gay Male and Lesbian Youth Suicide," *Report of the Secretary's Task Force on Youth Suicide* (Washington, D.C.: U.S. Department of Health and Human Services, 1989, 3-110 to 3-142.

63. G. Remafedi, J. A. Farrow, and R. W. Deisher, "Risk Factors for Attempted Suicides in Gay and Bisexual Youth," *Pediatrics* 87 (1991): 869–75.

64. Ibid., 874.

65. Trenchard, *Talking About Young Lesbians*, 36.

66. Savin-Williams, *Gay and Lesbian Youth*, 25.

67. Ibid.

68. Hunter and Schaecher, "Stresses."

69. G. Remafedi, "Moving toward a Healthy Paradigm of Teen Sexual Development," paper presented at the thirty-third annual meeting of the Society for the Scientific Study of Sex, Minneapolis, 1 November 1990.

70. Ibid.

71. Martin, "Learning to Hide." Martin and Hetrick, "Stigmatization." Hunter and Schaecher, "Stresses." M. Schneider and B. Tremble, "Gay or Straight? Working with the Confused Adolescent," *Journal of Social Work and Human Sexuality* 4 (1/2) (1986): 71–82. Rofes, "Opening Up the Classroom Closet." Gonsiorek, "Mental Health Issues."

72. H. L. Minton and G. J. McDonald, "Homosexual Identity Formation as a Developmental Process," *Journal of Homosexuality* 9 (1983/1984): 91–104.

73. Neisen, "Heterosexism."

74. Martin, "Learning to Hide."

75. Hunter and Schaecher, "Stresses."

76. Martin, "Learning to Hide." Martin and Hetrick, "Stigmatization." Hunter and Schaecher, "Stresses." R. Schaecher, "Stresses on Lesbian and Gay Adolescents," *Independent School* (Winter 1989): 29–34. Schneider and Tremble, "Gay or Straight?" Rofes, "Opening Up the Classroom Closet." Gonsiorek, "Mental Health Issues."

77. R. R. Troiden, "Homosexual Identity Formation," *Journal of Adolescent Health Care* 9 (1988): 105–13. R. R. Troiden, "The Formation of Homosexual Identities," *Journal of Homosexuality* 17 (1/2) (1989): 43–73.

78. Hunter and Schaecher, "Stresses."

79. Troiden, "Homosexual Identity Formation." Troiden, "Formation of Homosexual Identities."

80. Schneider and Tremble, "Gay or Straight?" 78.

81. J. Reid, *The Best Little Boy in the World* (New York: Ballantine Books, 1973).

82. Malyon, "The Homosexual Adolescent."

83. M. Kirk and H. Madsen, *After the Ball: How America Will Conquer Its Fear and Hatred of Gays in the 90's* (New York: Doubleday, 1989).

84. A. Fricke, *Reflections of a Rock Lobster* (Boston: Alyson, 1981).

85. Hippler, "Problem and Promise," 480.

86. K. McCaffree, personal communication, 12 December 1990.

87. G. M. Herek, "Gay People and Government Security Clearances: A Social Science Perspective, *American Psychologist* 45 (1990): 1035–42.

88. Schwartz, "Adolescent and Young Adult Sexuality," 173.

89. M. Fine and P. Rosenberg, "Dropping Out of High School: The Ideology of School and Work," *Journal of Education* 165 (1983): 257–72.

90. Hunter and Schaecher, "Stresses." Rofes, "Opening Up the Classroom Closet."

91. Dennis and Harlow, "Gay Youth and the Right to Education."

92. Whitlock, *Bridges to Respect,* 15–16.

93. Rofes, "Opening Up the Classroom Closet."

94. M. Foucault, *The History of Sexuality. Volume I: An Introduction* (New York: Vintage Books, 1978).

95. Savin-Williams, *Gay and Lesbian Youth.*

96. Ibid., 184.

97. Foucault, *History of Sexuality*

98. Schwartz, "Adolescent and Young Adult Sexuality," 147.

99. D. Kimmel, "Adult Development and Aging: A Gay Perspective," *Journal of Social Issues* 34 (1978): 113–30.

100. G. M. Herek, "On Heterosexual Masculinity: Some Physical Consequences of the Social Construction of Gender and Sexuality," *American Behavioral Psychologist* 29 (1986): 563–77.

101. P. R. Sanday, *Fraternity Gang Rape: Sex, Brotherhood, and Privilege on Campus* (New York: New York University Press, 1990).

102. Dennis and Harlow, "Gay Youth and the Right to Education."

103. Schwartz, "Adolescent and Young Adult Sexuality."

104. Ibid., 180–81.

105. Ibid., 241.

CHAPTER 11

*From field notes

1. See Barry Bluestone and Bennett Harrison, *The De-Industrialization of America* (New York: Basic Books, 1982).

2. Carol Axtell Ray and Roslyn Mikelson, "Restructuring Students for Re-structural Work: The Economy, School Reform, and Noncollege Bound Youth," mimeo, 8.

3. Estimates are fairly consistent regarding the new economy. See David Birch, "The Hidden Economy," *Wall Street Journal*, 10 June 1988, 23; Robert Shapiro and Maureen Walsh, "The Great Jobs Mismatch," *U.S. News and World Report*, 7 September 1987, 42–43; Sar Levitan and Isaal Shapiro, *Working but Poor: America's Contradiction*. (Baltimore: Johns Hopkins Press, 1987); as cited in Axtell and Mikelson, "Restructuring Students," 20.

4. Henry M. Levin and Russell Rumberger, "Education Requirements for New Technologies: Visions, Possibilities, and Current Realities," *Educational Policy* 1 (1987): 333–34.

5. Michael Apple, "American Realities: Poverty, Economy and Education," in *Dropouts from School: Issues, Dilemmas, and Solutions*, ed. Lois Weis, Eleanor Farrar, and Hugh Petrie (Albany: State University of New York Press, 1989), 205–25, as cited in Axtell and Mikelson, "Restructuring Students," 20.

6. Richard Edwards, *The Contested Terrain* (New York: Basic Books, 1979).

7. This is not to deny that many women do not rely on their wages alone but are, rather, enmeshed within a domestic economy that includes their husband's wages. Many women are not helped by a male wage, however, and the number of women also earning the sole family wage is rising.

8. This is not to deny the exploitation of the working class in the service of capitalist profits, but to quite frankly admit that many are far worse off in the economy than white working-class males.

9. See Lois Weis, *Working Class without Work: High School Students in a De-Industrializing Economy* (New York: Routledge and Chapman Hall, 1990); Mike Davis, *Prisoners of the American Dream* (London: Verso Press, 1986).

10. *Freeway Evening News*, magazine section, 5 June, 1983.

11. Occupations by year for Freeway Standard Metropolitan Statistical Area (SMSA), all persons. Data are reported in full by Lois Weis, *Working Class without Work*.

12. These figures are based on the same SMSA data as noted above.

13. See Paul Willis, *Learning to Labour: How Working Class Kids Get Working Class Jobs* (Westmead, England: Saxon House Press, 1977); J. C. Walker, *Louts and Legends: Male Youth Culture in an Inner City School* (Sydney: Allen & Unwin, 1988); R. W. Connell, "Live Fast and Die Young: The Construction of Masculinity among Youth Working Class Men on the Margin of the Labor Market," 1990 (mimeo).

14. Paul Willis, *Learning to Labour*, 49.

15. Angela McRobbie, "Working Class Girls and the Culture of Femininity," in *Women Take Issue,* ed. Women's Studies Group (London: Hutchinson, 1978); and Linda Valli, *Becoming Clerical Workers* (Boston: Routledge & Kegan Paul, 1986). It must be pointed out here that while this "ideology of romance" may be constructed with the hope of moving out of an oppressive home of origin and not, therefore, necessarily as "homebound," as has been seen by some investigators, it does, nevertheless, still tie women to the home of their future husband in much the same way as their mothers were tied. It is not, then, necessarily a celebration of their own home of origin, but may, rather, reflect a generally ill-founded hope that their future home will be different from (less oppressive than) that in which they grew up. Thus the identity uncovered by previous investigators is, indeed, homebound but may not reflect any particular attachment to the home of their father.

16. Karen Brodkin Sacks, ed., *My Troubles are Going to Have Trouble with Me* (New Brunswick: Rutgers University Press), 17–18. See also Alice Kessler-Harris, "Where Are the Organized Women Workers?" *Feminist Studies* 3 (1-2): 92–110, as cited in Sacks, *My Troubles,* 18.

17. Willis has suggested the possibility of white working-class men striving for more egalitarian gender relations. Unfortunately I could not disagree more. See Paul Willis, "Youth Unemployment: Thinking the Unthinkable," mimeo.

18. See, for example, Beverly Bryan, Stella Dadzie, and Suzanne Sharfe, *The Heart of the Race* (London: Virago, 1985); and Lois Weis, "Without Dependence on Welfare for Life: The Experience of Black Women in the Urban Community College," *The Urban Review,* 7 (1985): 233–56.

19. Paul Willis, "Youth Unemployment: Thinking the Unthinkable," 8.

20. Ray Raphael, *The Men from the Boys* (Lincoln: University of Nebraska Press, 1988), 157. For another interesting view of the production of masculinity, see David Gilmore, *Manhood in the Making: Cultural Concepts of Masculinity* (New Haven: Yale University Press, 1990).

21. See Alison Jones, " 'I Just Wanna Decent Job'—Working Class Girls' Education: Perspective and Policy Issues," in *Toward Successful Schooling,* ed. Hugh Lauder and Cathy Wylie (London: Falmer Press, 1990).

22. Based on a survey conducted in 1956, for example, Elizabeth Douvan and Joseph Adelson conclude that girls are much less clear about their future work than boys, and that adolescent females focus on marriage and motherhood as a life plan rather than the world of work. More recent studies such as those by Valli and McRobbie reach largely similar conclusions. See Valli, *Becoming Clerical Workers,* McRobbie, "Working Class Girls," and Elizabeth Douvan and Joseph Adelson, *The Adolescent Experience* (New York: John Wiley & Sons, 1966).

23. Weis, *Working Class without Work.*

24. For an extensive analysis of the teaching offered these students, see Weis, *Working Class without Work*.

25. Lawrence Miskel and David M. Frankel, *The State of Working America* (Washington, D.C.: Economic Policy Institute, 1990).

26. Linda Gordan and Allen Hunter, *Radical America* (November 1977–February 1978); 9–25, as cited in Edgar, "Reagan's Hidden Agenda: Racism and The New Right," *Race and Class* (3) (1981), 225.

27. Ibid., 225.

28. Gordan and Hunter, *Radical America*. See also Allen Hunter's further analysis of these issues in "Children in the Service of Conservation: Parent-Child Relations in the New Right's Pro-Family Rhetoric," Institute for Legal Studies, University of Wisconsin-Madison, 1988. He notes here that "the New Right's family is a politicization of the 1950s suburban family in which men worked, women stayed at home and took care of their children. Men are working, married heterosexuals; indeed, the New Right Vision is consonant with the dominant early 1950 view that 'adult masculinity was indistinguishable from the breadwinner role.' "

29. Andrew Koplind, *New Times*, 30 September 1977, 21–33, as cited in Edgar, "Reagan's Hidden Agenda," 225.

30. Michael Omi and Howard Winant, *Racial Formation in the United States* (Boston: Routledge and Kegan Paul, 1986). It is worth noting here that analysts suggest that similar trends are in evidence in the U.K. See Paul Gordan and Francesca Klug, *New Right, New Racism* (Nottingham, England: Russell Press, 1989).

31. Omi and Winant, *Racial Formation*, 120.

32. See Omi and Winant, *Racial Formation*, chap. 7.

33. It is noteworthy that in Buffalo, New York, two-thirds of the antiabortion protestors in recent months have been male, and the leadership is entirely male. These are fundamentalist groups rather than Catholic. Although I am not certain of the social class of these males, it is noteworthy that the group is so heavily male dominated. My thanks to Maxine Seller for pointing this out to me.

CHAPTER 12

1. See, for example, G. Natriello, A. Pallas, and E. McDill, "Taking Stock: Renewing our Research Agenda on the Causes and Consequences of Dropping Out," *Teachers College Record* 87 (1986): 4; and G. Wehlage, R. Rutter, G. Smith, N. Lesko, and R. Fernandez, *Reducing the Risk: Schools as Communities of Support* (London: Falmer Press, 1989).

2. M. Fine and P. Rosenberg, "Dropping Out of High School: The Ideology of School and Work," *Journal of Education* 165 (1983): 259.

3. R. Stevenson and J. Ellsworth, "Dropping Out in a Working Class High School: Adolescent Voices on the Decision to Leave." *British Journal of Sociology of Education,* in press.

4. Wehlage et al., *Reducing the Risk,* 48.

5. M. D. Hinds, "Cutting the Dropout Rate: High Goal but Low Hopes," *New York Times,* 17 February 1990, 1.

6. Ibid.

7. D. R. Grossnickle, *High School Dropouts: Causes, Consequences, and Cure.* (Bloomington, Ind.: Phi Delta Kappa Educational Foundation, 1986).

8. See, for example, J. N. Baker, "Helping Dropouts Drop In," *Newsweek,* 3 August 1987, 63; B. B. Remmes, "Why Kids Drop Out," *Newsweek,* 6 March 1989, 10–11; P. Skalka, "No One's a Born Loser," *Readers' Digest,* February 1989, 21–22; and B. Thompson, "The Only Failure Is Not To Try," *Christianity Today,* 17 October 1986, 34.

9. *U.S. News and World Report,* 5 June 1989, 49.

10. See, for example, *Newsweek,* 31 August 1987; and *New York Times,* 17 February 1990.

11. Wehlage et al., *Reducing the Risk.* 37.

12. Fine and Rosenberg, "Dropping Out of High School."

13. Ibid., 267.

14. J. Ogbu, "Class Stratification, Racial Stratification, and Schooling," in *Class, Race, and Gender in American Education,* ed. L. Weis (Albany: State University of New York Press, 1988); J. Ogbu, *The Next Generation: An Ethnography of Education in an Urban Neighborhood* (New York: Academic Press, 1974).

15. Wehlage et al., *Reducing the Risk,* 40.

16. Fine and Rosenberg, "Dropping Out of High School."

17. R. W. Rumberger, "High School Dropouts: A Review of Issues and Evidence," *Review of Educational Research* 57 (2) (1987): 101–121.

18. For example: Rumberger, "High School Dropouts," and Wehlage et al., *Reducing the Risks*

19. L. Weis, *Working Class without Work: High School Students in a De-Industrialized Economy* (New York: Routledge, 1990).

20. P. Willis, *Learning to Labour: How Working Class Kids Get Working Class Jobs* (Westmead, England: Saxon House Press, 1977).

21. Our reference to Willis's work should not be taken to suggest that we view this culture as worthy of emulation, since it was also wholly oppositional to females.

22. L. Weis, *Between Two Worlds: Black Students in an Urban Community College* (London: Routledge & Kegan Paul, 1985); Ogbu, *The Next Generation.*

23. Ogbu, "Class Stratification, Racial Stratification, and Schooling," 170.

24. Ibid.

25. J. Ogbu, "The Individual in Collective Adaptation: A Framework for Focusing on Academic Underperformance and Dropping Out among Involuntary Minorities," in *Dropouts from School: Issues, Dilemmas, and Solutions,* ed. L. Weis, E. Farrar and H. G. Petrie (Albany: State University of New York Press, 1989).

26. Ibid., 189.

27. For further discussion of this fracturing of the working class, both historically and as a result of the deindustrialization of the American economy, see Weis, *Working Class without Work.*

28. Ibid.

29. Ibid.

30. J. Anyon, "Workers, Labor and Economic History, and Textbook Content," in *Ideology and Practice in Schooling,* ed. M. W. Apple and L. Weis (Philadelphia: Temple University Press, 1983).

31. Fine and Rosenberg, "Dropping Out of High School," 259.

32. Stevenson and Ellsworth, "Dropping Out in a Working Class High School," 25.

CHAPTER 13

*I acknowledge funding for this work from the University of Pennsylvania Research Foundation and the Spencer Small Grant Program. A Spencer Postdoctoral Fellowship from the National Academy of Education, a University of Carolina Minority Postdoctoral Fellowship, and a Smithsonian Faculty Fellowship enabled me to work full-time on this study. I am grateful to Michelle Fine and Lois Weis for their comments on earlier drafts of this article and to Jeanne Newman for her transcription of the interviews.

1. B. Collier-Thomas, "The Impact of Black Women in Education: An Historical Overview," *Journal of Negro Education,* 51(3) (Summer, 1982): 173; Joint

Center for Political Studies, *Visions of a Better Way: Black Appraisal of Public Schooling* (Washington, D.C., 1989).

2. S. Lightfoot, *Worlds Apart: Relationships between Families and Schools* (New York: Basic Books, 1978); P. Sterling, *The Real Teachers: Thirty Inner-City Schoolteachers Talk Honestly about Who They Are, How They Teach, and Why* (New York: Random House, 1972); G. Lerner, *Black Women in White America: A Documentary History* (New York: Vintage, 1972).

3. R. Rist, "Student Social Class and Teacher Expectations: The Self-fulfilling Prophecy in Ghetto Education," *Harvard Educational Review* 40 (1970): 411–51; R. Rist, *The Urban School: A Factory for Failure* (Cambridge: MIT Press, 1973); P. Conroy, *The Water is Wide* (Boston: Houghton Mifflin, 1972); D. Spencer, *Contemporary Women Teachers: Balancing School and Home* (New York: Longman, 1986).

4. A total of nineteen teachers have been interviewed for this study. Fourteen are female and four are male. At the time they were interviewed, seven were elementary school teachers, five were teaching high school, and one was teaching junior high school. Four were retired at the time of their interviews. The remaining two were school administrators when they interviewed, though they had previously been teachers. All of the males teach high school or junior high school. The women teachers were almost evenly divided between elementary and high school levels: four were high school teachers and five were elementary school teachers. The teachers were raised in twelve states within five regions: the Northeast, Middle Atlantic, South Atlantic, West North Central, and West South Central. The regions were derived using 1989 109th Statistical Abstract. *Community nomination,* a term coined and a method of selection developed by this author specifically for this study, means that teachers were chosen by direct contact with African American communities. Periodicals, community organizations, and individuals provided the names of the teachers. Informants have been questioned about their family, childhood, and community life; their elementary, high school, college, and teacher training experiences; their decisions to become teachers; the various positions they have held; the changes they have observed during their lives and careers; and their philosophies and pedagogies of education. The interviews ranged from two to four hours in length, and where required, follow-up interviews, which build on previous sessions, have been conducted.

5. D. Tyack, *The One Best System: A History of American Urban Education* (Cambridge: Harvard University Press, 1984); V. P. Franklin, *The Education of Black Philadelphia: The Social and Educational History of a Minority Community 1900–1950* (Philadelphia: University of Pennsylvania Press, 1979); L. P. Curry, *The Free Black in America 1800–1850* (Chicago: University of Chicago Press, 1981); J. Anderson, *The Education of Blacks in the South, 1860–1935* (Chapel Hill: University of North Carolina Press, 1989); S. Ethridge, "The Impact of the 1954 Brown v. Topeka Board of Education Decision on Black Educators," *Negro Educational Review,* 30 (3–4) (1979): 217–32; M. Dilworth, *Teachers' Totter: A Report on Certification Issues* (Washington, D.C.: Institute for the Study of Educational Policy, Howard University, 1984).

6. L. E. Lomax, *The Negro Revolt* (New York: Signet Books, 1962), 269.

7. G. W. Streator, "The Colored South Speaks for Itself," in *A Documentary History of the Negro People in the United States, Volume 4: From the New Deal to the End of World War II*, ed. H. Aptheker (New York: Citadel Press, 1990).

8. Ibid.

9. All informants' names are pseudonyms to protect their identities. The place names remain unchanged. Information was gathered from the informants in face to face interviews with the author. Interviews took place between March 1988 and August 1991.

10. F. Jones, *A Traditional Model of Excellence: Dunbar High School of Little Rock, Arkansas* (Washington, D.C.: Howard University Press, 1981); T. Sowell, "Black Excellence—The Case of Dunbar High School," *Public Interest*, 35 (1974): 3–21; T. Sowell, "Patterns of Black Excellence," *Public Interest*, 43 (1976): 26–58.

11. R. Kluger, *Simple Justice* (New York: Vintage, 1975).

12. Ibid., 378–79.

13. Rist, "Student Social Class and Teacher Expectations"; Rist, *The Urban School;* Conroy, *The Water is Wide;* Spencer, *Contemporary Women Teachers.*

14. In a thorough analysis of all-Black Avery Institute from 1867 to 1954, *Initiative, Paternalism, and Race Relations: Charleston's Avery Normal Institute* (Athens: University of Georgia Press, 1990), Drago contends that despite the aristocratic ethos of the Charleston Black community, Avery Institute was able to imbue in its graduate a sense of service, whereby the majority of its students, including women, excluded from teaching in the all-Black public schools in Charleston until 1917, taught in the rural areas and small towns of South Carolina. Miss Ruthie, born into a family considered middle class by economic and social standards of early-twentieth-century Black Charleston, began working in Charleston County in 1928 and has been teaching in coastal South Carolina continuously since 1938.

15. For an excellent discussion of the way suburban districts have benefited by interdistrict plans at the expense of urban districts and students, see D. J. Monti, *A Semblance of Justice: School Desegregation and the Pursuit of Order in Urban America* (Columbia: University of Missouri Press, 1985). The declining numbers of Black teachers due to desegregation, especially the transfer of the most qualified Black teachers to predominantly white schools, is discussed in Ethridge, "Impact of Brown v. Topeka Board of Education," and D. Bell, *And We Are Not Saved: The Elusive Quest for Racial Justice* (New York: Basic Books, 1987). D. Bell, "Time for the Teachers: Putting Educators Back into the Brown Remedy," *Journal of Negro Education* 52 (3) (1983): 290–301.

16. Ethridge, "Impact of Brown v. Topeka Board of Education."

17. J. Stewart, K. Meier, and R. England, "In Quest of Role Models: Change in Black Teacher Representation in Urban School Districts 1968–86," *Journal of Negro Education*, 58(2) (1989): 140–52.

18. Tyack, *The One Best System*.

19. For information on the survey questions and results, see "Black Enterprise Survey: A View of the Past, a Look to the Future," *Black Enterprise* January (1990): 69–75. "Black Enterprise Survey Results," *Black Enterprise* August (1990): 85–94. The exact percentages of those polled are as follows: 63 percent believed that the quality of public school education for Black children had decreased in the past decade. Sixteen and one-half percent felt that the quality of public school education for Blacks had improved, and 17.9 percent of those responding to the questionnaire felt it had remained the same. Asked whether the quality of public school education for white students had improved during the same period, 32.2 percent felt the quality had increased, 22.2 percent felt it had decreased, and 37 percent felt it had remained the same. Asked to assess the improvement in education in the thirty-five years since, for Black children, 60 percent felt that the education was the same or worse, 44.5 percent of the respondents felt the education was worse, and 14.3 percent felt there was no change. The responses to the question of whether teachers were neglecting the education of Black and white children were as follows: for Black children in the respondent's community, 69.4 percent compared to 27.7 percent for white children in the same community; for Black children nationwide, 80 percent compared to 33 percent for white children.

20. B. Blauner, *Black Lives, White Lives: Three Decades of Race Relations in America* (Berkeley: University of California Press, 1989); M. Cohen, "Growing Up Segregated," *Emphasis Chapel Hill Sunday Newspaper*, 24 February 1991, C1–2.

21. H. Cruse, *Plural but Equal: A Critical Study of Blacks and Minorities in America's Plural Society* (New York: William Morrow, 1987); D. Bell, *And We Are Not Saved*.

22. Michele Foster, "The Politics of Race: Through African-American Teachers' Eyes," *Journal of Education*, 172(3) (1990:123–41); Michele Foster, "Connectedness, Constancy, and Constraints in the Lives of African-American Women Teachers: Some Things Change, Most Stay the Same," *NWSA Journal*, 3(2) (1991: 233–67); Michele Foster, "African-American Teachers and the Politics of Race," in *What Schools Can Do: Critical Pedagogy and Practice*, ed. K. Weiler (Albany, N.Y.: SUNY Press, 1991); Michele Foster, " 'Just Got to Find A Way': Case Studies of the Lives and Practice of Exemplary Black High School Teachers," in *Readings in Equal Education Volume 2: Qualitative Investigations into Schools and Schooling*, ed. M. Foster (New York: AMS Press, 1991), 276–309; Michele Foster, "Educating for Competence in Community and Culture: Exploring the Views of Exemplary African-American Teachers," in *Schooling, Culture and Liberation: Critical Essays on African-American Education*, ed. M. Shujaa (Chicago: African World Press, in press).

23. H. Giroux, *Schooling and the Struggle for Public Life: Critical Pedagogy in the Modern Age* (Minneapolis: University of Minnesota Press, 1988); S. Lightfoot, *Balm in Gilead: Journey of a Healer* (Reading, Mass.: Addison-Wesley, 1988).

24. M. Cohen, "Growing Up Segregated." Blauner, *Black Lives, White Lives;* Kluger, *Simple Justice;* S. Monroe and P. Goldman, *Brothers: Black and Poor* (New York: Ballantine Books, 1988); H. Baker, "What Charles Knew," in *An Apple for My Teacher: Twelve Authors Tell about Teachers Who Made the Difference,* ed. L. D. Rubin, Jr. (Chapel Hill, N.C.: Algonquin Books, 1987); M. Fields, with K. Fields, *Lemon Swamp: A Carolina Memoir* (New York: Free Press, 1985); S. Clark, *Echo in My Soul* (New York: E. P. Dutton, 1962); I. Reed, "Reading, Writing, and Racism," *San Francisco Examiner Image Magazine,* (August 19, 1990), 27–28.

CHAPTER 14

*I wish to acknowledge help from a number of people in the preparation of this paper. I am especially grateful to Michelle Fine for comments on earlier drafts, and to David Dan, Michele Foster, Susan Lytle, Rebecca Reumann, and Lois Weis.

1. Anthony Appiah, "The Uncompleted Argument: DuBois and the Illusion of Race," in *Race, Writing, and Difference,* ed. Henry Louis Gates (Chicago: University of Chicago Press, 1986), 36.

2. Cameron McCarthy, "Beyond the Poverty of Theory in Race Relations: Nonsynchrony and Social Difference in Education," in this volume.

3. Christine Slater and Carl Grant, "An Analysis of Multicultural Education in the United States," *Harvard Educational Review* 57 (November 1987): 422.

4. Ibid., 434–44.

5. For an exception, see Terry Dean, "Multicultural Classrooms, Monocultural Teachers," *College Composition and Communication* 40 (February 1989): 23–37, who quotes extensively from student writing.

6. McCarthy, "Beyond the Poverty of Theory"; Thomas Popkewitz, "Culture, Pedagogy, and Power Issues in the Production of Values and Colonialization," *Journal of Education* 170(2) (1988): 77–90.

7. McCarthy, "Beyond the Poverty of Theory."

8. Michelle Fine, "Why Urban Adolescents Drop Into and Out of Public High School," in *School Dropouts: Patterns and Policies,* ed. Gary Natriello (New York: Teachers College Press, 1987), 96.

9. David Lusted, quoted in Patti Lather, "Advocacy, Methodology, and Reflexivity: Postmodernism, Praxis, and Social Change," paper presented at the Tenth Annual Conference on Curriculum Theory and Classroom Practice, Dayton, Ohio, October 1988.

10. Elizabeth Ellsworth, "Why Doesn't This Feel Empowering? Working Through the Repressive Myths of Critical Pedagogy," *Harvard Educational Review* 59 (August 1989): 297–324.

11. See Roger Abrahams and John Szwed, "The Slave Accounts in Context, Two Extracts," in *After Africa: Extracts from British Travel Accounts of the Seventeenth, Eighteenth, and Nineteenth Centuries Concerning the Slaves, Their Manners, and Customs in the British West Indies,* ed. Roger Abrahams and John Szwed, assisted by Leslie Baker and Adrian Stackhouse (New Haven: Yale University Press, 1983), 1–49; Carol Stack, *All Our Kin: Strategies for Survival in a Black Community* (New York: Harper & Row, 1974).

12. Janet Helms, ed., *Black and White Racial Identity* (New York: Greenwood Press, 1990); Bailey Jackson and Rita Hardiman, "Racial Identity Development: Implications for Managing the Multiracial Workforce," in *NTL Managers' Handbook,* ed. Roger Ritvo and Alice Sargent (Arlington, Va.: NTL Institute, 1983), 107–120.

13. Peter McLaren, *Life in Schools* (New York: Longman, 1989); Stanley Aronowitz and Henry Giroux, *Education under Seige: The Conservative, Liberal, and Radical Debate over Schooling* (South Hadley, Mass.: Bergin & Garvey, 1985).

14. Gates, *"Race," Writing, and Difference.*

15. Gregory Ulmer, quoted in Later, "Advocacy," 7.

16. Ellsworth, "Why Doesn't This Feel Empowering?"; Patti Lather, *Getting Smart: Feminist Research and Pedagogy within the Postmodern* (New York: Routledge, 1991).

17. Lather, *Getting Smart,* 137.

18. Carol Stack, "Different Voices, Different Visions: Gender, Culture, and Moral Reasoning," in *Uncertain Terms: Negotiating Gender in American Culture,* ed. Faye Ginsburg and Anna Tsing (Boston: Beacon Press, 1990), 20.

19. Ulmer, quoted in Lather, "Advocacy," 8.

20. McCarthy, "Beyond the Poverty of Theory," 21.

21. Erik Erikson, *Childhood and Society,* 2d ed. (New York: Norton, 1964).

22. Michelle Fine and Nancie Zane, " 'Bein' Wrapped Too Tight': When Low-Income Women Drop Out of High School," in *Dropouts from School,* ed. Lois Weis, Eleanor Farrar, and Hugh Petrie (New York: SUNY Press, 1989), 23–53.

23. See Helms, *Black and White,* for further exploration of race as a counseling issue.

24. Fine and Zane, " 'Bein' Wrapped Too Tight,' " 44.

25. See Dean, "Multicultural Classrooms"; Shirley Brice Heath, *Ways with Words* (Cambridge, London, University of Cambridge Press, 1983); John Ogbu, *Minority Education and Caste: The American System in Cross-Cultural Perspective* (New York: Academic Press, 1978).

26. Regina Austin, "Sapphire Bound! (Minority Feminist Scholarship)," *Wisconsin Law Review* (May–June 1989): 562.

27. Zora Neale Hurston, "How It Feels to Be Colored Me," in *I Love Myself When I'm Laughing. . . .*, ed. Alice Walker (New York: Feminist Press), 152.

28. Appiah, "The Uncompleted Argument."

29. Henry Louis Gates, "Introduction: Writing 'Race' and the Difference It Makes," in *"Race," Writing, and Difference*, 1–20.

30. Krogman, quoted in Casas, quoted in Helms, *Black and White*, 3.

31. Helms, *Black and White*, 3.

32. Abrahams and Szwed, "Slave Accounts," 35.

33. Heath, *Ways with Words*.

34. August Wilson, "Interview," in Bill Moyers' *World of Ideas: Conversations with Thoughtful Men and Women about American Life Today and the Ideas Shaping Our Future*, 1st ed. (New York: Doubleday, 1989), 180.

35. John Ogbu, "Research Currents: Cultural-Ecological Influence on Minority School Learning," *Language Arts* 62 (December 1985): 860–69.

36. Christopher Miller, "Theories of Africans: The Question of Literary Anthropology," in *"Race," Writing, and Difference*, ed. Gates, 300.

37. Barbara Johnson, "Threshholds of Difference: Structures of Address in Zora Neale Hurston," in *"Race," Writing, and Difference*, ed. Gates, 324.

38. See Helms, *Black and White*, 50.

39. W. E. B. DuBois, *The Souls of Black Folk* (New York: Washington Square Press, 1970), 3.

40. See Hurston, "How It Feels," 154.

41. For further explorations, see Appiah, "Uncompleted Argument"; DuBois, *The Souls of Black Folk*.

42. James Lynch, "Human Rights, Racism, and the Multicultural Curriculum," *Educational Review*, 37(2) (1985): 141–52.

43. Ogbu, "Research Currents," 886–87.

44. Johnson, "Threshholds," 323.

45. Ibid.

46. Wade Boykin and F. Toms, "Black Child Socialization," in *Black Children: Social, Educational, and Parental Environments,* ed. Harriet McAdoo and John McAdoo (Berkeley: Sage, 1985), 43.

47. Miller, "Theories of Africans," 288.

48. Ogbu, "Research Currents."

49. Signithia Fordham, "Racelessness as a Factor in Black Students' School Success: Pragmatic Strategy of Pyrrhic Victory?" *Harvard Educational Review,* 58 (February 1988): 54–83.

50. See Stack, *All Our Kin;* Fine and Zane, " 'Bein' Wrapped Too Tight.' "

51. Austin, "Sapphire," 563.

52. M. Peters, "Racial Socialization of Young Black Children," in *Black Children;* ed. McAdoo and McAdoo, 172.

53. Austin, "Sapphire," 563.

54. Johnson, "Threshholds," 327.

55. Fordham, "Racelessness," 69.

56. Helms, *Black and White,* 28.

57. Beverly Gordon, "Toward Emancipation in Citizenship Education: The Case of African-American Cultural Knowledge," *Theory and Research in Social Education,* 12 (Winter 1985): 8.

58. See Lisa Delpit, "The Silenced Dialogue: Power and Pedagogy in Educating Other People's Children," *Harvard Educational Review,* 59 (August 1988): 280–98.

59. Carl Grant, "The Mediator of Culture: A Teacher Role Revisited," *Journal of Research and Development in Education* 11(1) (1977): 102–17.

60. See Ellsworth, "Why Doesn't This Feel Empowering?" for an example of this kind of scrutiny.

61. See Grant, "Mediator"; Michele Foster, "The Politics of Race: Through the Eyes of African-American Teachers," to appear in *Journal of Education* 72 (Spring 1991), for an example of African-American teachers exploring these and related issues.

62. Michelle Fine, "Making Controversy: Who's 'At Risk?' " *Journal of Urban and Cultural Studies,* 1(1) (1990): 63.

CHAPTER 15

1. Tribal people use both terms—*Native American* and *American Indian*—when speaking or writing about themselves. Consequently, I have used both terms interchangeably.

2. A. Astin, *Minorities in American Higher Education* (San Francisco: Jossey-Bass, 1982); R. Richardson and L. Bender, *Focusing Minority Access and Achievement in Higher Education* (San Francisco: Jossey-Bass, 1987).

3. W. G. Tierney, *Official Encouragement, Institutional Discouragement: Minorities in Academe, a Critical Analysis of Native Americans* (Norwood, N.J.: Ablex, forthcoming).

4. B. Wright and W. Tierney, "American Indians and Higher Education: A History of Cultural Conflict," *CHANGE* (March/April 1991): 11–18.

5. Astin, *Minorities in American Higher Education*, 23.

6. J. Fries, *The American Indian in Higher Education, 1976–76 to 1984–85* (Washington, D.C.: Office of Educational Research and Improvement, U.S. Department of Education, 1987), 31.

7. Ibid.

8. Bureau of the Census, *A Statistical Profile of the American Indian, Eskimo, and Aleut Populations for the United States, 1980* (Suitland, Md.: Bureau of the Census, 1985).

9. K. Tijerina and P. Biemer, "The Dance of Indian Higher Education: One Step Forward, Two Steps Back," *Educational Record* 68(4) 69(1) (1988): 86–93.

10. D. Birdsell, *Minorities in Higher Education* (Washington, D.C.: American Council on Education, 1984); J. Mingle, *Focus on Minorities: Trends in Higher Education Participation and Success* (Denver: Education Commission of the States, 1987).

11. D. Deskins, *Minority Recruitment Data* (Totowa, N.J.: Rowman & Allenheld, 1987).

12. A. Astin, *Preventing Students from Dropping Out* (San Francisco: Jossey-Bass, 1977); P. E. Beal and L. Noel, *What Works in Student Retention* (Iowa City, Iowa: American College Testing Program in the National Center for Higher Education Management Systems, 1980); W. G. Spady, "Dropouts from Higher Education: An Interdisciplinary Review and Synthesis," *Interchange* 1 (1970): 64–85; W. G. Spady, "Dropouts from Higher Education: Toward an Empirical Model," *Interchange* 2 (1971): 38–62; V. Tinto, "Dropout from Higher Education: A Theoretical Synthesis of Recent Research," *Review of Educational Research* 45 (1975): 89–125; V. Tinto, *Leaving College* (Chicago: University of Chicago Press, 1987).

13. R. Roosens, "Integration Processes—Adolescents from Minorities," unpublished manuscript; Center for Social and Cultural Anthropology, Catholic University, Leuven, Belgium, 1987; J. E. Rossmann and B. A. Kirk, "Factors Related to Persistence and Withdrawal among University Students," *Journal of Counseling Psychology* 17 (1970): 55–62; C. Sexauer, *Adult Baccalaureate Students: Who Are They? Why Do They Persist?*, Ph.D. dissertation, Pennsylvania State University, 1989.

14. V. Tinto, *Leaving College*, 84.

15. Ibid., 119.

16. Ibid., 95.

17. P. McLaren, "Schooling the Postmodern Body: Critical Pedagogy and the Politics of Enfleshment," *Journal of Education* 170(3) (1988): 62.

18. V. Deloria, *Custer Died for Your Sins* (New York: Macmillan, 1969); D. Brown, *Bury My Heart at Wounded Knee* (New York: Holt Rinehart & Winston, 1972); R. Andrist, *The Long Death: The Last Days of the Plains Indians* (New York: Collier Books, 1969).

19. Bureau of the Census, *A Statistical Profile*.

20. R. P. McDermott, "The Explanations of Minority School Failure, Again," *Anthropology and Education Quarterly* 18(4) (1987): 362.

21. G. Spindler and L. Spindler, "There Are No Dropouts among the Arunta and Hutterites," in *What Do Anthropologists Have to Say About Dropouts*, ed. G. and L. Spindler, 1–15 (New York: Falmer Press, 1989), 10.

22. Ibid., 13.

23. R. Pottinger, "The Quest for Valued Futures: Steps on a Rainbow Journey," *Journey of Navajo Education* 6(3) (1989): 3.

24. It is important to point out that even American Indian students who attend tribal colleges face similar cultural struggles and challenges. Tribal colleges began as institutions geared toward maintaining cultural values. However, these institutions exist in the system of American higher education; tribal colleges encounter tremendous obstacles with regard to the requirements placed on them by accreditation agencies. The funding formulas devised by the Bureau of Indian Affairs generated less income for the institutions in 1990 than they did in 1978, so that these colleges are currently the most seriously underfunded postsecondary institutions in the country. And for the most part, effective dialogues have not occurred with four-year institutions, so there are no transfer policies that insure academic support for Indian students when they move to a university.

Administrators, faculty, and staff at the tribal colleges also may not be in agreement about the purpose of education. Some tribal colleges mirror mainstream community colleges and maintain that their mission is to provide training and jobs; other tribal colleges believe that the purpose of the institution must be to maintain and strengthen tribal culture. Further, students who complete a degree at a tribal community college still encounter the same problems as Delbert and his friends faced; when tribal college students move to a four-year mainstream institution, they still must deal with assimilationist attitudes and structures. Consequently, although the tribal colleges have made significant strides since their founding over twenty years ago, the dream of tribal educators, that tribal colleges would solve the problems Indian students faced when they went to mainstream colleges, has not become a reality.

25. H. Giroux, "Border Pedagogy in the Age of Postmodernism," *Journal of Education* 170(3) (1988): 7.

26. W. G. Tierney, *Curricular Landscapes, Democratic Vistas: Transformative Leadership in Higher Education* (New York: Praeger, 1989).

CHAPTER 16

1. For trenchant critiques of "essentialist" approaches to race see Paul Gilroy, "Cruciality and the Frog's Perspective," *Third Text* 5 (Winter 1989): 33–44; Michael Omi and Howard Winant, *Racial Formation in the United States* (New York: Routledge & Kegan Paul, 1986); Barry Troyna and Jenny Williams, *Racism, Education, and the State* (London: Croom Helm, 1986); and Cornel West, "Marxist Theory and the Specificity of Afro-American Oppression," in *Marxism and the Interpretation of Culture,* ed. Cary Nelson and Lawrence Grossberg, (Urbana: University of Illinois Press, 1988).

2. Theresa Delauretis, *Alice Doesn't: Feminism, Semiotics, and Cinema* (Bloomington: Indiana University Press, 1984).

3. Carlos Cortes, "The Education of Language Minority Students: A Contextual Model," *Beyond Language: Social and Cultural Factors in Schooling Language Minority Students,* ed. California State Department of Education (Los Angeles: Evaluation, Dissemination and Assessment Center, California State University, 1986), 16.

4. Paul Gilroy, "Steppin' Out of Babylon: Race, Class, and Autonomy," in *The Empire Strikes Back,* ed. Centre for Contemporary Cultural Studies (London: Hutchinson), 278–314; and Julien Henriques, ed., *Changing the Subject: Psychology, Social Regulation, and Subjectivity* (New York: Methuen, 1984).

5. See Emile Durkheim, *The Evolution of Educational Thought: Lectures on the Formation and Development of Secondary Education in France* (London: Routledge & Kegan Paul, 1977); John Ogbu and Maria Matute-Bianchi, "Understanding Sociocultural Factors in Education: Knowledge, Identity, and School Adjustment," in *Beyond Language: Social and Cultural Factors in Schooling Language Minority Students,* ed. California State Department of Education; Thomas Popkewitz, ed., *The Formation of School Subjects* (London: Falmer, 1987).

6. Cameron McCarthy, *Race and Curriculum* (London: Falmer, 1990).

7. There are some very good examples of these more culturalist approaches to inequality in the writings of researchers such as Warren Crichlow, *A Social Analysis of Black Youth Commitment and Disaffection in an Urban High School,* Ed.D. dissertation, University of Rochester, 1990; Omi and Winant, *Racial Formation in the United States;* and Madan Sarup, *The Politics of Multiracial Education* (London: Routledge & Kegan Paul, 1986).

8. See Samuel Bowles and Herbert Gintis, *Schooling in Capitalist America* (New York: Basic Books, 1976).

9. Michael W. Apple, "Redefining Inequality: Authoritarian Populism and the Conservative Restoration," *Teacher's College Record* 90 (2) (1988), 167–84; and Phillip Wexler, *Social Analysis and Education: After the New Sociology* (New York: Routledge & Kegan Paul, 1987).

10. See Apple, "Redefining Inequality"; Henry Giroux, "Introduction," in Paulo Friere's *The Politics of Education* (South Hadley, Mass.: Bergin & Garvey, 1985), ix–xxvi; Philip Wexler, *Social Analysis and Education;* Geoff Whitty, *Sociology and School Knowledge* (London: Methuen, 1985).

11. Madan Sarup, *The Politics of Multiracial Education.*

12. Omi and Winant, *Racial Formation in the United States;* and Michael Burawoy, "The Capitalist State in South Africa: Marxist and Sociological Perspectives on Race and Class," in *Political Power and Social Theory,* ed. Maurice Zeitlin, 2: 279–335 (Greenwich, Conn.: JAI Press, 1981).

13. Stuart Hall, "Gramsci's Relevance to the Analysis of Race," *Communication Inquiry* 10 (Summer 1986): 5–27.

14. Julien Henriques, "Social Psychology and the Politics of Racism," in *Changing the Subject,* ed. Julien Henriques (London: Methuen, 1984), 60–89.

15. Stephen Gould, *The Mismeasure of Man* (New York: Norton, 1981); Marvin Harris, *The Rise of Anthropological Theory* (New York: Thomas Crowell, 1968); Omi and Winant, *Racial Formation in the United States.*

16. Edna Bonacich, "Capitalism and Race Relations in South Africa: A Split Labor Market Analysis," in *Political Power and Social Theory,* ed. Maurice Zeitlin, vol. 2; Eric Williams, *Capitalism and Slavery* (London: Andre Deutsch, 1964).

17. Omi and Winant, *Racial Formation in the United States.*

18. Ibid., 61.

19. Winthrop Jordan, *White over Black: American Attitudes towards the Negro, 1550–1812* (Baltimore: Penguin Books, 1969), 94–95.

20. Omi and Winant, *Racial Formation in the United States,* 61.

21. Abdul JanMohamed, "Introduction: Toward a Theory of Minority Discourse," *Cultural Critique* 6 (Winter 1987): 5–11; and Abdul JanMohamed and David Lloyd, "Introduction: Minority Discourse—What is to be Done," *Cultural Critique* 7 (Spring 1987): 5–17.

22. JanMohamed and Lloyd, "Introduction," 7.

23. Martin Carnoy, *Education and Cultural Imperialism* (New York: Longman, 1974); and John Ogbu, *Minority, Education, and Caste* (New York: Academic Press, 1978).

24. See Samuel George Morton, *Crania Americana or, a Comparative View of Skulls of Various Aboriginal Nations of North and South America* (Philadelphia: John Pennington, 1839); J. Eysenck and L. Kamin, *The Intelligence Controversy* (New York: Wiley, 1981); J. Gobineau, *The Inequality of Human Races* (London: Heineman, 1915); Arthur Jensen, "How Much Can We Boost IQ," *Harvard Educational Review,* Reprint Series no. 2 (1969): 1–23; Arthur Jensen, *Straight Talk about Mental Tests* (New York: Free Press, 1981); and Arthur Jensen, "Political Ideologies and Educational Research," *Phi Delta Kappan,* 65 (1984): 460.

25. Antonio Gramsci, *Selections from the Prison Notebooks* (New York: International, 1983), 108–10.

26. Manning Marable, *Black American Politics* (London: Verso, 1985); and Cornel West, "Marxist Theory and the Specificity."

27. Antonio Gramsci, *Selections From the Prison Notebooks,* 88.

28. Linda Grant, "Black Females' 'Place' in Desegregated Classrooms," *Sociology of Education* 57 (1984): 98–111; Mokubung Nkomo, *Student Culture and Activism in Black South African Universities* (Westport, Conn.: Greenwood Press, 1984); and Joel Spring, *American Education: An Introduction to Social and Political Aspects* (New York: Longman, 1985).

29. Omi and Winant, *Racial Formation in the United States,* 169.

30. See Michael W. Apple and Lois Weis, *Ideology and Practice in Schooling* (Philadelphia: Temple University Press, 1983).

31. Cameron McCarthy, *Race and Curriculum.*

32. Apple and Weis, *Ideology and Practice in Schooling,* 24.

33. Ibid.

34. Omi and Winant, *Racial Formation in the United States,* 52.

35. See E. P. Thompson, *The Making of the English Working Class* (New York: Vintage, 1966).

36. Apple and Weis, *Ideology and Practice in Schooling,* 25.

37. Emily Hicks, "Cultural Marxism: Nonsynchrony and Feminist Practice," in *Women and Revolution*, ed. Lydia Sargent (Boston: South End Press, 1981), 219–38.

38. See Adam Gamoran and Mark Berends, *The Effects of Stratification in Secondary Schools: Synthesis of Survey and Ethnographic Research* (Madison: National Center for Effective Secondary Schools, University of Wisconsin-Madison, 1986); Jeannie Oakes, "Tracking in Mathematics and Science Education: A Structural Contribution to Unequal Schooling," in *Class, Race, and Gender in American Education*, ed. Lois Weis (Albany, New York: State University of New York Press, 1988), 106–25.

39. Ray Rist, "Social Class and Teacher Expectations: The Self-fulfilling Prophecy in Ghetto Education," *Harvard Educational Review* 40 (1970): 411–51.

40. Stuart Hall, "The Toad in the Garden: Thatcherism among the Theorists," in *Marxism and the Interpretation of Culture*, ed. Nelson and Grossberg, 35–74.

41. John Fiske, *Television Culture* (London: Methuen, 1987).

42. Emily Hicks, "Cultural Marxism," 221.

43. J. Wellman, *Portraits of White Racism* (Cambridge: Cambridge University Press, 1977), 4.

44. Linda Grant, *Uneasy Alliances: Black Males, Teachers, and Peers in the Desegregated Classroom*, unpublished manuscript, University of Southern Illinois; and Rist, "Social Class and Teacher Expectations."

45. Gamoran and Berends, *Effects of Stratification*.

46. Sarup, *Politics of Multiracial Education;* Spring, *American Education;* and Troyna and Williams, *Racism, Education, and the State*.

47. K. Brown, "Turning a Blind Eye: Racial Oppression and the Unintended Consequences of White Non-racism," *Sociological Review* no. 33 (1985): 670–90.

48. J. Scott and T. Kerkvliet, eds., *Everyday Forms of Peasant Resistance in South East Asia* (London: Frank Case, 1986).

49. Emily Hicks, "Cultural Marxism."

50. Hall, "Teaching Race," in *The School in the Multicultural Society*, ed. A. James and R. Jeffcoate (London: Harper & Row, 1981), 68.

51. Ernesto Laclau and Chantal Mouffe, *Hegemony and Socialist Strategy: Toward a Radical Democratic Politics* (London: Verso, 1985).

52. Omi and Winant, *Racial Formation in the United States;* and Madan Sarup, *The Politics of Multiracial Education*.

53. Marable, *Black American Politics;* and Spring, *American Education*.

54. Spring, *American Education*.

55. Ibid., 105–6.

56. Ibid., 106.

57. Ibid., 106.

58. Ibid., 108.

59. Ibid., 108.

60. Grant, ''Black Females' 'Place,' '' 99.

61. Ibid.

62. Ibid., 102.

63. Ibid., 102.

64. Ibid., 102.

65. Ibid., 106.

66. Ibid., 107.

67. Grant, ''Uneasy Alliances.''

68. Grant, ''Black Females' 'Place','' 100.

69. Ibid., 103.

70. Ibid., 109.

71. Grant, ''Black Females' 'Place' ''; Grant, ''Uneasy Alliances''; and Spring, *American Education*.

72. Troyna and Williams, *Racism, Education, and the State*.

73. Stuart Hall, ''Race, Articulation, and Societies Structured in Dominance,'' in *Sociological Theories: Race and Colonialism*, ed. UNESCO (Paris: UNESCO, 1980), 339.

74. Grant, ''Black Females' 'Place' ''; Grant, ''Uneasy Alliances''; Spring, *American Education;* and Sarup, *The Politics of Multiracial Education*.

Contributors

Linda K. Christian-Smith is Associate Professor in the Department of Curriculum and Instruction at the University of Wisconsin in Oshkosh. She has extensive experience as a teacher of teen readers of romance novels and is a specialist in literature for young readers and in the sociology of curriculum.

Jody Cohen has taught English and Social Studies for a decade in urban schools. Currently, she is a doctoral candidate in the Language and Education Division of the Graduate School of Education at the University of Pennsylvania.

R. W. Connell is Professor of Sociology at University of California at Santa Cruz. He is currently involved in research on AIDS prevention, masculinity, sexuality, and social theory.

Jim Cummins is Professor at the Modern Language Center of the Ontario Institute for Studies in Education in Toronto, Canada.

Lisa D. Delpit is a Senior Research Associate at the Institute for Urban Research at Morgan State University.

Jeanne Ellsworth is a doctoral student in Social Foundations at the State University of New York at Buffalo and Research Assistant at the Buffalo Research Institute on Education for Teaching.

Michelle Fine is the Goldie Anna Charitable Trust Professor of Education at the University of Pennsylvania.

Michele Foster is Associate Professor of African American Studies and Education at University of California at Davis. She specializes in anthropological research with a particular focus on discourse analysis and classroom intervention.

411

Richard A. Friend is on the faculty of the Human Sexuality Program at the University of Pennsylvania and is Adjunct Assistant Professor in the College of Allied Health Sciences at Thomas Jefferson University.

Carol Gilligan is one of the founding members of the Collaborative Harvard Project on the Psychology of Women and the Development of Girls and is Professor of Human Development and Psychology at the Harvard Graduate School of Education.

Walter Haney is Associate Professor in the School of Education at Boston College and Senior Research Associate in the Center for the Study of Testing, Evaluation, and Educational Policy.

Cameron McCarthy is Assistant Professor in The Department of Education at Colgate University. He teaches Social and Political Foundations of Education.

Roslyn Arlin Mickelson is Associate Professor of Sociology and Adjunct Professor of Women's Studies at the University of North Carolina in Charlotte.

Melvin L. Oliver is Associate Professor of Sociology at the University of California in Los Angeles.

Mara Sapon-Shevin is Professor in the Division for the Study of Teaching at Syracuse University.

Stephen Samuel Smith is Assistant Professor of Political Science at Winthrop College in Rock Hill, South Carolina.

Robert B. Stevenson is Assistant Professor in the Department of Educational Organization, Administration, and Policy at the State University of New York at Buffalo.

William G. Tierney is Associate Professor and Senior Research Associate in the Center for the Study of Higher Education at Pennsylania State University.

Lois Weis is Professor of Sociology of Education and Associate Dean of the Graduate School of Education, State University of New York at Buffalo.

Index